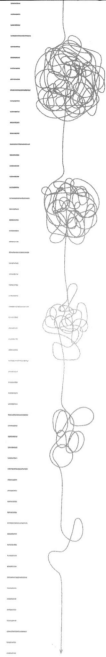

Davi

Peggy Parskey

Measurement Demystified

Creating Your L&D Measurement,
Analytics, and Reporting Strategy

ATD Press is an internationally renowned source of insightful and practical information on talent development, training, and professional development.

ATD Press
1640 King Street
Alexandria, VA 22314 USA

Ordering information: Books published by ATD Press can be purchased by visiting ATD's website at td.org/books or by calling 800.628.2783 or 703.683.8100.

Library of Congress Control Number: 2020946222

ISBN-10: 1-950496-85-6
ISBN-13: 978-1-950496-89-1
e-ISBN: 978-1-950496-86-0

ATD Press Editorial Staff
Director: Sarah Halgas
Manager: Melissa Jones
Community Manager, Learning & Development: Eliza Blanchard
Developmental Editor: Kathryn Stafford
Copy Editor: Jack Harlow
Text Design: Shirley E.M. Raybuck
Cover Design: Rose Richey

Printed by P.A. Hutchison Company, Mayfield, PA

Contents

Figures

Appendix C

Tables

Foreword

Talent development reporting informs organization leaders about how much the organization invests and how well investments in people pay off. Consumers of talent development data are C-suite executives who decide how and where to allocate organization resources. They are managers and supervisors accountable for business performance whose employees are participants of programs. They are the human resources business partners looking for solutions to their client needs. And they are employees who want insight into which programs can propel them along their development journey. Finally, consumers are the heads of learning, program owners, and facilitators who monitor learning investment progress and improve programs to drive even greater value. To steer consumers of data in the right direction, learning leaders need a reporting strategy built around a practical framework. This strategy should lead to reporting that makes it easy for data users to get the information they need when they need it, and understand what it means once they have it. This book describes how to develop such a strategy.

Progress With Measurement

The talent development industry is making progress in measurement. In 2010, ROI Institute partnered with ATD to conduct a first-of-its-kind study to determine what CEOs think about the learning investment. CEOs indicated the types of measures they were receiving and those they wished they were receiving to understand talent development's value. CEOs also ranked the measures in terms of their importance in resource allocation decisions. Of least importance were data describing inputs, efficiency, and participant reaction to learning; yet these were the data most executives reported receiving. Impact and ROI were the top two most important measures to CEOs, yet only 7 percent reported receiving impact data, and only 4 percent reported receiving ROI. This gap between what CEOs receive and what they want was a wake-up call for many talent development leaders.

Five years later, in 2015, *Chief Learning Officer's Business Intelligence Board Measurement and Metrics* study reported that 71.2 percent of 335 CLOs indicated they were either using or planning to use ROI as a measure of learning performance. In 2017, *Training* magazine's "Top 10 Hall of Fame" report acknowledged that the success of any program is based on whether it improves business results. Today, organizations recognized as *Training's* Top 125 must report how their talent development investments deliver business results to their organizations.

Progress with measurement was further evident in ROI Institute's 2020 benchmarking study. When comparing our recommended percentage of programs evaluated at the different levels to the survey respondents' results, we were happy to see the progress talent development is making in connecting programs to the business. While the percentage of programs evaluated at reaction and learning was lower than our recommendation, the rate of programs evaluated at impact and ROI was impressively higher. Survey respondents reported that they evaluated 37 percent of their programs to the impact level compared to our recommended 10 percent. They also said they evaluated 18 percent of their programs to ROI compared to our recommended 5 percent.

Despite this progress in measurement, there are still questions from many stakeholders regarding talent development's value and how best to allocate those resources. Why? Because reporting still fails to communicate performance effectively.

How Talent Development Reporting Fails

Talent development leaders have at their fingertips measures of activity, such as:

- number of programs
- number of employees reached
- numbers of employees participating
- learning assets produced
- spend per learning hour consumed.

These metrics, accessible in any learning management system, describe where funds are going, but not what the organization is receiving in return. These activity-based measures are easy to report, yet reporting them makes it difficult for others to recognize the learning investment's real value. For this reason, TD funding is an easy target when cost-cutting measures ensue. Activity-based reporting focuses on the learning leader as the consumer, ignoring other consumers' data needs.

Another way reporting fails is that even when the data reported are results-based versus activity-based, reports often omit targets. While some would argue targets are unnecessary, the question is, how does one define success if there is no basis for comparison? This omission of results-compared-to-target leaves the interpretation of success up to the consumer.

A third way reporting fails is that the data tend to be static. Measures and metrics with nice graphics make for an interesting report, but consumers sometimes struggle to understand the "so what?" of it all. Reporting data without insight offers little value.

Reporting fails to effectively communicate talent development performance because it, like evaluation, is often an afterthought. Yes, the easy data are automated and placed on dashboards, but the real value of reporting is when it clearly communicates information that can influence consumers who make the ultimate talent development funding decisions. These decision makers will certainly base decisions on activity; but these decisions are altogether different than those based on results.

A final reason for the failure in talent development reporting is the lack of standardization. This does not mean that every learning program should target the same outcomes; far from it. Program outcomes are relative to the organization and individual needs. However, is does raise the question: If financial statements for all organizations follow a similar format and include standard measures that describe investment performance, shouldn't talent development do the same? A common reporting framework enables any consumer of data, from any organization, to go immediately to the information most pertinent.

The Challenges

Talent development professionals must address several challenges to get reporting right. The first challenge is knowing the purpose of reporting measures. Goals for reporting vary from making the business case for investing in a solution to demonstrating the investment value. Sometimes reporting is merely an effort to monitor performance in measures. Defining the purpose of reporting helps address the second challenge—what to measure, given that there are so many possible measures.

A third challenge is knowing who is to receive the data and how to present it to offer insight, not just numbers. The fourth challenge is determining the appropriate timing and frequency of reporting. Should the data be reported instantaneously, monthly, quarterly, or on an ad hoc basis? A fifth challenge is where to find benchmark data to compare talent development performance.

A sixth challenge is in collecting, analyzing, and reporting data efficiently. Over the decades, our work at ROI Institute has led us to discover that a measurement and evaluation practice following the most robust of methodologies, such as the ROI Methodology, will only cost 5 percent of the talent development budget. Measurement, evaluation, and analytics, including reporting, does not have to be expensive, and it will not be costly if the reporting strategy follows a practical framework.

A final challenge talent development professionals face is technology. Finding the right technology that supports the reporting strategy is essential. Technology simplifies the reporting processes and helps reduce costs. Performitiv and Explorance Metrics-that-Matters not only support a common framework for reporting, they also include intelligence that offers insights to the output of the analysis, making the data reported useful. Other tools like Qualtrics are agnostic when it comes to a reporting framework, but they simplify analysis and offer insight not typically available in a survey tool. Tools such as Microsoft Business Intelligence, Tableau, and Qlik enable users to sort, compare, and visualize data in various ways, making them more meaningful than if they existed only on a spreadsheet. Selecting and investing in technology is an important consideration when developing a reporting strategy.

Why This Book

There have been many books on talent development measurement, evaluation, and reporting. I am fortunate to have been involved in many of them. My husband, Jack J. Phillips, wrote the first comprehensive book on training measurement, evaluation, and reporting in 1983, titled *Handbook of Training Evaluation and Measurement Methods,* now in its fourth edition. Together we have written many books on measurement and evaluation in talent development, including our most recent, *Proving the Value of Soft Skills,* which we published in 2020 with ATD. And there are many other books authored by us and others. One may wonder whether there is any need for another book describing frameworks, measures, and reporting for talent development. I would argue there is. Reporting results that matter to all talent development data consumers has been a long-time struggle for the field. Activity-based reporting is alive and well despite the progress in measurement.

Dave and Peggy's book, *Measurement Demystified,* addresses many of the challenges I've outlined here. It describes a practical framework for creating a talent development reporting strategy. From the book, you will learn why measurement is important, what measures matter, and the consequences of being overly focused on one type of measure over another. The book also provides examples of efficiency, effectiveness, and outcome measures, as well as a variety of different reporting formats. It also introduces the new International Organization for Standardization (ISO) Human Capital Reporting Standards, which can be used to help meet the new Securities and Exchange Commission rule mandating, for the first time, human capital disclosure by U.S. publicly traded companies.

Measurement Demystified serves as a primer to those people just entering the talent development field. Beginning this journey knowing the best way to report talent development performance will help frame the measures taken for each program evaluation. It also serves as a refresher for those who have been involved in designing standards around talent development reporting. Finally, the book serves as a booster for those with advanced capability in measurement and analytics. It provides new insights to developing reporting strategies that effectively inform decisions about the talent development investment.

Dave and Peggy have decades of experience in managing talent development functions as well as assessing, measuring, and evaluating talent development programs. Both have served in leadership roles for major corporations before taking on the responsibility of driving the Center for Talent Reporting. Their experience creating, consuming, and managing talent development data and helping others do the same gives them the right to write this book. I admire their passion for their work and their belief that what they do matters—because it does. Standardizing talent development reporting will make it easier for all consumers to know what they need to know about the talent development investment.

Call to Action

As you read this book, take note of what you learn and put it into action. Regardless of where you are along the measurement maturity continuum, there is always more to know, more to do, and a greater benefit you can bring to your organization and the individuals with whom you work. This book provides the tools, resources, and techniques to help demystify measurement for you, so that you can do the same for others.

Good luck with your talent development reporting journey, and remember: When it comes to demonstrating value, luck is not a factor, hope is not a strategy, and doing nothing is not an option. Change is inevitable, progress is optional, the next step is up to you.

Patti P. Phillips, PhD
CEO, ROI Institute
Board Chair, Center for Talent Reporting

Preface

*M*easurement Demystified is intended to meet an important, unfilled need in the learning and development (L&D) profession: a comprehensive and holistic introduction to the topics of measurement, analytics, and reporting. In fact, we hope this book becomes the first book you read on these topics. It is written to provide the foundation, framework, and language for you to gain a basic understanding of these areas and then apply that knowledge to create your own measurement and reporting strategy. Also, armed with this information, you will be prepared to appreciate the more advanced and in-depth coverage on topics such as the evaluation of learning programs.

The book is also written as a reference and performance support tool for the experienced learning practitioner, containing 120 learning measures, including efficiency measures, which are not the focus of other books on evaluation. You will find definitions and formulas for each measure, including recommendations for their use.

While comprehensive, the book is meant to be accessible to all, and no previous knowledge of L&D measurement is required. Step-by-step guidance is provided for selecting measures, creating reports, and crafting your own measurement and reporting strategy. In addition, more than 180 figures and tables are provided to enhance understanding and illustrate real-world application. Plus, a sample measurement and reporting strategy is included in the appendix along with a comprehensive glossary.

Measurement Demystified breaks new ground with the Talent Development Reporting principles (TDRp) framework for both measurement and reporting. This framework helps simplify the discussion of measurement, analytics, and reporting by providing a common language and an easy-to-use structure, consisting of four broad reasons to measure, three categories of measures, and five types of reports. The framework is employed throughout the book to provide an integrated, holistic approach to this important topic.

Notably, this is the first book to include the Association for Talent Development's benchmarks as well as the eight learning metrics recommended by the International Organization for Standardization (ISO), and it tackles unchartered territory with its comprehensive discussion of reporting. To our knowledge, no other book focuses on L&D reporting or provides a framework to help practitioners identify the type of report best suited to a particular need.

This book is about much more than evaluation. It is about all the reasons for measuring and how the measures should be used once they are obtained. In this book, we guide you on how to select, calculate, and use the measures, including how to use the reports to run learning like a business and deliver greater value. In sum, a more comprehensive introduction to these important topics will not be found elsewhere.

Introduction

The L&D profession has made steady progress over the last 60 years defining processes and introducing new concepts, systems, and tools. Many practitioners, though, still don't know where to start or how best to proceed with measurement, particularly with data analytics and reporting. For example, many are asked to create a measurement strategy or show the value of their investment in learning, but don't know how. And most L&D professionals have limited resources, which makes the task all the more challenging, especially considering the more than 180 measures we have identified that are available just for L&D. (We cover 120 in this book!)

We propose to simplify measurement, analytics, and reporting by applying a framework called the Talent Development Reporting principles (TDRp). Like any good framework, TDRp provides a common language for measures and the reasons for measuring. It recommends grouping measures into three categories, which will facilitate both the discussion and selection of measures. It also recommends a framework and common language for reporting based on the reasons for measuring. Moreover, TDRp breaks new ground by recommending the adoption of three standard reports for the management of individual programs and the entire department. TDRp also provides practical guidance on how to use the measures and reports to meet the needs of the various stakeholders in your organization.

Let's first offer a little history of how we got here before exploring TDRp in detail.

History

In 2010, a group of L&D leaders began discussing the need to create standards for measurement, reporting, and management within the industry. The discussions started casually among like-minded colleagues at conferences and centered on two key questions: Why is measurement capability in most organizations underdeveloped, and why does every organization spin its wheels creating its measurement approaches from scratch? The answer to both questions was the same: a lack of standards for measurement and reporting. Without standards, every talent function essentially had to start from scratch to first identify the measures that made sense in their organization and then design the appropriate reports that would provide insights for decisions and corrective action.

As the discussions widened to include a broader group of industry thought leaders, the realization hit: The Generally Accepted Accounting Principles (GAAP) employed by accountants in the United States (and International Financial Reporting Standards employed by accountants in the rest of the world) could be the inspiration for its mission. The rationale was: "If the GAAP framework for measurement and reporting works so well for accountants who also have hundreds of measures and numerous reports, why don't we have something like it for the learning profession?"

Moreover, they argued, accounting is not the only profession that has adopted frameworks and standards to help them organize vast amounts of data and provide a common language. Chemistry uses the periodic table; biology classifies organisms into kingdoms, phylum, families, and species; medicine classifies humans (and animals) by systems and organs. The founders of TDRp thought the time had come to develop a framework for learning.

The working group consisted of about 30 thought leaders and prominent practitioners, with Kent Barnett and Tamar Elkeles leading the effort (see sidebar). They recruited the experts shown in appendix A, including your authors, who helped conduct the research of current practices and wrote the whitepaper. After numerous revisions to the whitepaper, the group agreed on the key assumptions and principles, the three types of measures, and the recommended management reports (one of the five types of reports).

The Origins of TDRp
By Kent Barnett

In the fall of 2010, Tamar Elkeles, at that time the CLO of Qualcomm, and I, then CEO of KnowledgeAdvisors, were at lunch celebrating the retirement of Frank Anderson. Frank, the outgoing president of Defense Acquisition University, was a visionary and highly respected learning leader, so it was the perfect place to launch a strategic industry initiative. During our conversation, we agreed it was time to create standards to help us measure the impact and performance of L&D. We realized that the financial world had standardized reporting. By looking at the income statement, balance sheet, and cash flow statement, one could analyze the financial performance of any organization. Shouldn't we be able to do the same thing in learning?

Tamar and I agreed to co-chair a new council with the goal of creating standardized reporting for talent development. More than 30 thought leaders and leading organizations joined our effort, and out of that grew the Talent Development Reporting principles (TDRp). Most importantly, early on in the process Dave Vance accepted our offer to join us. As our work progressed, Dave took the lead and spearheaded the efforts to create the Center for Talent Reporting.

Ten years later, the TDRp framework is being adopted around the world and Dave Vance has turned the Center for Talent Reporting into an integral part of our industry's advancement.

The working group focused initially on L&D but quickly extended the principles to all core talent processes, defined as those processes that directly contribute to achieving high-level organizational outcomes. By mid-2012, we expanded TDRp to include talent acquisition, performance management, leadership development, capability development, and total rewards. (See appendix A for more detail.) In this book, we concentrate only on L&D. You can find the measures and sample reports for the other HR processes at CenterforTalentReporting.org.

Now that we had developed TDRp, it needed a home. The Center for Talent Reporting (CTR) was created in 2012 to be such a home and to advocate for TDRp's adoption. CTR would also provide resources to help the profession implement TDRp, including webinars, written guidance, workshops, and an annual conference.

With this background, let's turn to *Measurement Demystified*, which we wrote to help you, the L&D practitioner, better measure, analyze, report, and manage learning at both a program and department level, with the ultimate aim of delivering greater value to your organization.

About This Book

Our approach outlined in the following chapters will work for both small and large organizations, even if yours is an L&D staff of only one or two. Typically, smaller organizations will have fewer programs, so the number of measures and reports will also be smaller. Larger organizations will have greater complexity and require greater effort, so they will have to set some priorities. Even so, the guidance remains the same: Start small and grow. The approach also works for all types of organizations—for profit, nonprofit, government, education, and the military.

Our outlook on each topic is very practical. We all have limited resources, including limited time and imperfect data. We all operate in an environment of continual change and uncertainty. As practitioners, our goal is to do the best we can with what we have to help our organizations succeed. Consequently, we use imperfect and often incomplete data because that is usually better than the alternative, which is to do nothing. We plan, estimate, and forecast knowing that we will be wrong but, if we do it smartly, the effort will be worthwhile and contribute to our organization's success.

With that approach in mind, each chapter builds on the preceding chapters. You can jump directly to a chapter that interests you but, if you are not already familiar with all the reasons for measuring and the TDRp framework, we advise you to read chapter 1 first. Likewise, since we present a new framework for reporting, it will be helpful if you read chapter 8 before other chapters on reporting. After you are familiar with the framework and measures, you can use the book for performance support and go to the relevant section for definitions of measures or guidance on reports. Here is a description of the chapters:

In chapter 1, we start by discussing the many reasons to measure and then share the TDRp framework, classifying the reasons to measure into four categories to simplify communication and understanding. We provide a maturity model for measurement, employing the four broad reasons to measure, and classify measures into three types and reports into five types. The chapter ends with a discussion of the recently released International Organization for Standardization's (ISO) Human Capital Reporting Standards and their integration with TDRp.

Chapter 2 completes our foundational discussion of measurement by explaining the importance of including all three types of measures in a measurement strategy. In chapter 3 we begin our detailed discussion of measures by introducing efficiency (or activity) measures, which are by far the most numerous in the profession. We provide definitions and recommendations on 107 of these foundational measures, including those benchmarked by the Association for Talent Development in its annual *State of the Industry* report and those recommended by the ISO.

Chapters 4 and 5 explore effectiveness and outcome measures, the subjects of many books on evaluation. We provide a comprehensive introduction to these important measures and a discussion of the key differences between the Kirkpatrick and Phillips approaches. We define each measure and detail the options for calculation. We also include a list of measures that commonly benchmarked.

In chapter 6, we provide guidance on how to create a robust measurement strategy, including all the key elements. Then in chapter 7, we incorporate what we've learned so far to guide the reader in selecting the right measures based on their purpose for measuring. We provide examples of recommended measures for common programs and improvement initiatives.

Chapter 8 revisits the TDRp framework to explore the five different types of reports, employing the measures we've described so far. We suggest how to select the proper report to meet a specific need. Chapter 9 focuses on one type of report, the management report, and details the three specific management reports recommended for use in managing learning programs and department initiatives.

Chapters 10, 11, and 12 complete the exploration of reporting, first by providing guidance on creating a reporting strategy, and second by providing instruction on how to create values for the selected measures, including planning and forecasting. Some readers will find chapters 11 and 12 challenging, not because the concepts or measurements are difficult, but because there are so many options.

We end by sharing implementation guidance in chapter 13 and pulling all the elements of the book together in chapter 14. In addition to a history of the TDRp adoption, the appendix includes an example document of roles and responsibilities for L&D and goal owners, a sample measurement and reporting strategy, a sample project implementation plan, and a glossary.

To see how the concepts fit together, review the chapter layout here (Figure I-1).

Definitions of Terms We Use in the Book

The glossary provides definitions for more than 190 terms; here we share some of the most basic and important terms we use in the book.

We use the term *measure* as a noun to be synonymous with *metric* and *KPI* (key performance indicator). At one time, KPI might have been reserved for only the few key or important measures, but today it is commonly used for any measure.

Figure I-1. Chapter Layout

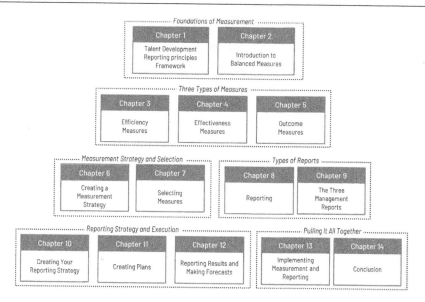

While many in the profession consider any operation involving numbers to be *analytics,* we reserve the term to mean higher-level analysis, often involving statistical tools. For example, we will not refer to determining the number of participants or courses as analytics. The same is true for reporting the average participant reaction for a program. In both cases, the value of the measure is simply the total or average of the measured values—no analysis required. In contrast, a detailed examination of any of the values of these measures, perhaps using their frequency distribution, the use of regression to forecast the value of a measure, or the use of correlation to discover relationships among measures will be referred to as *data analytics* or *analysis.*

Think of it this way: *measurement* provides the quantification of the measure, which is typically an input for analysis (the old term for analytics). There are exceptions, however, and sometimes analysis is required to determine the value of a measure (isolated impact, for example). In summary, simply measuring and reporting the value of a measure does not generally rise to the level of analytics; more than arithmetic is required to be considered analytics. (Figure I-2 describes the connections among measurement, analytics, methodologies, and reporting.)

With this context, we suggest the following definitions for these important terms:

- **Measure** (synonymous with metric and KPI). As a noun, it is the name associated with a particular indicator. For example, the number of participants is a measure. As a verb, it is the act of finding the value of the indicator.
- **Measurement.** The process of measuring or finding values for indicators.
- **Analytics** (synonymous with analysis). An in-depth exploration of the data, which may include advanced statistical techniques, such as regression, to extract insights from the data or discover relationships among measures.

The Institute for Operations Research and Management Science defines analytics as "the scientific process of transforming data into insights for making better decisions," but we believe this definition is overly restrictive. We agree that the intent of analytics is to provide insights, but the effort is not always directed toward decision making. Sometimes, the goal is simply a better understanding of the data or of relationships among multiple measures. Furthermore, an analytics effort may not always provide insights or lead to better decisions, just as an experiment may not always produce the hypothesized result.

While terms such as *program*, *initiative*, *course*, and *class* are often used interchangeably, we will define each specifically, borrowing from academic terminology:

- **Program.** A course or series of courses with similar learning objectives designed to accomplish a business or HR goal or meet an organizational need. For example, a program to improve leadership may comprise four related courses over a six-month period. At the university level, a program leading to a degree in economics may require 12 courses over a four-year period.

- **Course.** A class or series of classes, an online module or series of online modules, prework, post-work, performance support, discussion boards, and other types of learning to convey related and integrated content. For example, a course on leadership may consist of four hours of prereading, two online modules, four instructor-led classes, an online discussion board, and performance support. In a corporate environment, each course will have a specific designation in the learning management system (LMS). At the university level, students will enroll in specific courses each term such as Economics 101.

- **Class.** Each physical or virtual meeting of students where content is conveyed by an instructor. A course may consist of just one class if the content can be conveyed in one sitting or it may require multiple classes to convey all the content. At the university level, a semester-long course like Econ 101 might meet for two classes per week for 10 weeks. It is also possible that the number of students enrolled in a course exceeds the optimum class size, which necessitates multiple classes even if the content can be conveyed in a single sitting. So, a one-hour instructor-led course for 150 employees will require six classes of 25 each. The analogy at the university level is 300 students taking Econ 101 where enrollment is limited to 100 per class. In this case there will be three sections with 100 in each.

- **Online or e-learning module.** A single session of computer, tablet, or mobile-based instruction that may last from five or 10 minutes to an hour or more. Each online module will typically require the user to log in, with completion recorded in the LMS.

- **Initiative.** May be used in place of program but may also designate a coordinated series of actions to improve the effectiveness or efficiency of the L&D department. For example, there may be an initiative to reduce complaints about the LMS, lower department costs, or improve the application rate of learning in general across all courses. In this book we will use the term *program* when the effort addresses business or HR goals, or organizational needs like onboarding or basic skills training. We will use the term *initiative* when the effort is not directly aligned to business or HR goals or organizational needs, but instead focuses more on improving the efficiency or effectiveness of L&D department processes and systems or all programs.

Here are several other key terms and their definitions, which we will use frequently:

- **Learning and development.** The name of the professional field and many training departments dedicated to increasing the knowledge, skills, and capabilities of the workforce. Other names for L&D departments include training, organization development, and talent development, although the last two may include additional responsibilities such as succession planning.
- **Formal learning.** Learning that is structured and organized or directed by someone other than the learner. This includes instructor-led training (ILT) where the instructor is physically located with the participants, virtual ILT (vILT) where the instructor is at a different location than the participants, e-learning, structured coaching, and structured mobile learning.
- **Informal learning.** Learning that is not structured, organized, or directed by someone else. The participant learns on their own though self-discovery. This includes social learning, knowledge sharing, on-the-job learning, unstructured coaching, and personal learning through Internet or library exploration.
- **CLO (chief learning officer).** The person ultimately responsible for learning in an organization. This position may also be named vice president of training or director of training. If the person also has responsibility for other aspects of talent, the position may be called chief talent officer (CTO) or chief human resources officer (CHRO).
- **Employees or headcount.** The unique count of all employees at a point in time. Part-time employees are counted as well as full-time employees. Note: If an organization uses many contingent workers (temporary employees and contract workers), consideration should be given to using the term *workforce* (employees plus contingent workers) in addition to, or as replacement for, number of employees.
- **FTE (full-time equivalent).** This is a way of measuring full-time effort (40 hours per week x 52 weeks per year) when some employees are part-time and do not work 40 hours per week or 52 weeks per year. For example, if two part-time employees each work half-time, the full-time equivalent of their effort is 1.0 FTE.

Finally, throughout this book, we discuss the connections among the four foundational elements of TDRp:

- **Reporting**, which we define as an approach to structure measures and analysis to share results with stakeholders.
- **Measurement methodologies**, which we define as a process and suite of standards and tools that guide how practitioners execute a specific approach. The learning measurement profession uses several well-known methodologies such as:
  - Kirkpatrick Four Levels of Evaluation

- ◦ Phillips ROI Methodology
- ◦ Brinkerhoff Success Case Method.
- **Analytics** and **measurement**, the third and fourth components we defined previously.

In the interplay of these relationships, measurement is at the base, supplying the inputs to our methodologies (for example, Kirkpatrick or Phillips), as well as the analytics we employ (Figure 2). In some cases, however, the methodologies will dictate what measures we must use. Or, as we mentioned earlier, analytics may be required to compute a specific measure, such as the isolated impact of learning.

Figure I-2. The Interplay of Reporting, Analytics, Measurement, and Methodologies

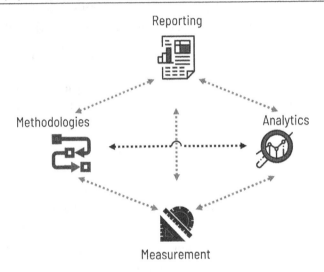

Reporting provides a way to display our data, ascertain trends, and provide insights into progress against targets or goals. Reports will often trigger a request for a deeper dive. Depending on how we have structured the reports, we may be able to drill down and get answers to our questions. In other cases, the reports may require additional analysis to understand the root causes behind observed results.

Conversely, a learning leader might formulate a hypothesis such as, "learners with low levels of management support are less likely to apply the learning." Through an impact study or ad hoc analysis, we can confirm or deny this hypothesis about manager support. The insights from the analysis may suggest ongoing reporting of new measures (for example, manager support). Moreover, the reports enable us to monitor results and determine if the hypothesis holds over time.

Understanding the interplay among the four elements of reporting, methodologies, analytics, and measures will help you see how you can navigate the implementation of TDRp within your own organization.

With all this in mind, let's get started.

PART I

Foundations of Measurement

CHAPTER 1
The Talent Development Reporting Principles (TDRp) Framework

The Talent Development Reporting principles (TDRp) framework simplifies the measurement, reporting, and management of learning. We use this framework throughout the book to provide a common language to help you understand the reasons to measure, select the right measures, and know how to share them in the right reports.

At its core, the TDRp framework answers three questions:

1. What are the reasons to measure?
2. What measures should I use?
3. What should I do with them once I have them?

We begin by addressing each of these questions, starting with the reasons to measure. We then discuss the complete TDRp framework and its relationship to other standard-setting efforts.

Reasons for Measuring

The starting point for all measurement and reporting strategies should be an answer to this question: "Why do we want to measure?" The answer will directly influence your choice of measures, how you use them, how you present them, and how frequently you report them.

There are many reasons for measuring, as shown in Figure 1-1. In some cases, we simply want to communicate results in a report, scorecard, or dashboard. In others, we want to answer questions that leaders have about the effectiveness of a specific initiative. Or we want to demonstrate value and the benefit provided by a curriculum or portfolio of programs, which will also help to build the case for new or additional investment.

Figure 1-1. Why Do We Want to Measure?

All of these are valid and may also depend on the specific needs of the organization. Whatever the reason, it is important to know the user and understand their needs. So, the recommended measures will always depend on the user and the context.

A Framework for Measurement

Given the many reasons to measure, it will be helpful to have a framework for measurement that highlights the most common reasons for measuring and segments the measures into fewer categories. Based on our experience, the reasons for measuring fall into four primary categories, which are an important part of the TDRp framework: **inform, monitor, evaluate and analyze,** and **manage.** Within each category, there are several specific reasons for measuring, each of which will guide your decisions on what data to collect, when to gather it, how to report it, and how to drive use of the data. Let's explore each of these major reasons and delve into the practices that organizations are most commonly using today.

Inform

The most common reason for measurement is to inform. Practitioners generate dashboards, scorecards, and reports to share activity, identify trends, answer questions, and surface opportunities for improvement. L&D teams also use the data to create their own internal benchmarks or submit their results to industry surveys for benchmarking.

When the purpose of measurement is to inform, L&D practitioners typically generate static reports shared via scorecards, dashboards, Excel spreadsheets, or even email updates.

Monitor

While informing is an important reason to measure, many leaders want to take a more active role in the process. When the purpose of measurement is to monitor, the recipients of the information want to know both what happened and how the results compare to a preestablished threshold, benchmark, or goal. Monitoring implies that a manager or leader wants to assess if the measure is meeting the threshold.

For example, an ongoing course's Level 1 participant reaction may be running in the 80–90 percent favorable range. L&D leaders have determined that they want to maintain it at 80 percent or higher. The measurement analyst would then generate a scorecard, which would highlight any Level 1 score below 80 percent. Alternatively, system administrators could program the system to generate a warning if the measure falls below 80 percent.

Another example could be monitoring participants for a course when all are expected to complete it. A monthly scorecard would show progress toward the 100 percent threshold and detailed reports could be generated showing those who have not yet completed it.

Evaluate and Analyze

Another common reason to measure is to evaluate and analyze. Efforts to determine the effectiveness of a program and demonstrate its value represent the primary activities for many measurement analysts.

Program evaluation is a major discipline within the measurement and evaluation field not only for profit-making organizations but also for nonprofit and government institutions. Because program evaluation is such an important driver of measurement, hundreds of books, whitepapers, and websites devote space to building competency and providing best practices for program evaluation.

While this has traditionally focused on evaluating the results of a specific program or initiative, measurement analysts are increasingly leveraging engagement, hiring, promotion, succession, and retention data to explore broader workforce trends. For example, large organizations with HR and talent data warehouses often examine the impact of engagement on employee productivity, or the relationship between manager effectiveness and attrition of high performers. Learning organizations are exploring the relationship between specific types of learning (for example, learning experience portals) and employee engagement and growth. Analysis that incorporates broader HR data provides important input for the learning strategy and processes to ensure access to the right learning at the right time by the right employees. As organizations accumulate greater volumes of data, improved data quality and accessibility of disparate data elements will enable increasingly more sophisticated analysis efforts.

Manage

The last reason for measuring is to manage programs, processes, people, and ultimately the L&D function. Management implies that leaders have established a plan, target, or goal for each measure and that L&D leaders have committed to actively managing the program or initiative throughout the year to deliver the planned results. While monitoring involves a threshold, which is near the historical value of the measure, leaders need to manage when the plan or goal represents a significant change from the status quo. In other words, you manage when you want to "move the needle" on a measure with an understanding that you may have to devote significant effort to effect the change.

The management process requires the creation of monthly reports showing at a minimum the plan, year-to-date (YTD) results, and a comparison of YTD results to plan. Ideally, the report will also show the forecast or value for the plan at year end if no special actions are taken. Since most L&D managers are not managing this way today, this reason for measuring represents the greatest opportunity for the use of measures.

In summary, each reason for measuring has an important role in enabling leaders, stakeholders, and initiative owners to keep abreast of progress, understand what's working and what's not, and make data-informed decisions about the actions needed to sustain the program or get it back on track (Figure 1-2).

Figure 1-2. The Four Reasons for Measuring

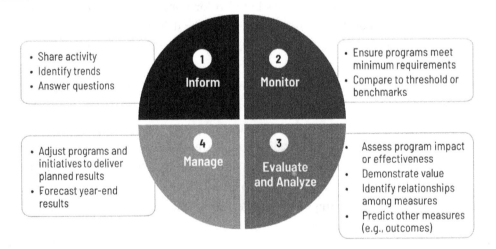

Measurement Maturity

Although all four categories represent important reasons to measure, their descriptions suggest a hierarchy of measurement purposes (shown in Figure 1-3), which will help organizations assess their measurement maturity and create their measurement strategy.

Figure 1-3. Hierarchy of Reasons to Measure

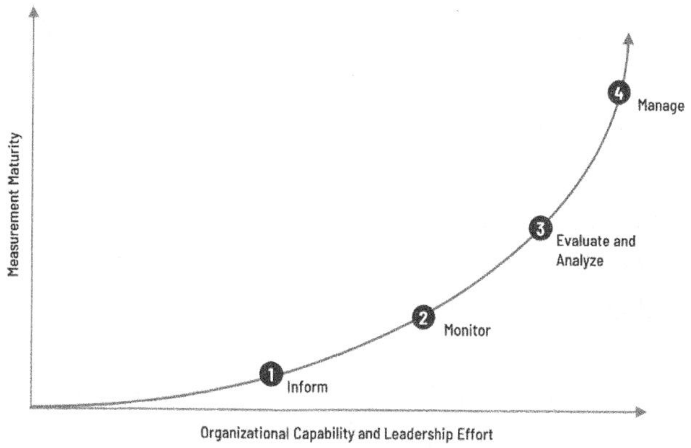

Informing

Informing represents the beginning of the measurement journey for organizations. At this level, leaders develop and report basic, foundational measures such as the number of courses and participants or the percentage of employees receiving training.

Monitoring

Monitoring represents the second logical step in the use of measures. When moving from informing to monitoring, the role and capabilities of leaders steps up a notch. At this level, leaders have identified not only the key measures, but also the acceptable levels for each of them. When the measure's value falls beneath the threshold, program owners are alerted that they need to take action.

Evaluating and Analyzing

Evaluating and analyzing is the third step in the hierarchy. At this stage, the organization uses measures to determine if a program is effective and what relationships (for example, correlations) exist among important measures. Evaluation and analysis is a big step up requiring considerably more effort and skill than monitoring.

At this step, leaders will often want a more robust set of measures. In the case of learning, they will go beyond reaction and learning data to measure application, impact, and return on investment (ROI). In addition to identifying relationships among L&D measures, analysts often examine the relationship between learning measures and HR or business measures. For example, leaders may ask, "Did the new product introduction training result in shorter sales cycle times or contribute to increased order levels in the first six months?" Or, leaders may ask, "Did learning contribute to higher employee engagement and retention?" When senior business leaders begin asking questions that they can't answer by simply monitoring basic data, L&D needs to build internal capability and the commitment to robust evaluation and analysis processes.

Managing

Managing is the highest-level reason for measuring programs, initiatives, processes, resources, and the overall L&D function. Managing requires that leaders first establish plans or targets for critical measures and then use monthly reported measures to determine if the program is on target to achieve the planned results. If not, managers need to take corrective action to get the program back on track.

Management is the most intensive use of measurement and requires the greatest skill and effort, but it also delivers the biggest payoff. As in any maturity model, management requires the foundational capability of the three other levels, particularly evaluation and analysis, to be effective.

While management seems like the obvious and logical level of measurement that leaders should aspire to achieve, many organizations have not fully embraced it. In fact, most measurement maturity models in the profession now list analytics and prediction (Level 3 in our model) as the highest level of maturity. The practice of setting plans and comparing results monthly to plan requires a level of business acumen, analysis, and discipline that many simply don't have or desire. Management also requires a tolerance for uncertainty and a willingness to be accountable. Chapter 9 on management reporting explores this topic of running learning like a business in greater detail.

The four reasons to measure hierarchy, along with descriptions of primary use, level of analysis, measurement frequency, and key elements, are shown in Table 1-1.

Table 1-1. Measurement Requirements at Each Maturity Level

Measurement Purpose	Primary Use	Level of Analysis	Measurement Frequency	Key Elements
Manage	• Identify if the program is delivering planned results and where adjustments are needed to meet goals.	High	Monthly	• Plan • YTD results • Forecast for measures being managed
Evaluate and analyze	• Analyze program and non-program data. • Explore relationships among measures. • Predict outcomes.	Medium to high	Based on business need	• Analytical methods (e.g., regression analysis, predictive modeling)
	• Evaluate the efficiency, effectiveness, or impact of a learning program.		End of program or pilot	• Six levels of evaluation (Level 0 to Level 5)
Monitor	• Determine if measure meets threshold or is within acceptable range.	Low	Monthly or quarterly	• Threshold or breakpoints for measures
Inform	• Answer questions, identify key trends, and share activity.	Low	As needed	• Specific measures or trends

Measurement Maturity (vertical label with upward arrow)

Copyright applied for by Center for Talent Reporting (2020). Used with permission.

The same measure may appear in each category but serve a different purpose. For example, the application of learning on the job could very well appear in each category. A leader may have a question about the level of job application across the organization (Inform). Leaders may set a minimum threshold for it and see that it is met each month (Monitor). For many programs, a goal owner may use application of learning as an indicator of program effectiveness (Evaluate) and want to understand if it is predictive of impact and perhaps employee retention (Analyze). For strategic programs, managers should actively manage the application rate monthly to ensure that the organization is achieving planned levels of application as part of an effort to achieve a business or HR goal (Manage).

At this point, you may be asking, where do reporting and analytics fit into the measurement hierarchy? The simple answer is that both reporting and analytics are methods that help achieve the purposes we have just described.

Reporting is a powerful means to highlight data anomalies or surface patterns in the data that program owners should address. John Tukey, an eminent 20th century statistician, said, "One great virtue of good graphical representation is that it can serve to display clearly and effectively a message carried by quantities whose calculation or observation is far from simple" (Tukey and Wilk 1965). We believe that all well-designed reporting can achieve this outcome, not simply those with graphical depictions.

Reporting is useful for all levels in the hierarchy, whether to inform through a standard scorecard or help manage a program through alerts when a measure is below is predetermined threshold. Reporting is critical to leaders and practitioners at all levels of the organization to meet their commitments and deliver quality programs.

Analytics is important at higher levels of the maturity curve, namely for evaluation, analysis, and management. Analytics is also required to answer multi-tier and complex questions. Reporting tends to answer questions such as "What just happened?" and "Where is the problem?" Analytics answers questions such as "Why is this happening?" or "What will happen if we don't make changes to our current processes or practices?" Analytics requires a deeper level of statistical analysis, often involving regression analysis or predictive modeling. Analytical methods are essential to verify the link between inputs, activities, output, impacts, and ultimate outcomes. And in turn, these causal links are most important for evaluation, analysis, and management. There are a variety of approaches that practitioners use for reporting and analytics (Table 1-2).

Table 1-2. The Role of Reporting and Analytics in the Measurement Hierarchy

Measurement Purpose		Types of Reporting		Types of Analytics
Manage	↑	• Management reports • Program evaluation reports	↑	• Optimization • Predictive modeling
Evaluate and analyze	Reporting	• Custom analysis reports • Static or dynamic dashboards	Analytics	• Statistical modeling • Forecasting/ extrapolation
Monitor	↓	• Scorecards • Alerts/exception reports	↓	
Inform		• Ad hoc reports		

(Measurement Maturity — vertical arrow on left)

In conclusion, the natural starting point in our journey to measure, report, and manage is to ask the fundamental question, "Why do we want to measure?" While the answer may not always lead to a unique set of measures, it will determine how we use the measures, how we present them, and how frequently we share them. In chapters 6 and 7, we employ the four broad reasons to measure to create a measurement strategy and select appropriate measures.

TDRp Measures

The second question answered by the TDRp framework provides a classification scheme for the measures themselves. For simplicity, we recommend three types of measures for L&D and HR: efficiency measures, effectiveness measures, and outcome measures (Table 1-3). Note this book focuses on measures and reports for L&D only. The Center for Talent Reporting (CTR) website provides measures and sample reports for other HR disciplines.

Table 1-3. The Three Types of TDRp Measures

Type	Description	Examples

Efficiency measures	Provide insight into the quantity of training delivered, its utilization, cost, and reach within the organization.	• Quantity
		  ○ Number of participants
		  ○ Number of courses
		  ○ Number of course hours
		  ○ Percentage of courses delivered on time
		• Utilization and reach
		  ○ Classroom utilization
		  ○ Instructor utilization
		  ○ Percentage of learners trained in target audience
		• Cost
		  ○ Total L&D spend
		  ○ Cost per learner

Effectiveness measures	Provide insight into the quality of the programs using models such as Kirkpatrick and Phillips	• Reaction • Learning • Application • Impact • ROI • Manager support
Outcome measures	Demonstrate the impact of learning on business or HR goals.	• Impact on sales growth • Impact on product quality • Impact on customer satisfaction • Impact on risk reduction

As we will discuss in chapter 2, these three types of measures, when used together, not only enable L&D functions to focus their energies but also mitigate unintended consequences when organizations focus only on one category of measure and ignore the rest.

Origins of the Three Types of Measures

The TDRp working group selected the three types of measures after reviewing the literature and discussing alternatives. David van Adelsberg and Edward Trolley had suggested two categories of effectiveness and efficiency in their 1999 book *Running Training like a Business.* Many practitioners followed their lead or settled on the same two categories independently. In this two-category framework, outcome or impact was included under effectiveness.

John Boudreau and Peter Ramstad developed the HC BRidge framework in their 2007 book *Beyond HR.* The framework focuses on impact (outcome) from a logic model perspective (Figure 1-4).

Figure 1-4. HC BRidge Framework Adapted From Boudreau and Ramstad

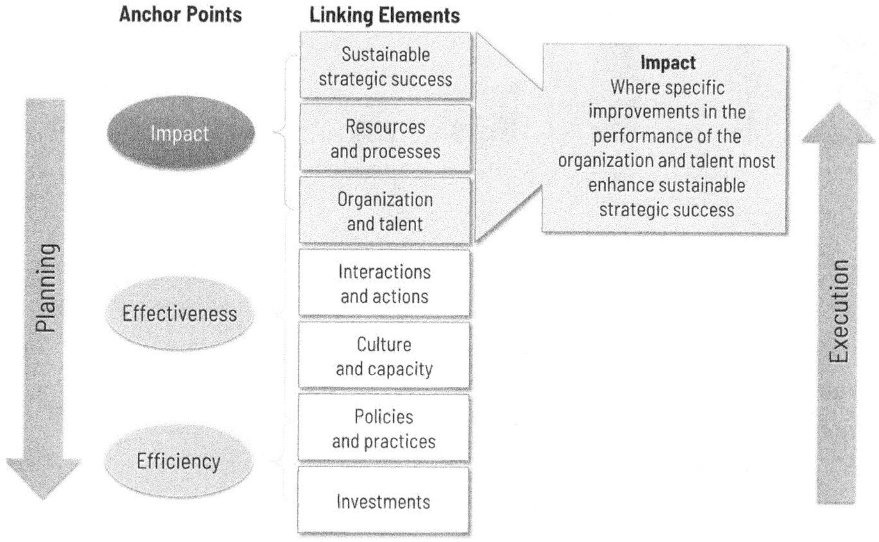

Boudreau and Ramstad's framework demonstrates that planning starts with identifying the business impact measures to ensure that L&D is focusing on those areas that create sustainable strategic advantage to the organization. With a clear focus on the areas leaders must address, planning then identifies the important talent pools that will drive that sustainable advantage. The organization should then ensure that their programs will align these talent pools and focus on building capability (human capacity). At this point, the focus shifts to the appropriate HR practices (such as L&D) that enable performance improvement along with the appropriate investments to realize the ultimate impact. In essence, the HC BRidge framework starts with the end in mind for planning and begins with the investments and HR practices for execution.

Research in 2010 by Jack Phillips confirmed the need to explicitly identify impact (outcome) as a separate category of measure (Phillips and Phillips 2010). He asked CEOs what measures they currently received from their learning department and what measures they would like to see. Their results are shown in Figure 1-5. The findings revealed a large gap between what organizations at the time measured relative to the needs of CEOs. It was clear that L&D needed to balance its measurement practices by including not simply efficiency measures (such as participation rates and costs) but also higher-level effectiveness measures (application, impact, and ROI).

Figure 1-5. What CEOs Want to See

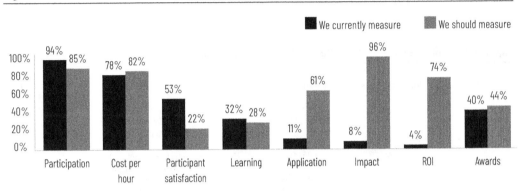

In light of the desire by CEOs to see impact, and the current state of not reporting it, and given its prominent role in any logic model like the HC BRidge model, the TDRp thought leaders and practitioners agreed that outcome (impact) should be a separate category of measure, even though it is the only measure in the category.

It is interesting to note that research conducted by the Association for Talent Development (ATD) found that most L&D departments were still not reporting impact to their CEO. The 2019 study, *Effective Evaluation: Measuring Learning Programs for Success*, showed that only 38 percent reported impact and 16 percent reported ROI.

As you might imagine, there are other frameworks, some with as many as nine categories of measures (Bersin 2008). The TDRp development team, however, believed that for a framework to be powerful and widely accepted, it must be easy to remember and simple to use. The working group agreed that three categories could encompass all relevant measures while meeting the design principle of simplicity and ease of use.

In chapters 2 through 5 we examine each type of measure in greater detail, including the commonly used measures in each category.

TDRp Reports

The third question answered by the TDRp framework is, "What should I do with the measures once I have them?" We recommend five broad types of reports to employ in presenting the measures: **scorecards, dashboards, program evaluation reports, custom analysis reports,** and **management reports**. Each has a specific purpose and is related to the reason to measure, as described in Table 1-4.

Table 1-4. Five Types of TDRp Reports

Type of Report	Description
Scorecards	These reports focus on **informing**. Typically static, they provide a snapshot of current performance compared to a threshold or benchmark. You can generate scorecards at any cadence, but in the L&D world, generally monthly or quarterly. If the scorecard includes a threshold, it may also be used for **monitoring**. Scorecards usually contain detailed data and are particularly useful for answering very specific questions or identifying trends or anomalies.
Dashboards	These reports are more advanced than scorecards and often contain visual displays. Unlike their static scorecard counterpart, dashboards may be continuously updated, depending on the reporting cadence of the underlying data. Dashboards may also be interactive, allowing the user to access detail or select measures. If the dashboard includes a threshold, it may also be used for **monitoring**. Dashboards usually contain summary measures rather than detailed data and therefore are especially well suited to briefing leaders.
Program evaluation reports	These reports present the results of a program **evaluation** to determine its efficiency, effectiveness, and impact, usually at the end of a program.
Custom analysis reports	These reports present the results of an **analysis** to determine the relationship among various measures or to predict the value of a measure based on its relationship with other measures.
Management reports	Management reports, as the name suggests, focus on enabling leaders to **manage** their business. They are produced at a predefined cadence (monthly or quarterly) and are typically static reports showing progress against plan and a forecast of year-end results. There are three types of management reports: the operations report, the program report, and the summary report.

Reports may now be added to the measurement requirements to explicitly show their relationship to the reasons for measuring. See the right-hand column in Table 1-5 for the type of report recommended for each reason for measuring.

Origins of the Five Types of Reports

While scorecards, dashboards, program evaluation reports, and custom analysis reports have been in use for many years, the literature did not reveal any management reports in common use that would be analogous to the three statements used by accounting. Consequently, TDRp thought leaders decided to focus on creating reports to manage. Following the lead of accounting, which employs three standard statements (income, balance sheet, and cash flow), TDRp recommends three management reports modeled on the work of several practitioners with the same type of format found in other department's monthly reports (like sales and manufacturing).

Table 1-5. Complete Measurement Requirements at Each Maturity Level

Measurement Purpose	Primary Use	Level of Analysis	Measurement Frequency	Key Elements	Shared In
Manage	• Identify if the program is delivering planned results and where adjustments are needed to meet goals	High	Monthly	• Plan • YTD results • Forecast for measures being managed	• Management reports
Evaluate and analyze	• Analyze program and non-program data • Explore relationships among measures • Predict outcomes	Medium to high	Based on business need	• Analytical methods (e.g., regression analysis, predictive modeling)	• Custom analysis reports
	• Evaluate the efficiency, effectiveness, or impact of a learning program		End of program or pilot	• Six levels of evaluation (Level 0 to Level 5)	• Program evaluation reports
Monitor	• Determine if measure meets threshold or is within acceptable range	Low	Monthly or quarterly	• Threshold or breakpoints for measures	• Dashboards • Scorecards
Inform	• Answer questions, identify key trends, and share activity	Low	As needed	• Specific measures or trends	• Dashboards • Scorecards

Measurement Maturity (vertical label with arrow on left)

Copyright applied for by Center for Talent Reporting (2020). Used with permission.

The Three Types of Management Reports

The **operations report** includes specific effectiveness and efficiency measures the chief learning officer (CLO) has chosen to manage for improvement or to hit a planned target (like number of participants). The report helps the CLO manage L&D initiatives and ensure that they are tracking to the plan. The CLO would receive a monthly operations report that would be reviewed with staff.

The **program report** depicts the key effectiveness and efficiency measures for the most important programs in support of achieving the outcome measure for a single goal. One program report will be generated and reviewed monthly for each high-level goal or need supported by learning. The report helps the goal owner, the program manager, and the CLO manage programs in support of important organizational goals, such as increasing sales by 10 percent.

The last management report is the **summary report**. The target audience for this report includes the CEO, chief financial officer (CFO), governing board, senior vice president of HR, L&D employees, and anyone else interested in a high-level overview of learning. This report shows the alignment of learning to organizational business and HR goals, the impact of learning on those goals, and key effectiveness and efficiency measures. The summary report would be used quarterly by the CLO to brief the CEO, senior leaders, and employees on the performance of L&D against its efficiency, effectiveness, and outcome goals. Management of programs and department initiatives takes place using the program and operations reports, while the summary report is a nontechnical report for sharing the plan and results. L&D would generate the summary report at least quarterly.

Following the format of other internal reports, each of the three management reports includes the plan or target, YTD results, and the forecast for each measure.

Chapter 9 covers these three types of management reports in more detail.

The Complete TDRp Framework

The complete TDRp framework is illustrated in Figure 1-6 and a description of each component follows.

Figure 1-6. The Complete TDRp Framework

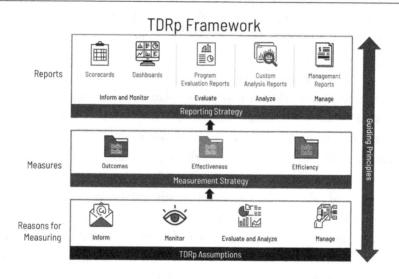

Reports

At the top of the framework are the outputs, which include five types of reports, each with a different intended purpose:

- **Scorecards** focus on informing but also may be used for monitoring.
- **Dashboards** also focus on informing but may also be useful for monitoring.
- **Project evaluation** reports focus on the results of a program evaluation.
- **Custom analysis reports** focus on results of an analysis to determine or use the relationship among various measures.
- **Management reports**, as the name suggests, focus on enabling leaders to manage their business.

Measures

Measures feed each type of report, depending on the reasons to measure. Efficiency and effectiveness measures should appear in all types of reports while outcome measures may only appear in program evaluation reports, custom analysis reports, or management reports.

Reasons for Measuring

There are four broad categories of reasons to measure: inform, monitor, evaluate and analyze, and manage. Since this is the starting point in any measurement and reporting strategy, it sits at the bottom.

TDRp Assumptions

Assumptions (at the base) provide the foundation. Four important assumptions underlie the TDRp framework and reflect the application of management principles to HR. Understanding these assumptions upfront should reduce potential misunderstandings and provide context for the other elements.

The first assumption clearly states the strategic role of HR; the second addresses the need for strategic alignment; the third addresses planning in an uncertain world; and the fourth acknowledges the role of competent managers:

1. The primary purpose of human capital initiatives and processes is to build organizational capability that enables the organization to achieve its goals or achieve its goals more quickly or at lower cost.

2. Whenever possible, human capital initiatives and processes should align strategically to the goals of the organization. HR leaders will meet proactively with stakeholders to discuss and agree on the role of initiatives and processes in meeting the organization's goals and will set appropriate goals for the initiative or process. Goal setting will involve uncertainty and will entail the use of estimates and forecasts.

3. The business environment is characterized by significant uncertainty and yet leaders must still establish plans with the best information available. Waiting for absolute certainty and perfection is not an option.

4. The recommended reports and the underlying data will be used appropriately by competent, experienced leaders to manage the function and meet agreed-upon goals and to continuously improve.

Guiding Principles

Guiding principles (right-hand arrow) provide direction for the standards, reports, and analysis just as GAAP (Generally Accepted Accounting Principles) and IFRS (International Financial Reporting Standards) provide direction for accounting concepts, statements, analysis, and reports. There are seven guiding and generally accepted principles for reporting at the executive level (program managers, goal owners, CLO, CFO, CEO):

1. Executive reporting should employ concise and balanced measures and a consistent and clearly defined format.
   - Key effectiveness, efficiency, and outcome measures should be reported and tracked on a regular basis.
   - Plans should be set for key outcome, effectiveness, and efficiency measures. Performance to plan should be tracked and reported.
   - Executive reports should include, at a minimum, results for last year, current year plan, current YTD results, and a current year forecast. Detailed reports typically include just the results, which may be daily, weekly, monthly, quarterly, or yearly.

2. Executive reports should be produced and communicated with a frequency and thoroughness to enable appropriate management of the function.

3. Executive reporting should include actionable recommendations.

4. Data integrity and completeness should be maintained.

5. Appropriate analytical methods should be employed.

6. The impact and value or benefit of initiatives and processes should be identified whenever appropriate, preferably by the stakeholder at the outset of the initiative.

7. The full costs of human capital initiatives and processes should be captured and reported whenever possible.

With the TDRp framework complete, we can now compare it to other frameworks and align it with these standards.

Integration of the TDRp Framework With Other Standard-Setting Efforts

The International Organization for Standardization (ISO) through its Technical Committee on Human Resources (TC260) is working to define and standardize measures for HR and to recommend measures for both internal and external reporting. *ISO Standard 30414:2018 Human Resource Management—Guidelines for Internal and External Human Capital Reporting* was published in December 2018 and represents the first set of voluntary reporting requirements for the field. (See sidebar for discussion of why standards for human capital measures matter.)

There are 59 measures in total with different reporting recommendations based on an organization's size. Internal reporting refers to reports that are shared inside the organization while external reporting refers to public disclosure, which in most cases would also include management discussion of the metrics. The distribution by HR cluster and the recommendations for reporting are shown in Table 1-6 (ISO 2018).

Table 1-6. Distribution and Recommended Reporting for ISO30414 Metrics

HR Cluster	Large Organizations		Small and Medium Organizations	
	Internal	External	Internal	External
Compliance and ethics	5	3	4	1
Costs	7	1	4	1
Diversity	5	5	4	0
Leadership	4	1	0	0
Organizational culture	2	0	2	0
Organizational health, safety, well-being	4	3	3	2
Productivity	2	2	2	2
Recruitment, mobility, turnover	15	5	3	1
Skills and capabilities	5	1	3	1
Succession planning	5	0	2	0
Workforce availability	5	2	5	2
Total	**59**	**23**	**32**	**10**

In this book, we focus on one of the five measures for compliance and ethics, which addresses training (for large organizations); two of the four measures for leadership, which address development (for large organizations); and all five measures for skills and capabilities (for large organizations; Table 1-7). Of these eight training-related measures, seven are efficiency measures and one is an outcome measure. In chapter 3, we highlight and define the efficiency measures; in chapter 5, the outcome measures.

Table 1-7. The Eight Training-Related ISO-Recommended Measures

Cluster and Measure	Type of Measure
Skills and Capabilities	
Total development and training cost	Efficiency
Percentage of employees who participate in training	Efficiency
Percentage of employees who participate in formal training	Efficiency
Average formal training hours per employee	Efficiency
Workforce competency rate	Outcome
Leadership	
Percentage of leaders who participate in training	Efficiency
Percentage of leaders who participate in leadership development	Efficiency
Compliance	
Percentage of employees who have completed training on compliance and ethics	Efficiency

A New Era for HR, A New Human Capital Reporting Standard

By Jeff Higgins, CEO, Human Capital Management Institute, and Member, ISO HR Standards Technical Advisory Group TC260

Why do standards for HR and human capital matter? More to the point, why does *ISO 30414 Human Resource Management—Guidelines for Internal and External Human Capital Reporting* matter? Why should organizations invest time and money to quantify the value of their human capital and report on their performance?

To answer this, it is important to understand the fundamental changes in how work is done that have occurred over the past 20 years. The rise of the computer, software, internet, big data, and other technology has forever changed the way organizations operate, with world economies shifting from industrial driven to technology and services driven. This can be proven simply by listing the top five most valuable companies in the world today: Apple, Amazon, Alphabet (Google), Microsoft, and Facebook. Only two of those existed 30 years ago, and none existed 50 years ago.

As demand for human capital data and metrics skyrocketed, there has been no agreement on what to measure or how to measure it. Without standards, a gap exists and organizations have been free to make up their own rules, or simply report nothing, ensuring continuing gaps or worse, confusion for interested investors, governments and other stakeholders on sustainability, comparability, accountability, and performance.

The ISO30414 human capital reporting standard addresses this measurement and disclosure gap with clear, cross-industry, comparable metrics in a global gold standard with differentiated requirements for organizations both large and small.

Why Standards for Human Capital Matter

There is broad agreement by investors, boards of directors, CEOs, CFOs, governments, HR, and workers that human capital has an impact on organizational success. CEOs frequently state "Our people are our most valuable asset," or "It all starts with people." Shouldn't such valuable asset information be disclosed to key stakeholders?

- The current disclosure gap obscures talent management effectiveness and material human capital risks to investors. With no visibility into the use of a firm's single largest expense, investors must rely on social media tidbits or simply make judgments on no information at all.
- In a world driven by services, data, and the Internet, most would agree that finding, hiring, motivating, and retaining top talent across the organization has equal or greater impact on success than other forms of capital (that is, equipment, real estate, debt, and equity).
- Organizations have a fiduciary duty to communicate existing and potential future risks deemed material to their business since regulatory securities commissions require extensive disclosure of all material items and major assets including financial, physical, and technological assets. Human capital clearly seems material to an organization's current and future success, therefore a fiduciary responsibility exists to provide greater disclosure to stakeholders.

- Today's environment shows increasing concern by policy makers, investors, and stakeholders on how organizations are managed from a governance and sustainability perspective.

ISO 30414 Human Resource Management—Guidelines for Internal and External Human Capital Reporting is a well-researched, rigorously constructed global standard for measuring, reporting, and disclosing human capital performance via standard metrics. The standard addresses both external and internal stakeholder needs, providing a means of disclosing material human capital risks and talent information externally while improving processes and performance internally.

Who can, in the end, argue with the validity of better information to measure, manage, and even predict workforce productivity and performance?

Regarding the ISO effort, the working group on metrics is considering a combination of two frameworks to further classify the measures. One framework is process focused on efficiency, effectiveness, and economy (cost) measures as three performance criteria. The second framework is a logic model or business activity descriptor model used globally by the performance auditing profession to audit the HR practices of organizations. This model consists of four categories of measures: input, process, output, and outcome.

The two frameworks combined would have seven categories and would offer greater granularity and specificity but would create a model too complex for most to remember or use. There is also duplication between the two frameworks. The result is that the measures are mapped from the seven potential ISO categories to the three TDRp categories (Table 1-8).

A practitioner may find these frameworks helpful in a particular project or with a particular client, but in this book, we use the three TDRp categories (efficiency, effectiveness, and outcome) as our measurement classification framework.

Table 1-8. Mapping: ISO Measurement Categories to TDRp Measurement Categories

ISO Category	TDRp Category
Performance Criteria	
Efficiency	Efficiency
Effectiveness	Effectiveness
Economy	Efficiency (cost is a TDRp efficiency measure)
Business Activity Descriptors	
Input	Efficiency (inputs like staff and costs are TDRp efficiency measures)
Process	TDRp efficiency and effectiveness measures are process measures
Output	Generally, a TDRp efficiency measure (e.g., number of employees trained)
Outcome	Outcome

Conclusion

This chapter introduced the TDRp framework. Even if you never create any of the TDRp management reports, the common language about measures will make it much easier for you to communicate with colleagues, identify holes in your existing strategy, and select the appropriate measures to meet your own needs. The chapter also introduced you to the new ISO standards for reporting and explained the relationship between ISO and TDRp categories. In chapters 2–5 we examine each type of measure in greater detail, including the commonly used measures in each category, as well as the eight learning-related ISO measures.

CHAPTER 2

Introduction to Balanced Measures

As we saw in chapter 1, the TDRp framework divides measures into three distinct categories: efficiency, effectiveness, and outcomes. Using these categories ensures that all measures have a home; that is, any measure you use in your organization will fit into one of these three categories.

The question we face is: Do we need measures in all three categories for all programs? Or can we pick and choose which categories of measures are most appropriate and leave it at that?

In this chapter, we make the case for why it is important to have both efficiency and effectiveness measures for all programs and provide guidance on when you should add outcome measures to the mix. We also highlight the unintended consequences of using only one category of measures.

The Consequences of Focusing on a Single Type of Measure

In this section we explore a little history for each type of measure and the unintended consequences of selecting just one. We start with efficiency measures.

Focus Only on Efficiency Measures

There is no mystery why organizations devoted and still devote significant energy to gathering efficiency measures. As we described in chapter 1 and will describe in detail in chapter 3, efficiency measures focus on *how much* and *how long*. These measures, even without technology, are easy to compile and compute. We can easily track how many employees attended our training programs, we can count how many courses we delivered, and we can compute the number of hours of training delivered. With a calculator we can then determine the hours delivered per employee and the average hours of delivery or class. If the raw counts are accurate, the ratios are simple.

With the introduction of the learning management system (LMS) in the late 1990s, organizations could now efficiently compute their efficiency measures. The LMS enabled calculations and reporting at scale, so learning functions used efficiency measures as their primary indicator of success. And when you augment that data with automated financial systems, these organizations now could compute not only throughput but also the direct costs of training and the investment per learner.

While reporting of efficiency measures took a giant leap forward in the early 2000s, organizations still faced challenges. First, many organizations failed to develop standard definitions for measures. For example, one organization with which Peggy consulted had more than 20 different definitions of headcount that varied by line of business or geographical region. A senior HR leader reported that it took more than 100 touches of the headcount data to compute a valid headcount statistic for the CEO. Beyond headcount, the organization didn't have common approaches for computing costs. So, creating comparable ratios of usage or investment were impossible.

Second, the data were typically not actionable. Few organizations we have encountered set throughput or financial goals beyond having an overall budget for learning. If the organization trained 1,000 employees in a new distribution process, no one knew if that was a good or bad number or what to do about it. The tendency was simply to report the data and take the "It is what it is" view of the result.

Finally, and most importantly, efficiency measures only tell part of the story. If your organization delivers 10,000 hours of training per year but has no indication of its effectiveness (aside from ad hoc and anecdotal feedback), it lacks any ability to determine if or where it should improve quality. And often, that lack of insight can lead to unintended consequences.

The most telling client example occurred in 2013 with a business unit within a Fortune 500 firm. Peggy's role was to improve knowledge-sharing processes within the customer contact center of this specific unit. The head of learning for the business unit, new to the firm, had decided that the learning organization had too many resources that were not delivering value. He focused solely on efficiency of the organization, namely, to deliver the most training at the lowest cost. He laid off or redeployed a number of employees and insisted that they reduce their design cycle time to better respond to client needs. Many of his employees, not trained in instructional design, did the best they could within the tight constraints set by their new leader.

As part of her consultant role, Peggy interviewed line employees to understand their onboarding experience and, in particular, how they applied training on the new features of the product at each product launch. They told her that they attended the formal training developed by the department head's staff but that it didn't meet their needs.

Their training lasted from five to 10 days, and the materials consisted of a huge binder filled with paper copies of all the slides. When employees got back to their jobs, they were overwhelmed by the sheer volume of material covered and had no easy way to reference specific sections they didn't understand or refresh their knowledge in areas they forgot. To address this problem, supervisors began to design and conduct "booster" sessions. When asked to describe the booster sessions, the employees reported that supervisors took the binders, separated out the materials into modules, added important tips and techniques, and then retaught the sessions to their employees. Peggy asked, "Are you the only group that is conducting booster sessions?" The response was "no." Most departments were replicating this "best practice" across the business unit.

Stop and think about what happened here. In the push for efficiency, the head of learning cut staff and reduced cost. On the key measures that management cared about, the department head was exceeding expectations. But in the process of cutting cost, he also cut capability. His people churned out substandard training that didn't meet the needs of the line employees, who then filled the gap by designing, developing, and conducting their own "booster" training. If we added up the costs associated with these "shadow" training organizations, it's likely that the head of learning wouldn't have looked so stellar on his primary metric: efficiency. Furthermore, if he had gathered at least some effectiveness data (however crude), he would have known that efficiency without effectiveness is no way to run a department. Here is how an L&D organization overly focused on efficiency without regard to effectiveness can create a downward cycle for itself (Figure 2-1).

Figure 2-1. Consequences of Being Overly Focused on Efficiency

Caution

Efficiency measures (activity, volume, reach, cost) are critical measures for learning but must be balanced with effectiveness measures to avoid unintended consequences.

Focus Only on Effectiveness Measures

As learning measurement became more common in the mid to late 1990s, many organizations began to realize that efficiency measures were necessary but not sufficient. Increasingly, organizations adopted the Kirkpatrick four levels of evaluation (more on that in chapter 4), to measure reaction, learning, and behavior and to discuss results. Some went further to measure the Phillips isolated impact instead of results for Level 4 and added ROI as a fifth level to the mix. Before learning evaluation systems became readily available, many organizations used paper surveys that were either manually tabulated or scanned and tabulated in Excel, often by third-party vendors.

The challenges with paper surveys were multifaceted. In some organizations, instructors were responsible for creating and reviewing their own "smile sheets" (as they were pejoratively called) and then taking action based on the class feedback. This approach prevented any data aggregation across the myriad instructors and classes taught. There was no way to look across all this data and find opportunities for improvement.

Other organizations took the scanning route, sending the completed "scantron" evaluations to a third party, which processed the paper forms and tabulated the results. By engaging a third party and mailing evaluations across the globe, the delay between delivery and publication of results became exceedingly long. At a minimum, weeks passed before the third party provided their findings. In some cases (as Peggy discovered in her own organization), evaluations took months to travel across the globe to the scanning center. The value of the data degraded as it aged, making it less likely that anyone would act on the findings.

About the time that the LMS was taking off and during the height of the dot-com boom, technology solutions were emerging to simplify the gathering of effectiveness data while also speeding the time to insight. SurveyMonkey formed in 1999 as an ad hoc online tool, Metrics That Matter launched in 2000 (originally a product of KnowledgeAdvisors, now part of a suite of integrated employee journey analytics offerings from Explorance), and other solutions followed. The LMS increasingly included basic survey capabilities to gather learner feedback.

Now effectiveness data could be gathered as easily as efficiency data. Online, self-serve systems reduced the administrative burden of collecting, scanning, and processing data and enabled learning organizations to provide results in a day or less rather than weeks or months.

However, effectiveness data, like efficiency data, has its challenges. To gather it at scale requires valid and reliable surveys. In Peggy's own organization at the time, senior learning practitioners questioned if the feedback received online would be fundamentally different from what a learner would record on a paper survey. Also, because surveys were self-report, colleagues questioned if they could rely on personal assessment of how much an employee learned, applied, and improved. While self-report was deemed acceptable for reaction data, clients often pushed back on the reliability of self-report for higher orders of evaluation such as application of learning and business results. Nevertheless, with scalable-data collection options limited, organizations increasingly adopted these methods for gathering effectiveness data.

In addition, L&D was hiring more people with degrees in instructional systems design and leveraging their skills and capabilities to create higher quality training. As a result, in many organizations effectiveness data began to be perceived as more important (and certainly sexier) than efficiency data. Unfortunately, when effectiveness trumps efficiency, the result is a more complex process, involving more people such as designers, subject matter experts (SMEs), and business leaders and considerably longer lead times. And the unintended consequence is that when L&D can't get its products out the door in a timely manner, shadow organizations emerge to fill the gap. Sound familiar? An overdependence on effectiveness measures had serious consequences for the L&D function over time (Figure 2-2).

Figure 2-2. Consequences of Being Overly Focused on Effectiveness

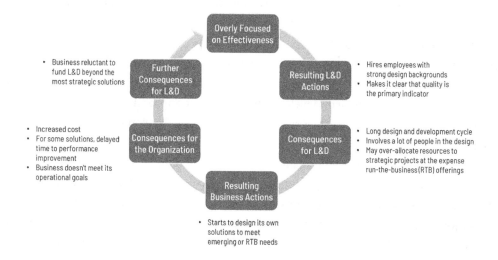

- Business reluctant to fund L&D beyond the most strategic solutions

Further Consequences for L&D

Overly Focused on Effectiveness

Resulting L&D Actions

- Hires employees with strong design backgrounds
- Makes it clear that quality is the primary indicator

- Increased cost
- For some solutions, delayed time to performance improvement
- Business doesn't meet its operational goals

Consequences for the Organization

Consequences for L&D

- Long design and development cycle
- Involves a lot of people in the design
- May over-allocate resources to strategic projects at the expense run-the-business (RTB) offerings

Resulting Business Actions

- Starts to design its own solutions to meet emerging or RTB needs

Focus Only on Outcome Measures

As L&D organizations continue to mature, they recognize that efficiency and effectiveness measures provide only a partial picture of their contribution to the enterprise. Measuring business results and demonstrating the impact of specific L&D programs on core business outcomes has been and continues to be the holy grail of the learning function.

The push for demonstrating L&D's link to the business is a healthy one. As the L&D function works closer with their business counterparts, it is being asked to account for the outcome: "We invested $250,000 in this solution, did it have an impact? And if it did, we need to show the evidence." Of the dozens of L&D professionals we meet every year, at some point nearly all of them tell us, "I have to show business impact."

The demand for this data comes from multiple places. First, business leaders rightly expect their learning counterparts to "operate like a business," meaning that they set clear performance goals, manage to those goals, and demonstrate that their investments have contributed to the overall health of the organization. Second, in a tight labor market, where securing the needed talent is becoming challenging, organizations must improve their performance from within. And how better to do that than train, develop, upskill, and reskill the existing workforce? L&D therefore needs to demonstrate that it is not only training employees but also improving their performance today and in the future.

Few would disagree that demonstrating L&D's impact on business results is a good practice. However, getting that data is often challenging. First, the outcome data are not always available, at least in the right form to demonstrate the tight link between a program and its business impact (outcome). Second, even if it is available, the approach to secure it for a specific program may not work for others; that is, gathering outcome data doesn't scale. Third, not all programs are designed to have a clear business outcome. Programs to develop better communication skills will certainly be linked to specific behavioral indicators, but the business outcome may be fuzzy or too many links away in the chain of evidence. Finally, in our experience, few L&D organizations have the discipline to consistently gather outcome data. Unlike effectiveness and efficiency data, which can be standardized across programs, expected outcomes depend on the program objective: Is the intent to improve productivity, reduce cost, drive growth, or minimize risk? Each objective requires a different suite of data elements. Incorporating outcome data into the mix takes discipline to identify the outcome before the program is designed, develop a measurement approach to isolate the impact of training, gather the right data at the right time, and finally, develop the analytics to demonstrate impact.

The challenge of using predominantly outcome data can be illustrated with a client story. This client housed its L&D function within the sales organization. Not surprisingly, business leaders wanted to know, "Has Program XYZ increased sales?" The L&D team had been doing a stellar job of linking their programs to improved business performance. The business, duly impressed, increased L&D's budget and increasingly integrated it into the planning cycle. Then something unexpected happened: Sales declined after L&D trained the sales associates. Should L&D take "credit" for that, too? After all, if it takes credit for the upside, then doesn't it bear some responsibility for the downside as well? The sales decline occurred in the spring of 2008. The recession had hit, and this company, a consumer products producer, was an early victim of the declining economy. The good news for L&D was that they also had a large volume of efficiency and effectiveness data. They could demonstrate that training had improved skills and individual performance. What they needed (and didn't have) was a mechanism to show that, without the training, sales would have declined even further. (See chapter 4 for a discussion on methods to isolate the impact of training on business outcomes.)

When an L&D organization focuses its energies on demonstrating outcomes to the exclusion of efficiency and effectiveness, we believe the function is no longer managing its day-to-day business. L&D needs both efficiency and effectiveness data to demonstrate that it is allocating its funds to the right programs for the right audiences and delivering value to learners and the business. It can't do that if it is only collecting outcome data that is not available until weeks or months after the conclusion of a program.

As we have shown in our discussion of efficiency and effectiveness data, focusing solely on outcome data has unintended consequences (Figure 2-3). While the example shown is extreme, L&D functions that eschew efficiency and effectiveness measures in favor of outcomes will miss out on important information and limit their ability to demonstrate to the organization that they can run their operation like a business.

Figure 2-3. Consequences of Being Overly Focused on Outcomes

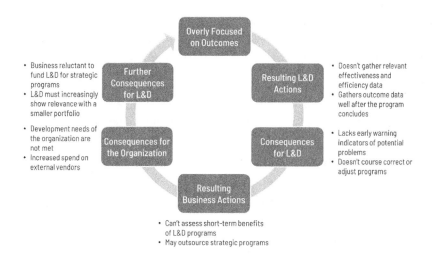

- Business reluctant to fund L&D for strategic programs
- L&D must increasingly show relevance with a smaller portfolio

- Development needs of the organization are not met
- Increased spend on external vendors

- Can't assess short-term benefits of L&D programs
- May outsource strategic programs

- Doesn't gather relevant effectiveness and efficiency data
- Gathers outcome data well after the program concludes

- Lacks early warning indicators of potential problems
- Doesn't course correct or adjust programs

The Solution: Be Purposeful About What You Measure

As we have shown throughout this chapter, the field of learning measurement has and continues to evolve. Measurement fads (yes, we do have those) come and go as do frameworks and approaches. But what never goes out of style is taking a deliberate and thoughtful approach to measurement. As we discuss in chapter 6, L&D professionals need to create program-level measurement strategies that contain:

- the reasons for measuring
- the users, why they want the measures, how they will use them, and the desired frequency
- the measures themselves, with specific measures identified for important programs or department initiatives
- use of sampling and expected response rates
- plans to collect and share the data
- resources required.

While we don't believe in a one-size-fits-all approach to measurement, we advise that three guidelines should inform the selection of measures: All programs should have a suite of efficiency and effectiveness measures; all strategic programs should have defined outcome measures; and non-strategic programs may not have an associated outcome measure.

First, every solution should have a suite of efficiency and effectiveness measures as part of the measurement strategy. As we have demonstrated, focusing only on efficiency or effectiveness measures produces unintended consequences that are avoided when both sets of measures are included in the plan. (See chapters 3 and 4 for a comprehensive set of efficiency and effectiveness measures.)

Second, for strategic solutions that advance the business strategy, every solution should have not only efficiency and effectiveness measures but also clearly defined outcome measures. For L&D, demonstrating the business impact of these types of training programs is very important. These programs should contribute, in a measurable way, to advancing the business strategy through improved financial outcomes (such as increased sales or profit), enhanced customer outcomes (such as new clients or increased loyalty of existing clients), operational outcomes (such as productivity or cycle time), or employee outcomes (such as engagement or retention of high performers).

For these programs, L&D should partner with the business outcome owner to determine how learning can best support the business goal. Also, the discussion with the business goal owner should inform not only what measures are in play but also how much the solution will contribute to those outcomes.

For example, let's return to the sales example described earlier. In this case, sales declined. L&D had not had the explicit discussion with the vice president of sales about how much their sales enablement program would or should impact sales. Instead, imagine they had agreed with the vice president of sales that their program would contribute to a 2 percentage point increase in sales relative to an overall target of a 10 percent increase in sales. When sales declined by 5 percent, they could have demonstrated (with the right data to isolate their impact) that sales would have declined by 7 percent had they not delivered the enablement program.

Third, recognize that not all solutions, particularly non-strategic programs, will yield a tangible business outcome. Solutions designed to "run the business" and focus on industry-standard skills are unlikely to have a clear business outcome. Compliance programs, for example, are intended to reduce organizational risk. But with a few exceptions, quantifying the direct link between a suite of compliance programs and an outcome can be challenging.

For example, one financial services firm ramped up efforts to ensure their frontline associates more consistently flagged customer money laundering activities. They developed an extensive suite of anti-money laundering training that was broadly rolled out across the firm. The L&D leaders felt that the best indicator of success was an increase in the volume of suspicious activity reports (SARs). However, training was not the only effort implemented to ensure that employees filed SARs. And, the timeframe between the training and the expected increase in SARs was uncertain. The organization would have been better served to evaluate whether employees were applying the skills attained and if their behaviors would lead to uncovering incidents of money laundering. These three guidelines are summarized in Table 2-1.

Table 2-1. Guidelines on Choosing Measures

Guidelines	Why	Benefits
All programs should have a suite of efficiency and effectiveness measures	Avoids unintended consequences of focusing simply on efficiency or effectiveness	Ensure L&D manages and monitors its operation
All strategic programs should have defined outcome measures	Ensures alignment of L&D with strategy priorities and that the organization is investing appropriately	Creates a collaborative partnership with the business and joint ownership for outcomes
Non-strategic programs may not have an associated outcome measure	The link between the program and business outcome is tenuous	Minimizes non-valued added measurement activities

Conclusion

In the three next chapters, we discuss the most common efficiency, effectiveness, and outcome measures and provide details about the specific types of measures you should consider when developing your measurement strategy. We then provide guidance on creating a measurement strategy and selecting the most appropriate measures based on your strategy and reasons for measuring. Throughout, remember that there are common measures but no magic list that you should always use. The key is to keep them balanced and ensure they are meaningful for your business to enable leaders to manage L&D efficiently and effectively to meet needs and advance business outcomes.

PART II

Measurement

CHAPTER 3
Efficiency Measures

Efficiency measures provide answers to the question, "How much?" How much activity has occurred (number of participants, courses, hours, and so forth), how much money has been spent, how much effort has been expended, how much of our target audience are we reaching (reach), how much time has been taken (cycle time), how much staff have we allocated, and how much of our resources (for example, facilities, faculty) are we using (utilization)? Efficiency measures are also called volume or activity measures, inputs, or Level 0 measures.

If the name of the measure starts with "number of," it is almost always an efficiency measure. In L&D, efficiency measures far outnumber effectiveness and outcome measures. In fact, of the 186 L&D measures in the CTR measures library, 144 are efficiency measures. In this chapter we describe 107 of the most commonly used efficiency measures for formal and informal learning, including all those that are benchmarked by ATD as well as those recommended by ISO. Our list of efficiency measures also includes other measures commonly used by organizations with which we work; measures shared by organizations in presentations, articles, award submissions, and workshops; and measures contained in *WLP Scorecard: Why Learning Matters* (Rivera 2007).

Most efficiency measures convey a message only when compared to a plan or benchmark. For example, you might consider your program to be efficient if it reaches a very high percentage of the target audience or if it comes very close to budget. Many efficiency measures also are a combination of two individual efficiency measures. For example, cost per learner divides cost by the number of learners and is readily benchmarked. Some efficiency measures, though, like a utilization rate, convey a sense of efficiency without comparison to an external benchmark.

While many of the efficiency measures can be applied broadly across the different types of learning, they vary considerably when measuring formal versus informal learning. Formal learning has distinct events, such as courses or classes. Informal learning is driven by the learner, not only when they choose to learn but also how. Consequently, activity and reach measures will be quite different between these two types of learning. We explore those differences throughout this chapter.

The categories and subcategories of efficiency measures are shown in Figure 3-1, but don't be overwhelmed by the large number of them. In chapter 7, we provide guidance on how to select the right measures.

Figure 3-1. Categories of Efficiency Measures

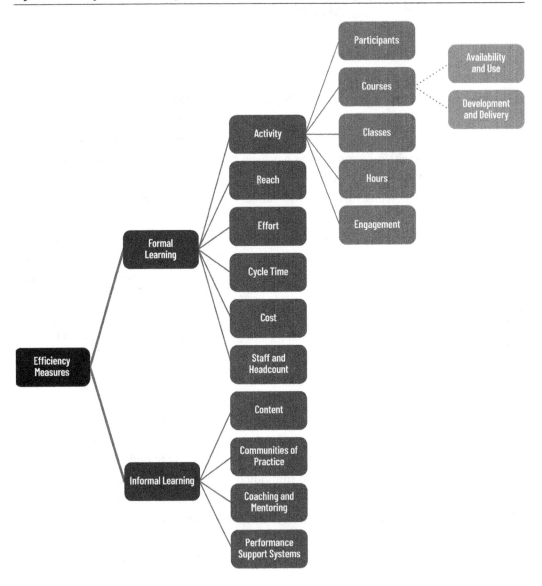

Additionally, seven of the eight ISO 30414:2018 standard metrics are found among these more than 100 efficiency measures; they are categorized in Table 3-1.

Table 3-1. Categorization of ISO Efficiency Metrics

ISO Metric Name	TDRp Measure Name	TDRp Category
1. Total development and training cost	Direct expenditure	Cost
2. Average formalized training hours per employee	Learning hours used per employee	Hours
3. Percentage of employees who participate in training compared with the total number of employees	Percentage of employees reached by formal training	Reach
4. Percentage of leaders who have participated in training	Subcategory of measure 3	Reach
5. Percentage of employees who participate in formalized training in different categories	Subcategory of measure 3	Reach
6. Percentage of employees who have completed training in compliance and ethics	Subcategory of measure 3	Reach
7. Percentage of leaders who have participated in leadership training	Subcategory of measure 3	Reach

Five of the seven measures shown are "reach" measures and will be discussed in the section on reach later in this chapter. The ISO measures for cost and hours will be addressed in their respective TDRp sections. The eighth ISO measure is workforce competency, which will be addressed in the outcome measures chapter. ISO-recommended measures are denoted by ISO 30414:2018.

As we list the types of measures in each category, we will denote measures benchmarked annually by ATD in their *State of the Industry* report using ATD BM. Benchmarking can provide valuable information about averages and the range of values for measures.

State of the Industry Report
By Maria Ho, Manager, ATD Research

ATD publishes its annual industry benchmarking report, *State of the Industry*, in December of each year. The report allows organizations to compare their talent development activities to those of other organizations, including winners of ATD's BEST Award (which recognizes organizations that use talent development to achieve enterprise-wide results).

The report analyzes 11 efficiency and expenditure indicators, including direct learning expenditure per employee, learning hours used per employee, and employees per talent development staff member. It also provides benchmarks for the percentage of the learning portfolio dedicated to 12 common content areas, the delivery methods for learning hours used and available, and organizations' use of 10 types of on-the-job learning. Benchmarking groups include all participating organizations, BEST winners, and industry and company size groupings.

According to the latest *State of the Industry*, in 2018, at the average organization, each employee used 34 hours of learning, and the average learning spend per employee was $1,299. ATD does note in the report that readers should consider their own organization's unique circumstances, which may be very different from those of the average participating organization.

Therefore, readers should not aim to replicate the averages in the report. Instead, ATD suggests that they use them to better understand their own activities and those of their peers.

The *State of the Industry* is available at TD.org/research.

Formal Learning Measures

We address formal learning measures first—activity, reach, effort, cycle time, cost, staff, and headcount—followed by informal learning measures.

Activity Measures

Activity measures for formal learning are the natural starting point because they are the most often reported efficiency measures. And of all the activity measures, the most common is the number of participants. We also examine measures for courses, classes, hours, and engagement.

Participants

Number of participants comes in two varieties: Unique Participants and Total Participants. For example, if Tonya takes two courses during the period, she would count as one unique participant with two instances of total participation. In other words, Total Participants equals two while Unique Participants equals one. To make life interesting there will always be multiple participants, so we will be interested in both total Unique Participants and total Total Participants. Since "total Total" is awkward, this measure is just called Total Participants. The formal definitions are:

Total Unique Participants: The unduplicated count of all participants. In other words, the number of unique (by name) participants.

Total Participants: All instances of participation, including multiple instances of participation by the same individual.

An LMS will report both total unique participants and total participants. If an LMS is not available and participant registration is recorded in a spreadsheet, the duplications will have to be removed manually. Table 3-2 shows the calculation of total unique participants and total participants.

When calculated manually, be aware that total participants can be summed over all periods, but unique participants cannot because the same individual may have taken courses in multiple periods. For example, in Table 3-2 notice that the total number of unique participants for the year is 9, not the sum of the unique participants for each quarter, which would be 6 + 5 + 1 + 2 = 14. Total participants, however, may always be easily calculated by summing the periods—7 + 6 + 2 = 2 equals 17, which is the correct total for total participants.

Why should we care about both of these measures? The simple answer is that they tell us different things about the operations of L&D and each one is needed for planning. The measure of unique participants identifies the size of the target audience for a program or curriculum. Larger target audiences will often have more disparate needs resulting from different roles, geographies, or levels in the organization. The number of performance consultants and level of front-end analysis may increase with larger, more diverse target audiences and unique participants. Total participants, on the other hand, has implications for delivery resources. Unless every program is self-paced, increased numbers of total participants will inevitably require larger delivery resource commitments, including instructors, facilities, schedulers, and web-based tools.

Table 3-2. Calculation of Total Unique Participants and Total Participants

	1st Quarter		2nd Quarter		3rd Quarter		4th Quarter		Total	
	Course A	Course B	Course A	Course B	Course A	Course B	Course A	Course B	Course A	Course B
Employee 1	X			X					X	X
Employee 2			X					X	X	X
Employee 3	X			X					X	X
Employee 4										
Employee 5			X	X					X	X
Employee 6	X	X							X	X
Employee 7		X					X		X	X
Employee 8		X	X						X	X
Employee 9					X	X			X	X
Employee 10	X								X	

	1st Quarter	2nd Quarter	3rd Quarter	4th Quarter	Total
Unique Count	6	5	1	2	9
Total Count	7	6	2	2	17

Recommendation

Collect and report both total unique participants and total participants for all programs and for the enterprise as a whole at least monthly. Each measure answers a different but important question:

- The measure of total unique participants answers: "How many people were touched or reached by learning?"

- The measure of total participants answers: "How much learning activity took place?" The L&D budget and items like number of instructors, number of classrooms, and amount of development and delivery typically depend on the number of total participants.

Beyond simply counting attendance, L&D and their business counterparts are often interested in knowing the completion rates for specific courses. Many organizations also measure the level of no-shows. Online or virtual instructor-led training (vILT) courses are particularly prone to employees registering but never showing up. When the no-show rate gets high, some L&D functions charge the business for no-shows who don't cancel at least 24 hours in advance of the course.

To compute these measures, we need to distinguish between the number who registered, the number who attended the course (even in part), and those who completed it. Using these measures, we can then compute:

Target Audience for the Course: The intended audience for the course. For compliance or mandatory courses, it's the number who are directed to take the course.

Registrations: Count of unique participants registered or scheduled for a course.

Attendees: Count of unique participants who attended the course. These individuals may not complete the course, but they showed up at some point during its delivery.

Attendee Rate: Attendees ÷ Registrations (expressed as a percentage).

No Show Rate: 100% – Attendee rate.

Completions: Count of unique participants who attended and completed a course.

Drop Out Rate: 100% – (Completions ÷ Attendees, expressed as a percentage)

Completion Rate: Completions ÷ Target audience for the course. This measure shows the percentage of the target audience that competed the training.

As with other measures, some practitioners may wish to report by the modality of the learning: instructor-led training (ILT), virtual instructor-led training (vILT), online or e-learning (also called web-based training or WBT), mobile learning, or blended learning (any combination of ILT, vILT, e-learning, or mobile learning). These measures are also often broken out by region, business unit, brand, role, and so forth.

Recommendation

- Measure no-shows for ILT and vILT to pinpoint where issues arise so leaders can develop a mitigation plan. No-show rates help L&D leaders better manage economies of scale. High levels of no-shows affect use of resources, both instructors and facilities.

- Compute completion rates for certain types of learning like compliance training, basic skills training, and advanced skills training, where it is important that the participant be exposed to all the content in the course.
- When the module or course, or especially performance support tool, is designed for the participants to jump in, find what they need, and jump back out, organizations need not compute completion rates.

Courses

There are two important types of course measures. The first addresses availability and usage; the second, development and delivery.

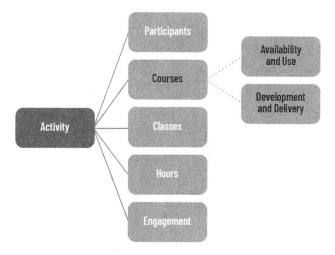

Definitions of Terms

While terms such as *program*, *course*, and *class* are often used interchangeably, we define each specifically, borrowing from the academic terminology.

- **Program:** A course or series of courses with similar learning objectives designed to accomplish a business or HR goal or meet an organizational need. For example, a program to improve leadership may comprise four related courses over a six-month period. At the university level, a program leading to a degree in economics may require 12 courses.
- **Course:** A class or series of classes, an online module or series of online modules, prework, post-work, performance support, discussion boards, and other types of learning to convey related and integrated content. For example, a course on leadership may consist of four hours of pre-reading, two online modules, four instructor-led classes, an online discussion board, and performance support. In a corporate environment, each course will have a specific designation in the LMS. At the university level, students will enroll in specific courses each term, such as Economics 101.

- **Class:** Each physical or virtual meeting of students where content is conveyed by an instructor. A course may consist of just one class if the content can be conveyed in one sitting or it may require multiple classes to convey all the content. At the university level, a semester-long course like Econ 101 might meet for two classes per week for 10 weeks for a total of 20 classes. It is also possible that the number of students enrolled in a course exceeds the optimum class size, which necessitates multiple classes even if the content can be conveyed in a single sitting. So, a one-hour instructor-led course for 150 employees will require six classes of 25 each. The analogy at the university level is 300 students taking Econ 101 where enrollment is limited to 100 per section. In this case, there will be three sections with 100 students in each.

Availability and Use

The number of courses available and the number used are very popular activity measures. There are three key course measures.

Courses Available or Offered: Total courses available = ILT courses available + vILT courses available + e-learning courses available + mobile learning courses available. Total number of unique courses available for enrollment during the period of measurement. For example, a course that is open for registration in December 2020 but not offered until February 2021 would count as a course available in 2021 but not in 2020. A course that is open for enrollment but ultimately canceled due to low or no registration still counts as an available course since it was offered. A course planned but never opened for enrollment does not count as an available course.

Courses Used or Consumed: Total number of unique courses that had participants.

Percentage of Courses Used: Courses used ÷ Courses available (expressed as a percentage)

Another common use of course measures is to determine the mix of learning by modality—ILT only, vILT only, e-learning only, mobile only, and blended learning—as shown in Figure 3-2 and described below

Percentage ILT Only: ILT courses ÷ Total courses (expressed as a percentage)

Percentage vILT Only: vILT courses ÷ Total courses (expressed as a percentage)

Percentage E-Learning Only: E-learning courses ÷ Total courses (expressed as a percentage)

Percentage Mobile Learning Only: Mobile learning courses ÷ Total courses (expressed as a percentage)

Percentage Blended Learning: Blended courses ÷ Total courses (expressed as a percentage)

Figure 3-2. Example of Chart With L&D Mix of Courses by Delivery Modality

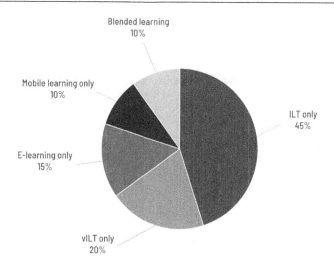

Recommendation

Report course measures such as number available, number used, and utilization rate at least annually. These are foundational for an L&D department. Further, if the department has a goal to shift the mix of learning from one modality to another, then the percentage mix by modality should be reported annually and perhaps monthly. For example, many departments are trying to shift from a reliance on ILT to more vILT, e-learning, mobile learning, and blended learning.

Development and Delivery

This second set of course measures addresses the development and delivery of courses, including whether they were on time.

> **Total Courses Developed:** Total number of new and updated courses during a period. The number of new courses and the number of updated courses may be reported separately.

> **Completion Date for Development:** The date development is to be completed. Used for an individual course. Year-to-date (YTD) progress may be expressed as the percentage complete.

> **Total Courses Developed Meeting Deadline:** Total number of new and updated courses completed on or before the deadline established by the stakeholder and learning staff.

> **Percentage of Courses Developed Meeting Deadline or Percentage of On-Time Completion for Development:** Total courses developed meeting deadline ÷ Total courses developed (expressed as a percentage).

Total Courses Delivered: Total number of courses delivered, including e-learning courses made available online.

Completion Date for Delivery: The date delivery is to be completed for an individual course. (YTD progress may be expressed as percentage complete.)

Total Courses Delivered Meeting Deadline or Percentage On-Time Completion for Delivery: Total number of courses delivered on or before the deadline established by the stakeholder or learning staff.

Percentage of Courses Delivered Meeting Deadline: Total courses delivered meeting the deadline ÷ Total courses delivered (expressed as a percentage).

Recommendation

Use on-time development and delivery measures whenever a deadline commitment is made to a goal owner or stakeholder. For example, when developing or delivering just one course for a goal owner or stakeholder, the measure may simply be the completion date. In this case, YTD progress may show percentage progress toward completion and the date once completed. These measures appear in almost all program reports. (See chapter 9 for examples of on-time measures and completion dates.)

Classes

Class measures are less common than course measures but still have a purpose in managing the L&D function. The most common class measures are:

Total Classes: Total number of classes that were held. For example, if course A has five classes, course B has three classes, and course C has one class, the total number of classes for the three courses is 5 + 3 + 1 = 9.

Class Size: Number of participants in an ILT or vILT class.

Average Class Size: Sum of class sizes ÷ Total classes. The simple average of all class sizes.

Classes Canceled: Number of classes that were open for enrollment but later canceled.

Percentage of Classes Canceled: Classes canceled ÷ Total classes (expressed as a percentage).

Recommendation

Consider class-based measures if there is an issue with very small or very large class sizes or if classes are being canceled due to participants not showing up.

Hours

Some common hourly measures include unique hours available, total hours consumed, and learning hours used per employee:

Unique Hours Available (or Offered): Total number of hours available for formal learning. This is typically a one-time count made annually, answering the question, "How many hours of learning were available for people to take last year?" The total is calculated as the sum of the hours for each unique course offered regardless of whether it is subsequently canceled (in other words, the sum of the hours of all classes for all available courses). Typically, a standard duration is set for an e-learning or mobile course and the standard duration is assumed for all participants of that course. (For example, a typical standard duration is 30 minutes, meaning that participants, on average, are expected to engage the e-learning class for 30 minutes.)

Unique Hours Used (or Consumed): Total number of unique hours in courses that had participants. This is typically calculated annually. For example, suppose five two-day ILT courses were available (offered) for the week but two canceled for low enrollment. The hours of formal learning available would be 80 hours (5 courses × 16 hours per course), and the unique hours used would be 48 hours (3 courses × 16 hours per course).

Percentage of Unique Hours Used: Unique hours used ÷ Unique hours available (expressed as a percentage). This measure is usually calculated annually. In the example above, it would be 48 hours ÷ 80 hours = 60%.

Total Hours Used (or Consumed): Total number of hours that participants were engaged in formal learning (accessed or completed courses). This measure is often reported monthly as well as annually. The total is calculated as the sum of each participant's total number of hours in courses. Using the above example, suppose that there were 20 participants for the first course, 10 for the second, and 25 for the third. The total hours of formal learning used would be (20 participants × 16 hours) + (10 participants × 16 hours) + (25 participants × 16 hours) = 320 hours + 160 hours + 400 hours = 880 hours.

Learning Hours Used per Employee: Total hours of learning used ÷ Number of employees. Alternatively, Total hours of learning used ÷ Number of FTE employees (ATD BM). Many organizations used to set a goal of 40 hours per employee per year. This is typically an annual measure.

Note

This is identical to the ISO 30414:2018 standard measure Average Formalized Training Hours per Employee, which is recommended for internal reporting by all organizations (ISO 2018, 25). ISO recommends using headcount in the denominator but allows for FTE (full-time equivalent) to be used as well. Given the two definitions of employee, a report should always indicate which definition is used. Further, if an organization has a large contingent workforce, consideration should be given to using workforce as the denominator where workforce includes contingent workers in the number of employees. (Contingent workers are temporary and contract workers.) The selection of the denominator depends on how much training contingent workers need (if they need a lot, include them). Regardless of which denominator is chosen for the summary measure, it is recommended the measure also be shown by category of workforce: full-time employees, part-time employees, temporary workers, and contract workers.

Recommendation

These are all foundational measures for an L&D department and should be reported and analyzed at least annually. At a minimum, the ISO recommended measure for average formal training hours per employee should be reported.

Six other useful measures involving hours are:

Learning Hours Used per Participant: Hours of learning used ÷ Number of unique participants.

Learning Hours Available per L&D Staff Member: Unique hours available ÷ FTE learning staff (ATD BM).

Learning Hours Used per L&D Staff Member: Total hours used ÷ FTE learning staff (ATD BM).

Reuse Ratio: Total hours used ÷ Unique hours available. This ratio indicates the intensity of use or how many times one hour of learning is used. Note that this measure is not referring to how much content from the previous year is repurposed or reused for the coming year.

Percentage of Unique Hours Available by Delivery Type: Unique hours available for learning type ÷ Total unique hours available. This measure provides the percentage or share of learning offered by delivery type (modality) and is typically measured annually.

For example, ILT may make up 54 percent of all unique learning hours available, e-learning 38 percent, and vILT 8 percent. *Note: ATD refers to this measure as Average Percentage of Formal Learning Hours Available via Different Delivery Methods (ATD BM).*

Percentage of Total Hours Used by Delivery Type: Total hours used for learning type ÷ Total hours used. This measure provides the percentage or share of learning used by delivery type (modality) and may be reported monthly as well as annually. For example, ILT may make up 60 percent of learning hours used, e-learning 25 percent, and vILT 15 percent. *Note: ATD refers to this measure as Average Percentage of Formal Learning Hours Used via Different Delivery Methods (ATD BM).*

Recommendation

Report measures for hours used regularly if the department has a goal to shift the mix of learning from one modality to another. For example, many departments are trying to shift from a reliance on ILT to more vILT, e-learning, and blended learning. The hours may tell a different story than the number of courses, so the recommendation is to report both.

Engagement

In addition to the efficiency measures covered under Participants and Courses, there are several measures that are specific to e-learning. These can be collected if the course is developed with xAPI (experience API), a software that provides insight into the learner's interaction with the content. Some learning platforms also offer the same measurement capability. Common measures include:

Learner Engagement: Number of interactions with the content.

Course Duration: Time spent on the course.

Topic or Task Duration: Time spent on a particular topic, task, or subset of the course.

Learner engagement may also be reported by topic or section, just as duration.

In addition, xAPI enables organizations to aggregate data from different systems (for example, customer relationship management systems, LMSs, learning simulations systems, and data from call-listening sessions) to create the full picture of a learner's performance.

Reach Measures

Reach shows the number or percentage of people touched by learning. It is a measure of the breadth or dispersion of learning within the organization. Reach answers the question of whether learning is broad based (reaching most employees) or more narrowly focused (reaching only a few).

Employees Reached by L&D: The number of unique employees who participated in formal or informal learning that was sponsored, conducted, or managed by the learning function. For example, any employee who took a course from the learning function, engaged in a community of practice sponsored by the learning function, or used a performance support tool designed by the learning function would count.

Employees Reached by Formal Training: The number of employees who participated in formal training. In practice, it may be difficult to identify employees who used a knowledge-sharing platform or a performance support tool. In this case, the measure might simply reduce to those reached by formal training, which is tracked in the LMS.

Percentage of Employees Reached by L&D: Employees reached by L&D ÷ Number of unique employees (expressed as a percentage).

Percentage of Employees Reached by Formal Training: Employees reached by formal training ÷ Number of unique employees (expressed as a percentage).

Note

This measure is identical to the ISO 30414:2018 standard measure Percentage of Employees Who Participate in Training Compared With Total Number of Employees per Year (ISO 2018, 25; "Technical Specification on Metrics for Skills and Capabilities" forthcoming.)

In addition to reporting this measure at a high level for all employees, we also recommend that L&D generate a report by category of employee. For example, the report might show the percentage of management versus non-management employees reached by learning. The report might also show percentage reached by business unit or region or by age or another common demographic.

ISO 30414:2018 recommends one such demographic in particular for internal reporting by large organizations, namely leaders (ISO 2018, 16)

Percentage of Leaders Who Participate in Training: Number of leaders who participate in formal training ÷ Number of leaders, expressed as a percentage.

This measure may also be reported by category. For example, the percentage taking compliance, basic skills, onboarding, or leadership. Reporting by category is identical to the ISO 30414:2018 measure Percentage of Employees Who Participate in Formal Training in Different Categories, where each organization defines the categories of greatest relevance (ISO 2018, 25; "Technical Specification on Metrics for Skills and Capabilities" forthcoming.)

ISO 30414:2018 recommends two categories for internal reporting by large organizations—compliance and ethics and leadership development:

Percentage of Employees Who Have Completed Training on Compliance and Ethics: Number of employees who have completed training on compliance and ethics ÷ Number of unique employees assigned to the training (expressed as a percentage; ISO 2018, 12).

Percentage of Leaders Who Have Participated in Leadership Development Programs: Number of leaders who have participated in leadership development programs ÷ Total number of leaders (expressed as a percentage; ISO 2018, 16).

There are two other important measures of reach:

Employees With Development Plan: The number of unique employees who have a personal development plan.

Percentage of Employees With Development Plan: Employees with development plan ÷ Number of unique employees, expressed as a percentage.

Recommendation

Report reach at least annually; it is another foundational measure for an L&D department. The CEO at Caterpillar, where David was president of Caterpillar University from 2000 to 2007, was always very interested in the percentage of employees reached by learning because he wanted to ensure that all employees had learning opportunities. Since compliance training may constitute a large percentage of training taken, reach should also be reported separately for compliance and noncompliance-related training, preferably with a breakdown by category as recommended by ISO, including leadership. Per the ISO standard, the percentage of leaders who have completed leadership training should also be reported. Lastly, the percentage of employees with a development plan is also a very important measure and should be reported at least quarterly if not monthly.

Effort Measures

Effort is a measure of the amount of work required to plan, design, develop, deliver, measure, and manage learning, and is usually expressed in hours or days. For example, if one learning staff member spends 200 hours on learning program A and another spends 60 hours on that program, the total effort spent on program A is 260 hours.

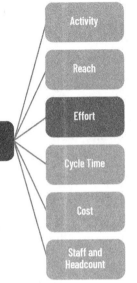

Effort to Create New Courses: The effort required to plan, design, and develop a new course, including the performance consulting (expressed in hours or days).

Effort to Update Existing Courses: The effort to plan, redesign, and redevelop an existing course (expressed in hours or days).

Recommendation

Use effort measures to plan the resource requirements for your future programs.

Cycle Time Measures

Cycle time is the time elapsed from the beginning of a defined process to its completion. Tracking cycle times and comparing to internal history and external benchmarks provides an opportunity to improve efficiency.

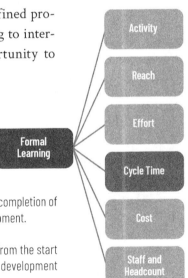

Cycle Time for Performance Consulting: The time in days from the first meeting with a goal owner to discuss how learning may help meet their need (start of needs analysis) to the completion of the needs analysis and hand off to design and development.

Cycle Time for Handoff to Design: The time in days from the completion of the performance consulting to the start of design and development.

Cycle Time for Design and Development: The time in days from the start of design and development to the completion of design and development (goal owner agrees the course is ready for deployment).

Cycle Time for Handoff to Delivery: The time in days from the completion of design and development to the delivery of the course (first day of ILT or vILT class, or the first day the e-learning is available).

Cycle Time for Delivery: The time in days from the start of delivery to the completion of delivery.

Total Cycle Time: The time in days from the first meeting with the goal owner to completion of delivery. Total cycle time is the sum of the previous five components.

Recommendation

Measure cycle times to determine your opportunities for improvement if you are not meeting promised completion dates or if you want to become more agile.

Cost Measures

There are a number of popular cost measures employed in L&D. We explore 16, including eight that are commonly benchmarked, beginning with the most important cost measure.

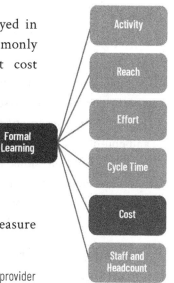

When computing costs, expenditures both for formal and informal learning should be included in the totals. We highlight where informal learning costs may show up differently than formal learning within each of the major categories below.

Most L&D departments report a high-level cost measure such as direct expenditure:

Direct Expenditure: Internal costs + External service provider expenditures + Tuition reimbursement expenditures. This includes expenses incurred by the organization for the planning, design, development, delivery, management, and measurement of formal and informal learning. Direct expenditure also includes expenditures by staff in the learning departments for performance consulting, reinforcement of learning, and general management of the learning function. Put another way, direct expenditure includes all the expenses (entire budget) of all learning departments within an organization plus any identifiable expenditures on learning that occur outside the learning departments plus tuition reimbursement expenditures (wherever they are budgeted).

In terms of the financial reports for a learning function, the following types of expenditures are included in direct expenditure:

- **Internal cost.**
  - ◦ Labor and related expense (salaries plus employer paid taxes, benefits, bonuses, profit sharing).

- Overhead expense, including office supplies, dues, subscriptions, printing, mailing, phone, computer, equipment leases, travel and entertainment, consultants, other external service providers, classroom rental, utilities, and training (for the L&D staff).
  - Internal charges. In many organizations, the L&D department is charged by the organization for occupancy-related expenses. There may also be internal charges for IT, HR, accounting, legal, and so forth. These may appear under "Overhead" in a monthly department expense statement or be shown separately, but they should be included.
- **External services and technology platform expenditures.** The amount spent on contract services from learning providers or technology vendors outside the company. While this category is part of the internal cost's overhead expenses, it is often also reported separately. It includes expenses for partners, vendors, and consultants who design, develop, and deliver or administer learning as well as providers of learning systems (LMS, LCMS, and so forth), technology platforms (for example, learning experience platforms), and applications for specific needs (such as a performance support system or coaching program platform).
- **Tuition reimbursement expenditure.** Reimbursements to employees for degree and non-degree educational programs at educational institutions, including programs for professional education and certification. It is understood that tuition reimbursement may not fall within the scope of all L&D functions.

Direct expenditure may also be calculated by summing the expenditures of all learning functions, all spending on training outside learning functions, and tuition assistance.

> **Direct Expenditure:** All expenses of all learning departments + Expenditures on learning outside learning departments + Tuition reimbursement expenditures.

> **Note**
>
> This measure is identical to the ISO 30414:2018 standard measure Total Development and Training Cost (ISO 2018, 25; "Technical Specification on Metrics for Skills and Capabilities" forthcoming.) ISO recommends this important measure for external reporting by all organizations. See the next section for a discussion on total cost and why the ISO nomenclature may be confusing in this instance.

Conceptually, there are two other important learning-related costs, but both are difficult to measure and consequently seldom reported.

> **Learner's Travel-Related and Fee Expenses:** The travel-related cost for participants to attend either in-house or external learning programs plus the program-related costs

of external programs (for example, the registration fee to attend a three-day leadership program). It is often difficult to obtain this cost data, although some organizations provide a check box on travel expense forms to indicate the expense is related to learning.

Opportunity Cost: The value of what is given up or foregone in choosing one course of action over another. In the context of learning, opportunity cost is the value of what the participants would have been doing if they were not in class. Salespeople would be closing deals, engineers would be designing product, and so forth, which is why they were hired in the first place. So, the organization loses their work contribution when they participate in a learning program.

What Is the Value of the Opportunity Cost?

The opportunity cost should be at least what the organization is paying them, and if it is not, then the employee should be reassigned, retrained, demoted, or fired because it does not make economic sense for the organization to pay the employee more than they are worth.

Thus, at a minimum, opportunity cost can be calculated as the value of the participant's time in class and in transit. This can be found as hours multiplied by the labor and related hourly rate. For example, the opportunity cost of 100 salespeople (each earning $50 per hour in salary and benefits) in a two-day ILT with 30-minute travel time each way would be:

$$= 100 \times [(2 \text{ days} \times 8 \text{ hours per day}) + (0.5 \text{ hour per trip} \times 4 \text{ trips})] \times \$50 \text{ per hour}$$

$$= 100 \times 18 \text{ hours} \times \$50 \text{ per hour}$$

$$= \$90{,}000$$

In some cases, the opportunity cost will exceed the value of the participant's time and can be more accurately determined. For example, the organization may be able to estimate the value (impact on net income) of the lost sales from having 100 salespeople in training for two days. In this case, and assuming this estimate exceeds the value of their time, the estimate should be used as the opportunity cost. (See Vance [2017] for more on opportunity cost.)

Opportunity cost should also be calculated for organizations that employ a "leaders as teachers" model. In this case, the value of a leader's time will not be captured in a learning department expense statement but it does represent a cost to the organization, especially if very senior leaders dedicate much time to teaching. In other words, their time is not free.

So, the most comprehensive measure of cost would be total cost, which includes learner's travel-related expenses and opportunity costs. Total cost for learning in an organization includes all learning related costs except those outside the learning function(s) for management and reinforcement of learning (which generally would be too difficult to obtain). Cost breakdown is shown in Figure 3-3; by formula it would be:

Total Cost: Direct expenditure + Learner's travel costs and fees + Opportunity cost.

Figure 3-3. Components of Total Cost

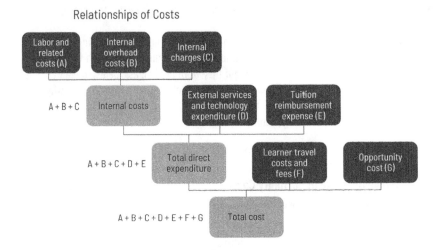

Important cost-related measures for L&D that derive from direct expenditure include:

Direct Expenditure per Employee: Direct expenditure ÷ Number of employees. Alternatively, Direct expenditure ÷ Number of FTE employees (ATD BM). Because there are two potential ways to define employee, the report should always specify which definition is used. Like our earlier discussion about hours per employee, this measure should also be calculated for contingent workers if company-provided training is important for their performance on the job.

Since the average decreases with organization size due to economies of scale and since it varies significantly by industry, ATD also reports the following two comparisons:

Direct Expenditure per Employee by Organization Size: Reported for organizations with fewer than 500 employees, 500-9,999 employees, and 10,000 or more employees (ATD BM).

Direct Expenditure per Employee by Industry Grouping: This measure is reported for four different industry groupings: finance, insurance, and real estate; healthcare and pharmaceutical; manufacturing; and software, information, broadcasting, and telecommunications (ATD BM).

Other cost-related measures include:

Direct Expenditure per Learner: Direct expenditure ÷ Number of unique participants.

Direct Expenditure as a Percentage of Revenue: Direct expenditure ÷ Organization (company) revenue (ATD BM).

Direct Expenditure as a Percentage of Payroll: Direct expenditure ÷ Organization (company) payroll (including benefits; ATD BM).

Direct Expenditure as a Percentage of Profit: Direct expenditure ÷ Organization (company) profit (or surplus).

Percentage of Expenditure for Tuition Reimbursement: Direct expenditure for tuition reimbursement ÷ Total direct expenditure (ATD BM).

Percentage of Expenditure for External Services: Direct expenditure for external services ÷ Total direct expenditure (ATD BM).

Cost per Learning Hour Available: Direct expenditure ÷ Unique hours available (ATD BM).

Cost per Learning Hour Used: Direct expenditure ÷ Total hours used (ATD BM).

Average Development Cost of a New ILT or vILT Course: Direct expenditure of developing new ILT or vILT courses ÷ Number of new ILT or vILT courses.

Average Development Cost of a New E-Learning Course: Direct expenditure of developing new e-learning courses ÷ Number of new e-learning courses developed.

Cost Reduction: A reduction in direct expenditure cost or a component of direct expenditure or opportunity cost.

In the next section, we focus on the efficiency measures for informal learning. We will not cover cost measures specifically, not because they do not have associated costs, but because we believe that the taxonomy we outlined in Figure 3-3 applies to informal learning as well. For example, consider the implementation of a mentoring program. The costs associated with the program would include internal resources to design, develop, and implement the program. If L&D purchased software to match mentors and mentees, this cost would be included in the technology expenditures. Finally, if the organization hired external resources to mentor employees in specific roles, these expenditures would be addressed in the external services category. We recommend that organizations incorporate costs for all programs, be they formal or informal in their cost calculations.

It is evident from the list of measures that numerous benchmarks are available for direct expenditure. Some organizations benchmark annually while others only do so periodically. In either case, the following caveats are important to keep in mind when comparing to benchmarks:

1. Compare to organizations of a similar size because economies of scale will almost always drive average costs down for larger organizations.
2. Compare to others within your industry because averages vary significantly by industry.
3. Remember that a benchmark average should not necessarily be your goal. Many organizations with higher than benchmark spending adopt a goal to reduce their own spending toward the benchmark, which is often a mistake. The benchmark, while informative, is nothing more than an average, and the optimum level of L&D

expenditure for your company may be above or below the average. It should be above the average if you have very challenging organizational goals or a relatively less experienced and proficient workforce. It should be below the average if you have less challenging organizational goals or a more experienced and proficient workforce. No one outside your organization can tell what the right level of expenditure is for your organization for the coming year, and you should not aspire to be average.

Recommendation

Measure direct expenditure at least annually, even if some assumptions or estimates are required. This is a foundational efficiency measure, and your CEO will expect it. More mature organizations also measure opportunity cost. Typically, learners' travel-related costs are very difficult to measure because they are not learning department expenses and consequently are seldom measured. It will also be helpful to track direct expenditure per employee and direct expenditure as a percentage of either payroll or revenue through time to gauge whether the investment in learning and development is keeping pace with the growth in employees and with organization size.

L&D Staff and Employee Headcount Measures

There are numerous common measures for staff and headcount. These are the most popular:

FTE L&D Staff: Number of staff in all learning functions expressed as full-time equivalent (FTE). For example, three full-time staff and one part-time staff person who works 20 hours per week (20 hours ÷ 40 hours = 0.5 FTE) would be 3.5 FTEs.

Unique L&D Staff: The unique number of learning staff, including part-time employees. In the example, the number of unique staff would be four.

Total Hours for L&D Staff: The sum of each staff member's employed hours in a period. A full-time staff member is typically paid for 52 weeks × 40 hours per week = 2,080 hours per year. A part-time employee may be paid for work 20 hours per week or 1,040 hours per year. Typically, an estimate is made of total hours available annually.

Total Hours Used by L&D Staff: The sum of each staff member's actual hours used to plan, design, develop, deliver, reinforce, measure, and manage learning. Typically, these hours are tracked and recorded on a daily or weekly basis. Time for holidays, vacation, and sick time as well as time for staff meetings, performance management, and training is not included.

Activity

Reach

Effort

Formal Learning

Cycle Time

Cost

Staff and Headcount

Percentage of L&D Staff Hours Used: Total hours used ÷ Total hours, expressed as a percentage. Typically, this comes out to 60–70 percent. This measure is important for calculating the burden rate.

FTE Employees: The size of the organization's workforce measured as the average number of FTE employees over the year. The count should include employees of consolidated domestic and international subsidiaries, part-time and seasonal employees, and officers. The count should not include contracted workers, consultants, vendors, board members, or employees of unconsolidated subsidiaries. Most organizations report employee counts on a monthly basis, so total employees will be found as the simple average of the counts for the 12 months. Some organizations may not provide the FTE for part-time employees. In this case, estimate the FTE for part-time employees from the total number of part-time employees. (Note: Since ATD uses FTE rather than headcount, this measure for FTE Employees is identical to ATD's Workforce Size measure.)

Unique Employees: The size of the organization's workforce measured as the count of all full-time and part-time employees throughout the year. Due to turnover, this count will exceed the number of employees on the payroll at the end of the year. For example, if employees A–D were on the full-time payroll all year, Employee E left in March, part-time Employee F started in June, and full-time Employee G started in December, the unique employee count is seven and the year-end count is six.

Employees per L&D Staff Member: FTE employees ÷ FTE learning staff (expressed as a number to one decimal place; ATD BM). Both the numerator and denominator are best expressed in FTE, but may also be calculated as the number of unique employees divided by the number of unique L&D staff members.

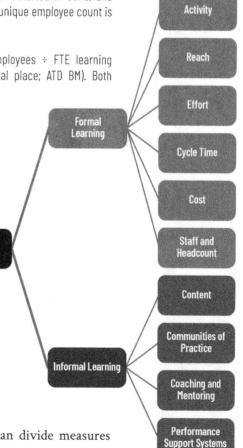

> **Recommendation**
> Report the total and unique learning staff at least annually. Many L&D departments also report employees per L&D staff annually. Utilization of staff hours is less common.

Informal Learning Measures

Unlike formal learning with a few modalities but a common set of measures, informal learning comes in many shapes and sizes. Rather than divide measures into categories like activity and reach, for this section, we focus on the measures associated with four common types of informal learning: content, communities of practice, coaching and mentoring, and performance support.

Content Measures

Learning organizations are increasingly creating learner experience portals (LXPs) as a single source of information that may range from whitepapers, tools or job aids, videos, or links to relevant training. LXPs typically track which documents employees access and share, and may identify how much time a user spends on a specific page. The challenge is that LXPs contain thousands of documents that are being accessed each day by employees. It's impossible to track the details associated with every piece of content, so organizations must make choices about what provides useful insight for decision making.

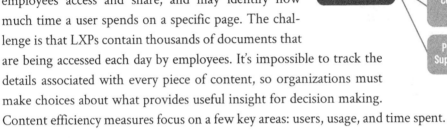

Content efficiency measures focus on a few key areas: users, usage, and time spent.

Users

When organizations develop content portals (or LXPs), they may initially target specific audiences such as sales professionals, client-support personnel, or R&D. Over time, organizations will broaden their reach, and it's important to understand if the target audience is actually using the resources. These measures are focused on a suite of communities; however, they could be used for specific communities as well.

> **Target Audience Size:** Approximate number of employees in the target audience for the communities overall.

> **Unique Users:** Number of unique employees who have accessed the content within the period.

> **Percentage Reach:** Unique uses ÷ Target audience size.

> **Total Users:** Number of total employees who have accessed content within the period. This allows for a unique employee to access multiple pieces of content and to access the same piece of content more than once.

Usage

Organizations devote significant resources to acquiring, developing, curating, and managing content. Consequently, L&D needs to determine what is being used and what is not being used.

> **Total Number of Documents Available:** Total number of documents (across all types of documents) available in a given period.

Total Number of Documents Accessed: Total number of documents (across all types of documents) accessed in a given period.

Percentage of Documents Accessed: Total number of documents accessed ÷ Total number of documents available (expressed as a percentage).

Average Documents Accessed: Total number of documents accessed ÷ Number of unique users. This measure can be subdivided as shown:
- Average number of documents accessed by type (for example, job aid versus whitepaper).
- Average number of documents accessed by modality (for example, document, blog, or video).
- Average number of documents accessed by community.

Top 25 Most Common Documents Accessed: By document, identify documents with the largest number of hits.

Time Spent

Time spent on a site can mean different things: Users might be engaged and find the content useful, or they might be spending a lot of time searching for content without finding what they need. While time alone doesn't tell the whole story, it is important to track it to understand the behaviors of employees and how they use the site.

Average Time Spent on the Site: Total time spent on the site ÷ Number of unique users.

Recommendation

For organizations that have created a knowledge portal (or implemented an LXP), track at least the number of users (relative to the target audience) and the usage. Duration data are helpful when combined with effectiveness measures to characterize the behavior of employees when accessing content.

Communities of Practice Measures

Etienne Wenger defined communities of practice (CoPs) as groups of people who share a concern or a passion for something they do and learn how to do it better as they interact regularly (David 2014). In business settings, communities often form to advance knowledge in a specific industry, domain (for example, technical specialty), or practice (such as project management). Communities facilitate knowledge sharing, not only through content but also via people-to-people connections and online or in-person discussions. While CoPs have existed for years, the ability to track them has improved significantly with the use of online platforms. Some CoPs use sophisticated platforms that provide discussion forums, blogging, messaging, content reviews, and news feeds. Others are smaller scale, using messaging apps to enable like-minded employees to interact. For this book, our focus is on a suite of measures that are independent of the platform being used.

The following provide a starter set of efficiency measures for CoPs. If your organization is a heavy user of CoPs, you may want to add to this list to capture the diversity of activity within the communities.

Total Communities of Practice: The number of unique communities of practice in the organization.

Active Communities of Practice: The number of communities where there has been activity within a defined time period (month, quarter, or year); activity would include discussions, requests for help, providing help, identification of experts, or contributions or access to stored knowledge.

Percentage Active Communities of Practice: Active communities of practice ÷ Total communities of practice (expressed as a percentage).

Unique Community of Practice Members: The total number of unique individuals who are members of at least one community of practice.

Unique Active Community of Practice Members: The total number of unique individuals who have engaged in discussions, requested or provided help, served as experts, or contributed or accessed knowledge within a defined time period.

Percentage Active Community of Practice Members: Active community of practice members ÷ Total community of practice members (expressed as a percentage).

Total Community of Practice Members: The total number of individuals who are members of a community of practice. This measure allows for individuals to be members of multiple communities.

Recommendation

All seven measures are highly recommended for monthly reporting if there is a department goal to increase the use of communities of practice. If not, then these measures should be reported at least quarterly if COPs play an important role in the organization's overall learning strategy.

Coaching and Mentoring Measures

While coaching and mentoring occurs informally in all business settings, we examine measurement in specific programs developed to match mentors or coaches with employees who will benefit from guidance in specific areas (for example, leadership or people management). Structured coaching and mentoring programs usually engage a program coordinator and develop processes to recruit and train mentors, vet mentees, and provide support for employees engaged in the program.

Efficiency measures for coaching or mentoring networks focus on how many individuals are engaged, the ratio of mentors to mentees, the frequency of meetings, and the duration of time in the program. We recognize that coaching and mentoring are very different types of activities and different skills and processes are involved. However, for the sake of measurement, we group these two types of programs together.

Number of Coaches or Mentors: The number of individuals who have been approved to act as a coach or mentor in the program.

Number of Coachees or Mentees: The number of individuals who have been selected to receive coaching or mentoring in the program.

Ratio of Coaches (Mentors) to Coachee (Mentee): Total coachees or mentees ÷ Total coaches or mentors.

Average Time in the Program for Coaches or Mentors: Total months of engagement for all coaches or mentors ÷ Number of coaches or mentors. This is the average amount of time (usually in months) that a coach or mentor has been engaged in the program.

Average Time in the Program for Coachees or Mentees: Total months of engagement for all coachees or mentees ÷ Number of coachees or mentees. This is the average amount of time (usually in months) that a coachee or mentee has been receiving coaching or mentoring in this program.

Frequency of Meetings: Number of meetings per period between the coach or mentor and coachee or mentee.

Duration of Meetings: Average time of meetings (virtual or in person) of coach or mentor and coachee or mentee.

Recommendation

All seven measures are highly recommended for monthly reporting if a coaching or mentoring network has been established to achieve a department goal for building organizational competency. If not, these measures should be reported at least quarterly if coaching or mentoring networks play a role in the organization's overall learning strategy.

Performance-Support Specific Measures

Performance support refers to the tools that learners use at the time of need to perform a task, which may be as simple as a checklist. Performance support is particularly valuable when a task requires multiple steps (especially if they must be completed in a particular order) or infrequently used instructions.

For example, performance support may be helpful for managers who need to enter performance ratings for their employees into the organization's HR system annually. While not complex, this involves multiple steps and very specific instructions, all of which occur just once per year. Managers could be sent to a class to learn how to enter the ratings, but it would take time and most would quickly forget the steps. Instead, a performance support tool would supply the information managers need when they need it. Performance support tools are also critical for employees in customer call centers who must answer a wide variety of questions from many customers in a short span of time.

Some measures for performance support include:

Performance Support Tools Available: Number of performance support tools available.

Performance Support Tools Used: Number of performance support tools used.

Percentage of Performance Support Tools Used: Performance support tools used ÷ Performance tools available (expressed as a percentage).

Unique Performance Support Users: Number of people using at least one performance support tool.

In addition to being a standalone tool, performance support can also be included in course design, to be used during the course or for reference afterward. This is a form of blended learning, just like employing both e-learning and instructor-led learning in a program. A measure for this would be:

Percentage of Courses With Performance Support: Number of courses with a performance support tool ÷ Total number of courses (expressed as a percentage).

Recommendation

All five of these measures should be reported if the learning strategy calls for performance support.

Conclusion

This concludes our description of the most common efficiency measures. No organization would ever use all of these or even half. The goal is to identify the right measures to support the learning strategy, which in any year is typically focused on some, but certainly not all, of these measures.

The most common efficiency measures are shown in Table 3-3. These represent the most commonly used efficiency measures and include all the efficiency measures benchmarked by ATD and recommended by the ISO 30414:2018 standard. Additional efficiency measures may be found in the CTR measures library.

Table 3-3. Most Common L&D Efficiency Measures

Measure Name	Unit of Measure	Benchmarked by ATD	Recommended in ISO 30414
Participants			
Total participants	Number		
Total unique participants	Number		
Registrations	Number		
Attendees	Number		
Completions	Number		
Attendee rate	Percent		
No show rate	Percent		
Completion rate	Percent		
Courses			
Courses available	Number		
Courses used	Number		
Percentage of courses used	Percent		
Percentage ILT	Percent		
Percentage vILT	Percent		
Percentage e-learning	Percent		
Percentage mobile	Percent		
Percentage blended	Percent		
Total courses developed	Number		
Total courses developed meeting deadline	Number		
Percentage of courses developed meeting deadline	Percent		
Completion date for development	Date, percent complete		
Total courses delivered	Number		
Total courses delivered meeting deadline	Number		
Percentage of courses delivered meeting deadline	Percent		
Completion date for delivery	Date, percent complete		

Table 3-3. Most Common L&D Efficiency Measures (cont.)

Measure Name	Unit of Measure	Benchmarked by ATD	Recommended in ISO 30414
Classes			
Total classes	Number		
Average class size	Number		
Classes canceled	Number		
Percentage of classes canceled	Percent		
Hours			
Unique hours available or offered	Hours		
Unique hours used or consumed	Hours		
Percentage unique hours used or consumed	Percent		
Total hours used or consumed	Hours		
Learning hours used per employee	Hours	Yes	Yes
Learning hours used per participant	Hours		
Learning hours available per L&D staff member	Hours	Yes	
Learning hours used per L&D staff member	Hours	Yes	
Reuse ratio	Ratio		
Percentage unique hours available by delivery type	Percent	Yes	
Percentage total hours used by delivery type	Percent	Yes	
Engagement			
Learner engagement (number of interactions)	Number		
Course duration	Minutes		
Topic or task duration	Minutes		
Reach			
Employees reached by L&D	Number		
Employees reached by formal training	Number		
Percentage of employees reached by L&D	Percent		
Percentage of employees reached by formal training	Percent		Yes (five measures)
Employees with a development plan	Number		
Percentage of employees with a development plan	Percent		
Total users who have accessed content	Number		
Effort			
Effort to create new courses	Hours		
Effort to update existing courses	Hours		

Table 3-3. Most Common L&D Efficiency Measures (cont.)

Measure Name	Unit of Measure	Benchmarked by ATD	Recommended in ISO 30414
Cycle Time			
Performance consulting	Days		
Handoff to development	Days		
Design and development	Days		
Handoff to delivery	Days		
Delivery	Days		
Total	Days		
Cost			
Direct expenditure	Dollars		Yes
Learner's travel and fee expenses	Dollars		
Opportunity cost	Dollars		
Total cost	Dollars		
Direct expenditure per employee	Dollars	Yes	
Direct expenditure per learner (unique)	Dollars		
Direct expenditure as a percentage of revenue	Percent	Yes	
Direct expenditure as a percentage of payroll	Percent	Yes	
Direct expenditure as a percentage of profit	Percent		
Percentage of direct expenditure for tuition reimbursement	Percent	Yes	
Percentage of direct expenditure for external services	Percent	Yes	
Cost per learning hour available	Dollars	Yes	
Cost per learning hour used	Dollars	Yes	
Average development cost for new ILT or vILT course	Dollars		
Average development cost for new e-learning course	Dollars		
Cost reduction	Dollars		
Learning Staff and Employee Headcount			
FTE L&D staff	Number		
Unique L&D staff	Number		
Total hours for L&D staff	Hours		
Total hours used by L&D staff	Hours		
Percentage of L&D staff hours used	Percent		
FTE employees	Number	Yes	
Unique employees	Number		
Employees per L&D staff member	Number	Yes	

Table 3-3. Most Common L&D Efficiency Measures (cont.)

Measure Name	Unit of Measure	Benchmarked by ATD	Recommended in ISO 30414
Content (Learning Experience Platforms)			
Target audience size	Number		
Unique users	Number		
Percentage reach	Percent		
Total number of documents available	Number		
Total number of documents accessed	Number		
Percentage of documents accessed	Percent		
Average number of documents accessed	Number		
Top documents accessed	Number		
Average time spent on site	Number		
Communities of Practice			
Total communities of practice	Number		
Active communities of practice	Number		
Percentage active communities of practice	Percent		
Total community of practice members	Number		
Active communities of practice members	Number		
Percentage active community of practice members	Percent		
Coaching or Mentoring Network			
Number of coaches or mentors	Number		
Number of coachees or mentees	Number		
Ratio of coaches or mentors to coachees or mentees	Number		
Average time in the program	Months		
Average time in meetings	Hours		
Frequency of meetings	Number		
Performance Support Measures			
Performance tools available	Number		
Performance tools used	Number		
Percentage of performance tools uses	Percent		
Percentage of courses with performance support tools	Percent		
Unique performance support users	Number		

We're now finished with efficiency measures, which are the most numerous measures in L&D and the foundation of any measurement strategy. Next, we examine effectiveness measures which are more powerful and form the basis for the evaluation of learning programs.

CHAPTER 4
Effectiveness Measures

Effectiveness measures are designed to measure and improve the quality of a program or course, in contrast to efficiency measures, which are primarily focused on activity.

In L&D, we are fortunate to have a framework for the five basic types or levels of effectiveness measures. This five-level framework reflects the work of Raymond Katzell and Don Kirkpatrick beginning in the 1940s and 1950s and Jack Phillips beginning in the 1970s. This framework serves as a base or starting point for chapters 4 and 5, which represent our interpretation, synthesis, and extension of their important work. The reader is encouraged to explore the many excellent books on program evaluation by Katzell, Kirkpatrick, and the Phillipses to gain an in-depth understanding of the topic, including how they define and use each level to deliver more impactful training.

We first explore the history of evaluation for context and perspective, then describe each of the five levels of effectiveness measures in detail, noting some key differences between the two measurement pioneers.

The Five Levels of Effectiveness Measures

The story begins with Raymond Katzell, a respected industrial-organizational psychologist, who wrote an article in 1948, "Testing a Training Program in Human Relations," and another in 1952, "Can We Evaluate Training?" on the topic of evaluation. In these articles, Katzell presented the four steps to evaluation. In 1956, Don Kirkpatrick wrote an article entitled "How to Start an Objective Evaluation of Your Training Program," where he presented Katzell's "Hierarchy of Steps." (The four steps later were referred to as levels by the practitioners themselves). Kirkpatrick shared Katzell's work in conferences throughout the 1950s and then in late 1959 and early 1960 published four consecutive monthly articles in ATD's magazine, focusing on a different step each month. The four steps became known as the four levels, and the profession had its first model for evaluation. (Kirkpatrick didn't credit Katzell in the articles for reasons that are not understood. Katzell, however, does not appear to have complained.)

Jack Phillips began using the four levels in practice in the 1970s and came to realize that the profession needed to isolate the impact of learning on the results and then take measurement to the next level by calculating the return on investment (ROI) for the learning program, just as organizations do for other important investments. In his ground-breaking and extremely comprehensive 1983 book, *Handbook of Training Evaluation*, Phillips introduced ROI as Level 5 and a new definition for Level 4. This was the first book on training evaluation in the United States. Jack and his wife, Patti, continue to refine and improve the Phillips model with more than 100 books or articles published on evaluation. The original handbook is now in its fourth edition.

In the 1960s, 1970s, and 1980s, Kirkpatrick was a professor at the University of Wisconsin. He didn't publish any additional articles until his retirement in 1993. In 1994, he published his first book on evaluation, *Evaluating Training Programs: The Four Levels*, and continued to advocate the four levels until his death in 2014. Kirkpatrick is the one who popularized the four levels and created a lasting measurement framework. Don's son Jim, and Jim's wife, Wendy, carry on the work and have continued to publish and improve the Kirkpatrick model.

The L&D profession widely uses each of these models. It is important to understand that the two models define Level 4 very differently and that only the Phillips model takes steps to attribute improvement in business measures to programs and demonstrate the financial return on investment (Level 5; Table 4-1).

The TDRp framework adopts the Phillips model with isolated impact for Level 4 and ROI for Level 5, but gratefully acknowledges the contribution of Don Kirkpatrick and the fine work by Jim and Wendy, especially with regard to the critical role of establishing a close partnership with the goal owner and ensuring that the learning is actually applied and meets stakeholder expectations.

Table 4-1. Measurement Levels of Kirkpatrick and Phillips

Level	Kirkpatrick / Katzell	Phillips
Level 1	Reaction	Reaction
Level 2	Learning	Learning
Level 3	Behavior	Application
Level 4	Results	Business impact
Level 5	N/A	Return on investment (ROI)

Similar to efficiency measures, we have developed a taxonomy for effectiveness measurement (Figure 4-1). We examine the five levels starting with Level 1. The taxonomy shows the key elements for Levels 1, 3, and 4 as well as greater detail for several levels.

As with efficiency measures, benchmarks are available for many of the effectiveness measures. While ATD does not provide benchmarks for effectiveness measures, other organizations do. One such organization is Explorance, with a product called Metrics That

Matter (MTM), which Dave used at Caterpillar and Peggy used at Hewlett-Packard. MTM provides the ability to automatically survey participants, collect the data in a warehouse, and generate reports. They began collecting data in 2001 and now have data on hundreds of organizations, providing a rich source of benchmark information. While the wording of their questions is proprietary, we will denote measures where benchmark data are available from MTM by including (BM MTM) in the applicable measure details. (Performitiv is another company that provides benchmark data.)

Figure 4-1. Categories of Effectiveness Measures

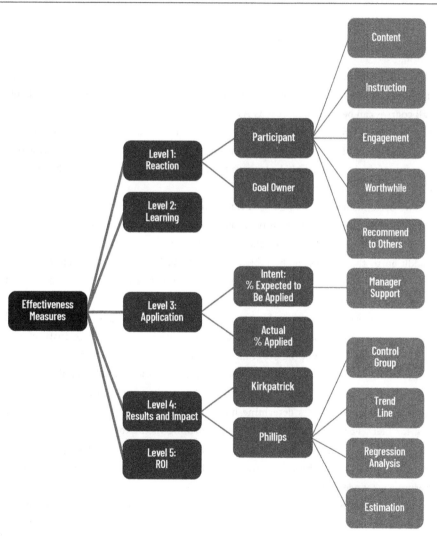

Benchmarks

By John Mattox II, PhD, Former Head of Talent Research, Explorance

A benchmark is usually the average score for a given measure, and it provides a valuable point for comparison. It is similar to a performance outlier in that it offers a point of reference. Benchmarks show average performance, whereas outliers show superlative or very poor performance. Benchmarks are valuable because they provide a point of comparison to determine if performance is at, above, or below par.

Once a course is developed and deployed, it is difficult to know whether it is good or even good enough. There are many ways to determine if learning is leading to performance improvement and eventually attainment of organizational goals. One of the most practical approaches is to gather opinion data from learners immediately after training.

The MTM system from Explorance is designed to deploy validated surveys with consistent measures allowing users to benchmark their course against others. It is scalable so all courses can be evaluated. Just as ATD provides valuable benchmarks for efficiency measures, MTM provides benchmarks for effectiveness measures. Notably, learning is only one aspect of HR that encompasses the employee learning journey. Measures across all aspects of the journey should be gathered. (See Table 4-5 at the end of the chapter for a list of measures benchmarked by MTM.)

Two basic calculations can be used for Likert scale questions: the average score and the sum of the percentages in the top two boxes (for example, 4 and 5 on a 5-point scale). The MTM system allows users to choose either of these calculations for comparison. In addition to the metrics in the table, the MTM methodology and system calculates proprietary, derived metrics such as percentage of performance improvement and estimated ROI aligned to the Phillips methodology.

While it is valuable to know how a course (or instructor) is performing compared to the benchmark, the decisions that follow are more important. If an instructor is underperforming, what will the program manager do to help the instructor improve? If the instructor and the courseware are outperforming the benchmark, but application and performance are underperforming, what will the program manager change?

Benchmarks help leaders determine how to manage the curriculum and prioritize work for L&D. For the programs that are performing in the top 10–15 percent of the curriculum, leaders should focus on deployment to rest of the target audience. Don't revise; just deploy. For the programs in the bottom 10–15 percent, leaders need to determine what needs to be retired because it is stale or no longer valuable; they also need to determine what needs revision because the content is needed (for example, aligned to business needs), but ineffective. Because budgets and resources are limited, the middle section of programs between the top and bottom 15 percent are intentionally left alone, adhering to the adage, "If it ain't broke, don't fix it." The advantage of having benchmarks is that they facilitate decision making.

Our discussion of effectiveness begins with the Level 1 measures, which subdivide into participant measures and those for the goal owner.

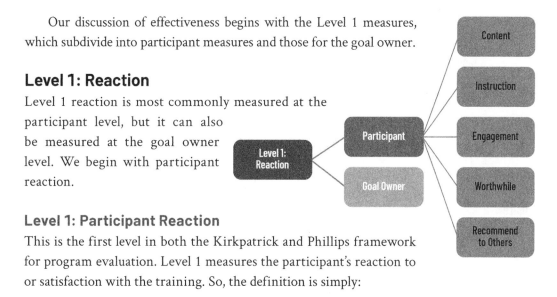

Level 1: Reaction

Level 1 reaction is most commonly measured at the participant level, but it can also be measured at the goal owner level. We begin with participant reaction.

Level 1: Participant Reaction

This is the first level in both the Kirkpatrick and Phillips framework for program evaluation. Level 1 measures the participant's reaction to or satisfaction with the training. So, the definition is simply:

> **Level 1: Participant Reaction:** The participant's reaction to the training. Both Kirkpatrick and Phillips refer to Level 1 as Reaction.

Historically, data were gathered from a paper survey administered after the course (sometimes referred to as a smile sheet), but now Level 1 is more commonly measured by electronic surveys (called post-event surveys) sent after an ILT course is finished or embedded at the end of an online course. Typical response rates may be 20–40 percent, which is sufficient as long as there are at least 30 responses, and the respondents are believed to be a good representation of all participants. Of course, the level of confidence in the survey results will be higher if the sample size is larger and if the response rate is higher.

The purpose of Level 1 is to elicit immediate feedback on the course so that course owners can make the necessary changes before deploying the same course to others. A well-designed survey may uncover the following types of issues:

- The needs analysis was flawed (or the program objectives were not aligned to business requirements).
- The program was poorly designed or delivered.
- The course communications did not clearly articulate expectations to participants.
- The wrong audience attended the course.

Level 1 surveys often ask questions in five key areas (Figure 4-2):

> **Content:** These questions address the quality of training materials and job aids. Content questions also address the relevance of the content to the learner's role and development needs (BM MTM).

> **Instruction:** These questions focus on the quality of the instruction, including the instructor's knowledge and ability to engage the learners (BM MTM).

Engagement: These questions focus on the extent to which the course design balanced presentation with hands-on activities, if the delivery approach challenged the learners, and if learners had opportunities to ask questions (BM MTM).

Worthwhile: These questions address the value of the course to the learner, either for their current role or their long-term career goals. These questions serve to uncover if the time spent by the learner was a worthwhile use of their time (BM MTM).

Recommend: Many organizations now include a "recommend" question on their Level 1 survey. We discuss this type of question later in the chapter (BM MTM).

Figure 4-2. Common Level 1 Question Areas

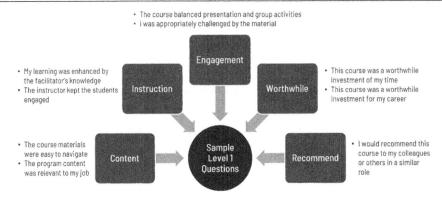

Note: MTM also provides a benchmark for the average of all Level 1 questions.

Level 1 reaction is not an indicator of impact or value and should never serve as a substitute for Levels 4 and 5. For this reason some practitioners have stopped collecting it, but this is ill advised. Since Level 1 provides valuable information about the design, content, delivery, and audience, it should always be a part of your evaluation strategy.

Research on the validity and reliability of scales has shown that five-or seven-point scales are optimal (Krosnick and Presser 2010). We recommend a five-point Likert agreement scale with points labeled: strongly agree, agree, neutral, disagree, strongly disagree. Some organizations use seven-point scales, but these scales tend to only label the end points (strongly agree and strongly disagree), leaving the respondent to interpret what the middle five points mean.

We do not recommend even-numbered scales because they may introduce bias by forcing a respondent who is truly neutral to select a positive or negative answer. We also advise against 10- or 11-point scales due to their complexity, with the exception of the Net Promoter Score (NPS). The NPS question: "What is the likelihood that you would recommend X [*this course, this program*] to a friend or colleague?" has become popular recently in learning since many organizations use it for customer feedback. NPS uses an 11-point scale (0–10), which we generally don't recommend. However, if NPS is the organization's standard way of measuring satisfaction, then it would make sense to use the 11-point scale for learning as well since leaders are already familiar with it.

If you are not familiar with survey design, we suggest you educate yourself on this topic, particularly if you are going to develop your own questions. (See appendix F for a list of resources on survey design.)

Often, organizations will agree on a set of 5 to 10 core questions they will use for all courses. This standardization enables comparability among courses and tracking trends over time. Building on the core questions, they will add questions that are specific for different learning modalities (for example, ILT, vILT, e-learning, mobile-learning, or blended courses) to solicit feedback specific to each modality. Other questions may focus on specific content.

Organizations do not need to administer the Level 1 survey to all participants for all courses, because that may lead to survey fatigue and poor-quality feedback in some organizations. Instead, we suggest organizations consider sending surveys to a sample or subset of the population who took the course. This approach works well if the response rates are 30 to 40 percent, and if the overall population size is large (for example, more than 100 participants). Furthermore, sending surveys to participants in a course that has been taught by the same instructor for many years is unlikely to reveal any issues, except perhaps the wrong audience. So, in this case, the organization could administer the survey periodically rather than after each delivery.

Participant Reaction Calculation Methods

Here we share two common methods for calculating Level 1 participant reaction: percent favorable and average score.

Method 1: Percent Favorable or Percent Checking Top Two Boxes

Typically, participants will be given a range of answers (for example, strongly agree to strongly disagree) and be asked to select the one that best represents their opinion. This method of calculating a Level 1 score adds up all the participants who selected the top two answers or boxes (typically, strongly agree and agree) and divides by the total number of responses. A five-point scale is recommended, but some use a seven-point scale. (Some of those who use a seven-point scale count the top three boxes as favorable.) By formula, assuming a five-point scale:

> **Level 1: Reaction Percent Favorable for One Question:** (Number selecting agree + Number selecting strongly agree) ÷ Total number of respondents (expressed as a percentage).

For example, on a particular question, suppose 87 participants selected 4 (agree) or 5 (strongly agree), and 13 selected 1 (strongly disagree), 2 (disagree), or 3 (neutral). The total number of responses is 100 (87 + 13). Method 1 would calculate the percent favorable rating for that question as 87 ÷ 100 or 87 percent favorable. This example is also represented in the first row of Table 4-2.

When multiple questions are asked, use a simple average to combine the percent favorable for each question. The average percent favorable for all 10 questions in Table 4-2 is 89 percent, so the reported Level 1 score for this program would be 89 percent.

> **Level 1: Reaction Percent Favorable for All Questions:** Sum of percent favorable for each question ÷ Number of questions (expressed as a percent).

It is also instructive to analyze the results by question to pinpoint specific problems. Table 4-2 clearly shows a major issue with question 10, where the overall percent favorable rating drops to 69 percent. Further analysis shows there is a bimodal distribution (two peaks or humps) with a significant number (31) responding with a disagree or strong disagree. In this case, further analysis is warranted to understand the underlying problem.

Table 4-2. Calculation Methods

	Number of Respondents for Each Rating						Method 1	Method 2
Question	1 Strongly Disagree	2 Disagree	3 Neutral	4 Agree	5 Strongly Agree	Total Responses	Percent Favorable	Average Score
1	2	3	8	75	12	100	87%	3.9
2	1	1	4	80	12	98	94%	4.0
3	2	1	10	74	11	98	87%	3.9
4	0	0	2	45	53	100	98%	4.5
5	1	0	2	36	60	99	97%	4.6
6	2	1	5	41	50	99	92%	4.4
7	2	1	3	23	71	100	94%	4.6
8	0	1	7	45	47	100	92%	4.4
9	2	3	15	65	15	100	80%	3.9
10	19	12	0	12	57	100	69%	3.8
Total	31	23	56	496	388	994	89%	4.2

Method 2: Average Score

The average score is another common method for calculating Level 1 scores. This method assigns a value to each answer or box (for example, 1 for strongly disagree to 5 for strongly agree). The Level 1 score for one question is calculated as the simple average of all the participants' responses to that question, reported to one decimal point. For example, if there were five participants in a program and their responses were 4, 3, 5, 4, 3, method 2 would report 3.8 for Level 1 for that question $(4 + 3 + 5 + 4 + 3) \div 5 = 19 \div 5 = 3.8$.

By formula:

> **Level 1: Reaction Average Score for One Question:** Sum of all responses ÷ Number of respondents.

Row 1 in Table 4-2 shows the average of 3.9 for 100 respondents for question 1.

If the data are already grouped by rating as shown in Table 4-2, a weighted average can be used to calculate the average. By formula:

> **Level 1: Reaction Average Score for One Question:**
> = [(Number who selected rating 1 × 1) + (Number who selected rating 2 × 2) + (Number who selected rating 3 × 3) + (Number who selected rating 4 × 4) + (Number who selected rating 5 × 5)] ÷ Number of respondents
> = [(2 × 1) + (3 × 2) + (8 × 3) + (75 × 4) + (12 × 5)] ÷ 100
> = [2 + 6 + 24 + 300 + 60] ÷ 100
> = 392 ÷ 100
> = 3.9.

Use the same simple average methodology shown in Method 1 to find the average score for all questions for all participants. This is illustrated in the last column of Table 4-2, where the average score for all 100 participants for all questions is 4.2. By formula:

> **Level 1: Reaction Average Score for All Questions:** Sum of average score for each question ÷ Number of questions.

This method also allows calculation of the average score for each respondent. Simply find the average response for all the questions answered. By formula:

> **Level 1: Reaction Average Score for One Participant:** Sum of all responses ÷ Number of questions answered.

The case where Participant 2 does not answer all the questions is illustrated in Table 4-3. The denominator for Participant 1 is 10 because they answered all 10 questions. The denominator for Participant 2 is six because this individual left four questions unanswered.

Table 4-3. Results When All Questions Are Not Answered

Question	Participant 1 Ratings	Participant 2 Ratings
1	5	5
2	4	4
3	5	N/A
4	3	N/A
5	4	4
6	5	N/A
7	3	3
8	3	3
9	4	4
10	5	N/A
# of Responses	10	6
Average	4.1	3.8

The percent favorable method is often easier for others to understand because they don't need to know the scale to interpret it. When you use the average score, the reader will need to know something about the scale (was it five or seven points; was it an agreement or satisfaction scale). The percent favorable score is also easier to explain. For example, what does a 3.8 mean on a five-point scale, sort of agree? When you are communicating with business leaders, it will be a lot easier to convey the meaning behind the result using the percent favorable score. At Caterpillar, we shared Level 1 using percent favorable on a five-point scale.

Recommendation

Use Level 1 reaction for all courses but not necessarily for every class or every participant. Be clear about what information you want from Level 1 and what you will do with it. Use a five-point scale and sample when appropriate. Clearly state which method you are using to calculate Level 1.

For a complete analysis, you should share the distribution as well as the average. As you can see in Figure 4-3, both Course A and Course B had a 70 percent favorable rating. However, for Course A, those who didn't score a 4 or 5 selected the neutral score of 3, resulting in an average of 4.0 for this course. For Course B, several individuals gave a very low rating, resulting in an average of 3.6, which should trigger further investigation into the underlying cause behind the low scores.

Figure 4-3. Score Distribution of Two Courses

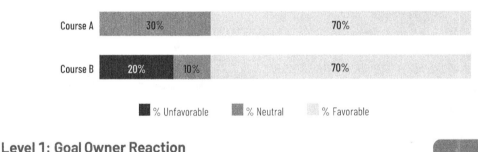

Level 1: Goal Owner Reaction

Goal owner reaction measures how satisfied the goal owner is with L&D. A goal owner is the highest-level leader accountable for an organizational goal. For example, the goal owner for a learning program to increase sales might be the senior vice president of sales. This measure seeks to determine what that high-level leader thinks of the L&D department.

Level 1: Goal Owner Reaction:
The goal owner's satisfaction with L&D.

The purpose of this measure is to discover opportunities for improvement and to strengthen your partnership with goal owners and senior leaders. The questions, of course, are different than for participant reaction. Common questions include:

- Did L&D meet the agreed-upon deadlines for development and delivery?
- Did the program stay within its budget?
- How was L&D to work with?
- Would you recommend L&D to others in the organization?
- Open-ended question: How could L&D improve?

For comparability, we recommend that you use a five-point scale, or whatever scale you are using for your participant reaction data.

Typically, you would measure goal owner reaction at the end of a program after results have been obtained (or not), although for long duration programs we recommend measuring it at six-month intervals.

Goal Owner Reaction Calculation Methods

If this measure is reported for just one goal owner, use the simple average of all questions for the summary measure but also show the reaction for each question. Be sure to also report any answers to the open-ended questions.

To combine the reactions for multiple goal owners, use a simple average, same as for participant reactions. Make sure to also include a summary of the answers to open-ended questions.

Recommendation

We highly recommend L&D leaders assess goal owner opinions of L&D. They certainly have opinions about L&D so why not discover what they are and address any that are not favorable? It is very easy to administer a four- or five-question survey, particularly if you only have a few goal owners.

Level 2: Learning

Level 2 of the Kirkpatrick and the Phillips frameworks measures how much participants have learned, usually via a test at the end of the course or multiple tests embedded throughout the course. Level 2 may also measure the improvement in skill or change in attitude. The definition for Level 2 is simply:

> **Level 2: Learning:** The extent to which participants improve knowledge, increase skill, or change attitude. Both the Kirkpatrick and Phillips frameworks refer to Level 2 as "learning."

The purpose of Level 2 is to ensure participants have learned the required knowledge or skill or can demonstrate the new attitude in class. (Demonstration on the job will be Level 3.) This is particularly important for compliance courses and others where some minimum level of learning will be required to perform a task successfully. Level 2 is typically employed for compliance and basic skills courses and may be appropriate for about 40-50 percent of all other courses aligned to specific goals. (This percentage excludes general course offerings and catalogs of e-learning courses where tests are not given.)

A low Level 2 learning score may also indicate a problem the program manager needs to address—confusing content, poorly worded questions in the test, the wrong target audience (they can't relate to the content or the questions), or lack of proper motivation by their manager for taking the course (they don't know why it is important). Like a low average Level 1 score, a low average Level 2 score calls for immediate management action to understand and correct the issue.

Level 2 is not an indicator of impact or value and should never be used in place of Levels 4 and 5.

For knowledge transfer, L&D organizations typically administer a test to determine the amount of knowledge acquired. Your survey tool can generate a score reflecting how many questions each participant answered correctly. For skill development, you may opt to use a behavioral observation approach. In this case, the grade reflects the percentage of new skills or level of proficiency demonstrated by the participant. Change in attitude may be measured by answering questions or observation, and the grade reflects the percentage of desired attitudes exhibited by the participant. Some organizations measure skills both before and after a class, course, or program. Typically, the goal owner or SME will establish a minimum passing score, which participants must exceed to successfully complete the course.

Another way to evaluate learning is to use a "then and now" approach to testing. With this approach, students only take one assessment at the conclusion of the class. They must determine what they knew before coming to the class ("then") and what they now know ("now"). This approach is referred to as a retrospective pretest (Wingate 2016). The benefit, as discussed by Theodore Lamb (2005), is that it avoids what is called the response-shift effect. Before attending the program, learners don't know what they don't know. In many cases, learners overrate their abilities on a pretest, causing the pre-post difference to be small. When using a retrospective pretest, on the other hand, the learner is quite aware of what they didn't know (after learning the material) and can provide a more meaningful rating for their "before" knowledge.

Level 2 may also be measured more generically by adding a question to the post-event survey that asks participants to what extent they have gained new knowledge. A five-point Likert scale is recommended. This is benchmarked by MTM.

Level 1: Reaction

Level 2: Learning

Effectiveness Measures

Level 3: Application

Level 4: Results and Impact

Level 5: ROI

Level 2 Calculation Methods

Next, we discuss five Level 2 calculation methods.

Method 1: Percentage Who Passed

This is one of two common methods for presenting Level 2 scores. Typically, the goal owner or SME sets a minimum threshold that the learner is expected to achieve for the test (for example, 85 percent or 17 questions answered correctly out of 20). Performance above the threshold constitutes a passing score. The percentage who passed is calculated as the number of participants performing above the threshold divided by all the participants in the class, course, or program.

For example, suppose 16 out of 20 participants scored above the threshold. Method 1 would report an 80 percent pass rate ($16 \div 20 = 80\%$).

Method 2: Average Score

The second common method for presenting Level 2 scores for a class, course, or program is to calculate the simple average of all the participants' scores, where each participant's score is expressed as the percentage of correct answers. This average is often compared to the goal owner's threshold.

For example, suppose the test scores (average percent correct) for five participants in a class were 90 percent, 60 percent, 70 percent, 80 percent, and 70 percent. Method 2 would report that the average score was 74 percent $[(90\% + 60\% + 70\% + 80\% + 70\%) \div 5 = 370\% \div 5 = 74\%]$.

Method 3: First-Time Pass Rate

This is an adaptation of Method 1 to provide actionable information when participants are required to keep taking the course until they pass. In this case, by definition, 100 percent of participants will ultimately pass, so the final pass rate doesn't convey any useful information about content, target audience, and so forth. First-time pass rate is calculated as the number of participants whose test score on their first attempt exceeds the threshold divided by all participants in the class, course, or program.

Method 4: First-Time Average Score

This method may be used instead of Method 3 to indicate if there are any issues that need to be addressed when participants are required to take the course until they pass. This measure is calculated the same way as the average score in Method 2.

Method 5: Likert Scale

This is a generic method to ascertain participant opinions of how much they learned. A five-point scale is recommended. The question might be worded, "I have gained new knowledge by taking this course."

Recommendation

Level 2 learning is an important effectiveness measure and should be reported for the courses where a test or check on learning is appropriate. The percent who passed measure is probably easier for most to understand than average score, which requires knowledge about the scale and the desired threshold. Use the first-time pass rate if a passing score is mandatory.

Like Level 1, you should also analyze the distribution to determine if some participants are performing considerably worse than others, indicating that corrective action needs to be taken regarding the content, delivery, test questions, or audience.

Level 3: Behavior and Application

Although the Kirkpatrick approach refers to Level 3 as behavior, both the Kirkpatrick and Phillips approaches focus on application: what participants did on the job with their changed behavior. In other words, how did they apply what they learned? We will use the word *application*, but clearly the change in behavior is key:

> **Application:** The application of new knowledge, skills, or attitudes by the participants when they return to their job. Application is measured as the *application rate*, which is defined later in this chapter.

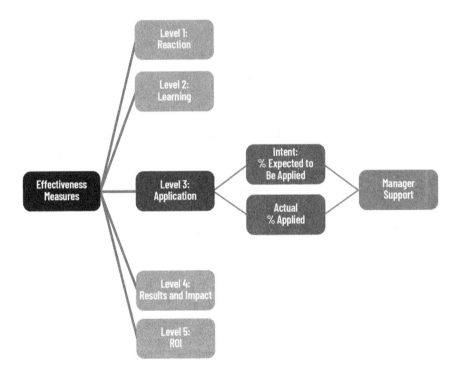

The purpose of measuring Level 3 is to ensure that participants actually applied what they learned. It is not only possible but very often the case that participants liked the training (Level 1) and learned (Level 2) but did not apply it. In other words, their behavior did not change in any measurable way. And if they did not apply the knowledge, it cannot have any impact on organizational goals or needs. This "wasted" learning is called *scrap learning*, which is defined simply as:

> **Scrap Learning:** 1 – Application rate (expressed as a percentage). For example, if the application rate is 55 percent, then the scrap rate is 45 percent.

Research by MTM based on millions of data points for organizations that do not measure scrap learning shows an average scrap rate of 45 percent (Mattox, Parskey, and Hall 2020). Others have estimated the scrap rate to be as high as 85 percent. It seems safe to say that only about half of the learning today is applied.

As mentioned, high scores for Level 1 reaction and Level 2 learning do not guarantee application. Kirkpatrick (2006) explains it this way:

> In order for change to occur, four conditions are necessary:
> 1. The person must have a desire to change.
> 2. The person must know what to do and how to do it.
> 3. The person must work in the right climate.
> 4. The person must be rewarded for changing.

Level 2 may measure point 2, but the other three factors depend primarily on the participant's supervisor and organizational culture and are not captured by Level 1. For learning to be successfully applied, the supervisor needs to be supportive before and after the formal learning occurs. This includes explaining why the content is important before the course and reinforcing the application after the course. While this sounds simple, these four conditions are often not met in the real world, where supervisors are often not briefed on the program or expectations and have limited time to spend with their employees.

Level 3 is important because it is the first level that correlates directly with impact. Generally, where there is application there is also impact. While there may be cases where impact does not follow application, we know for sure that without application of learning there will be no impact from learning. So, it is critical to measure application to drive scrap down but also as a leading indicator of Level 4 impact.

Low Level 3 scores combined with good scores for Levels 1 and 2 for application may indicate the following issues:
- low or nonexistent supervisor support for the training
- inadequate or nonexistent reinforcement of the training on the job by the supervisor (no rewards or recognition for application or no negative consequences for failing to apply)

- no opportunity to apply what they've learned on the job
- lack of resources, tools, or processes to apply the learning.

Other causes of low application rates could be that the content was confusing, the instruction was poor, the audience was wrong, or the material was not relevant, but these issues should have been revealed by low Level 1 scores. It's also possible that participants simply did not learn the required knowledge, skill, or attitude, but this should have been revealed by low Level 2 scores.

Application may be measured at the end of a course by asking participants about their intent to apply what they learned. It can also be measured after the participants have had time to apply their new knowledge on the job, typically two to three months after the course. (Research indicates that about 80 days are required to embed a new behavior.) This will be a measure of actual application.

Increasing the Use of Level 3 Application

By Ken Phillips, PhD, Chief Executive Officer, Phillips Associates

Application of training program content back on the job is one of the three critical pieces of evidence CEOs most want to see from their L&D investments, according to research conducted by the ROI Institute. (The other two are evidence of business results and return on investment.) ROI Institute research also found that only 11 percent of CEOs were receiving job application data from their learning and development department.

The crucial question, of course, is how can L&D start providing this information? The simple answer, to borrow a phrase from Nike, is to "just do it!" However, if history is a predictor of the future, that isn't likely to happen. Three different research studies conducted by ATD between 2009 and 2019 on the state of measurement and evaluation of learning found no significant change in the percentage of organizations measuring learning at Level 3. Specifically, the studies found that in 2009, 55 percent of organizations evaluated some learning programs at Level 3; in 2015, it was 60 percent, and in 2019 it was 54 percent. These numbers are both noteworthy and concerning. Of particular concern is that despite the countless number of presentations delivered and articles and books published on the topic of evaluating training at higher levels during this same period, the numbers remain essentially unchanged.

This raises another question: Is a new approach needed for measuring the application of training back on the job? The short answer is "no." The five-level evaluation model provides an easy to understand, logical way to look at measuring and evaluating learning, and it has broad acceptance throughout the L&D community. However, what is needed is an innovative new way of measuring the application of learning back on the job.

I've been working on just such a methodology for the past several years; it's called Predictive Learning Analytics. A unique feature of the method is that it has two phases. First, it identifies the underlying causes of scrap learning at an individual and supervisor level, indicating which participants are most and least likely to apply what they learned and which managers are inclined to provide strong or weak support.

While pinpointing the underlying causes of scrap learning is valuable, of even greater significance is being able to measure, monitor, and manage the targeted corrective actions taken to address the underlying causes. This process comprises the second phase of the Predictive Learning Analytics methodology. Like phase one, it uses data to determine how well each corrective action is working, and where any tweaks or adjustments, if any, are required.

It stands to reason that if L&D professionals had a direct, proven way to measure the application of training back on the job, they would be inclined to use it. By using this methodology or a similar data-driven approach, L&D professionals should be positioned to give CEOs the information they want: evidence of application of training back on the job.

Level 3 Calculation Methods

There are a variety of methods to measure behavior change or application. Here we discuss a leading indicator, intent to apply, and three ways to determine the actual application rate.

Intent to Apply

It is a best practice to measure the intent to apply as soon after course completion as possible. Intent to apply is a leading indicator of actual application, so it serves as an early warning of potential actual application issues. After all, if participants don't think they will apply it, they most likely won't, resulting in a high scrap rate. The question is generally included in the post-event survey where Level 1 questions are asked.

The actual wording of the question to measure intent to apply depends on the complexity of the content and learning objectives. For a single course with a narrow learning objective, the question may simply be: "Will you be able to apply what you learned in this course on the job?" Intent to apply is calculated as the percentage answering "yes":

> **Intent to Apply:** Number of participants who answered yes ÷ Total number of participants who responded (expressed as a percentage and rounded to the nearest whole number). For example, if 63 participants answered yes and 22 answered no, the intent to apply would be 74 percent (63 ÷ 85).

A Likert scale may also be used instead of a simple Yes/No, where the scale runs from strongly disagree to strongly agree: "I will be able to apply what I learned in this course on the job."

> **Intent to Apply:** Number of participants who selected the top two boxes on a five-point scale (or top two or three boxes on a seven-point scale) ÷ Total number of participants who responded (expressed as a percentage and rounded to the nearest whole number).

If the course has multiple learning objectives and especially if it has a longer duration, it may be better to ask about the percentage of content applied: "What percentage of the content from this course will you be able to apply?" (BM MTM)

Intent to Apply: Average of the participants' planned application rates.

In an automated survey, a decile scale is typically used, providing 10 percentage point increments from 0 percent to 100 percent. For example, if the responses from five participants were 80 percent, 40 percent, 70 percent, 0 percent, and 90 percent, the average would be: (80% + 40% + 70% + 0% + 90%) ÷ 5 = 56%. Note that participants reporting no intent to apply are still counted in the denominator. In this case, it may be helpful to remind participants of the major topics covered before they answer the question. If the program manager wanted more specific information on application by learning objective, multiple questions could be asked with one for each objective.

Note

Some practitioners follow the convention that any question eliciting a participant's reaction is a Level 1 question. Accordingly, they would classify this application question as a Level 1 question. Others include "planned action" with "reaction" in the definition of Level 1, and intent to apply would be a planned action. In any case, we would all agree it is an important measure and should be included in the post-event survey. For this book, we consider both the intent to apply and the actual application to be Level 3 measures, so the reader can always associate application with Level 3.

Actual Application Rate

Actual application may be determined by observation, demonstration, or survey, and is usually measured two to three months after the course. This provides time for the participant to change their behavior. Of course, despite best intentions, many will not actually apply what they learned or only apply a small percentage. So, the actual application rate will generally be lower than the intent to apply.

For some types of learning, actual application must be checked immediately after the training. For example, supervisors will listen in or observe as new call center employees or bank tellers address customer questions to ensure they are providing the correct information.

Observation

For some types of learning—like safety training, machine operation, or consultative selling skills—a supervisor may observe whether employees are doing what they were taught. The actual application rate is calculated as the percentage of those observed who applied what they were taught.

Actual Application Rate: Number of participants observed correctly applying the taught knowledge, skills, or attitude ÷ Total number of participants who were observed (expressed as a percentage and rounded to the nearest whole number).

The supervisors will need to be briefed on exactly what behaviors to look for and should be given a scoring tool.

Demonstration

For some other types of learning content, like leadership development, participants are asked to create an individual action plan outlining the specific steps they will take to implement what they learned. This plan is then shared with a supervisor with whom they have regular meetings to discuss progress. This provides an opportunity to measure actual application, either by asking the participant if they have completed their action plan or by asking their supervisor if the participant has completed their action plan. The actual application rate is calculated as the percentage of participants who have completed their plan, or alternatively, what percentage of their plan has been completed.

> **Actual Application Rate:** Number of participants who have completed their action plan ÷ Total number of participants (expressed as a percentage and rounded to the nearest whole number).

Alternatively, if the components of an action plan can be measured, then the actual application rate may reflect the percent completed:

> **Actual Application Rate:** Average percent completion (rounded to the nearest whole number).

Survey

The most common methodology is to use a survey to ask participants about their application. In contrast with the intent to apply question in the post-event survey, the question on actual application is asked in a follow-up survey, which may contain only this question and perhaps one or two others. The questions should mirror the intent to apply questions asked immediately following the training with the verb tense changed from future to past.

Just as with intent to apply, the wording of the question to measure actual application depends on the complexity of the training and learning objectives. For a single course with a narrow learning objective, the question may simply be: "Have you applied what you learned in the course on the job?"

Of course, you should remind the participant what course you are asking about and perhaps what they were supposed to learn so they can more accurately answer the question. The actual application rate is calculated as the percentage answering "yes":

> **Actual Application Rate:** Number of participants who answered "yes" ÷ Total number of participants who responded (expressed as a percentage and rounded to the nearest whole number).

A Likert scale may also be used instead of a simple Yes/No where the scale runs from strongly disagree to strongly agree: "I have applied what I learned in this course on the job."

> **Actual Application Rate:** Number of participants who selected the top two boxes on a five-point scale (or top two or three boxes on a seven-point scale) ÷ Total number of participants who responded (expressed as a percentage and rounded to the nearest whole number).

If the course has multiple learning objectives and especially if it has a longer duration, it may be better to ask about the percentage of content they applied: "What percentage of the content from this course have you been able to apply on the job?" (BM MTM). In an automated survey a decile scale is typically used, with increments provided from 0 percent to 100 percent. The actual application rate is calculated as the average percentage applied:

> **Actual Application Rate:** Average of the participants' actual application rates, rounded to the nearest whole number.

In this case, because it has been two to three months since they completed the course, it will be necessary to remind participants of the major topics covered before they answer the question. If the program manager wanted more specific information on application by learning objective, multiple questions could be asked with one for each objective.

Manager Support

We have discussed the importance of manager support, particularly as it pertains to application. In the best of all worlds, employees would have a discussion with their manager before the training to understand how the manager expects it to be applied. During training, employees would keep those goals in mind to ensure that they learn what the manager expects. After the training, the employee would meet with the manager to discuss expectations for application and specific approaches to apply and reinforce what they learned. Clearly, what we've outlined doesn't happen as frequently as it should. Pressing day-to-day priorities or simply a lack of interest by either the manager or employee may push these discussions off the list of things to do.

However, we also know that manager support is key to application. A comprehensive study by the analytics provider Explorance, *Predictive Learning Impact Model* (2019), found that manager support had a significant influence on the level of application by learners after a program. We recommend that L&D professionals include a question about manager support on both a post-event survey (immediately after a class) and on a follow-up survey (administered 60-90 days after completing the course). Manager support questions should address expectations for application and if the manager and employee have discussed the training and how it will be applied.

> **Manager Support:** My manager has communicated their expectations about how I will apply this training on the job.

Level 3 application should be measured for all important learning programs. At a minimum, intent to apply should be asked in the post-event survey along with Level 1 questions. Actual application should be measured by observation, demonstration, or survey for the most important programs, where it is crucial to deliver planned results (Level 4). If direct observation or demonstration of actual application are not available, a survey tool like SurveyMonkey can easily be employed to survey the participants. There is really no excuse for not measuring application for key programs.

Level 4: Results and Impact

We are finally ready to address learning's impact on business results. As we noted at the beginning of the discussion for effectiveness measures, Kirkpatrick and Phillips define Level 4 differently. The primary difference is whether the impact of learning can be isolated from other factors that may also contribute to achieving the business results. For example, if sales increase 5 percent after a training program, how much of the 5 percent was due to training and how much to other factors? Other factors might include the economy, a new incentive compensation system, a new supervisor, new employees in the group, a new workstation, and so forth.

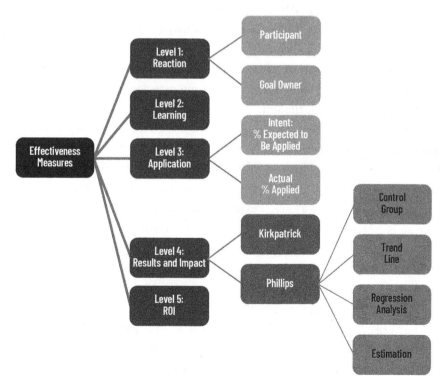

The Kirkpatricks and the Phillipses fundamentally disagree about the need and wisdom of isolating the impact of training. The Kirkpatricks do not advocate ever trying to do this, even if a naturally occurring control group is available. Instead, they focus on first defining and then meeting the expectations of the goal owner in terms of improvement in the goal itself (for example, sales) or leading indicators (such as the number of leads). In other words, they look for a correlation between training, leading indicators, and the business measure that would allow a reasonable person to conclude that training contributed to the results. In this approach, the impact of training is not isolated from other factors and consequently no net benefit of training can be calculated. There will be evidence but no proof of training impact. Instead, a compelling chain of evidence from Levels 1, 2, and 3 could be provided along the following lines:

1. If the proper needs analysis was done and the goal owner (such as the head of sales) and learning professionals agreed on what behaviors needed to change, and
2. If both parties worked diligently and in partnership, including reinforcement of the learning by the participant's supervisors, and
3. If the right audience took the training (number and type of audience, which are Level 0 measures), liked it, thought it was relevant (Level 1), and
4. If the participants learned what they needed (Level 2), and
5. If their behaviors changed in the intended way and they could successfully demonstrate the desired behavior (Level 3), and
6. If the business metric (in this case, sales) showed improvement following the training, then
7. It would be reasonable to assume that training contributed to the results (Level 4).

We think most would agree that a compelling case could be made for training if these conditions are met. Notice, though, that the Level 4 result is not a number. Instead, the focus of the Kirkpatrick approach is on meeting the goal owner's expectations that training would make a difference.

Unlike the Kirkpatricks, the Phillipses believe that the impact of learning can and should be isolated from other factors, at least for the most important training programs. We share their methodology here. Their position is supported by executives who call for a connection between learning and improvements in business measures.

Thus, we employ the Phillips definition of Level 4. That said, meeting goal owner expectations is critical, and one that most L&D organizations still are not doing today, so for most of them, that in itself would be an important accomplishment.

Level 4 impact is so important that in the TDRp framework we have called it out from other effectiveness measures and made it a separate category called outcome. So, Level 4 will do double duty as both an effectiveness measure and as an outcome measure. Furthermore, impact will usually be the only true outcome measure. It is that important.

Following the Phillips approach, we offer this definition for impact:

> **Impact:** The isolated contribution of learning on achieving a business (organization) goal or meeting a business (organization) need. Where "isolated" means the contribution of just learning, apart from all the other factors that also contributed to achieving the business goal or meeting the business need.

The purpose of Level 4 is to answer the all-important question from goal owners, senior leaders, and others: "Did learning make a difference in achieving our results?" The Phillips approach will answer this question quantitatively with a number like a 3 percent increase in sales due just to learning or a 20 percent contribution toward achieving the goal. The Kirkpatrick approach will answer the question qualitatively by building a convincing chain of evidence to demonstrate the likely impact of learning.

If the Phillips approach is employed, impact can be used to determine Level 5 net benefit and the return on investment (ROI), which in turn will answer the question: "Was the investment in learning worth the cost?"

The issue of isolating the impact of learning from all other factors remains one of the most contentious in our field. The methodology is simple and straightforward, but many are not comfortable with the concept. The Kirkpatricks would say that even if it were possible to isolate the impact, it should not be done. They worry that L&D will claim credit for the isolated impact of learning when, in fact, it will only be successful if both the goal owner and L&D work together as partners to ensure that the right target audience is selected, the right communication is provided to the learners in advance, the training is properly designed and delivered, and the new knowledge is reinforced by the goal owner once the learners are back on the job. If L&D were to claim sole credit, the L&D department could alienate the goal owner and damage the partnership.

In our view, the Kirkpatricks are absolutely correct that learning will only be successful if there is a close partnership between the goal owner and the L&D department. After all, the target audience reports to the goal owner and not L&D. Only the goal owner can require their employees to apply what they've learned to achieve the desired impact. Consequently, we agree that L&D should never claim credit for the results or impact. The credit must always be shared, and both L&D and the goal owner should be credited for successful learning. In other words, it is the learning, not the L&D department, which leads to the results or impact.

With this important insight in mind, we continue to explore the two approaches.

Level 4 Calculation Methods

In this section, we first explore how the impact of learning can be calculated. Following this discussion, we share our thoughts on when and how you might use the Kirkpatrick approach.

The Phillips Approach

Jack Phillips first described his approach to calculate impact by isolating the contribution of learning in his 1983 *Handbook of Training Evaluation and Measurement Methods*. The current, fourth edition describes six methods to isolate the contribution of learning—control group, trend line, regression, estimation, expert, and customer input (Phillips 2016). They are listed in order of credibility, with the first, a control group, being the most credible. We provide a short description of the first five, but the interested reader is encouraged to consult the Phillips book for a comprehensive and detailed discussion.

Control Group

A control group remains the gold standard to isolate the contribution of learning from all other factors. Using this methodology, training is given to one group (the experimental group) and not provided to another group (the control group). If the two groups are identical in all ways except for the training, then it follows that any difference in performance between the two groups must be due to that. For example, suppose that sales training is provided to one group of sales representatives and their sales increase 10 percent following the training. If sales for the control group increase only 6 percent, then training must explain the 4 percentage point difference. In other words, the impact of training was a 4 percent increase in sales, meaning that sales increased 4 percent solely due to the training. The remainder of the sales increase (6 percent) for the experimental group and the entire 6 percent increase in sales for the control group would be due to nontraining factors, such as a growing economy, new products, or a new sales incentive plan.

While everyone agrees that this is the best approach, it is often challenging to implement in the real world. If the target audience for the program is small, the organization generally wants to provide it to everyone as soon as possible so the training can contribute to results across the board. Leaders would be reluctant to withhold training from half of the target audience simply to create a control group. Furthermore, the single greatest factor in determining whether training has an impact is generally the leader, and the participants in the control group will typically report to a different leader than those in the experimental group, which means that the two groups are not identical in every way except the training.

These objections may be overcome if there is a very large target audience. In this case, the training may not be provided to everyone at the same time, so there might be an opportunity for a "naturally occurring" control group that does not receive the training in the beginning. Also, if the target audience is large enough such that participants report to many different leaders, we might assume that on average the leadership quality for the control and experimental groups is the same, removing this as a confounding factor.

Trend Line

In the Phillips methodology, trend line analysis is simply a comparison of the projected results without training to the actual results with training. To project results without training a trend line is fitted through the actual results and then extended a year into the future. The difference between the projected results and the actual results represents the impact of training as long as nothing else of significance happened while the training was being provided, which would also have influenced the results.

The method works if two conditions are met. First, the pretraining trend would have continued if the training had not been conducted. Second, in the post-training period, no other influences have entered the process apart from the training.

Let's consider an example. Quarterly injuries are plotted over five years ending on December 31, 2019 (Figure 4-4). A trend line is visually fitted to the data and extended through 2020. Training is provided in January 2020, and the results are shown. Not surprisingly, the training leads to a significant decrease in injuries. The trend line projects quarterly injuries for 2020 of a little below 20 each quarter, for a total of 77 injuries for the year. Actual injuries for the year were 54, so trend line analysis indicates that training reduced injuries by 23.

This method can easily be accomplished by creating a chart of the actual results before and after training, and then using a ruler to fit a line through the two sets of data points. While easy to do, the resulting placement of the lines is somewhat subjective and may be difficult if the data do not "line up" nicely.

Figure 4-4. Example Using a Trend Line to Forecast Safety Without Training

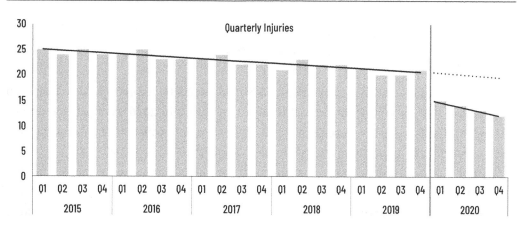

Regression

Regression is a statistical technique to fit a line through a series of data points. Instead of visually fitting the line as in the trend line method, regression uses a standard statistical technique to provide the best fit possible. The result is an equation that describes the relationship between the business result (such as sales) and the multiple factors that explain changes in the business result (for example, market growth, advertising, and special promotions). This equation can then be used to forecast the value of the business metric without training for the coming year. The difference between the forecasted level for the business metric and the actual is the isolated impact of training because the regression considered all the other factors.

For example, suppose we believed three variables or factors could explain or predict sales, which is to say that changes in these three explanatory variables would explain the changes in sales. The three variables could be advertising, special promotions, and market growth. (The model will tell us if these turn out to be good predictors. If they are not, we would look for others.) The regression equation would take the form of:

Sales = A + (B × Advertising) + (C × Special promotions) + (D × Market growth).

A statistics package would estimate the value of the coefficients (A, B, C, and D), which do the best job predicting sales over the historical period for which we have data (2010–2019). Armed with these four coefficients and the actual values for advertising, special promotions, and market growth for 2020, sales can be predicted without training for 2020. Let's suppose the model estimates the coefficients to be:

- A = 300
- B = 0.05
- C = 0.07
- D = 30

And further that in 2020:

- Advertising = $10,000
- Special promotions = $7,000
- Market growth = 1.5%

Then predicted sales for 2020 = 300 + (0.05 × 10,000) + (0.07 × 7000) + (30 × 1.5)

= 300 + 500 + 490 + 45

= $1,335.

The regression model predicts sales of $1,335 in 2020. Assuming sales had been entered into the model in thousands, this means that sales in 2020 were predicted to be $1,335,000. If sales actually were $1,500,000, then we would conclude that sales training was responsible for a $165,000 increase in sales ($1,500,000 – $1,335,000).

While statistically appealing, especially as it can include numerous variables and has statistical rigor, this method requires someone who understands the factors influencing sales growth to identify the key explanatory variables (the measures besides training that could influence the business result). Due to its complexity, unless the organization employs a data scientist, this method generally requires the assistance of a consultant.

Estimation

When a control group, trend line analysis, or regression are not feasible, estimation from the most credible sources is the next best approach. It is simple to do and does not require hiring consultants or performing a regression analysis.

Essentially, this method uses the insights of those who know best to estimate the isolated impact of learning. (You might think of this as the "wisdom of crowds" method, after the 2005 book of the same name by James Surowiecki.) Furthermore, the method considers that self-reported data may be biased and that the estimates are just that—estimates—and not actual values. In his 1983 book, Phillips introduced the confidence factor as an ingenious method to correct for the likely self-reporting bias.

Participants in a program are often asked for their estimate of the program's impact but supervisors, leaders, and other could also be asked. Here is how it works. Each participant in the sample is asked two questions, which can be built into a follow-up survey administered 60 to 90 days after the training:

- What percentage of your performance improvement since the training do you believe is due to just the training?
- How confident are you in this estimate?

The generic term "performance improvement" is used in the example but can be replaced with more specific wording such as "increase in sales." An 11-point scale from 0 percent to 100 percent with 10 percentage point increments can be used for both questions. The two answers are then multiplied together to calculate the confidence-adjusted isolated impact of training. Last, the confidence-adjusted isolated impacts are averaged across the sample to find the average for the group. Table 4-4 shows an example for five participants (in practice at least 30 should be used unless the course had fewer than 30 participants, in which case a very high response rate is needed).

Table 4-4. Participant Estimation Method Calculation

Participant	Impact of Training	Confidence in Estimate	Confidence-Adjusted Isolated Impact
John	80%	70%	56%
Sue	60%	50%	30%
Gaj	90%	80%	72%
Tonya	0%	N/A	0%
Jose	50%	40%	20%
Average			35.6%

We see that John thought the training was very impactful (80 percent) and was fairly confident (70 percent) about the 80 percent estimate. Multiplying the estimate by the confidence factor reduces the 80 percent to 56 percent, which allows for self-reporting bias. Sue was less impressed by the training and also less confident. Gaj thought the training was very impactful and felt very confident about his estimate. In contrast, Tonya thought the training was a complete waste of time (0 percent impact), so we don't need to ask her how confident she is about the 0 percent. Jose thought it was impactful but was not confident about his estimate, so his resulting score is only 20 percent.

The average for the group is 35.6 percent, which means that on average the group attributes about 36 percent of their increase in sales due just to the training. That means the other 64 percent was due to the other factors such as the economy, new sales representatives, or a new supervisor. If sales for the five participants increased by 9 percent, then training alone was responsible for a 3.2 percent sales increase (35.6% × 9%) or about a third of the total 9 percent increase.

A best practice would be to share this result with head of sales and the sales supervisors to assess if they believe it is reasonable (the voice of the experts!). The 3 percent increase in sales due just to training could then be revised up or down based on the expert's opinion. Alternatively, you could ask the supervisors the same questions and average their confidence-adjusted isolated impact with participants before sharing with the head of sales. In this case, the estimate from the supervisors could be weighted equally with that from the participants or the two samples could be weighted (for example, 75 percent for the participants and 25 percent for the supervisors).

If the target audience for the training has fewer than 30 participants, theoretically all participants will need to provide their estimates for the result to be statistically significant. In the real world, though, we would just like most of the participants to respond if the audience size is less than 30 (like 12 out of 15 or 15 out of 20). If the target audience is more than 30, but fewer than 30 respond, you can still use the resulting impact as long as you have a very high response rate (like more than 70 percent) and more than 15 or 20 respond.

As you can see, the method is easy to use and does not require any advanced statistics, which is why it is such a popular approach to isolating impact. You can also employ this approach immediately after the training to provide an initial estimate of the anticipated isolated impact. This is analogous to the "intent to apply" question for application. The wording of the question simply needs to be modified to the future tense:

- How much do you believe your performance will improve due to just the training?
- How confident are you in this estimate?

This question would be included along with the Level 1 questions and the intent to apply question in the post-event survey distributed immediately after the course. We will refer to this as the initial estimate of impact and the measure after 90 days as the final estimate of impact:

> **Initial estimate of impact:** Average of the participant's confidence-adjusted isolated impacts × Expected result, based on questions in the post-event survey. (BM MTM)

> **Final estimate of impact:** Average of the participant's confidence-adjusted isolated impacts × Actual result, based on questions in the follow-up survey. (BM MTM)

The final estimate of impact questions along with the actual application question would be included in the follow-up survey distributed about 90 days after the training.

Expert

The simplest, although not the most robust, method for isolating the impact of learning is to ask an expert. The expert typically would be the goal owner or someone in the goal owner's department. If we want to know the isolated impact of a sales training program, the single best person to ask would be the head of sales, or someone else in sales close to the program like the sales supervisor. While this approach is very subjective, it does have the advantage that the estimate of isolated impact comes from a trusted, credible, and often senior leader.

Alternatively, an expert other than the goal owner might provide guidance. For example, this might be a consultant who specializes in the area and who has experience with similar programs in similar settings.

The Importance of Isolating Impact

By Jack J. Phillips, PhD, Chairman, ROI Institute

Determining the effect of your program on the impact measure is absolutely necessary. Evaluators must isolate the effects of the program from other influences to validate and accurately report the program's success. If the program effects are not isolated, no business link can be established, and there will be no proof that the program actually influenced the measures. The evidence will show only that the program might have made a difference. Results have improved, but other factors might have influenced the data.

Isolating program impact acknowledges that other influences are almost always present and multiple factors generate business results. Other processes and programs are usually present to improve the same outcome metrics targeted by the program. Additionally, the other factors and influences have their own protective owners who will insist that it was their processes that made the difference. Some of them will even suggest that the results are due entirely to their efforts, and they may present a compelling case to executives stressing their achievements.

Isolating the effects of the program on impact data is an achievable task. It can be accomplished in all situations with a reasonable degree of accuracy. The challenge is to develop one or more specific techniques to isolate the effects early in the program planning process. Fortunately, a variety of isolation techniques are available to facilitate the procedure in every case. These techniques include both quantitative methods and qualitative methods.

Every few years, ROI Institute conducts a highly comprehensive benchmarking study to obtain data that show what is occurring and the progress being made by ROI Methodology users. The *2019 ROI Institute Benchmarking Study* asked the question, "When isolating the effects of the programs on improvement of key measures, what percentage of time do you use the following techniques?" Figure 4-5 reveals the response of the 246 participants and provides insight into the frequency of use for each technique.

Figure 4-5. Techniques for Isolation

When isolating the effects of programs on improvement in key measures, what percentage of the time do you use the following techniques?

Technique	Percentage
Participant estimates	57%
Manager estimates	49%
Senior manager estimates	42%
Trend line analysis	40%
Customer input	38%
Expert input	37%
Control Grups	34%
Mathematical modeling	28%

When this data is compared to previous studies, we see the use of control groups, trend line analysis, and mathematical modeling have increased. This is encouraging, and likely the payoff of analytics programs being available in organizations. These three methods are the most credible approaches. When these numbers are totaled, it yields 102 percent. If these methods work each time, then there is no need to use estimates. However, the most credible approaches don't always work in the end and estimates are needed.

We recommend considering and pursuing multiple isolation methods to tackle this important issue. When multiple methods are used, the most credible is used. If more than one is credible, the most conservative method should be used in the ROI calculation. (Conservative means the one with the lowest ROI.) The reason is that a conservative approach builds acceptance. Deciding on which techniques to use should be based on each method's feasibility, accuracy, credibility, cost, and time requirement.

Thoughts on the Kirkpatrick Approach

We close the section on Level 4 measures by returning to the Kirkpatrick approach.

While we recommend using isolated impact for Level 4, there may be occasions where the isolation methodology does not resonate with leaders or where it does not seem appropriate. For example, some organizations do not have a clearly defined business metric, making it impossible to calculate the isolated impact. Training missions in the military offer one such example where the mission or business objective is to train. Of course, the ultimate objective is to win wars, but this is hard to measure and would not lend itself to the participant estimation method described. Instead, the best course of action may be to reach agreement on a measurable expectation, such as achieving an average score of 4.5 on a 5-point scale for readiness of the troops from the commander who receives them when their training is complete. In this case, the receiving commander takes the place of the goal owner and training should try to meet their expectations. Readiness in this case would be the results measure, but there is no attempt to measure the isolated impact of training on readiness, which will also depend on the capabilities of the recruits coming into training and other factors. Levels 1, 2, and 3 should be available to craft a compelling chain of evidence that expectations were met.

Another approach is to ask a question on improved job performance as part of the follow-up survey. While not specifically recommended by the Kirkpatricks, it does address results from a personal point of view and could be viewed as another link in the chain of evidence. The question might take the following form: "My job performance has improved as a result of taking this course."

The responses would be scored on a five- or seven-point Likert scale and shared as the percentage who reported improved job performance. The question could also be modified to ask about expected job performance improvement and asked as part of the post-event survey.

A final note on the Kirkpatrick approach. They employ a term called ROE, which they define as return on expectations. While this is not a number like ROI, it is a way to focus attention on the goal owner's expectations for learning and whether the joint effort between the goal owner's organization and the L&D department was successful in meeting those expectations. It is a concept rather than a measure and consequently there is no formula to calculate it. Figure 4-6 shows we might use a compelling chain of evidence for Levels 0–3 (recall that Level 0 from chapter 3 is synonymous with the efficiency measure) to demonstrate that learning met the expectations of the goal owner.

In this example, we think most would agree that the goal owner's expectations for training were met. They were clearly met in terms of the Level 0-3 targets and the plans for supervisor engagement, which comprise the chain of evidence. Sales increased by 9 percent, which is better than the 5 percent gain last year without the training, and the goal owner, Branson, is happy with the learning effort by both the L&D department and her supervisors. Of course, it may be the case that the increase in the sales growth rate from 5 to 9 percent was due to factors other than training, like a pick-up in the economy or a failing competitor, which can be addressed through the Phillips' isolated impact methodology.

Figure 4-6. Simple Example of the Chain of Evidence Approach

Context	• Business goal: Increase sales by 10% • Goal owner: Branson, SVP of Sales • Prior year: Company did not achieve goal to increase sales by 10%; sales rose 5% • Needs analysis: Sales representatives would be more successful if they knew the latest product features and if they had consultative selling skills
Expectations of Goal Owner	• Goal owner and L&D agree that the right training on product features and consultative selling skills and proper reinforcement by sales supervisors will enable the company to increase sales by 10%

Plan and Target	• Provide training to 100 sales representatives on product features and consultative selling skills by March 31 (Level 0 measures)
	 • Targets:
	   ○ Level 1: 90% favorable rating
	   ○ Level 2: Average score of more than 85% on first attempt for knowledge checks on product features and consultative selling skills training
	   ○ Level 3 intent to apply: 80% of participants intend to apply consultative selling skills (in a post-event survey)
	   ○ Level 3 actual application: 70% of participants have applied the consultative skills after 90 days (in a follow-up survey)

Roles	• L&D: Design, develop, and deliver training • Sales: Subject matter experts • Branson: Communicate importance of the training, expectations from the training to sales supervisors and sales reps • Sales supervisors: Meet with the reps immediately after training to answer questions and reinforce the concepts • Sale supervisors: Provide ongoing coaching
Results	• Business results: 9% sales increase • Level 1: 88% favorable • Level 2: 86% on first attempt • Level 3 intent to apply: 82% • Level 3 actual application: 72%, meeting plan • Supervisors: 90% met with reps immediately after training and all provided ongoing coaching for two months

Recommendation

Impact should be calculated for all programs in support of key organizational goals, especially those of the CEO. For example, if L&D has the opportunity to help the organization achieve its sales, quality, productivity, cost, or employee engagement goals, the impact of learning should be calculated not only to determine the actual impact but also to learn how it might be done better in the future. Calculation of impact may not make sense or be appropriate for other types of learning like team building, basic skills, or compliance training. This learning is more operational or tactical in nature and generally does not have a CEO-level goal.

Level 5: ROI

The purpose of ROI is to determine if the training was worth doing. Put differently, ROI will demonstrate the bottom-line value of the program. It is possible that the participants liked the program and would recommend it (high Level 1 reaction), learned the content and demonstrated mastery (high Level 2 learning), applied it on the job (high Level 3 actual application), and improved their performance in key business measures (Level 4 actual impact), but the training still should not have been conducted. This will be the case when the cost of the program exceeds its value, which can occur more often than you might think once the total costs of learning are included. Bottom line, ROI answers the question of whether there was enough benefit to warrant the cost.

This is one of the key insights from Jack Phillips and reflects the idea that L&D should be run like a business, meaning the benefit of a program should exceed its cost. It is not sufficient that participants like it, or they learn, or even that they apply the new knowledge to improve their performance. The learning program must pay for itself to be worth doing, just as other programs in our organizations are expected to show a positive ROI.

Another important reason for undertaking an ROI analysis is to learn more about the benefits and costs of a program and, even more importantly, identify opportunities for improvement in future programs. There are always opportunities to improve and a good ROI study will almost always provide insights on what could be done in the future to increase benefits or reduce costs.

Definition and Level 5 Calculation Methods

By formula, ROI is defined as:

> **Return on Investment (ROI):** Net program benefit ÷ Program cost (expressed as a percentage).

Other important terms are:

> **Net Program Benefit:** Gross program benefit - Program cost.

> **Gross Program Benefit:** Monetary value of the isolated impact of learning.

> **Program Cost:** All the costs associated with the training including the needs analysis, design, development, delivery, measurement, and management as well as the opportunity cost of the participant's time, travel costs and even the evaluation cost. If components are outsourced, then add the cost to purchase or deliver content. (**Note:** This definition for program cost is the same as the definition provided earlier for total cost under the efficiency measures, but here the focus is on the cost for a program rather than cost for all learning.)

> **Opportunity Cost:** Value of participant's time spent away from their job in training or traveling to and from training. Also includes the value of a leader's time if the course is taught by a leader.

We next explore net program benefit and program cost in more detail.

Net Program Benefit

Let's begin with the monetary (dollar) value of the Level 4 impact. Once the improvement in a business measure has been isolated to the program, the measure must be converted to money and then annualized to be used in the ROI numerator. There are a number of ways to convert a measure to money. In the ideal situation, you simply use a standard value for the measure as set by the organization. For example, if you are evaluating a sales training program that targets sales to new customers, your unit of measure would be one sale to a new customer. The value of a sale is the gross profit of that sale. Let's say you increase sales of widgets by $5,000 per month. The monetary benefit to the organization is the margin gained after accounting for cost of doing business. If the gross profit margin is 20 percent, then the organization made $1,000 from that increase in sales. Therefore, the monetary benefit of the training is $1,000 per month. Multiply that by 12 and that is a $12,000 added value to the organization. This value would be the gross benefit of the program.

If you are working with measures other than sales, you would also look for standard values to use as the basis for converting measures to money. For example, if you are running an effective meeting skills program and the objective is to reduce the time (in hours) a person spends chairing meetings each month, the unit of measure might be one hour of time. To convert time to money, you would use the standard value of time, which is how much you pay (salary plus benefits) the individuals whose time you are trying to save.

When standard values are not available, other techniques exist, including historical costs, expert input, databases, connecting soft measures to hard measures more easily converted to money, and estimates.

The results of ROI Institute's *2019 Benchmarking Study* are shown in Figure 4-7. The results indicate the frequency with which respondents to their survey reported using the different techniques to convert a measure to money.

Because ROI represents the gain over and above the cost of a program, the gross monetary benefit must be converted to net program benefit before being inserted into the ROI formula. To calculate net benefit, simply subtract the program cost from the gross monetary benefit. So, net program benefit is the value to the organization of the learning program after all the costs associated with it have been subtracted. This brings us to program cost.

Program Cost

First, appreciate that a learning program involves more than just design, development, and delivery. Someone (hopefully!) spent time talking to the goal owner at the beginning and then performing a needs analysis to determine if training is needed. Someone has to manage the program from start to finish and work closely with the goal owner. And someone needs to measure it and generate reports.

Figure 4-7. Methods to Convert Data to Money

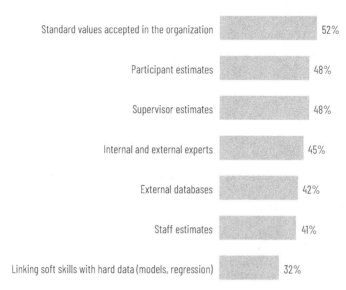

When converting data to money, what percentage of the time do you use the following techniques?

Standard values accepted in the organization	52%
Participant estimates	48%
Supervisor estimates	48%
Internal and external experts	45%
External databases	42%
Staff estimates	41%
Linking soft skills with hard data (models, regression)	32%

Source: ROI Institute, 2019 ROI Methodology Benchmarking Study. Used with permission.

Second, the cost of learning includes more than just the salary of staff working on the program. A complete accounting of cost must include the costs related to salary (like employer-paid taxes, healthcare, and pension) plus a portion of all the overhead in the department (such as office space charges, telephone, copiers, travel, and supplies). So, a fully burdened labor and related rate is required to calculate the cost of a program. This fully loaded rate is typically two to three times an employee's salary. (Your accountants can help you calculate this. See Vance 2017, chapter 1, for a detailed description of the calculation.)

For example, suppose the average salary of the team working on the learning program is $30 per hour. The fully burdened rate would likely be $60 to $90 per hour. Let's use $90. If the team spends 100 hours on the program, the program cost would be 100 hours × $90 per hour = $9,000 + Any direct costs for items like materials, room rental, and so forth. If direct cost was $5,000 then program cost would equal $9,000 + $5,000 = $14,000. Travel costs for the participants and trainers should also be included in the program cost.

Third, we need to add the opportunity cost, which is an economic concept rather than an accounting concept. When participants take time away from their jobs to receive training, there is a cost to the organization in forgone work. They are not performing the job they were hired to do, so a complete accounting of cost needs to add in the value of the work not done. For example, a salesperson is not closing deals; thus the company is less profitable during the time of the training.

Opportunity cost is usually estimated conservatively as the Participant's salary and benefits × Hours away from job. Use of the participant's salary ensures that their value is appropriately captured. After all, the opportunity cost for a purchasing agent is much different than that of a graphic designer. For example, if the average participant's salary and benefits are $35 per hour and 100 people attend a four-hour course with one hour of travel time, the opportunity cost for the program would $35 per hour × 5 hours × 100 participants = $17,500. For large programs, especially for senior-level employees, the opportunity cost is often the largest cost and may exceed the combined cost for design, development, and delivery.

ROI and Other Calculations

With terms defined, ROI can now be calculated. Using the examples described, assume the following and then calculate net benefit and ROI: gross benefit is $50,000 and program cost is $31,500.

> **Net Program Benefit:** Gross program benefit − Program cost = $50,000 − $31,500 = $18,500.

> **ROI:** Net benefit ÷ Program cost = $18,500 ÷ $31,500 = 0.59 or 59%.

The ROI of 59 percent means that for every dollar invested in this program, the organization will get its investment back plus an additional 59 cents. The goal is to have a positive ROI, which indicates that the net benefit is positive and that the gross benefit exceeds the total cost.

An older measure involving these same terms is the benefit-cost ratio, which is simply a different way of expressing the same information.

> **Benefit-Cost Ratio:** Gross program benefit ÷ Program cost (usually shown to two decimal points).

A benefit-cost ratio of 1.0 means that the gross program benefit (before subtracting the costs) equals the cost, so the goal is to have a benefit-cost ratio greater than 1.0. Using data from our example, the benefit-cost ratio is 1.59:

> **Benefit-Cost Ratio:** $50,000 ÷ $31,500 = 1.59.

In other words, the program benefits are about one and a half times as great as the costs. Notice that the benefit-cost ratio and ROI are mathematically related:

> **ROI:** Benefit-cost ratio − 1 (expressed as a percentage) = 1.59 − 1 = 0.59 or 59%

The primary purpose of ROI and the benefit-cost ratio is to demonstrate value and identify opportunities for improvement. At Caterpillar, we conducted more than 15 ROI studies and learned important lessons from each one, which helped us improve our learning going ahead. ROI should also be employed proactively in the planning stage using forecast of benefits and costs to ensure that the benefits are likely to exceed the costs. In fact, it will be the most important element in any business case.

Recommendation

Calculate ROI for very expensive programs or for any program where it is important to better understand the relationship between benefits and costs. ROI should not be used defensively to prove the worth of a program or a department when the program is not aligned to key organizational goals and where there is not a good partnership with the goal owner and other stakeholders. In other words, even a very high ROI will generally not make up for poor planning and the lack of strong partnership with the goal owner and senior leaders, and in this case senior leaders are unlikely to be convinced by any ROI regardless of how high it is. (See Vance 2017, chapter 8, for more on the use of ROI.)

The Importance of Demonstrating ROI in Learning

By Patti P. Phillips, PhD, Chief Executive Officer, ROI Institute

In recent years, a change has occurred in organizational accountability, especially toward investments in people, programs, projects, and initiatives. Program sponsors and those who have responsibility for program success have always been concerned about the value of their initiatives. Today, this concern includes financial impact—the actual monetary contribution from a project or program. Although monetary value is a critical concern, it is the comparison of this value with the program costs that captures stakeholder attention—and translates into ROI.

Implementing an evaluation and measurement process for learning programs has earned a place among the critical issues in the talent development field. For decades, this topic has been on conference agendas and discussed at professional meetings. Journals and newsletters regularly embrace the concept. Professional organizations have been created to exchange information on measurement and evaluate and provide significant coverage of the topic. Hundreds of books have been published, with the first book of case studies describing how organizations apply the concept arriving in 1994, edited by Jack J. Phillips and published by the American Society for Training and Development (now, ATD).

Although interest in the topic has heightened and much progress has been made, it is still an issue that challenges even the most sophisticated and progressive L&D departments. While some professionals argue that having a successful evaluation process is difficult, others are quietly and deliberately implementing effective evaluation systems. The latter group has gained tremendous support from the senior management team and has made much progress.

Regardless of the position taken on ROI, there are good reasons to pursue it as part of your evaluation strategy:

- **To improve programs.** This has always been our preferred reason for tackling impact and ROI analysis. In the past, talent development professionals focused their efforts on improving the learner experience and ensuring that participants learned the delivered content. While this focus is important, executives and key sponsors (those who provide the support and funds) would prefer to see outcomes beyond learning—they want evidence that learning contributes to the improvement in key organizational measures. And, when a program does not contribute to the target measures, resulting in a less than desired ROI, leaders want to know why it happened and how to improve results. An ROI study will answer both questions.

- **To satisfy key stakeholders.** Programs have many stakeholders, but no one is more important than those who sponsor, support, or provide the budget or funds for programs. These individuals want to see the business connections of programs. Even if you are in a government or nonprofit organization, costly, strategic programs must drive improvement in measures of output, quality, cost, time, customer satisfaction, job satisfaction, work habits, and innovation. Demonstrating the impact and ROI of your programs communicates to stakeholders that you are listening to them, observing what is happening in your organization, and allocating resources to the programs that best align with their strategy.

- **To make a difference in the organization.** Prior to my work in measurement and evaluation in talent development, I worked on the business side of the organization. In that capacity, we had to demonstrate impact and be concerned with benefits as compared to costs. Our focus was on outcomes, results, and accomplishments. It wasn't always easy, but it felt good because we could see that we were moving the needle on measures that mattered to the organization. Talent development professionals who demonstrate the impact and ROI of their major projects feel the same way. By evaluating programs to impact and ROI, it is easy to see that you are making a difference in the organization.

- **To maintain or enhance your budget.** This is the number one reason we see ROI being implemented globally. Whether in good times or bad, protecting funds is top of mind of many functional leaders. When the threat of economic downturn exists, L&D is often first to see their funds get cut. This is primarily because executives only see activity-based evidence of learning's contribution, such as the number of people trained, hours spent in training, and overall satisfaction with the programs. Activity reflects cost, costs get cut. One of the best ways to convince executives that L&D is not a cost, but rather an investment, is to demonstrate the results of that investment in terms that resonate with them. These terms include the actual ROI.

- **To change the perception of the L&D function.** Investment in L&D should be something executives want to do because it makes good business sense. Unfortunately, there is still a mindset that investment in learning is something that executives must do, but they do so at a minimal level. It is as if they perceive L&D as a necessary evil. We have had too many executives say, "We know we have to fund training and teach people how to do their jobs, but beyond that, we are very selective in how we spend our dollars." Being selective is good; basing that selection on mere intuition or macro-level studies is insufficient. But if that is all they have on which to base their decisions, then that is how they will decide. Integrating measurement rigor within the L&D function and showing the connection of programs to the business is the best way to change the perception of L&D as a necessary evil to that of a necessary business driver.

While not all programs require evaluation to the impact and ROI levels, those that do, are the initiatives that should drive change in the organization. Waiting to pursue impact and ROI until one of these opportunities presents itself is a shortsighted and risky approach. The time to begin developing capability, putting systems in place, and integrating impact and ROI into your measurement mix is before you ever need it.

Conclusion

In this chapter we introduced you to the most common effectiveness measures and their nuances, with a goal of providing a solid foundation upon which you can build by reading more from the Phillipses, Kirkpatricks, and others. While there are only five levels (Levels 1–5), effectiveness measures are much more powerful than efficiency measures (Level 0) and are the primary measures used to evaluate program success and determine program value. The most common effectiveness measures and their MTM benchmarks are summarized in Table 4-5.

Table 4-5. Most Common L&D Effectiveness Measures

Measure	Unit of Measure	Benchmark Available From Explorance MTM
Level 1: Participant Reaction		
Quality of content	Score or percent selecting top two boxes	Yes
Quality of instructor	Score or percent selecting top two boxes	Yes
Learner engagement	Score or percent selecting top two boxes	Yes
Worthwhile	Score or percent selecting top two boxes	Yes
Recommend	Score, percent selecting top two boxes, or Net Promoter Score calculation	Yes
Overall assessment	Score or percent selecting top two boxes	
Total for Level 1	Average of measures	Yes
Level 1: Goal Owner Reaction	Score	
Level 2: Learning		
Gained new skills or knowledge	Score or percent selecting top two boxes	Yes
Pre- and/or post-test	Score or number of attempts	
First-time pass rate	Percent	
Level 3: Application		
Intent to apply (from survey at course completion)	Percent who intend to apply or percent content to be applied	Yes, for percent content to be applied
Actual application (after three months)	Percent who applied it or percent content applied	Yes, for percent content applied
Manager support	Score or percent selecting top two boxes	Yes

Table 4-5. Most Common L&D Effectiveness Measures (cont.)

Measure	Unit of Measure	Benchmark Available From Explorance MTM
Level 4: Impact		
Actual impact using a control group	Same as supported goal	
Estimated impact from trend line or regression analysis	Same as supported goal	
Initial estimate by participants (end of course)	Same as supported goal	Yes
Final estimate by participants (after three months)	Same as supported goal	Yes
Level 5: ROI		
ROI	Percent	
Gross program benefit	Dollars	
Net program benefit	Dollars	
Program cost	Dollars	
Benefit-cost ratio	Ratio	

Table 4-5 includes the five most common high-level effectiveness measures employing the Kirkpatrick and Phillips frameworks, as well some common subcategories for Level 1 and the key measures required to calculate ROI for Level 5. The profession today focuses its measurement efforts primarily on Levels 1 and 2, although most organizations are planning to do considerably more with Levels 3–5. The unit of measure for Level 4 will always be the same as the organization goal it is supporting. Typically, goals for sales, costs, productivity, and safety are expressed in percentages (such as a 5 percent increase in sales), while goals for quality, customer or patient satisfaction, employee engagement, and leadership are expressed in percentage points (such as a 2-point increase in customer satisfaction).

We turn our attention next to a short but in-depth discussion of outcome measures, which are the third type of TDRp measure. The preferred outcome measure is the Phillips Level 4 isolated impact, so Level 4 does double duty as both an effectiveness and outcome measure.

CHAPTER 5
Outcome Measures

Outcome measures show the impact of a program on an organizational goal or need. Ideally, the impact is the isolated impact of learning using the Phillips definition of Level 4, as discussed in chapter 4, to show the difference made by training in achieving the organizational goal or meeting the organizational need. In this chapter we explore these quantitative measures in greater detail and suggest a qualitative approach that represents a middle ground between the Phillips and Kirkpatrick methodologies. We also consider the application rate as a leading indicator when isolated impact is not achievable for outcome measures and the special case of competencies.

The Importance of Outcome Measures

Outcome measures are a critical type of measure. As we discussed in chapter 1, some programs are strategic in nature, meaning they are directly aligned to the goals of the organization. These strategic programs should have outcomes. Other programs are more tactical or operational in nature. They are still very important but will likely not have outcome measures.

The expectations are different for each type of program. A tactical or operational program is expected to be efficient and effective. A strategic program is expected to be efficient and effective as well, but it should also generate an outcome—a contribution toward achieving an organizational goal. The right audience could have taken the training, they could have liked it, learned from it, and applied it, but all this great training still might not have helped the organization achieve its goals or meet its needs. For strategic programs, L&D is not funded or staffed simply to be efficient and effective. The business invests in L&D because it believes that the right learning program can help it succeed if it is properly aligned, designed, delivered, and reinforced. This success is measured in outcomes.

CEOs are particularly focused on outcomes. Recall from chapter 1 that research by Jack Phillips clearly showed CEOs are most interested in seeing Level 4 impact, which is the preferred outcome measure. In fact, almost every CEO who responded wanted to see impact. They want to know what difference L&D is making, specifically how much it is contributing to their goals and meeting key needs.

It is for this reason that Level 4 isolated impact has been elevated to its own category of measure in TDRp. The L&D profession must focus more on this measure and share it with senior leaders. Yes, strategic programs should be run efficiently and effectively (Levels 1–3), but most importantly, these programs must deliver impact and value (Levels 4 and 5). They must contribute to outcomes.

Most Common Outcome Measures

The name of an outcome measure for learning is simply "Impact of learning on _____," where the business or HR measure to be improved by learning fills in the blank. For example, if content was designed to improve sales, then the outcome measure would be "impact of learning on sales." If it is designed to increase employee engagement, then the outcome measure is "impact of learning on employee engagement."

Since learning content can be designed to support any business or HR goal, the list of potential learning outcome measures is long. The most common, however, are included in Figure 5-1.

Outcome measures are specific to each organization and will exist whenever learning can support an organizational goal or need. The natural starting point in identifying outcome measures is the CEO's goals, followed by the head of HR's goals, followed by goals of other senior leaders. If learning can support these goals, then there should be an outcome measure for it.

The unit of measure for the outcome measure is the same as the unit of measure for the organizational outcome. A sales goal is usually expressed as a percent increase, so the unit of measure for the learning outcome measure (impact of learning on sales) would be percent as well (for example, a 4 percent increase in sales due to learning). Patient and customer satisfaction goals are usually expressed in terms of percentage

Figure 5-1. Most Common Learning Outcome Measures

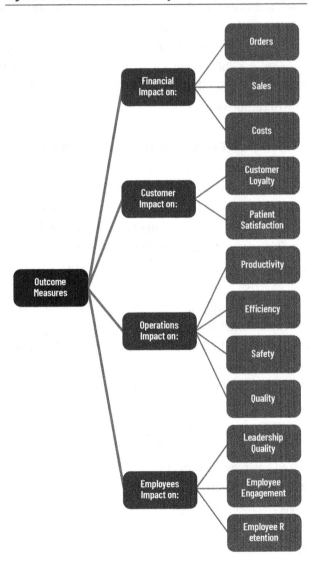

points of improvement, such as a 2-point increase in customer satisfaction. The outcome measure will be in the same unit of measure (points). Adopt whatever your organization is using as the unit of measure for the organizational goal or outcome for the learning outcome.

Types of Outcome Measures

There are two types of outcome measures: quantitative and qualitative.

Quantitative Outcome Measures

The first type of outcome measure is quantitative—the Phillips Level 4 isolated impact discussed in detail in the last chapter. This type is expressed in numbers and has both a percentage contribution from training and the resulting impact on the business measure. For example, if a sales training program contributed 20 percent (which might come from using a control group or from using the participant estimation method) toward achieving a 10 percent increase in sales, the resulting impact on sales would be 20% × 10% = 2% higher sales due just to training. By formula:

Impact of Learning on Sales:
= Percentage contribution from learning × Actual sales results
= 20% × 10%
= 2% higher sales due to learning.

Our focus will be on the learning outcome measure, but know that an outcome measure for the organization also exists. It is called the organization (or business) outcome measure. Examples include sales, productivity, quality, number of injuries, cost, patient satisfaction, customer satisfaction, employee engagement, and leadership.

Qualitative Outcome Measures

The second type of outcome measure is qualitative. Here, the concept of isolation is still used, but adjectives are used instead of percentages for the isolated contribution, and there is no resulting isolated impact. We recommend using a three-point scale to make this approach manageable. The most common scale is low/medium/high, but any adjectives will work. High is interpreted to mean learning was responsible for contributing at least 50 percent of the result, medium implies a contribution of 20–50 percent, and low implies a contribution of less than 20 percent. If learning were thought to have been the major driver and itself responsible for achieving most of the goal, it would have made a high contribution. If learning was not responsible for achieving most of the goal, but still played a very important role, it would have made a medium contribution. If learning played a relatively minor but still important role, then it would have made a low contribution. Alternatively, you could use adjectives such as important, very important, and significant.

Qualitative outcome measures are particularly useful in the planning stage when L&D is working with a goal owner to agree on the role and expected impact of learning.

Drawing on the Kirkpatrick model, L&D and the business goal owner would agree upfront on the expectations for learning (high, medium, or low). Results would be measured against those expectations using the same qualitative outcome measure discussed during planning. Notice that the absolute meaning of the adjective (such as high) is not as important as the agreed-upon meaning before the program is launched. In other words, qualitative outcome measures will work as long as L&D and the goal owner or stakeholder agree on expectations and what their chosen adjective means to them. Last, from a planning point of view, the choice of high/medium/low will directly determine the level of effort by both parties and the completion date. (High impact typically can only be achieved through deployment in the first quarter of the fiscal year.) We'll discuss this further in chapter 11 on creating plans.

Warning

Levels 0, 1, and 2 are not good leading indicators for Level 4 impact. The number of participants (Level 0), the reaction score (Level 1), and the learning results (Level 2) are not predictive of Level 4 impact. It is true that if no one takes the course there will be no impact. It is also true that if participants did not find the content relevant or did not learn, there will likely be no impact. Unfortunately, however, the reverse does not hold. There are numerous instances where the right audience completed the program, liked it, and learned it, yet there was no application or impact. Senior leaders know this, which is why they want to see application and especially impact. Simply sharing the number of participants and Level 1 scores will never take the place of Level 3 and 4 measures, and should never be used to demonstrate the impact or value of learning.

Application Rate as a Leading Indicator

It may not always be possible to use either a quantitative or qualitative outcome measure in planning. Perhaps the goal owner is not comfortable with either the concept of isolated impact or the methodology to calculate it (quantitative) or characterize it (qualitative). In other cases, the L&D staff is not comfortable having the isolated impact discussion with the goal owner. Rather than abandoning the concept of agreeing on expectations for learning, we recommend using the application rate as a leading indicator of outcome.

In learning, the Level 3 application rate is the best leading indicator for Level 4 isolated impact because we know that if there is no application, there is no impact (outcome). We also know that usually when there is application, there is at least some impact. So, while it is possible to have application without impact, application is in most cases an excellent next-best measure for reaching agreement with the goal owner on expectations for learning. (There is a detailed discussion in chapter 11 about reaching agreement with the goal owner.) Agreement on a Level 3 application rate will facilitate a discussion on roles and responsibilities, timing, and level of effort—just like a discussion to agree on Level 4 impact.

Flexibility in Creating Outcome Measures

Sometimes a situation will arise where a senior leader has goals or needs that are lower level or more transactional in nature. These goals may even involve measures that in the TDRp framework are efficiency or effectiveness measures. For example, a senior leader may have a goal to reduce the duration of a program by 25 percent, which would typically be an efficiency measure. Or, the leader may have a goal to improve the participant reaction by 10 points for a very important program, such as onboarding. Typically, this would be an effectiveness measure.

Our advice is to follow the direction of the leader and adapt TDRp to the needs of the situation. If a leader says reducing duration or improving reaction is one of their top business goals, then treat them as outcomes. Don't tell them that according to a book you just read their goals are not really outcomes. If it is an important goal or outcome to them, it is an important outcome for you.

This flexibility will be important when we start creating reports showing outcome measures. In this case, we would show "reduction in program duration" and "improvement in participant reaction" as "headline" measures, taking the place of an outcome measure of success, rather than as efficiency or effectiveness measures.

Recommendation

Outcome measures for learning should be calculated and shared with senior leaders (CEO, CFO, governing boards, goal owners, or business unit leaders) whenever learning can support an important organizational goal or need. This is the measure that CEOs most want to see. Sharing it with them shows that L&D is aligned to their goals and is contributing to the success of the organization. No other efficiency or effectiveness (Levels 1–3) measure has this same power. Typically, an L&D organization will only have only a handful of outcome measures, so the task isn't as daunting as it may appear. And the future of L&D in many organizations may well be determined by whether the senior leaders believe learning is contributing to the organization's bottom line success.

The Special Case of Competency Measures

Competency measures present a special case in our discussion of outcome measures. In most learning programs, improved competency in itself is not the intended goal or outcome. Rather, based on the needs analysis conducted during the planning stage, L&D identifies gaps in employee competencies, which must be closed if the goal (such as increased sales) is to be achieved. Here, competencies are best viewed as a means to an end rather than the end.

Consequently, the outcome measure focuses on the organizational goal or need and not on the competencies.

There are special cases, however, where the goal truly is to improve competency. In these cases, a higher competency level is the end goal. One such case is basic skills training. No one would argue that new employees typically need basic skills before they can start work. The basic skills are not directly aligned to any company goals, but many organizational goals, such as revenue and quality, would nevertheless be adversely affected over time if new employees did not acquire the necessary skills. This is especially true in retail industries like restaurants, department stores, and banking. It is also very true for knowledge-based businesses such as consultancies, where the product provided to clients is knowledge.

For these types of learning programs, then, what should be used for outcome measures? We suggest choosing measures that capture the satisfaction of the senior leaders with the training. This may be considered a "next best measure" for the unmeasurable Level 4 isolated impact. For example, L&D might ask the leaders of new employees who have just received basic skills training about their proficiency on the job. Do they have the skills necessary to complete their first tasks and be a successful member of the team? Of course, they will continue to learn on the job, but the question is how well prepared they are when they arrive at their first duty station. Leaders will have an opinion on this because they are observing the new employees every day.

Another example of this situation is basic training and even the first training after basic training in the military. In this case, the training command provides the training. What is an appropriate outcome measure? Since there is no good way to isolate the impact of basic training on winning wars, the training command could survey the supervisors who receive their trainees and ask about their preparation. The desired outcome, then, is a well-prepared force. This incorporates the voice of the customer, who in this case is the receiving unit.

Note

In the December 2018 standard for human capital reporting, the ISO identified the workforce competency rate as a metric that should be reported internally by large organizations. The purpose of the metric is to understand the competency level for the workforce in total as well as the competency levels for categories of employees. The formula is:

Workforce Competency Rate: Average of employee competency ratings.

Employee competency ratings may be based on an objective assessment (using a test instrument) or a subjective assessment by the employee or supervisor. A five-point scale is recommended, as shown in Figure 5-2.

The most appropriate competency level for each sales representative could be found by asking the employee or the supervisor to select the level that best describes the representative's level of competency. Once a level has been determined for each representative in the department, they are averaged to determine the workforce competency rate for that category of sales representatives. This competency rate could then be combined with rates from other groups using weighted averages by group size to determine the competency rate of the entire organization.

Figure 5-2. Example of a Five-Point Competency Scale for Sales Representatives

	Level 5 • Recognized as a company expert and extremely knowledgeable about all aspects of sales • Teaches and mentors others • Represents the company on national and international advisory bodies
	Level 4 • Excellent knowledge of the industry, selling skills, and product features • Significant selling experience (more than 10 years) with all levels of customers, including the largest and most complex accounts
Increasing Levels of Confidence and Competence	**Level 3** • Good knowledge of the industry, selling skills, and product features • Four to 10 years' selling experience • Retained the largest accounts
	Level 2 • Good knowledge of the industry, selling skills, and product features • One to three years' selling experience • Able to sell to small customers and assist with larger customers
	Level 1 • Basic knowledge of the industry, selling skills, and product features • Little or no experience selling • Not ready to interact with customers

Conclusion

This chapter concludes our discussion of the three types of measures. Throughout this chapter and chapters 3 and 4, we have described more than 100 efficiency measures, more than 10 effectiveness measures, and a suite of outcome measures. Clearly, the L&D profession does not lack measures, and there are more in the CTR measures library if those in this chapter do not meet your needs. These chapters have provided standard names, definitions, and formulas, which are based on the work of the measurement pioneers in our field (Kirkpatrick and Phillips) for the effectiveness measures and ATD, which provides benchmarks for many of the efficiency measures. It is our hope that this work will contribute to the growing standardization of measures, which is important for a mature profession.

Next, we use these measures and the TDRp framework to create a measurement strategy.

CHAPTER 6
Creating a Measurement Strategy

I n this chapter we explore how to create a measurement strategy, starting with its elements and the specific steps to create it. Typically, a user will create a measurement *and reporting* strategy, and we begin by exploring the reasons to have one. After that, though, this chapter will only focus on the measurement strategy; chapter 10 will add the reporting strategy. We also discuss the creation of a measures library as a single, safe source for the selected measures. By the end of this chapter, you should be well positioned to create the framework for a measurement strategy. Then chapter 7 drills down on how to select the appropriate measures for different types of programs. A sample measurement and reporting strategy is provided in appendix C.

Why a Measurement and Reporting Strategy Is Important

Up to this point, we have presented the reasons for measuring and provided a comprehensive list of measures. The next question is, what do you do with it all? You aren't going to use every measure we provided nor are you going to measure every program or department initiative the same way. Also, what may be appropriate for a mature organization with hundreds of programs and thousands of learners may not be appropriate for a small organization just getting started with measurement.

A measurement and reporting strategy signals to the business and L&D stakeholders that you are purposeful in your measurement efforts and that their engagement matters. Moreover, a measurement and reporting strategy provides several other benefits, as shown in Figure 6-1.

Figure 6-1. Benefits of a Measurement and Reporting Strategy

First, the strategy ensures you and the business are aligned on what success looks like for any given program or suite of programs. Second, it provides clarity and helps you focus your energies on measuring those factors that matter to both L&D and business sponsors. Third, the strategy creates ownership and accountability for success. If the measurement plan requires observational feedback or reinforcement from the managers of participants, then the program goal owner must ensure that the managers understand the expectations and are committed to meeting them. Fourth, the strategy identifies the budget and resources required for execution. The funding and resources may come from L&D, HR, or the business, depending on the complexity of the plan. Being clear on what's required is essential to the strategy's success. Finally, the measurement and reporting strategy provides guidance and ensures continuity over time. A good strategy provides a clear road map for the department to follow and is invaluable when there is staff turnover. And with a measurement and reporting strategy document, a new person can come into a measurement and analytics position and easily understand the plan for the year, the key users, what they want, and the agreed-upon measures.

In short, the measurement and reporting strategy lays out the why, what, when, how, and who to ensure that the measurement and reporting commitments made can be realized.

Steps to Create a Measurement Strategy

Now that we have explored what a measurement strategy entails and what should be included in a written document, let's look at the steps to create one from the point of view of the measurement head or analyst who would normally be tasked with creating it. There are eight basic steps to create a good measurement strategy (Table 6-1).

Table 6-1. Steps to Create a Measurement Strategy

Step	Objective
1. Talk with the CLO	• Understand department goals, initiatives, and priorities
2. Talk with directors, program managers, and other users	• Develop deeper understanding of programs and initiatives • Identify measurement requirements and expectations
3. Reflect on what you heard and create a draft strategy	• Synthesize requirements • Create a measurement strategy reflecting the needs of the CLO, directors, and program managers
4. Present to directors and program managers for feedback	• Ensure measurement strategy accurately captures director and program manager requirements • Get director and program manager to sign off on the measurement strategy
5. Incorporate their feedback	• Update measurement strategy incorporating director and program manager feedback
6. Present to CLO for feedback	• Ensure measurement strategy reflects CLO's requirements
7. Incorporate CLO feedback	• Update measurement strategy incorporating CLO feedback
8. Present final document for approval	• Finalize measurement strategy • Ensure L&D leadership commitment to the strategy

The first step is to meet with the CLO to discover the department goals and initiatives for the coming year. Which director or program manager will be responsible for each goal and initiative? What are the CLO's expectations for a measurement strategy? Does the CLO already have some measures in mind? How frequently would the CLO like to see the measures reported? If there is a governing board for learning, the CLO should be able to convey any measurement needs from the board.

The second step is to talk with all the CLO's direct reports and any directors or program managers who are not direct reports. These are the managers responsible for programs and initiatives, and they, along with the CLO, will be the primary users of the measures. This is an opportunity to learn more about the programs and initiatives. Ask about their expectations for the measurement strategy. What measures will they need? How will they use them? How often do they need to be reported? Also talk with users outside L&D to discover their needs and how they will use the measures.

The third step is to reflect on what you heard. What measures did they request? Are those the best measures for the intended use? What additional measures would you suggest? We are assuming here that the program managers are working closely with organizational goal owners and stakeholders, like the vice president of sales and the head of HR, and they can represent the needs of these senior leaders. If that is not the case, the measurement professional may need to engage the CLO for direction on measures that would be of interest to goal owners. In a small organization, the measurement specialist may have direct contact with goal owners if there aren't any program managers. Based on what was learned in these conversations, the measurement professional should be ready to draft a strategy. It should contain the seven elements discussed in the next section.

The document or PowerPoint outlining the strategy should begin with an introduction (executive summary covering all major points if it is a long document or presentation) and should end with a conclusion. The introduction, reasons for measuring, and conclusion need to be particularly strong. If the CLO runs L&D like a business, these three sections need to be in the language of business, meaning that the business case for investing in measurement must be clear. That means no appeals to approve the measurement strategy because "It is the right thing to do" or "We need the data" or "The best organizations do it." The case must be made that it is worth doing, which gets back to the reasons for measuring. The strongest arguments for measuring will always be that it is necessary to deliver planned program and initiative benefits, measure and analyze programs and initiatives to identify opportunities for improvement and optimize results, and ensure critical measures are in an acceptable range. Informing will not be a compelling reason to invest any more than the absolute minimum required to answer the questions.

The fourth step is to share the draft with the program managers and directors for their feedback and then incorporate it. It is better to do this before sharing with the CLO in case you misunderstood some of their programs or initiatives, or in case they disagree with your proposed measures for them.

The fifth step is to resolve any misunderstandings and disagreements and share a revised draft with them that they hopefully will support in front of the CLO. You may go through a few iterations before you have their support, and the CLO may need to resolve several issues.

The sixth step is to share the revised draft with the CLO. Let them know that you have already shared it with the directors and program managers and incorporated their feedback. Also tell the CLO if there are any unresolved issues.

The seventh step is to incorporate the feedback from the CLO.

The eighth step is to present the revised document to the CLO for final approval. This might also take place during the CLO's staff meeting so all direct reports are present. If any final changes are required coming out of this meeting, make them and present again for final approval. We recommend you put the date of final approval on the document and then share a copy of the document with everyone who was involved and others for whom the document would be helpful, like measurement staff.

Elements of a Measurement and Reporting Strategy

Now that you know why you should create a measurement and reporting strategy, and how to do it, let's discuss what to include in your strategy. At a minimum, a solid strategy has seven elements:

1. a clear articulation of the reasons for measuring
2. the users, why they want the measures, when they need the data, and how they want to see it reported
3. the measures overall with specific measures identified for important programs or department initiatives.
4. how you plan to collect the data, including the use of sampling and expected response rates
5. the types of reports you will use to communicate to stakeholders
6. how you plan to share the data
7. the resources you require to execute and sustain measurement and reporting over time.

This chapter focuses on the first four elements, which make up the measurement strategy. Chapter 10 covers types of reports and how you plan to share the data, which form the reporting strategy will take, and the final element, which addresses the resources required for the combined measurement and reporting strategy.

We assume that the final measurement and reporting strategy is a written document but it may also be a PowerPoint presentation. The central elements are the same for either, but a written document typically allows for more detail and a better record of the strategy. We have included a sample written measurement and reporting strategy in appendix C.

Discussion of the Four Reasons for Measuring

The first section in your written measurement and reporting strategy should be the reasons to measure. As we introduced in chapter 1, there are four broad reasons to measure: inform, monitor, evaluate and analyze, and manage each with its own set of activities as shown in Figure 6-2.

Figure 6-2. Reasons for Measuring

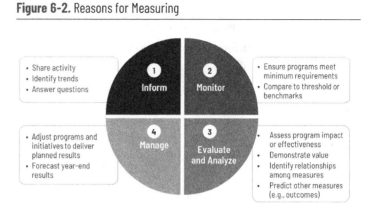

These four reasons are important because they will guide your selection of the appropriate report as well as the frequency of measurement. This connection between reason to measure and report selection is shown in Table 6-2.

Table 6-2. Measurement Requirements for Each Level of Maturity

Measurement Purpose	Primary Use	Level of Analysis	Measurement Frequency	Key Elements	Shared In
Manage	• Identify if the program is delivering planned results and where adjustments are needed to meet goals	High	Monthly	• Plan • YTD results • Forecast for measures being managed	• Management reports
Evaluate and analyze	• Analyze program and non-program data • Explore relationships among measures • Predict outcomes	Medium to high	Based on business need	• Analytical methods (e.g., regression analysis, predictive modeling)	• Custom analysis reports
	• Evaluate the efficiency, effectiveness, or impact of a learning program		End of program or pilot	• Six levels of evaluation (Level 0 to Level 5)	• Program evaluation reports
Monitor	• Determine if measure meets threshold or is within acceptable range	Low	Monthly or quarterly	• Threshold or breakpoints for measures	• Dashboards • Scorecards
Inform	• Answer questions, identify key trends, and share activity	Low	As needed	• Specific measures or trends	• Dashboards • Scorecards

(Left side vertical label: Measurement Maturity)

Copyright applied for by Center for Talent Reporting (2020). Used with permission.

It is important to walk the reader through the reasons to measure for your organizations, explaining each reason, ideally with some examples from your own organization. (Note: all four may not apply.) The discussion need not be long but also should not be skipped because it sets the foundation for all that is to come. It also provides the high-level business case for measurement, and that business case will be stronger if the primary reasons to measure are to manage and to evaluate and analyze. We return to this hierarchy in chapter 8 on reporting and displaying data.

A Note on the Importance of Measurement

Many leaders view measurement as optional, something that learning professionals want to do for their own reasons. It is critically important for L&D leaders to make the case that measurement is not optional. In fact, programs will not deliver the planned impact without measurement, meaning that organizational goals may not be achieved. Without measurement, you have no indication of the efficiency, effectiveness, or impact of your programs. Without measurement, you have no data to inform improvement efforts. Without measurement no one will ever know if a program was worth doing or whether a similar program should be repeated in the future. Without measurement, there is no way to ensure critical measures remain above, below, or within bounds, and consequently, no warning when management actions are required to address the issue. Last, without measurement, there is no data and no accountability. No other part of business would be run without data and neither should L&D. Make the case for measurement as a business necessity. It is not optional.

Discussion of Users

The second element your measurement and reporting strategy and the written document is a discussion of the users, their reasons for measuring, the desired frequency of the measures, and what they want to see in their reports. In a smaller organization, this may be combined with the first section, but in larger organizations it is best to have a separate section with details by major user or at least category of user. View the first section as a high-level overview of the reasons to measure and the second section as the detail that can be operationalized in the strategy to ensure that all stakeholder needs are met.

This section, then, is an opportunity to list the key users, what they need to see, how often they would like to see it, and in what form they want to see it. This discussion with key users is an excellent opportunity for L&D staff to better understand their stakeholders and what they want from measurement and learning. Here are three important considerations for measurement and reporting users outside the L&D department:

1. **Have a discussion with users at least annually and more often when there is a new stakeholder or a new program.** This discussion is critical to understand what success looks like to the goal owner, what their needs are,

and what they would like to see. Without this discipline, you may be creating reports to answer questions a leader, now gone, raised years ago. The report stays in production and lands on the desk of the successor who didn't ask for it and often has no idea what to do with it. Then L&D wonders why this person doesn't appreciate the wonderful report. Leaders change. Needs change. Questions change. It is extremely important to make the effort to refresh your strategy with your stakeholders on a regular basis.

2. **Start by asking them to share their goals and plans for the coming year.** Explore any business challenges they are facing in their department. This information provides invaluable context and will help inform what measures are most appropriate to the leader. Don't ask what they want to measure; often they have no idea and may ask you what you think they should measure, especially if it is a new leader or if their responsibilities or programs have changed. After you understand their business priorities, you can turn to the discussion of training and what will be required to meet their expectations. At this point, you will likely want to share information about the program and the key business and learning measures (for example, number of participants, completion date, application rate, and impact). Typically, measures will flow naturally from this more focused discussion. When you begin talking about their priorities and challenges, the measures become more meaningful to the stakeholder. It will also become apparent what data they require to monitor or manage the program to successful completion.

3. **Don't assume the discussion is over if they suggest a measure, especially if they suggest one right away.** There is a danger that they will suggest a measure they know or have been using for years, but there may be a better one for their purpose. Of course, since they are not L&D measurement experts, they don't know about it. So, be sure to ask them why they want that measure and how they will use it. Their answer may confirm it is the right measure or it may lead you to suggest better measures.

This discussion should take the same form with leaders inside L&D, but it should also be easier. Ask the CLO and the directors or program managers about their goals and plans for the year. Get into specifics, which is where measures will surface. Just as with leaders outside L&D, this discussion should uncover key efficiency measures like participants, completion dates, and cost, as well as key effectiveness measures like Levels 1–5. You should summarize the results of these discussions in a simple user needs analysis (Table 6-3).

The three primary users of measures within L&D are the CLO, program managers, and directors. CLOs have the broadest need for measures because they have responsibility for everything that goes on in the department. Program managers, who oversee programs in support of identified goals and needs, need measures to manage but also to evaluate, analyze, optimize, and improve. Directors, for our purposes, will be the senior L&D leaders with responsibility for department processes, systems, and improvement initiatives. For example, a CLO might have a director who is responsible for technology (like the LMS), another responsible for planning and budgeting, and another responsible for measurement. The CLO is also likely to give program managers and directors additional responsibilities to lead improvement initiatives outside their own area, such as leading an effort to improve Level 3 application across all programs.

The goal owners for major programs and their staff will also be interested in measures as they jointly manage the program for their employees. Higher-level leaders like the head of HR, CFO, and CEO will be interested in what the department is accomplishing at both an aggregate level and for the key, aligned programs.

Table 6-3. User Needs Analysis

User	Needs
CLO	• Know what the department is accomplishing • Monitor certain measures to ensure their acceptability • Determine if programs and initiatives are efficient, effective, and producing desired outcomes • Identify opportunities for improvement and optimization • Manage programs and initiatives to successful conclusions
Program managers	• Manage programs to deliver planned results • Evaluate the efficiency and effectiveness of programs • Ensure planned outcomes are delivered • Identify opportunities for improvement and optimization
Directors	• Manage department initiatives to deliver planned results • Evaluate the efficiency and effectiveness of department initiatives • Identify opportunities for improvement and optimization
Goal owners and their staff	• Manage programs to deliver planned results • Ensure planned outcomes are delivered • Identify opportunities for improvement and optimization
Head of HR, CFO, CEO, and the governing board	• Know what the department is accomplishing • Determine whether programs and initiatives are efficient, effective, and producing desired results

The Recommended Measures

The next element of the strategy and document lists the recommended measures, including the programs or department initiatives employing the measures. A summary of measures by type is recommended to start, followed by a more detailed listing showing measures by program or department (Table 6-4). Here, "department" refers to an improvement initiative at the department level in some process or system, or an initiative to improve an efficiency or effectiveness measure across all programs.

Table 6-4. Summary of Measures to Use

Type of Measure	Unit of Measure	Use at What Level?	
		Program	Department
Efficiency Measures			
Unique participants	Number	Y	Y
Total participants	Number	Y	Y
Completion rate	Percent	Y	Y
Percentage on time development	Percent	Y	Y
Percentage on time delivery	Percent	Y	Y
Reach	Percent	Y	Y
Percentage of learning by modality	Percent	N	Y
Direct expenditure	Dollars	Y	Y
Number of documents available	Number	N	Y
Number of documents used	Number	N	Y
Percentage of documents used	Percent	N	Y
Number of unique documents used	Number	N	Y
Effectiveness Measures			
Participant Level 1 reaction	5-point scale	Y	Y
Goal owner reaction	5-point scale	Y	Y
Level 2 learning	Score	Y	Y
Level 3 intent to apply	Percent	Y	Y
Level 3 actual application	Percent	Y	Y
Outcome Measures			
Level 4 initial estimate of impact	Same as supported goal	Y	N
Level 4 final estimate of impact	Same as supported goal	Y	N

The summary list should include all the measures that will be used either at the program level or at the department level where data are aggregated across multiple programs for department-wide initiatives like increasing the percentage of e-learning. Following TDRp, there should be a balance of measures. In other words, in addition to the nearly always present efficiency measures, there should also be effectiveness measures. If the learning organization has an opportunity to support key organizational goals from the CEO or business unit leaders, there should also be outcome measures.

While Table 6-4 provides a good summary, it does not provide the detail needed for an analyst to know exactly how individual programs are to be measured or how the CLO wants initiatives measured. In this case, you should create a more detailed list, arranged by program or measure, which will be the heart of the measurement strategy. The list could be arranged by program or by measure. The two approaches are illustrated in Table 6-5.

Table 6-5. Two Approaches to Listing Recommended Measures

By Program or Department

Program or Initiative	Department-Wide
Program A	Unique participants
Unique participants	Total participants
Total cost	Reach
Level 1 participant and goal owner	Percentage on-time of completions
Level 2	Direct expenditure
Level 3 intent and actual	Aggregate Level 1 goal owner
Program B	Aggregate Level 2
Unique participants	Aggregate Level 3 intent
Total participants	Aggregate Level 3 actual
Completion rate	Percentage of courses by modality .
Percentage of on-time completion	Number of documents available
Total cost	Number of documents used
Level 1 participant and goal owner	Percentage of documents used
Level 2	Percentage of unique documents used
Level 3 intent and actual	
Program C	
Unique participants	
Percentage of on-time completion	
Total cost	
Level 1 participant and goal owner	
Level 2	
Level 3 intent and actual	
Level 4 initial and final estimates	

Table 6-5. Two Approaches to Listing Recommended Measures (cont.)

By Measure

Efficiency Measure	Program A	Program B	Program C	Department-Wide
Unique participants	X	X	X	X
Total participants		X		X
Total cost	X	X	X	
Completion rate		X		
Percentage of on-time completions		X	X	X
Reach				X
Direct expenditure				X
Percentage of courses by modality				X
Number of documents available				X
Number of documents used				X
Percentage of documents used				X
Percentage of unique documents used				X
Effectiveness Measure	**Program A**	**Program B**	**Program C**	**Department-Wide**
Level 1 participant reaction	X	X	X	
Level 1 goal owner reaction	X	X	X	X
Level 2	X	X	X	X
Level 3 intent and actual	X	X	X	X
Level 4 initial and final estimates			X	

An alternative to listing the measures is to include them in a matrix, such as the measurement strategy matrix in Table 6-6 (which uses different data). Programs and department initiatives are listed as rows and the measures are listed as columns with groupings for the three TDRp types of measures. This matrix also includes additional measures at the bottom for all learning.

The matrix would certainly be more suitable for a PowerPoint presentation. In either case, notes would also need to be added about frequency. For example, "All measures will be reported monthly" or "N/A indicates that data are not available, or the sample size is too small to be meaningful."

Either approach satisfies our requirement that a measurement analyst reviewing the strategy will be able to determine which measures are to be employed for which programs with what frequency.

In chapter 7, we provide recommendations on the minimum measures to include for specific types of programs.

Table 6-6. Measurement Strategy Matrix

Programs or Measures	Effectiveness Measures				Efficiency Measures						Outcome Measures	
	Level 1	Level 2	Level 3	Level 5	Unique and Total Participants (#)	Courses (#)	Hours (#)	On-Time Development	On-Time Delivery	Cost	Phillips Impact	Kirkpatrick Results
Strategic Programs												
Consultative selling skills	X	X	X	X	X	X	X	X	X	X	X	
Product features training	X	X	X	X	X	X	X	X	X	X	X	
Safety training	X	X	X	X	X	X	X	X	X	X	X	
Design for manufacturing	X	X			X	X	X	X	X	X		X
Six-sigma	X	X	X	X	X	X	X	X	X	X		X
Intro to supervision	X		X	X	X	X	X	X	X	X	X	
Intro to management	X		X	X	X	X	X	X	X	X	X	
Programs to Meet Identified Needs	X	X¹	X		X	X	X	X	X	X	X¹	X¹
Unaligned, Discretionary Programs	X²				X	X	X	X	X	X		

Additional Enterprise-Wide Measures
- Utilization rates for ILT and e-learning
- Percentage of engaged employees reached by L&D
- Percentage of engaged employees with individual development plans

Note: ¹ *Where appropriate.*
² *Asked as part of the annual employee engagement survey.*

Data Collection

At this point in our strategy development, we know why we are measuring, who the users are, and what the measures will be. To operationalize the strategy though, you still need to know exactly how the data will be collected. This is the fourth element in both the development of our strategy and in creating the written document. We need to explore how the data are collected, including a discussion of sampling and response rates.

Most efficiency measures come from department or company systems, including the LMS, knowledge sharing platform, portal analytics, and performance support platform. Other efficiency measures like cost, percentage on-time completion, and cycle time will come from other systems or an Excel spreadsheet, where the measures are tracked manually.

Effectiveness measures for Levels 1, 3, and 4 will generally come from surveys and be captured in a database by the organization or its vendor. In a small organization the results of the surveys may be captured in Excel spreadsheets. Level 2 test results may be captured in an LMS or other system if the tests were automated. The Level 5 effectiveness measure, ROI, is often calculated in a spreadsheet with input from the outcome measure, Level 4 impact. Table 6-7 is an example of a data sources table.

Sampling is often used to reduce survey fatigue for Levels 1, 3, and 4. If sampling was used, a short discussion

Table 6-7. Sample Data Sources

Type and Name of Measure	Source
Efficiency Measures	
Formal Learning	
Unique participants	LMS
Total participants	LMS
Completion rate	LMS
Percentage on-time completion	
Development	Spreadsheet
Delivery	Spreadsheet
Cost	
Direct expenditure	Spreadsheet
Total	Spreadsheet
Reach	LMS or spreadsheet
Percentage of learning by modality	LMS
Informal Learning	
Number of documents available	Portal analytics
Number of documents used	Portal analytics
Percentage of documents used	Portal analytics
Number of document users	Portal analytics
Effectiveness Measures	
Formal Learning	
Participant reaction (Level 1)	Vendor or evaluation system
Goal owner satisfaction (Level 1)	Internal survey or spreadsheet
Learning (Level 2)	
Score	LMS or testing system
Application rate (Level 3)	
Intent to apply	Vendor or evaluation system
Actual application	Vendor or evaluation system
ROI	Spreadsheet
Informal Learning	
Participant reaction (Level 1)	Vendor or evaluation system
Outcome Measures	
Impact (Level 4)	
Initial estimate	Vendor or evaluation system
Final estimate	Vendor or evaluation system

should be included describing where and how it was employed. Some organizations send the post-event and follow-up surveys to just a sample or subset of all unique participants for a course or program. The sample should be selected randomly and be of sufficient size to yield statistically significant results, and the same sample should be used for both the post-event and follow-up surveys. Other organizations deploy the surveys selectively (not randomly) based on the course, instructor, and recent feedback. For example, if the same instructor has been teaching the same course with the same content to the same type of audience for the last five years, and if past surveys have not indicated any issues, the organization may simply skip this course in its surveying. Or, if there are limited survey resources, the organization may choose to rotate courses or survey every second or third offering.

A related issue is the response rate for electronic surveys. Many organizations either use a tool like SurveyMonkey or partner with a vendor to conduct learning surveys. Although some organizations report response rates greater than 90 percent, most experience response rates of 20–30 percent, which is not a problem if the number of respondents is large enough to be statistically significant. The minimum number of respondents from a course with more than 30 participants is 30 (this allows us to assume the population is normally distributed and allows us to use the sample average as a good estimate of the true but unknown population average). A larger sample size will produce a more accurate estimate of the true average with greater confidence. In other words, the error margin around the average for the measure will get smaller as the sample size increases. Table 6-8 shows the relationship between sample size and error margin at a 95 percent confidence level for samples with a mean (average) of 4.0 and a standard deviation of 0.77.

Table 6-8. Sample Size and Error Margins

Sample Size	Error Margin	95% Confidence Interval Around Average
30	0.28	3.72–4.28
50	0.31	3.79–4.21
100	0.15	3.85–4.15
200	0.11	3.89–4.11
300	0.09	3.91–4.09
500	0.07	3.93–4.07
1,000	0.05	3.95–4.05

With a sample size of 30, we can be 95 percent certain that the true average (from the population) lies between 3.72 and 4.28, which is the same as saying 4.0 plus or minus 0.28. If we could get 100 responses, the error margin would be cut in half, and the confidence interval shrinks to between 3.85 and 4.15. Notice that the rate of improvement in shrinking the error margin is much larger with smaller sample sizes (nearly a 50 percent reduction when the sample size increases by 70; from 30 to 100) than with larger sample sizes (only a 45 percent reduction in error margin when the sample increases by 700; from 300 to 1,000).

You might ask what happens when the course has fewer than 30 participants. If we got a 100 percent response rate there would be no worry at all because we would have data on the entire population. The reported average for Level 1 reaction or Level 3 application would be the true average. However, in the real world that seldom happens. Instead, we get a response rate less than 100 percent, which means that we must work with a sample, and the sample size falls below the magic number of 30. In this case, we would like a response rate as high as we can reasonably get. If the response rate is 27 out of 30, that is a 90 percent response rate, and most leaders would make decisions based on the reported average for the measure. The same is true if the response rate is 70 percent on 30 and probably even 50 percent.

As the number of participants in the course shrinks, a higher response rate would be required for a decision maker to have confidence in the reported measure. For example, if there are only 15 participants, it would be nice to have at least 10 responses. There are no hard and fast rules here because we are already below the minimum number of 30 needed to assume we are dealing with a normally distributed population. However, since our goal is not to publish an academic article on the program but simply to evaluate and manage it, in the real world we typically are willing to go with responses under 30 if the response rate is above 50–70 percent. Table 6-9 shows how we would treat data when working with small populations and varying response rates, but this a subjective matter for each leader.

Since both sampling and response rates are issues that often arise in measurement work, it is recommended that the measurement strategy include a description of how each is used, including average response rates, number or percentage of courses where sampling is used, and minimum response rate thresholds for courses with fewer than 30 participants.

Table 6-9. Subjective Confidence Levels for Measures From Small Populations

Population	Responses	Response Rate	Subjective Confidence Level	Act on Data?
30	30	100%	Very high	Yes
30	24	80%	High	Yes
30	15	50%	Medium	Maybe
30	9	30%	Low	No
20	16	80%	High	Yes
20	10	50%	Medium	Maybe
20	6	30%	Low	No
10	8	80%	High	Yes
10	5	50%	Low	No
10	3	30%	Very low	No

Your Measures Library

Although not part of creating the written document, we recommend that your strategy includes the creation of a measures library, which is a single, safe source for all learning measures. These libraries are usually Excel spreadsheets with rows for the measures and columns for the key information about the measures. This is considered a best practice in the field.

There are several benefits to creating and maintaining a measures library. First, it provides a safe, durable repository for the selected measures. Staff have worked hard to select the right measures, but the staff who did the original work are likely to move on at some point. In the absence of a library, you can easily lose institutional knowledge and future staff may have to recreate the work.

Second, there is often disagreement about which measures to select, how to define them, how to measure them, and how to use them. Once you have resolved these issues and captured the results in the library, there is less chance you will waste time in the future revisiting them. Instead, the CLO and measurement staff can simply remind everyone that they had discussed the issue previously and settled with the results captured in the measures library.

Columns for the library should include all the categories of interest for an organization's measurement strategy. Column headings for a starter measures library are shown in Table 6-10 and categorized by commonly or less commonly used. Mature organizations might add other columns such as criticality of the measure, frequency of collection or generation, ease of collection, quality of the measure, start date for data series, or subcategory (helpful when there are many measures).

Table 6-10. Column Headings for a Measures Library

Column Heading	Notes
Common Headings	
Measure	Use TDRp or ISO names, if possible, to promote standardization
Type of measure	Efficiency, effectiveness, or outcome
Category	Further breakdown of the "type" (e.g., cost, utilization, job application)
Formal or informal	Does this measure apply to formal learning, informal learning, or both?
Primary users	Program managers, directors, CLO
Description	Use the TDRp or ISO description, if possible, to promote standardization
Formula	Use the TDRp or ISO formula, if possible, to promote standardization
Source system	System or database that generates the data
Less Common Headings	
Data type	Survey item, ratio, count, calculated field
Data granularity	Enterprise only, business unit, or department level
Data collection priority	Importance of this measure to the organization (H/M/L)
Data collection method	Automated or manual
Ease of collection	Amount of effort required to gather the data for this measure (H/M/L)
Data quality	Indicates the reliability of the data available (H/M/L)

A measures library is simplest to create early in your measurement journey when there are just a few measures. Then it is easy to add a few each year. For organizations with many measures already, we suggest you start with the most important measures and build from there. An example of a simple measures library is shown in Table 6-11.

Table 6-11. Simple Measure Library

Measure	Measure Type	Category	Formal or Informal	Primary Users (Roles)	Description	Formula	Data Source
Percent of knowledge and skills expected to be used	Effectiveness	Application on the job	Formal	CLO, program managers	Survey question: What percent of the knowledge and skills learned in this training will you use on the job?	Average percentage across all respondents	Evaluation system
Net Promoter Score	Effectiveness	Internal customer satisfaction	Both	CLO, program managers	Survey question: How likely are you to recommend this training (workshop) to a friend or colleague? (0 = not at all likely; 10 = extremely likely)	NPS formula: Promoters – Detractors	Evaluation system
Vendors meeting or exceeding SLAs	Effectiveness	Other	N/A	L&D operations manager	Percent of vendors who meet or exceed their contractual service level agreements	Number of vendors meeting SLAs ÷ Number of total vendors	Vendor management system
Courseware quality	Effectiveness	Quality or reaction	Formal	Program managers	Post-event survey scores for Kirkpatrick Level 1 courseware question category (See Acme Evals-PES)	Average scores or percentage of learners selecting top two box answers for courseware category on post-event survey	Evaluation system
Instructor quality	Effectiveness	Quality or reaction	Formal	Instructor manager	Post-event survey scores for Kirkpatrick Level 1 instructor question category (See Acme Evals-PES)	Average scores or percentage of learners selecting top two box answers for instructor category on post-event survey	Evaluation system
Hours/employees trained per year	Efficiency	Activity	Both	L&D operations manager	Uses unique participants	Start with the U.S. population and then move to global	LMS
Number of courses used	Efficiency	Activity	Formal	Program managers	Number of courses that had at least one registration		LMS
Number of hours of training received	Efficiency	Activity	Formal	CLO, operations manager	Total participant hours of training (attended)	Sum of hours of training for all participants in the period (all training types)	LMS
Number of courses delivered	Efficiency	Activity	Formal	CLO, program managers	Total number of courses delivered	Sum of unique course titles delivered in the period	LMS

Table 6-11. Simple Measure Library (cont.)

Measure	Measure Type	Category	Formal or Informal	Primary Users (Roles)	Description	Formula	Data Source
E-learning abandonment rate	Efficiency	Activity	Formal	Program managers	This matters for courses intended for training		LMS
Facility utilization rate	Efficiency	Activity	Formal	Operations manager	Percent of facility used for training (based on number of classrooms)	Number of classrooms used vs. Number of classrooms available	LMS
Total participants	Efficiency	Activity	Formal	CLO, operations manager	Number of students attending all courses in a period (total)	Sum of participant counts for all courses in the period (= course throughput)	LMS
Unique participants	Efficiency	Activity	Formal	CLO, operations manager	Number of students attending all courses in a period (unique)	Count of unique participants trained in the period	LMS
Solution time to market (cycle time)	Efficiency	Time	Formal	CLO, program managers	Time to market for learning programs	Time from request to initial deployment of learning program	TBD
Impact on customer satisfaction	Outcome	Customer	Both	CLO, program managers	Results of transactional survey at time of interaction	NPS score	CRM
Impact on new customer growth	Outcome	Customer	Both	CLO, program managers	Number of new customers gained in prior period	Number of new customers ÷ Number of existing customers	CRM
Impact on employee turnover	Outcome	Learning and growth	Both	CLO, program managers	Number of employees leaving the organization	Number of employees leaving ÷ Number of employees	HRIS
Impact on employee engagement index	Outcome	Learning and growth	Both	CLO, program managers	Results of the engagement survey	Computation of engagement index (based on a suite of specific questions)	Survey system
Impact on first call resolution rate	Outcome	Operations	Both	CLO, program managers	Percent of calls resolved on the first call	Number of calls resolved on the first call ÷ Number of total calls	Call center management system
Impact on average time to settle a claim	Outcome	Operations	Both	CLO, program managers	Amount of time to settle the claim from the point received	Number of days between receipt of claim and payment to insured	Claims management system

You may also find the CTR measures library to be useful. This library contains more than 700 measures across all aspects of HR with about 170 for learning (not including leadership development, which is separate category in TDRp). The column headings for the CTR library are shown in Table 6-12.

Table 6-12. Column Headings in the CTR Measures Library

Column Heading	Notes
Talent process	L&D, leadership development, talent acquisition, performance management, capability management, total rewards
TDRp category	Efficiency, effectiveness, or outcome
TDRp subcategory	A further breakdown such as cost, courses, or Level 1
Metric tier	1, 2, or 3 indicating importance
Description	A short description of the measure
Measure	Use TDRp names, if possible, to promote standardization
Formula	Use the TDRp formula, if possible, to promote standardization
Defined by	Source for formula (e.g., author, book, organization)
Demographic splits	Common ways to "slice and dice" the measure
Identify to	References to other sources that have defined the measure
Similar to	References to other sources that have defined the measure similarly, but not identically

Conclusion

With the conclusion of this chapter, you should now have a good understanding of the elements in a measurement strategy and how to create the written document to share your measurement strategy. You should be ready to select your measures and to create a measures library. The next chapter will provide guidance to select measures by program and initiative.

CHAPTER 7
Selecting Measures

We are now ready for the hardest part of creating a measurement strategy—selecting the measures. As we noted in the introduction, we have identified more than 180 measures for L&D and more than 700 for all of HR. So, the profession does not lack measures! Instead, the challenge is to select the right measures for the coming year or two, understanding that the measurement strategy will evolve in future years, requiring different measures. Moreover, the goal is to select the smallest number of measures required to meet your needs. There is no extra credit for selecting hundreds of measures, most of which would go unused but require valuable time to generate.

The purpose of measuring provides some guidance in the selection of measures, but as noted earlier, the same measure can serve different purposes. Table 7-1 gives some general selection guidance based on the purpose of measuring.

Table 7-1. Guidance on Measurement Selection by Purpose for Measuring

Measurement Purpose	Measures	Comments
Manage	• Same as evaluate	Same as evaluate
Analyze	• Typically, the CLO will decide which measures to analyze; they may include efficiency, effectiveness, and outcome measures	
Evaluate	• Efficiency measures: participants, completion rate, on-time completion, cost • Effectiveness measures: Levels 1–3 (minimum); Level 5 for key programs • Outcome measures for key programs; isolated impact (Level 4) if possible	
Inform and monitor	• Efficiency measures (e.g., participants or courses) • May also include basic effectiveness measures (e.g., Levels 1, 2, and 3)	Determine what leaders want to see and provide it

As you can see, the same measure may be employed for all purposes, especially the most common efficiency and effectiveness measures.

Our approach will be to first select measures for strategic programs, which are directly aligned to organizational goals. The same measures will be employed for most programs, but there will be some differences. The purpose of these measures will be to inform, monitor, evaluate or analyze, and manage; they will be used primarily by the program manager and CLO. Second, we will examine measures for non-strategic programs, which are not directly aligned to organizational goals. Like strategic programs, they typically contain multiple courses. The measures will be similar to those for aligned programs except there usually will be no outcome measure. Third, we will examine measures for courses of general interest, which are typically taken at the discretion of the employee. These are often referred to as general studies courses. Fourth, we will suggest measures to be used at the department level to inform, monitor, analyze, and manage measures across many programs as well as measures for improvement initiatives in L&D processes and systems. Last, we will suggest some other common measures often used by the CLO. The plan is shown in Table 7-2.

Recommendation

Ensure that you have a robust measurement strategy. As explained in chapter 2, such a strategy should contain all three types of measures (efficiency, effectiveness, and outcome), not necessarily for one program or initiative but certainly across all programs and initiatives. A strategy with only efficiency or only effectiveness measures would be unbalanced, regardless of the reason for measuring (except perhaps to inform and monitor if the focus was only on one type of measure). And a strategy with no outcome measures indicates an L&D department that was not well aligned to the organization since learning should always be able to support at least one strategic or organizational goal.

Table 7-2. Plan for Measuring Programs, General Studies Courses, and Department Initiatives

Focus for Measurement	Type of Measure		
	Efficiency	Effectiveness	Outcome
Programs			
Strategic (aligned)	Yes	Yes	Yes
Non-strategic	Yes	Yes	No
General Studies			
Individual courses	Yes	Minimum Level 1	No
Suites of courses	Yes	Minimum Level 1	No
Department Initiatives			
Across multiple programs	Yes	Yes	Maybe
For process or systems improvement	Yes	Yes	No

Measures for Programs

The right combination of measures for a program depends on the program, the purpose and goals of the program, and the reason for measuring the program. The result may be:

- efficiency and effectiveness measures
- efficiency and effectiveness measures plus an outcome measure.

We will refer to programs directly aligned to organizational goals as strategic programs. By organizational goals we mean those set by the CEO, business unit leader, or head of HR—such as a 10 percent increase in sales, a 5 percent increase in product quality, or a 2 percentage point increase in employee engagement. Directly aligned programs would be designed specifically to help achieve these goals. An example would be a sales training program to help sales representatives close more deals. And, if it is an organizational goal, there should be an outcome measure.

We will refer to programs not directly aligned to top-level goals as non-strategic programs. While not directly aligned, these programs nonetheless are very important to the success of the organization, and in some cases, may be more important than the strategic programs. Examples include basic skills training and compliance.

In both cases, we are talking about structured programs, which usually consist of multiple courses in a particular order covering multiple learning objectives. We will address measures for individual courses after discussing measures for both types of programs. Let's start with the strategic programs.

Strategic Programs (Directly Aligned to Organizational Goals)

Measures for consideration are shown by category in Table 7-3. Any given program may not employ all these measures, depending on the specific program, resources, priorities, and other considerations.

Table 7-3. Recommended Measures for Programs Directly Aligned to Organizational Goals

Efficiency Measures	Effectiveness Measures	Outcome Measures
• Unique participants • Total participants* • Completion rate • Completion date† • Cost	• Level 1 participant reaction • Level 1 goal owner reaction • Level 2 learning • Level 3 intent to apply • Level 3 actual application • ROI	• Level 4 actual impact from control group or • Level 4 actual impact from trend or regression or • Level 4 initial estimate of impact and • Level 4 final estimate of impact

Notes:

If a program consists of just one course, the number of unique and total participants will be the same. If there are multiple courses for the same audience, then in theory Total participants = Unique participants × Number of courses. In practice, participants may not start or complete every course, so measured total participants may be less.

†*Completion date or on-time completion is a measure of the program's progress in meeting development and delivery deadlines, so there may be a measure for each.*

While these are the common measures for formal learning, there may also be informal learning integrated into the program, and occasionally, performance support may eliminate the need for any formal learning. So, the measures in Table 7-4 may be employed in addition to those measures listed by category.

Table 7-4. Measures of Informal Learning for Strategic Programs

Efficiency Measures	Effectiveness Measures
Content	
• Unique users • Percentage reach • Total number of documents available • Total number of documents accessed • Percentage of documents accessed • Average number of documents accessed • Average time spent on site	• Participant reaction to content
Communities of Practice	
• Total number of community of practice members • Active community of practice members • Percentage of active community of practice members	• Participant reaction to community of practice resources and activities
Performance Support	
• Performance support tools available • Performance support tools used • Unique performance support tool users • Total number of performance support tool users • Percentage of performance support tool users	• Participant reaction to performance support tools
Coaching or Mentoring	
• Number of coaches/mentors • Number of coachees/mentees • Ratio of coaches/mentors to coachees/mentees • Average time in program • Average time in meetings • Frequency of meetings	• Participant reaction to coaching • Participant reaction to mentoring • Coach/mentor reaction

Just as informal learning should always be considered when designing a program, so should the informal learning measures. While it does not make sense to repeat the list in Table 7-4 for each program, you should select the appropriate informal learning measures whenever informal learning is part of the program.

With this in mind, the following examples illustrate the selection of measures for formal learning in programs that are directly aligned to organizational goals.

Sales Training Programs

Since sales training programs are typically directly aligned to an important organizational goal, all the key effectiveness and outcome measures are employed (Table 7-5). If resources do not permit using all the measures, the recommendation is to measure intent to apply and initial estimate of impact as part of the post-event survey and then skip the follow-up survey.

Table 7-5. Recommended Measures for Sales Training Programs

Efficiency Measures	Effectiveness Measures	Outcome Measures
• Unique and total participants • Completion rate • Completion date • Cost	• Level 1 participant reaction • Level 1 goal owner reaction • Level 2 average score on first attempt or number of attempts required to pass • Level 3 intent to apply • Level 3 actual application • ROI	Impact of learning on sales • Level 4 actual impact from control group or • Level 4 actual impact from trend or regression or • Level 4 initial estimate of impact and • Level 4 final estimate of impact

Quality, Efficiency, and Other Productivity Training Programs

Since quality, efficiency, and other productivity training programs are typically directly aligned to an important organizational goal, all the key effectiveness and outcome measures are employed, just as with sales training (Table 7-6). If resources do not permit using all the measures, the recommendation is to measure intent to apply and initial estimate of impact as part of the post-event survey and then skip the follow-up survey.

Table 7-6. Recommended Measures for Quality, Efficiency, and Other Productivity Training Programs

Efficiency Measures	Effectiveness Measures	Outcome Measures
• Unique and total participants • Completion rate • Completion date • Cost	• Level 1 participant reaction • Level 1 goal owner reaction • Level 2 average score on first attempt or number of attempts required to pass • Level 3 intent to apply • Level 3 actual application • ROI	Impact of learning on goal • Level 4 actual impact from control group or • Level 4 actual impact from trend or regression or • Level 4 initial estimate of impact and • Level 4 final estimate of impact

Safety Training Programs

Since safety training programs generally are directly aligned to an important organizational or business unit goal, all the key effectiveness and outcome measures are employed (Table 7-7). If resources do not permit using all the measures, the recommendation is to measure intent to apply and initial estimate of impact as part of the post-event survey and then skip the follow-up survey.

Table 7-7. Recommended Measures for Safety Training Programs

Efficiency Measures	Effectiveness Measures	Outcome Measures
• Unique and total participants • Completion rate • Completion date • Cost	• Level 1 participant reaction • Level 1 goal owner reaction • Level 2 average score on first attempt or number of attempts required to pass • Level 3 intent to apply • Level 3 actual application • ROI	Impact of learning on safety • Level 4 actual impact from control group or • Level 4 actual impact from trend or regression or • Level 4 initial estimate of impact and • Level 4 final estimate of impact

Leadership Training Programs

Leadership programs are a little different from most other L&D programs (Table 7-8). The completion rate may not be measured or reported because it is assumed all leaders will complete it, and knowledge tests usually are not given, so there is no Level 2. In some organizations the leadership score on the employee engagement survey is used as the organizational goal. At Caterpillar, there were seven questions on leadership and these formed a leadership index, which served as the measure for leadership. With this, Level 4 could be measured. Most organizations, however, do not try to measure the isolated impact on a leadership score but can still measure the isolated impact of leadership training on revenue, cost reduction, and so forth. If resources are limited, the Level 4 and 5 measures can be skipped, especially if the program has excellent senior leadership support.

Table 7-8. Recommended Measures for Leadership Training Programs

Efficiency Measures	Effectiveness Measures	Outcome Measures
• Unique and total participants • Completion date • Cost	• Level 1 participant reaction • Level 1 goal owner reaction • Level 3 intent to apply • Level 3 actual application • ROI	Impact of learning on leadership score (used by some organizations) • Level 4 actual impact from control group or • Level 4 actual impact from trend or regression or • Level 4 initial estimate of impact and • Level 4 final estimate of impact

Non-Strategic Programs

The list of recommended measures for programs not directly aligned to organizational goals is the same, except there will be no outcome measures because the program is not designed to directly contribute to achieving an organizational goal (Table 7-9). Examples of non-strategic programs would be onboarding, basic skills training, team building, communication skills, data literacy, IT skills, and career exploration. These are all important programs and should increase workforce competency, which should in turn improve performance, which should help the organization achieve its goals, but the impact is indirect compared to a sales training program, which should directly lead to higher sales.

Table 7-9. Recommended Measures for Programs Not Directly Aligned to Organizational Goals

Efficiency Measures	Effectiveness Measures	Outcome Measures
• Unique participants • Total participants • Completion rate • Completion date • Cost	• Level 1 participant reaction • Level 1 goal owner reaction • Level 2 learning • Level 3 intent to apply • Level 3 actual application • ROI	• May include a competency measure

Just as with strategic programs, the measures for informal learning listed in Table 7-4 should be considered whenever informal learning is part of the program design.

Depending on the program, there may be a measure of competency, which in some cases could be a proxy for an outcome measure. As discussed in chapter 5, an increase in competency is usually a means to the end of improving performance, which is the outcome. However, there are circumstances where the program is very important, and the isolated impact of learning is difficult or impossible to measure. In these cases, a measured improvement in competency may serve as a proxy for the unmeasurable outcome.

With a caveat to also consider the informal learning measures shown earlier, the following examples illustrate the selection of measures for programs not directly aligned to organizational goals.

Compliance Programs

Typically, compliance programs are not directly aligned to an organizational goal. For compliance programs, the most important measures are unique participants and completion rate (to make sure the right employees completed the course), as well as the final test score for each employee to prove that they passed the course (Table 7-10). These measures are required for the organization's legal defense. Other measures will be helpful in evaluating and managing the program. Often, Level 3 is not measured for compliance, but it should be for those programs that are important to the organization's culture like sexual harassment. In these cases, actual application may also be worth measuring.

Table 7-10. Recommended Measures for Compliance Programs

Efficiency Measures	Effectiveness Measures	Outcome Measures
• Unique and total participants • Completion rate • Completion date • Cost	• Level 1 participant reaction • Level 1 goal owner reaction (perhaps) • Level 2 individual score on final test, average score on first attempt or number of attempts required to pass • Level 3 intent to apply	• Generally none, but could be reduction in violations or percent of complaints

Six Sigma, Lean, and Other Process Improvement Training Programs

Although these programs are typically not directly aligned to an organizational goal and thus do not normally have an outcome measure, their highly quantitative nature and focus on customer voice lends them to isolated impact and thus ROI (Table 7-11). All the key effectiveness measures can still be employed, but there may not be an outcome measure, although the goal owner may believe it will contribute to achieving a quality or productivity goal. If resources do not permit using all the measures, the recommendation is to measure intent to apply and initial estimate of impact as part of the post-event survey and then skip the follow-up survey.

Table 7-11. Recommended Measures for Process-Improvement Training Programs

Efficiency Measures	Effectiveness Measures	Outcome Measures
• Unique and total participants • Completion rate • Completion date • Cost	• Level 1 participant reaction • Level 1 goal owner reaction • Level 2 average score on first attempt or number of attempts required to pass • Level 3 intent to apply • Level 3 actual application • Level 4 isolated impact on various organizational metrics like sales or cost • ROI	• Impact of learning on process improvement • Productivity • Quality

Basic Skills Training Programs

Basic skills training programs are not typically directly aligned to an organization or business unit goal. Basic skills training enables employees to meet the minimum requirements of their jobs. In some cases, this training is provided during the onboarding period to ensure they can perform the job for which they were hired. In other cases, basic skills training addresses changing job requirements or preparation for a new role. Some organizations like those in the restaurant industry complete basic training in just a few hours. Other professions such as accounting, consulting, and the military send their employees to in-house or external training that may last weeks or months.

Because basic skills programs can vary significantly in length, you should include a duration measure or time to proficiency. For Level 1, the opinion of the trainee's current or receiving supervisor is particularly important and may serve as a headline measure of success (Table 7-12).

Table 7-12. Recommended Measures for Basic Skills Training Programs

Efficiency Measures	Effectiveness Measures	Outcome Measures
• Unique and total participants • Duration of program • Completion rate • Completion date • Cost • Time to proficiency	• Level 1 participant reaction • Level 1 receiving supervisor reaction • Level 2 individual score on final test, average score on first attempt or number of attempts required to pass • Level 3 intent to apply	• None, unless some measure of competency or a measure of satisfaction from the receiving unit is used

Reskilling Programs

Reskilling programs are not typically directly aligned to an organization or business unit goal. Like basic skills training programs, reskilling programs may last for weeks or months, so duration measure is common. Likewise, some measure time to proficiency, especially when it is self-paced. For Level 1, the opinion of the supervisor receiving the re-skilled employee is particularly important and may serve as a headline measure of success (Table 7-13).

Table 7-13. Recommended Measures for Reskilling Programs

Efficiency Measures	Effectiveness Measures	Outcome Measures
• Unique and total participants • Duration of program • Completion rate • Completion date • Cost • Time to proficiency	• Level 1 participant reaction • Level 1 receiving supervisor reaction • Level 2 individual score on final test, average score on first attempt or number of attempts required to pass • Level 3 intent to apply	• None, unless some measure of competency or a measure of satisfaction from the receiving unit is used

IT and Other Professional Skills Training Programs

IT and other professional skills training programs are not typically aligned to an organization or business unit goal. This category of programs includes professional skills such as IT, accounting, purchasing, logistics, finance, and HR. For Level 1, the opinion of the professional leader, like the head of IT as well as supervisors in that area, is particularly important and may serve as a headline measure of success (Table 7-14). From time to time, these programs may be aligned to an organizational goal (like reducing the cost of purchased material), and in these cases there will be an outcome measure.

Table 7-14. Recommended Measures for Professional Skills Training Programs

Efficiency Measures	Effectiveness Measures	Outcome Measures
• Unique and total participants • Completion rate • Completion date • Cost	• Level 1 participant reaction • Level 1 senior professional leader (e.g., head of IT or accounting) and supervisor reaction • Level 2 individual score on final test, average score on first attempt or number of attempts required to pass • Level 3 intent to apply • Level 3 actual application	• None, unless some measure of competency is used

Onboarding Programs

Onboarding programs are very similar to basic skills training programs; they are not typically directly aligned to an organization or business unit goal. They are longer than most courses and are often required before a new hire can perform the job for which they were hired, so a duration measure is common. Unlike basic skills training, there usually would not be a time to proficiency measure and there may not be any knowledge tests. For Level 1, the opinion of the supervisor receiving the new employees is particularly important and may serve as a headline measure of success (Table 7-15).

Table 7-15. Recommended Measures for Onboarding Programs

Efficiency Measures	Effectiveness Measures	Outcome Measures
• Unique and total participants • Duration of program • Completion rate • Completion date • Cost	• Level 1 participant reaction • Level 1 receiving supervisor reaction • Level 2 individual score on final test, average score on first attempt or number of attempts required to pass	• None unless the satisfaction of the receiving supervisor is used

This concludes the section on program measures. Generally speaking, there will always be at least one efficiency and one effectiveness measure, and it is hard to imagine programs for which there would not be two or three of each. Program measures almost always should include a mix (Table 7-16). If the purpose is to evaluate, these measures will be shared in a program evaluation report. If the purpose is to manage, they will be shared in a program report. Both reports are explored in chapter 9.

Table 7-16. Summary of Recommended Core Program Measures

Efficiency Measures	Effectiveness Measures	Outcome Measures
• Unique and total participants (if multiple courses) • Completion rate • Completion date (on-time completion) • Cost	• Level 1 participant reaction • Level 1 goal owner reaction • Level 2 (learning) if appropriate • Level 3 (intent to apply) • Level 3 (actual application) for key programs	• Program specific (measure of impact if aligned to strategic program)

Measures for General Studies Courses

Next, we examine measures for courses not directly aligned to organizational goals and not part of structured programs to address organizational needs. These are often referred to as general studies and include courses like team building, communications, and cultural awareness. They are important and will indirectly contribute to a better workforce, but they do not directly contribute to the organization's top goals or an important need like onboarding or basic skills training. Examples of unaligned programs in the previous section included the same courses, but the difference is how they are organized. Typically, a program will consist of multiple courses and be designed to meet some need. Often the courses will be mandated or strongly recommended. In contrast, general studies courses are offered individually and are completely at the discretion of the employee. Most general studies courses today are online and self-paced, but some are still instructor led like communications and teambuilding.

Given these differences, only basic efficiency measures and a Level 1 effectiveness measure are recommended for these courses. Since they are not directly aligned, there will be no Level 4 and no outcome measure. It is usually not worth it to measure Level 3, so the measurement strategy is very simple.

Individual General Studies Courses

Because it is just one course, total participants will equal unique participants (Table 7-17). Since it is not directly aligned to any organizational goal and being managed, there is usually no need to measure completion rate or date. Cost may be measured. Level 1 participant is the only effectiveness measure that may be worth measuring, since it would be interesting to know if the learner thought it was worthwhile. If they don't, the course should be updated or replaced. If Level 1 data can be easily obtained, then measure Level 1. If it is expensive and time consuming, your measurement effort is better spent on the aligned programs and department improvement initiatives.

Table 7-17. Recommended Measures for a General Studies Course

Efficiency Measures	Effectiveness Measures	Outcome Measures
• Unique participants	• Level 1 reaction	• None

Suites of E-Learning Courses

Many organizations pay vendors to provide hundreds of e-learning courses for their employees to take at work, from home, or on the road. The organization may pay by course or by seat and often can swap courses in and out on a quarterly basis. This can be a very cost-effective way to provide quality learning to employees if the utilization rate is high.

Since we are now analyzing a suite of courses, the number of total participants is just as important as the number of unique participants as many employees may take more than one course. The average number of courses used per employee is another way to measure the intensity of usage, and the percentage of employees who accessed at least one course is a measure of the breadth of usage. It is also important to manage course utilization, so number and percentage of courses used are usually measured (Table 7-18). These measures provide guidance on swapping out less used courses for those with potentially better demand.

Table 7-18. Recommended Measures for Suites of E-Learning Courses

Efficiency Measures	Effectiveness Measures	Outcome Measures
• Unique participants • Total participants • Number of courses used per employee • Percentage of employees who have accessed at least one course • Number of courses used • Percentage of courses used	• Level 1 participant reaction measured periodically for entire suite of courses, not for each course • Level 1 manager reaction to the suite of courses	• None, unless the courses are deployed to increase employee engagement or retention, in which case these could be outcome measures

Level 1 participant reaction may be obtained if the question can be appended to the end of each course. If this is not possible, then conduct a periodic survey to obtain feedback on all the general studies courses in the suite taken in the last six or 12 months. Instead of asking about each course, ask about satisfaction with the suite of courses and whether the suite provides enough general learning opportunities. Additional questions might include satisfaction with the breadth of courses offered and an open-ended question on suggestions for other courses. It would also be good to get feedback from managers who have responsibility for employee development because these courses will be used heavily for general development in employee individual development plans.

Department Initiatives

We now turn our attention to initiatives that represent improvements in L&D processes and systems, or in aggregate measures of efficiency and effectiveness across all programs. The CLO decides on the initiatives for the year and sets a target or goal for improvement. In other words, these initiatives will be managed. (The last section of this chapter addresses other measures of interest to a CLO that may not be managed.)

If the initiative is to improve an efficiency or effectiveness measure, then the primary focus will be on that particular measure. If the initiative is to improve a process or system (like the LMS), then the primary focus will be on measures related to the particular process or system.

For department improvement initiatives, this general guidance will make selection of the appropriate measures easier:

- Choose the measure that is the target of the improvement initiative. This will be the primary measure.
- Consider adding a complementary measure to identify unintended consequences.
  For a primary effectiveness measure, this will be an efficiency measure. For a primary efficiency measure, this will be an effectiveness measure.
- Consider adding ancillary measures, which provide additional context.

An example of an unintended consequence would be a drop in the satisfaction with e-learning programs (complementary measure) as a result of introducing a lot of new (primary measure) but lower quality e-learning content.

The selection of the primary measure is always easy. It is simply whatever the CLO says. If they say the goal is to increase the percentage of e-learning, the percentage of e-learning is the primary measure. If they say the goal is to increase the average Level 1 reaction across all courses, the primary measure is Level 1 reaction. Selection of the complementary measure is trickier and often requires experience to know what the likely unintended consequences could be.

We start with improvement initiatives across all courses and then address improvements to processes and systems.

Improvement Initiatives Across All Courses

Following are some examples of initiatives across all courses.

Increase the Percentage of E-Learning

The primary measure is the percentage of e-learning because that is what the CLO said it was. From experience, an emphasis on a quantity measure may lead to a deterioration in an effectiveness measure, so it would be wise to keep a close watch on learner satisfaction with e-learning (Table 7-19).

Table 7-19. Recommended Measures for Increasing the Percentage of E-Learning

Efficiency Measure (Primary)	Effectiveness Measure (Complementary)
• Percentage of e-learning by number of courses or hours or participants)	• Level 1 participant reaction with e-learning

Increase Satisfaction With E-Learning

In this case, the primary measure is satisfaction with e-learning because that is the goal of this initiative. From experience, an emphasis on a quality measure may be associated with a deterioration in an efficiency measure, so it would be wise to keep a close watch on e-learning usage (Table 7-20). For example, suppose the increase in e-learning satisfaction occurs because all the low-rated e-learning courses are removed. That would be one way to increase the average satisfaction but is probably not what the CLO intended.

Table 7-20. Recommended Measures for Increasing Satisfaction With E-Learning

Efficiency Measures (Complementary)	Effectiveness Measure (Primary)
• Participants for e-learning • Percentage of e-learning • Number of e-learning courses	• Satisfaction with e-learning: Level 1 participant reaction with e-learning

Increase On-Time Program Deliveries

The primary measure is the percentage of on-time deliveries because that is the goal from the CLO. What could go wrong as this goal is pursued? For one, the staff may rush out new programs before they are ready, which is likely to show up as a drop in participant satisfaction and ultimately a drop in goal owner satisfaction. So, Level 1 becomes the complementary measure to watch (Table 7-21).

Table 7-21. Recommended Measures for Increasing On-Time Program Deliveries

Efficiency Measures (Primary)	Effectiveness Measure (Complementary)
• Percentage on-time program deliveries • Note: track both promised and actual completion deadlines	• Level 1 goal owner reaction • Level 1 participant reaction

Increase Overall Participant Satisfaction With Learning

Context: Assume Level 1 participant reaction has declined over the past two years. Analysis indicates that participants are unhappy with the old-style courses and the quality of the instructor's in-class performance. Plans have been put in place to upskill the course designers and provide coaching to the instructors. At the same time, a new LMS is being installed.

This example shows a particular situation but illustrates how ancillary measures can be used to present a holistic picture. The primary measure is satisfaction with all learning because that is goal of this initiative. The most important complementary measures are probably the percentage of learning by modality since a change in the mix could produce an improvement of Level 1. For example, if e-learning has a lower Level 1 than ILT, simply reducing the percentage of e-learning could increase Level 1. In this case, no actual improvement occurred in either e-learning or ILT.

There are a number of ancillary measures that may be of interest in this particular example. One is the installation of a new LMS, which can easily impact Level 1 scores regardless of efforts to improve Level 1 for ILT. If the transition is messy and courses are not available, participants could reflect that in their Level 1 feedback. Since improvement is dependent on designers taking the new courses and instructors receiving coaching, both bear watching (Table 7-22).

Table 7-22. Recommended Measures for Increasing Participant Learning Satisfaction

Efficiency Measures (Complementary)	Effectiveness Measure (Primary)
• Percentage of ILT and e-learning by participants, courses, and hours	• Satisfaction with learning: Level 1 participant reaction with all learning, ILT, and e-learning
Potential Measures (Ancillary)	
• Installation date for new LMS • Number of designers taking new design courses • Completion date for designers to complete new courses	• Number of instructors selected for coaching • Completion date for coaching targeted instructors

Increase Overall Application Rate

Assume Level 3 actual application has been falling, and the CLO has directed staff to undertake an initiative to improve communication by the goal owner with the target audience and influence the goal owners to do a better job reinforcing the learning (Table 7-23).

Table 7-23. Recommended Measures for Increasing Overall Application Rate

Efficiency Measures (Complementary)	Effectiveness Measure (Primary)
• None	• Level 3 intent to apply • Level 3 actual application
Potential Measures (Ancillary)	
• Percentage of key programs with communication plans by goal owner in place at launch • Percentage of key programs with reinforcement plans in place at launch • Percentage of key programs where reinforcement occurs	• Number of instructors selected for coaching • Completion date for coaching targeted instructors

This example reflects another very specific situation but illustrates how ancillary measures can help present a holistic picture. The primary measure is application, which will be measured both ways. Intended application will serve as a leading indicator of actual application. No true complementary measures have been identified, but several important ancillary measures have been, and these are taken directly from the action plan for this initiative. The first measures whether the goal owner has communicated, and the last two measure how the goal owner is performing on reinforcement. These all will be leading indicators for application.

Improvement Initiatives in L&D Processes and Systems

Last, we examine the selection of measures for process or system improvements. These will often involve very specific measures, which may not be as common and consequently not discussed in chapter 3. The approach, however, will be the same as in the previous section. The primary measure will come directly from the CLO's goal, and it may be helpful to identify an ancillary measure of interest or a complementary measure to guard against unintended consequences.

Increase LMS Uptime

Like our other examples, the primary measure comes directly from the CLO establishing a goal to increase LMS uptime. No complementary measure has been identified that may deteriorate because of increasing LMS uptime, but if resources must be redirected to work on the LMS uptime issue, it is possible that another measure could be adversely affected. An improvement in LMS uptime should result in higher user satisfaction, so that is included as an ancillary measure (Table 7-24).

Table 7-24. Recommended Measures for Increasing LMS Uptime

Efficiency Measure (Primary)	Effectiveness Measures (Ancillary)
• LMS uptime (percent of time LMS is available)	• User satisfaction (a Level 1 type measure applied to the LMS)

Reduce Average Help Desk Call Time

In this case, the objective is to reduce the average time of help desk calls. The danger, of course, is that the reduction in average call time will reduce the quality of the support (providing brief, incomplete guidance or not asking if there are any other issues), so user satisfaction should be measured to ensure the quality does not suffer. Depending on the plan to reduce call time, there may be other ancillary measures to monitor or manage as well. For example, if the plan includes posting FAQs, then an ancillary measure may be the number of FAQs and their completion date. If the plan is to provide better scripts for the help desk staff, then an ancillary measure would be the completion date for the scripts and perhaps training on the new scripts (Table 7-25). Each of these ancillary measures will help leaders manage the action items to reduce the average call time.

Table 7-25. Recommended Measures for Reducing Call Time

Efficiency Measures (Primary)	Effectiveness Measures (Complementary)*
• Average help desk call time	• User satisfaction with help desk
Potential Measures (Ancillary)	
• Number of FAQs posted • Completion date for FAQ posting	• Completion date for new scripts • Completion date for training on new scripts

Increase the Use of Informal Learning

Assume the CLO wants to increase the use of communities of practice, portal content, and performance support. Efficiency measures such as usage will provide insight into the adoption of these informal learning methods. However, the CLO also understands that usage without positive perceptions will not be sustainable. As a result, the CLO suggests that the organization also select one or two complementary effectiveness measures (Table 7-26).

Table 7-26. Recommended Measures for Increasing the Use of Informal Learning

Communities of Practice

Efficiency Measures (Primary)	Effectiveness Measures (Complementary)
• Number of communities of practice • Active communities of practice • Unique Users	• User reaction to communities of practice

Content

Efficiency Measures (Primary)	Effectiveness Measures (Complementary)
• Number of documents available • Number of documents accessed • Unique users • Total users	• User reaction to content

Performance Support

Efficiency Measures (Primary)	Effectiveness Measures (Complementary)
• Number of performance support tools available • Number of performance support tools used • Unique users • Total users	• User reaction to performance support

This concludes our section on department initiative measures to be managed. There will always be a primary measure, which is the goal of the CLO. It may be either an efficiency or effectiveness measure. It would be wise to supplement the primary measure with a complementary one that will help identify a potential unintended consequence of the initiative. And consider whether any ancillary measures would be useful.

The primary measures will be shared in the operations report, which is discussed in chapter 9.

Other Measures the CLO May Request

While we have already discussed many measures and applications, there are still other measures that a CLO may want to see on a monthly, quarterly, or annual basis. Unlike the measures in the last section on improvement initiatives, these may not always be managed. Sometimes they will simply be used to inform or monitor and, if the results are not acceptable, may be moved over to the "manage" category.

Here, then, are some examples of these other measures to round out our chapter on measurement selection.

Portfolio Analysis

Typically, the CLO will be interested in the mix of courses, hours, and participants by modality. By definition, these measures will be aggregated across all courses for which there are data:

- courses available
- percentage of courses used
- percentage of courses, hours, and participants by modality
- percentage of courses by area or discipline.

In addition, some learning organizations segment their learning portfolio based on the program purpose, such as increased sales or enhanced employee productivity. In this case, the CLO might be interested not only in efficiency measures for each portfolio, but also effectiveness measures to enable comparisons across programs with a similar purpose.

Course Management

CLOs are also usually interested in some measures of course management such as:

- total courses developed
- percentage of courses developed meeting the deadline
- total courses delivered
- percentage of courses delivered meeting the deadline
- classes canceled
- percentage of classes canceled
- effort to create new courses
- effort to update existing courses.

Reach

Another set of common measures focuses on reach or the number or percentage of employees touched by learning. As we discussed in chapter 3, reach is a measure of the breadth or dispersion of learning within the organization. Reach answers the question of whether learning is broad based (reaching most employees) or more narrowly focused (reaching only a few). These types of measures are often of interest to senior leaders:

- employees reached by L&D
- employees reached by formal learning
- percentage of employees reached by formal learning
- employees who have accessed content
- employees with a development plan
- percentage of employees with a development plan.

Cost

The CLO and the CFO are always interested in cost measures. The most common include:

- direct expenditure
- opportunity cost
- direct expenditure per employee
- direct expenditure per unique learner
- direct expenditure as a percentage of revenue, payroll, or profit
- percentage of direct expenditure for tuition reimbursement
- percentage of direct expenditure for external services.

Informal Learning

The discussion in this section so far has focused primarily on measures for formal learning, but informal learning measures are becoming increasingly common. Content, a community of practice, performance support, or coaching should be added to the lists of measures that a CLO would like to see for the purposes of informing or monitoring. A complete list was included in Table 7-4, and a shorter list was provided in the discussion about increasing the use of informal learning in the previous section on department initiatives.

This concludes our discussion of other measures a CLO might want to see to inform or monitor. Note that measures to manage department improvement initiatives were discussed in the previous section. These measures should come up in the discussion with the CLO at the start of the measurement strategy process and could include any of the efficiency or effectiveness measures identified in chapters 3 and 4. These additional measures to inform or monitor would appear in scorecards or dashboards.

Conclusion

You should now be ready to create the measurement portion of your measurement and reporting strategy. Our advice is to start with a few measures and gradually grow your strategy through time, both in terms of number of measures and complexity. It is much better to execute a lean strategy successfully than fail to execute a grandiose strategy. A successfully executed lean strategy will produce results, give everyone valuable experience using the measures, and build internal expertise and credibility. In contrast, failure to execute a complex strategy may lead leaders to question the ability of the team to produce results and make it more difficult to win approval for strategies in the future.

With our measures selected, we are now ready to explore how the measures are used in reports. Chapter 8 introduces the five types of reports and chapter 9 focuses on the highest use of measures for management reporting.

PART III

Reporting

CHAPTER 8
Reporting

Congratulations! You have now selected measures to include in your measurement strategy for the coming year or perhaps just measures to meet a specific need. The next order of business is to decide what to do with them once the data are available. How should you share this information? What format should you use? This chapter provides answers to these questions, starting with a return to the measurement hierarchy for guidance on reporting. We recommend different types of reports depending on the purpose and user of the report, and we share examples to help you understand the options.

Types of Reports and Data Displays

We start by admitting that there is no standard definition in our field for the terms *report, scorecard*, or *dashboard*. We use *report* generically to mean any display of data for purposes of this chapter. A report may just be a display of data or it may be a written document containing data. We reserve *scorecard* to refer to a tabular or table-like display of data that contains only the results (history) for the measures. It may also contain a threshold if the purpose is to monitor.

We use *dashboard* to mean a higher-order report than a scorecard, although it may still be tabular in format. A dashboard may be interactive, allowing the user to drill down into the data, or it may contain a visual display of data like a bar chart, line graph, or speedometer. It may also contain a threshold if the purpose is to monitor.

Last, we reserve *management report* to mean a report that shows the plan (synonymous with goal or target) for a measure, YTD results, YTD results compared to plan, forecast for how the measure is likely to end for the year, and a comparison of forecast to plan. A management report may also have interactive capabilities and visual displays, but the defining characteristics are inclusion of plan, YTD results, and forecast for each measure. The characteristics for each of these reports are described in Table 8-1.

Table 8-1. Characteristics of the Three Most Common Types of Reports

Report Type	Table-Like Display	Visual Display	Interactive	Values for			
				Threshold	Plan	YTD Results	Forecast
Scorecard	Yes	Maybe, paired with a table	No	Maybe	No	Maybe	No
Dashboard	Often	Typically	Often	Maybe	Maybe	Maybe	No
Management	Yes	Maybe	Maybe	No	Yes	Yes	Yes

Since there is no standard, organizations often use these terms differently, and some reports will not fit neatly into our classification scheme. Regardless of nomenclature, though, we want to make the point that not all reports are equal, and reports have different characteristics, which will be important as we recommend the best ones to use in different circumstances. Furthermore, in the TDRp framework, reports are used at all maturity levels (scorecards for lower maturity and management reports for higher maturity). This contrasts with many who do not differentiate by type of report and instead classify all reporting as a low maturity-level activity.

In addition to displaying data in tables, charts and graphs can supplement the table or can replace the table entirely. Bar charts are common in our field and lend themselves to comparisons of several measures for the same time period or one or several measures over time. Likewise, graphs display data for one or more measures over time, particularly when there are numerous data points (like monthly data over three years or more).

We continue our discussion of the different reports by returning to the measurement hierarchy first shared in chapter 1 (Table 8-2). Recall that the hierarchy is based on the reasons to measure, and the reason to measure will dictate the type of report to use.

Table 8-2. Measurement Requirements and the Impact on Reporting

Measurement Purpose	Primary Use	Key Elements	Shared In
Manage	• Identify if the program is delivering planned results and where adjustments are needed to meet goals	• Plan • YTD results • Forecast for measures being managed	• Management reports
Evaluate and analyze	• Analyze program and non-program data • Explore relationships among measures • Predict outcomes	• Analytical methods (e.g., regression analysis, predictive modeling)	• Custom analysis reports
	• Evaluate the efficiency, effectiveness, or impact of a learning program	• Six levels of evaluation (Level 0 to Level 5)	• Program evaluation reports
Monitor	• Determine if measure meets threshold or is within acceptable range	• Threshold or breakpoints for measures	• Dashboards • Scorecards
Inform	• Answer questions, identify key trends, and share activity	• Specific measures or trends	• Dashboards • Scorecards

Measurement Maturity (vertical axis label with upward arrow)

Copyright applied for by Center for Talent Reporting (2020). Used with permission.

In this chapter, we focus on each measurement purpose and the reports that typically serve that purpose.

Reporting to Inform

As we discussed in chapter 1, the most common reason to measure is to inform or answer questions, identify trends, and share activity. Sometimes, the question is very simple: "How many courses were used last year?" In this case, you may simply provide the answer in person or in an email—no table required. More often, though, the question is more complex, or the answer would benefit from some detail. For example, the user might want to see the breakdown of courses used by type or subject matter, and it might be useful to show the answer for both unique and total courses. In this case, you would display the data in a table or scorecard but sometimes in a graph or chart as well.

Scorecards are an effective way to inform. They are one of the most common reports and are a natural starting point for our examination of reporting options to inform. At its simplest, the scorecard is simply a table of historical results. Typically, the x-axis (horizontal) is time and the y-axis (vertical) is the name of the measure. Table 8-3 shows a simple example for unique courses used by type of learning.

Table 8-3. Example of a Simple Scorecard

Unique Courses Used by Type of Learning								
		Course Count						
Measure	Unit of Measure	Jan	Feb	Mar	Apr	May	Jun	Total Unique Courses YTD
ILT only	Number	15	15	14	12	11	9	23
vLIT only	Number	1	1	2	2	3	3	3
E-learning only	Number	9	10	11	11	12	13	15
Blended	Number	1	1	2	2	2	3	3
Total courses		26	27	29	27	28	28	44
		Percent of Total for the Month						
Measure	Unit of Measure	Jan	Feb	Mar	Apr	May	Jun	Percent of YTD Total
ILT only	%	58%	56%	48%	44%	39%	32%	52%
vLIT only	%	4%	4%	7%	7%	11%	11%	7%
E-learning only	%	35%	37%	38%	41%	43%	46%	34%
Blended	%	4%	4%	7%	7%	7%	11%	7%
Total courses		100%	100%	100%	100%	100%	100%	100%

Note: Since the table displays unique courses, the YTD total eliminates duplicates across months.

Since the purpose of a scorecard is to answer questions, a table like this is appropriate if the CLO asked to see a breakdown of courses used by type of learning for the first six months of the year. This table provides that information very clearly answers the following types of questions:
- How many courses were used in June? (Answer: 28)
- How does that compare to the first five months? (Answer: Down from March but up from January, February, and April)
- What type of course has been more popular over the first six months? (Answer: ILT at 52 percent but e-learning has gradually increased in popularity, surpassing ILT in May)
- Is there a trend? (Answer: Yes. E-learning, vILT, and blended have increased since the start of the year.)

It is a best practice to always add a note if something in the table is likely to confuse the user. In this case, a user may have quickly noticed that the YTD column does not appear to be summing the six months correctly. Rather than waiting for them to point this out (or just assume you made an error), it would be wise to explain it. In this case, the measure is unique courses used, not the total, so just like with unique participants, you cannot simply sum the amounts across time periods because that will result in duplicates being counted. In other words, there were only 23 unique (by name) ILT courses used in the first six months. They were never all used in the same month, and each month would have a slightly different list of courses used. Using an LMS or a spreadsheet is essential to obtain the unique count.

This scorecard includes the YTD column, which we always recommend when displaying partial-year data, so the user does not have to calculate it manually.

In many cases, the report recipient will want to review trends. While the table includes the percentage of total courses delivered by modality, it's easier to see the trend via a graph (Figure 8-1).

Figure 8-1. Graphical Depiction of Trends

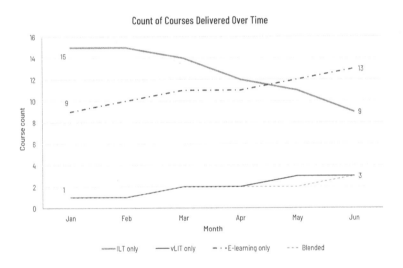

In our client work, we are often asked when it's appropriate to use a table versus a graph or bar chart. We suggest the following:
- A table is best when:
  - You need to look up specific values.
  - Users need precise values.
  - You need to compare related values (for example, sales in Q1 versus Q2).
  - You have multiple data sets with different units of measure.
- A graph or bar chart is best when:
  - You have large data sets.

◦ You want to reveal relationships among multiple values (similarities and differences).

◦ The shape of the graph tells the story.

Often, our clients need to see the specific values and the overall trends in an easy-to-read view. In this case, use both the table and the graph. Your users will thank you.

We depict a slightly more complex scorecard in Table 8-4. The CLO requested a report showing the historical results for the organization's effectiveness measures during the last six quarters.

Table 8-4. Example of a More Complex Scorecard

Measure Name	Unit of Measure	Effectiveness Measures							
		2019					2020		
		Q1	Q2	Q3	Q4	Avg	Q1	Q2	YTD
Level 1: Participant Reaction									
Quality									
Content	% of top two boxes	74%	75%	77%	83%	77%	87%	87%	87%
Instructor	% of top two boxes	76%	79%	80%	74%	80%	84%	85%	85%
Delivery	% of top two boxes	78%	82%	85%	84%	82%	86%	85%	86%
Environment	% of top two boxes	78%	79%	82%	85%	81%	85%	84%	85%
Subtotal for quality	Average of measures	77%	79%	81%	82%	80%	86%	85%	86%
Alignment	% of top two boxes	75%	75%	78%	79%	77%	87%	88%	87%
Recommend to others	% of top two boxes	78%	79%	83%	88%	82%	90%	91%	90%
Relevance to job	% of top two boxes	82%	82%	83%	85%	83%	85%	86%	85%
Worthwhile investment of time	% of top two boxes	74%	75%	79%	82%	78%	85%	86%	85%
Total for Level 1 Participant Reaction	Average of measures	77%	78%	81%	83%	80%	86%	87%	86%
Level 1 Goal Owner Reaction	**% of top two boxes**	73%	73%	77%	77%	75%	77%	77%	77%
Level 2 Learning	**Score on first attempt**	75%	75%	79%	82%	78%	83%	83%	83%
Level 3 Application									
Intent to apply	% of content applied	79%	79%	81%	85%	81%	86%	87%	87%
Actual application	% of content applied	58%	60%	62%	65%	61%	76%	80%	78%

This view answers the following questions:

- What is the average Level 1 participant reaction score for 2019 and for the first six months of 2020? (Answer: 80 percent for 2019 and 86 percent for 2020.)
- What are the lowest and highest components of Level 1 participant reaction for 2020? (Answer: Four components tie for lowest score at 85 percent favorable—instructor quality, environment quality, relevance to job, and worthwhile investment—and recommend to others is the highest at 90 percent.)

- Is goal owner satisfaction improving in 2020? (Answer: It improved slightly from Q4 2019 to Q1 2020 but did not increase any further in Q2.)
- Has the application rate improved over the last six quarters? (Answer: Yes. Intent to apply improved from 79 percent to 87 percent while actual application improved from 58 percent to 78 percent.)

Notice that in both examples the scorecard did not contain a threshold, plan, or target values. Consequently, a user could not say whether the values were good or bad, just whether they were improving or deteriorating. There is no information on what the L&D department wanted to achieve. For example, did the department intend to move away from ILT and toward vILT, e-learning, and blended? Is the department actively trying to improve Level 1 scores or did this improvement just happen on its own?

In summary, if a scorecard is going to inform, it must provide information about relevant measures in a way that recipients can easily interpret and identify where to take action.

> **Note**
>
> This scorecard raises the issue of when to use a simple versus weighted average. We use a simple average here to provide the average for 2019 for each component, which means each value is weighted equally. An alternative would be to use a weighted average where the weight is the number of respondents each quarter. If one quarter had a lot more respondents than other quarters, the value for that quarter would receive a heavier weighting. Likewise, the average for the Level 1 subcategory of quality is the simple average of the subcategory components (content through environment). And the average for Level 1 participant reaction is the simple average of the five components (quality, alignment, recommend, relevance, and worthwhile investment).
>
> An analyst could choose to weight the categories differently to give some more weight than the others. Typically, simple averages are employed but the option always exists to weight. If that's what you decide to do, be sure to disclose that in a note because the reader will assume you have used a simple average.

Reporting to Monitor

The next use of measures is to monitor or determine if a measure meets a threshold or is within an acceptable range. Scorecards with thresholds and dashboards with thresholds are well suited to this purpose.

Many scorecards and dashboards will use color coding to indicate satisfactory, marginal, or unsatisfactory results. The color coding may include predefined thresholds or may use the concept of a "heat map," which assigns colors (typically green, yellow, and red) based on the distribution of the data. The thresholds, however, are generally not equivalent to a target or plan. That is, the colors merely make it easier to assess the level of performance. Table 8-5 is an example of such a scorecard. (Note that the colors have been adjusted to grayscale for printing; light gray represents green, medium gray is yellow, and dark gray is red.)

Reporting

Table 8-5. Example of a Scorecard With Color Coding

Departmental Dashboard								
	JAN	FEB	MAR	APR	YTD	Green	Yellow	Red
Efficiency Measures								
LMS uptime (percent)	99.5%	98.0%	99.1%	99.4%	99.0%	>99%	97-99%	<97%
Help desk call time (minutes)	11.5	10.5	9.8	9.7	10.4	<10 min	10-20 min	>20 min
Help desk wait time (minutes)	2.2	0.8	1.6	2.3	1.7	<1 min	1-2 min	>2 min
Percentage of on-time completions (percent)		75.0%	79.2%	81.5%	78.6%	>90%	80-90%	<80%
Effectiveness Measures								
Level 1 reaction: percent of top two boxes	75.0%	81.5%	82.0%	82.0%	80.1%	>80%	70-80%	<70%
Level 2 learning: first-time pass rate	79.0%	85.0%	90.5%	91.0%	86.4%	>90%	80-90%	<80%
Level 3 application: percent of content applied		58.0%	61.5%		59.8%	>60%	40-60%	<40%

Note: In this table, light gray represents green, medium gray represents yellow, and dark gray represents red.

In this scorecard, leadership sets thresholds (shown at right) for each measure. These thresholds then determine the status or color for each measure. For example, the threshold for LMS uptime is 99 percent, meaning that the expectation is for the system to be available 99 percent of the time. Values between 97 percent and 99 percent signal a warning and are not expected to occur very often. A value in the red is a cause for concern and requires immediate attention.

LMS uptime has been green and meeting expectations every month except February, where it slipped into the yellow. Help desk wait time, on the other hand, is not doing well. It is very erratic, meaning the process is not under control, has registered two months of red, only one green, and is not showing any sustained improvement. So, management needs to address and improve help desk wait time and percentage on time completions. Other measures are doing well and show sustained improvement.

This type of scorecard, particularly if it is color coded, is very popular since it is so easy to use, and it clearly shows when a measure is out of an acceptable range. Also, the use of color coding can improve the usefulness of the report. Without at least some context (what does "good" look like?), the data on the report has limited value, particularly to a recipient who may not even have asked for the report.

Dashboards often look like a scorecard but usually provide drill down capability to examine select measures or a specific timeframe. They often include visual displays such as bar charts or line graphs. Some have "speedometer" dials, which show activity. Like scorecards, if dashboards are used to monitor, they will also include a threshold, which is an acceptable range for a measure or a minimum or maximum value so a user can see if the measure is in compliance or not. The thresholds are predefined and may use benchmarks to compare results to a broader population.

The Use of Benchmarks

As we mentioned in chapters 3 and 4, benchmarks are extremely helpful to gauge your performance against other organizations. ATD and Explorance provide robust benchmarks they continually refresh to reflect shifting trends in L&D.

We recommend that L&D use benchmarks to help leaders set appropriate goals for their organizations. In some cases, the benchmark may become the goal, which is acceptable as long as the decision is intentional. However, leaders should not simply make the goal to equal the benchmark. Rather, they should adjust the goal to reflect the maturity of their organization and its ability to meet or exceed a specific threshold at a particular point.

Dashboards for monitoring (like scorecards) are best employed when the measures historically have been in an acceptable range and are likely to remain within an acceptable range going forward. This is often the case for effectiveness measures, especially Level 1 participant reaction, where many organizations consistently receive high marks. They may average 4.5 on a 5-point scale with little variability around the average (most responses fall between 4.2 and 4.8). So, it would be unusual to have a value below 4.2, and accordingly, 4.2 is set as the threshold value. The program manager and CLO want to receive an alert when a value falls below 4.2—if they don't hear otherwise they will assume everything remains within the acceptable range.

Dashboard designs vary considerably. Reporting users often want fewer tables and more visualization. To respond to this demand, L&D technology providers have customized their dashboards to include combinations of colorful visual displays and often graphs. In some cases, these dashboards are simply glorified scorecards with no thresholds, interactivity, or drilldown capability. The difference is that dashboards convey some information graphically, which also means that dashboards often contain much less specific information than scorecards, given the limit on how much information they can display visually.

As vendors respond to client needs, they have increasingly provided dashboards that provide thresholds as well as drill down capability. The example dashboard in Table 8-6 shows Level 1 participant reaction average scores for the first three quarters, where the threshold or minimally acceptable score is 4.2. View 1 of the dashboard shows the high-level view of the results across all quarters. When you examine the data, it's clear that something happened in Q2 causing program scores to decline by 0.3 point from Q1. If you are monitoring these programs, you might want to know if the problem occurred for all programs and courses or only a subset.

When you double click on "All Programs," the dashboard will display the results of Program A and Program B (view 2). While the scores of both programs declined in Q2, the larger drop was for Program B, which declined by 0.4 point versus the overall 0.3 point average. At this point, you would likely want to explore if all courses in Program B had similar declines. To do so, you would double click on Program B so the dashboard displays the results of two courses, Course B1 and Course B2 (view 3). Clearly, Course B2 is pulling down the average. What you might not know is that the initial rollout of Course B2 occurred in Q2 with a score of 3.9. So, we are seeing not a decline in the scores from Q1 to Q2, but rather the introduction of a new course, which impacted the overall average. When you double click on Course B2, it's obvious that all three instructors (D, E, and F) had similar scores (view 4). The next step would be to investigate Course B2 and identify why it did not meet the threshold overall.

While this dashboard enables drill down, it doesn't color code the results, requiring a bit more work on the part of the user to compare the actuals to the threshold. Table 8-7 is a dashboard with drill down capability and color-coded scores to facilitate easy comparison to plan. This dashboard focuses on Level 1 content questions only.

Walking through the example, you

Table 8-6. Dashboard With Drill Down Capability

Level 1: Reaction—Average for All Questions							
View 1							
Program Title	**Threshold**	**Q1**	**Q2**	**Q3**	**Q4**	**YTD**	
All programs	4.2	4.5	4.2	4.4		4.3	
View 2							
Program Title	**Threshold**	**Q1**	**Q2**	**Q3**	**Q4**	**YTD**	
Program A	4.2	4.4	4.3	4.4		4.3	
Program B	4.2	4.5	4.1	4.4		4.3	
All programs	4.2	4.5	4.2	4.4		4.3	
View 3							
Program Title	**Threshold**	**Q1**	**Q2**	**Q3**	**Q4**	**YTD**	
Program B	4.2	4.5	4.1	4.4		4.3	
Course B1	4.2	4.5	4.4	4.6		4.5	
Course B2	4.2		3.9	4.2		4.1	
View 4							
Program Title	**Threshold**	**Q1**	**Q2**	**Q3**	**Q4**	**YTD**	
Program B	4.2	4.5	4.1	4.4		4.3	
Course B2	4.2		3.9	4.2		4.1	
Instructor D	4.2		3.9	4.3		4.1	
Instructor E	4.2		3.8	4.1		4.0	
Instructor F	4.2		4.0	4.3		4.2	

Table 8-7. Example of Dashboard Drill Down by Content With Color (Views 1 and 2)

Level 1: Reaction—Average for All Questions						
View 1						
Program Title	**Threshold**	**Q1**	**Q2**	**Q3**	**Q4**	**YTD**
All programs	4.2	4.2	4.2	4.3		4.2
View 2						
Program Title	**Threshold**	**Q1**	**Q2**	**Q3**	**Q4**	**YTD**
Program A	4.2	4.1	4.1	4.2		4.1
Program B	4.2	4.3	4.3	4.4		4.3
All programs	4.2	4.2	4.2	4.3		4.2

Note: light gray = green; medium gray = yellow; dark gray = red

encounter possible pitfalls when simply monitoring results versus managing them. In Table 8-7, view 1 only shows the total for all programs where the YTD average of 4.2 indicates that the threshold is being met and no further investigation is necessary. However, averages can be deceiving. When you double click on "All programs" in view 1 to see the details by program (view 2), you discover that Program B seems to be doing well (at or above the threshold), but Program A is falling behind.

You now double click Program A in view 2, which brings up the detail for Program A (view 3; Table 8-8). Here you find that the 4.1 score for Program A results from a mix of courses and instructors who are exceeding the threshold (Instructors A, C, E and F), those who are a bit below (Instructor D), and one who is underperforming considerably (Instructor B). Had you only looked at the top-line results, you might not have uncovered areas for further action.

You now feel you've done your due diligence and that you don't have to investigate further. Program B is doing great, right? Well, maybe not.

Return to view 2 and double click on Program B. In view 4, you'll see that the averages masked courses that were underperforming (Table 8-9). Course 2 is at risk, below threshold, or just barely meeting for all instructors.

The point of this example is that when you choose to monitor results, do not assume that the average is telling the full story. Explore beyond the top-line result to uncover emerging issues early that require less drastic corrective action.

Table 8-8. View 3: Result of Double Clicking on Program A in View 2

			Quarter			
	Threshold	Q1	Q2	Q3	Q4	YTD
Program A	4.2	4.1	4.1	4.2		4.1
Course 1	4.2	4.1	4.1	4.2		4.2
Instructor A	4.2	4.8	4.6	4.6		4.7
Instructor B	4.2	3.1	3.3	3.8		3.5
Instructor C	4.2	4.4	4.3	4.2		4.3
Course 2	4.2		4.1	4.2		4.2
Instructor D	4.2		3.8	4.1		4.0
Instructor E	4.2		4.3	4.3		4.3
Instructor F	4.2		4.3	4.3		4.3

Note: light gray = green; medium gray = yellow; dark gray = red

Table 8-9. View 4: Result of Double Clicking on Program B in View 2

			Quarter			
	Threshold	Q1	Q2	Q3	Q4	YTD
Program B	4.2	4.3	4.3	4.4		4.3
Course 1	4.2	4.3	4.6	4.6		4.5
Instructor A	4.2	4.6	4.8	4.8		4.7
Instructor B	4.2	3.9	4.2	4.3		4.1
Instructor C	4.2	4.5	4.7	4.6		4.6
Course 2	4.2		4.0	4.2		4.1
Instructor D	4.2		3.9	4.2		4.0
Instructor E	4.2		3.8	4.0		3.9
Instructor F	4.2		4.2	4.3		4.3

Note: light gray = green; medium gray = yellow; dark gray = red

---

Note

Since monitoring implies that the values are expected to fall in an acceptable range, most values in a dashboard should be in the green or yellow. If a scorecard or dashboard is predominantly red, leaders have set the threshold too high for monitoring. If the wto manage the measure to a higher level and will require a management report rather than a scorecard or dashboard to achieve the desired result.

Next, we provide examples of actual dashboards. They all include visually appealing displays of data and some include thresholds or small tables as well.

The oil company Marathon provides an example of a dashboard for an organization just beginning the measurement journey (Figure 8-2). When they first began measuring they had no benchmarks but simply collected data. By year two, they had sufficient efficiency and effectiveness data so that they could set individual and department thresholds or goals and use the dashboard to monitor.

Figure 8-2. Sample Dashboard From Marathon

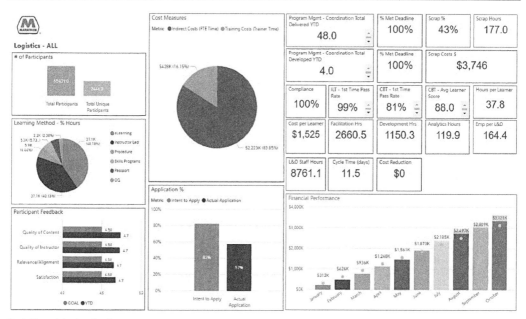

Used with permission from Marathon.

Figures 8-3 and 8-4 are two dashboards from the solution provider Explorance that illustrate what can be generated for a client with a measurement and reporting tool, in this case Metrics That Matter (MTM), which we introduced in an earlier chapter. Both dashboards contain visual displays of the data as well as simple tabular presentations; each is interactive, allowing the user to select the time period. The custom dashboard illustrates what the CLO and program managers would use to monitor the key measures of net promoter score and scrap learning with some detail for each (Figure 8-3). Details on business results (1) and application challenges (2) are found on the left-hand side.

The dashboard provides six views chosen by the client to monitor progress:

1. The top left panel identifies the top three business results reported across all courses. For this client, the top results are teamwork/office dynamics, patient satisfaction, and productivity.

2. The middle left panel shows the barriers to application reported across all programs. More than 53 percent of participants reported having no challenges, whereas 26

percent reported not having enough time and 13 percent could not apply the learning because it conflicted with their current work processes.

3. The bottom left panel shows a 12-month trend of two indicators, job impact and perceived value, compared to the corporate university benchmark that is available in the MTM database.

4. The top middle panel shows the courses that reported the most unapplied learning (scrap) ordered from most scrap to least scrap.

5. The top right panel depicts instructor Likert scores from lowest to highest (Note: we have replaced the names for confidentiality).

6. Finally, the bottom right panel shows the trend of Net Promoter Score over the past 12 months compared to the corporate benchmark.

Figure 8-3. Custom Dashboard From Metrics That Matter

Used with permission from Explorance.

It's worth noting that while the dashboard provides information and is useful for monitoring, this particular company is very focused on managing their learning business. As a result, key measures like scrap and NPS fall within a very narrow range.

The dashboard in Figure 8-4 is designed to be shared with senior leaders like the CEO, CFO, and business unit heads. It highlights the four key measures that senior leaders care about:

1. The top left panel shows the overall usage of learning by purpose of the training: operational efficiency, mitigate risk, foundational skills, and drive growth. This view provides insight into the type of training that the organization is consuming.

2. The second panel to the right shows the overall scrap rate for L&D in that period. The green dot denotes that scrap rates are lower than the corporate benchmark (a lower value of scrap is good).

3. The third panel to the right depicts the overall performance improvement as calculated by the MTM system. The green dot also shows that training across the enterprise in the reported period is above benchmark.

4. The panel on the top right shows the overall net promoter score, which is also above benchmark.

5. The final view on the bottom right depicts the scrap rates for all of L&D over the past 12 months compared to the corporate benchmark. As you can see, this organization had scrap rates that fell below the benchmark for every month in the past year.

Figure 8-4. Executive Dashboard Template

Used with permission from Explorance.

These views are customizable. Over time, L&D and business stakeholders may decide to focus on different efficiency and effectiveness measures, enabling L&D to replace the existing panels with data that is relevant to their business objectives.

Reporting to Evaluate and Analyze

The need to evaluate programs and analyze a variety of data represent the next category in our reasons to measure. We recommend sharing program evaluation results in a program evaluation report and custom analysis results in a custom analysis report. We start with program evaluation reports.

Program Evaluation Report

The in-depth evaluation of a specific program is often summarized in a program evaluation report. The report may take the form of a short, written report or a PowerPoint presentation. In either case, it should include the following information:

- The goal or need addressed by the program (like a goal to increase sales by 10 percent)
  - The mutually agreed-upon planned impact (the Phillips approach) or expectations (the Kirkpatrick approach) from the goal owner (like the head of sales) and L&D
- The plan to achieve the impact or meet expectations. This might include:
  - Description and size of the target audience
  - Brief description of the training solution
  - Planned completion date
  - Planned completion rate
  - Plans for the goal owner to communicate the importance of the learning program, expectations for it, and reinforcement plans
  - Planned cost
- Results of the implementation
  - Key efficiency measures such as:
    » Number of participants versus plan
    » Actual completion date versus plan
    » Completion rate versus plan
    » Cost versus plan
    » Key communication and reinforcement initiatives
  - Key effectiveness measures such as:
    » Participant reaction
    » Learning
    » Application rates
    » Manager support
- Results for the business outcome measure (like a 9 percent increase in sales)
  - The isolated contribution of learning on the business goal (the Phillips approach, like 3 percent higher sales due to learning) or a discussion of whether the goal owner expectations were met (Kirkpatrick approach)
- The ROI on the program (if the Phillips approach is used)
- Lessons learned.

Figure 8-5 shows a three-slide presentation for a sales training initiative. The number of slides or length of the written summary will of course depend on the audience and the purpose of the briefing. Use what is common in your environment. Figure 8-5 might be appropriate for a 15-minute high-level briefing to the CEO or for sharing in an all-employee meeting for the L&D department. A more detailed summary would be appropriate for briefing the head of sales or for an after-action review by L&D. The basic elements remain the same, however.

Figure 8-5. Three-Slide PowerPoint Program Evaluation Report

2019 Sales Training Initiative	
• Goal: 　○ Help achieve the company goal of 10 percent higher sales • Solution: 　○ Consultative selling skills 　○ Product features training 　○ Coaching 　○ Supervisor reinforcement 　○ Enhanced incentives for reps and supervisors • Sales and learning department agreed these two programs would contribute to 3% higher sales • Target audience: 　○ all 73 sales representatives	• Approach: 　○ Consultative selling skills program leveraged best practices of most successful sales representatives 　○ Vice president of sales clearly articulated expectations to all sales representatives • Timeline: 　○ Jan. 1 - Feb. 28: 80 hours of training per rep 　○ Mar. 1 - June 30: Individual coaching and reinforcement by sales supervisors 　○ Monthly meetings between reps and supervisors to review progress

Summary and Opportunities for Additional Research	
• Training completed on time and at budgeted cost of $325,000 • Response: 　○ Training was well received, and application rate was high 　○ 90 percent agree that the training was a worthwhile investment and would recommend it to others 　○ 84 percent had applied key concepts and 100 percent had demonstrated capabilities in articulating the product features after 90 days	• Sample feedback: 　○ "One of the best programs I have ever attended. The content was clear, powerful, and relevant. Instructors were great and I really appreciated the coaching afterward. The program enabled me to increase my sales by at least 20%." 　○ "I strongly recommend this program to anyone who wants to dramatically improve their performance." • With the help of this program, sales increased 11% for the year, exceeding the plan of 10%

Results	
• The sales and learning department believe this initiative, including the effort by the sales supervisors to reinforce the learning and hold their reps accountable, contributed at least **3% higher sales** • This increase in sales resulted in an additional **$585,000 in gross profit** • This program contributed **$260,000 to net profit*** • The **ROI** was conservatively estimated at **80%**	• Lessons learned: 　○ Executive sponsorship and supervisor reinforcement is critical 　○ Further gains from the learning are possible in 2020 　○ Participant feedback provided numerous ideas for improvement 　　　*After subtracting the costs associated with the training.*

Custom Analysis Report

Custom analysis reports are used to share the results of one-off analysis projects like a special analysis exploring the relationship between the number (or type) of courses used and employee engagement (or retention).

Like program evaluation reports, these may be written documents or PowerPoint presentations and will vary in length and detail depending on the topic, audience, and purpose of the briefing. The elements for a custom analysis report for a one-off analysis might include:

- The research question to be answered (for example, is there a relationship between amount or type of learning and employee engagement and retention?)
- Brief description of the analysis:
  - Methodology
  - Data
  - Problems encountered and steps taken to address issues
- Results
- Opportunities for additional research.

Figure 8-6 shows a PowerPoint custom analysis report.

Figure 8-6. Sample PowerPoint Custom Analysis Report

Analysis of the Relationship Between Learning and Employee Engagement and Retention		Data and Methodology	
Hypotheses: • More learning will lead to higher rates of employee engagement and retention • Self-directed learning will have the strongest relationship with engagement and retention, followed by program-related learning • Compliance training will have no relationship	**Background:** • Other organizations are beginning to report finding these relationships • The literature on employee engagement and retention supports the hypothesis for self-directed learning	Data pulled from the corporate HRIS and LMS for last year by employee on: • Engagement • Retention (here on Dec 31?) • Number of courses and hours used • Type of course • Number of documents accessed on the portal • Demographic data	**Methodology:** • Cross-sectional analysis using correlation and regression • Analysis for the enterprise as well as key demographics, such as business unit, region, age, years of experience, gender, salary grade, and performance rating • Control for leader trust

Results		Summary and Opportunities for Additional Research	
Statistically significant and positive relationship found between: • Self-directed learning and engagement • Program-related learning and employee engagement Relationship strongest for: • Young employees • New employees based in North America	No relationship found between: • Compliance training and engagement • Self-directed learning and retention • Program-related learning and retention Other findings: • Gender did not appear to influence the results • Stronger relationship at lower salary grade	**Summary:** • The hypothesis was confirmed for the relationship between learning and engagement for self-directed and program-related learning • Employees find these two types of learning to be of high value • As expected, compliance training does not lead to higher engagement • A year may be too short of a period to test the impact on retention	Opportunities for further research: • Expand the time period to test for impact on retention Actions for next year's business plan: • Increase spending on discretionary learning • Increase marketing of discretionary learning

You could also generate a custom analysis report to share the results of department initiatives to improve efficiency and effectiveness across all programs. This type of custom report might address:

- The need (like a desire to improve level application across all programs)
- The planned actions
  - Specific actions or tasks
  - Task owners
  - Completion deadlines
  - Resources required
- The results
- Lessons learned
- Recommendations for next year if the goal is not realized.

Reporting to Manage

The highest-level reason for measuring is to manage, which means delivering planned results. This effort requires the results from evaluation and analysis as well as data that otherwise may have simply been used to inform. As we have mentioned before, you can use the same measure for all four purposes. However, when you select a measure to manage (versus inform or monitor), you will share and report it quite differently. Management requires a separate set of reports to support the concept of running L&D like a business; we will introduce them in this chapter but provide more detail in chapter 9.

A management report is appropriate when the purpose is to improve the value of a measure or attain a certain value. This purpose stands in contrast to monitoring where the purpose was to ensure that a measure remained within an acceptable range. Management implies that leaders are not satisfied with historical results and are willing to dedicate resources to "move the needle" or make improvements. Accordingly, managers will implement programs to achieve the planned results, and a program manager will be accountable for achieving them. Again, this is in contrast to monitoring, where leaders did not develop any specific programs to improve the measure. Instead, leaders expected the measure would remain within an historically acceptable range. If leaders wish to improve a measure, they will have to expend the effort to manage the program and consequently will require management reports.

Management reports are specifically designed to meet the needs of leaders, and thus the format for management reports for L&D will be like reports for sales, manufacturing, and other organizational functions since all leaders have similar needs. A management report should contain:

- Last year's actual results, if available
- Plan or target for this year
- Year-to-date (YTD) results
- Comparison of YTD results with plan
- Forecast for the year-end value of the measure
- Comparison of forecast to plan.

The last two items involving forecast may not be present and sometimes there is no historical data, but for a management report, you must include the plan and YTD results.

A management report organizes the data by type of measure, and often by program or initiative as well. The simple report shown in Table 8-10 is organized just by type of measure—the name of the measure is on the left followed by the unit of measure, 2020 Actual, 2021 Plan, 2021 YTD Results, YTD Results Compared to Plan, 2021 Forecast, and Forecast Compared to Plan. To use a management report, start by looking at last year's actual results and the plan for this year. These two columns will tell a story, namely, what the CLO or program manager wants to accomplish in the new year. In this case, the plan is to increase the number of unique participants to 600 and dramatically increase the total number of participants to 1,800, implying each unique participant will take an average of three courses (1,800 ÷ 600 = 3). Leaders are very unhappy with last year's 49 percent on-time completion rate and have targeted 80 percent for this year. The department is planning to spend an additional $55,000 this year to make all the planned improvements and to reach more participants.

Table 8-10. Sample Management Report

Results Through June						2021		
	Unit of Measure	2020 Actual	Plan	YTD Results	YTD Results Compared to Plan	Forecast	Forecast Compared to Plan
Efficiency Measures							
Number of unique participants	Number	541	600	524	87%	600	100%
Number of total participants	Number	1,234	1,800	1,456	81%	1,700	94%
On-time completions	%	49%	80%	71%	9% below	75%	5% below
Direct expenditure	Dollars, thousands	$345	$400	$195	49%	$400	100%
Effectiveness Measures							
Participant reaction	% favorable	72%	80%	75%	5% below	80%	On plan
Goal owner reaction	5-point scale	3.5	4.0	3.8	0.2 below	4.0	On plan
Learning	% passed	87%	95%	93%	2% below	95%	On plan
Intent to apply	% who intend to apply	76%	85%	84%	1% below	85%	On plan
Actual application	% who did apply	51%	70%	55%	15% below	60%	10% below
Outcome Measures							
Impact of learning on sales	% increase in sales	1%	3%	1.6%	1.4% below	2.5%	0.5% below
Impact of learning on injuries	% decrease in injuries	5%	10%	8%	2% below	12%	2% above
Impact of learning on leadership	Point increase in leadership score	1 pt	2 pts	1 pt	1 pt below	2 pts	On plan

In similar fashion, the plan for effectiveness measures calls for improvement across the board as well as a first-time score for goal owner satisfaction of 4.0. The CLO wants an 8 percentage point increase in participant reaction, an 8 percentage point increase in pass rates, a 9 percentage point increase in intent to apply (measured in the post-event survey), and a whopping 19 percentage point increase in actual application (measured in the follow-up survey).

The department supports three key outcomes in 2021 and has worked with the goal owners to establish mutually agreeable plans for the impact of learning. In 2021, the learning plan is to increase sales by 3 percent, decrease injuries by 10 percent, and improve the leadership score on the employee engagement survey by two points.

That is the plan. Now, leaders need to know how they are doing. More specifically, how are they doing year-to-date, and are they likely to make plan for the year based on all that is known so far? The June YTD Results and YTD Compared to Plan columns help answer the first question, while the Forecast and Forecast Compared to Plan columns help answer the second question.

In Table 8-10, the YTD results indicate that good progress is being made toward plan for most measures except actual application, which has improved only slightly in six months, to 55 percent. Apparently, this is turning out to be more difficult than anticipated. Intent to apply is nearly at plan, so the focus for further analysis must be on what happens when employees go back to their workplace. They may not be receiving the support, tools, time, or resources they need to apply what they learned. In addition, total number of participants, percent on-time completion, and sales are behind plan YTD and not expected to make plan.

The forecast column answers the ultimate question about whether the organization will achieve its plan. The forecast is simply how the year is likely to end for a measure if leaders take no special action. In other words, if the original plan to improve the measure is executed in the remaining months of the year, and given what is now known about achieving the plan, how will the year likely end? In our sample report, all measures are forecast to end the year on or near plan except for total participants (6 percent below plan), percentage on-time completion (5 percent below plan), participant reaction (2 percent below plan), and actual application (10 percent below plan). Armed with this report, leaders can focus their efforts on better understanding why these measures are not forecast to make plan and the special actions that could be undertaken to get back on plan. This is the essence of active management and running learning like a business, which will be explored further in the next chapter.

Conclusion

In this chapter we examined the five most common types of reports to share measures. Even more importantly, we identified the most appropriate type of report to use based on the reasons for measuring. Our hope is that the framework and terminology for reporting we introduced will become standardized and provide a common language for the profession since none exists today for this important topic. We would also note that while L&D has made great progress in creating ever better dashboards, much less progress has been made in creating and using management reports, which represents one of the greatest opportunities for the profession going forward.

With this overview of reporting, we are now ready to explore the three TDRp reports for management in the next chapter.

CHAPTER 9
The Three Management Reports

In this chapter we explore the three TDRp management reports—the program report, the operations report, and the summary report—which we introduced in chapter 1. These reports are specifically designed to enable L&D leaders to run learning like a business, so it will be helpful to begin by briefly describing what we mean by that.

Running Learning Like a Business

A foundational belief underlying TDRp is that learning, and all HR functions, should be run like a business. By this we mean that HR and L&D leaders should manage their functions with business-like discipline. In its simplest form this requires that leaders set a plan at the start of the year with specific, measurable goals, and then execute the plan with discipline throughout the year to come as close as possible to delivering the planned results. This is exactly the same discipline that our colleagues use in other departments such as sales and manufacturing. This approach creates accountability for creating a good plan and executing it, both of which are necessary if L&D is to earn and keep a seat at the table.

We also assume that the appropriate performance consulting and needs analysis are done at the beginning of each engagement and both formal and informal learning solutions are considered. The expectation is that many learning programs will contain a blend of both formal and informal learning, so the resulting recommendations may include ILT, vILT, e-learning, mobile, content on the employee's portal, communities of practice, and performance support.

We examine this approach for strategic programs (aligned directly to organizational goals to deliver agreed-upon outcomes), non-strategic programs (important programs but not usually aligned directly to a top goal), and department initiatives (designed to improve the efficiency and effectiveness of all programs or department processes) as shown in Table 9-1. For each, we discuss creating the plan first, followed by its disciplined execution, including the recommended management report.

Table 9-1. Recommended Reports

Type of Program	Type of Report
Strategic programs	Program report
Non-strategic programs	Program report
Department initiatives	Operations report

Strategic Programs

We define strategic programs as learning programs that directly align to the top goals of the CEO and head of HR. These programs will address the most important priorities of the organization included in its business plan. Examples of these high-level goals typically involve revenue, quality, efficiency, leadership, engagement, and retention.

The Plan

Running learning like a business starts with creating a good business plan for the year. The plan should support the vision and mission statements for both the department and the organization. Further, since L&D is a support function, the plan needs to align with the organizational goals for the coming year. Some L&D departments have the opportunity to be more strategic than others, but every department should look for opportunities to directly support the organization's goals for the coming year as well as future years.

The first step is for the CLO to meet with the CEO well before the new year begins to discover three things:

- the organization's goals for the new year
- the goal owner for each goal
- the CEO's priorities for the goals.

Following this discussion, the CLO should have a prioritized list of goals and goal owners. Next, the CLO needs to talk with the head of HR to learn about the HR goals for next year and their priorities. (In many organizations, the L&D function dedicates considerable effort onboarding employees, or providing basic skills training to new employees, advanced skills training to experienced employees, and compliance training to all employees. These important activities should also be captured and will be discussed in the next section on non-strategic programs.) An example of the results from the first step for an L&D department focused just on business and HR goals is shown in Table 9-2.

Table 9-2. Top Organizational Goals for the Next Fiscal Year

Priority	Business Goals	Goal Owner
1	Increase sales by 10%	SVP of Sales: Kronenburg
2	Reduce injuries by 20%	SVP of Manufacturing: Swilthe
3	Reduce operating costs by 5%	COO: Goh

Priority	HR Goals	Goal Owner
1	Increase employee engagement by 3 points	SVP HR: Wang
2	Decrease regrettable turnover by 5 points	SVP HR: Wang
3	Implement new performance mgt system	SVP HR: Wang

The second step is to meet with each goal owner to determine if L&D has a role to play in achieving the goal or meeting the need. Sometimes it will, other times it will not. If it appears that learning programs may help achieve the goal, the L&D team can pursue it further with the goal owner's staff.

The third step, assuming learning has a role to play, is for the CLO to meet again with the goal owner and share the recommendations of L&D and the goal owner's staff. Several meetings may be required before all parties are comfortable with the agreed-upon learning initiatives.

The fourth step is to reach agreement on all the specifics (such as target audience, timing, learning objectives, and modality), roles and responsibilities of both parties, an outcome measure (or other measure of success), and a plan or target for all key efficiency and effectiveness measures required to achieve the outcome. This step is critical to running learning like a business because this is where the learning function and the business agree on specific, measurable goals. L&D cannot set these without input from others since the goal owner and supervisors in the goal owner's organization will play a significant role in communicating the reasons for the training, selecting the right audience, ensuring the audience takes the program, and most importantly, reinforcing the learning after the participants return to their jobs. In other words, a strategic learning program (one aligned directly to a goal of the organization) will only succeed if both parties plan and execute it.

Table 9-3 on the next page illustrates a well-conceived learning plan to help achieve the sales goal of the organization. At the top is the organizational goal or outcome (increase sales by 10 percent) and the name of the goal owner. (Since we are running learning like a business, the plan is business-centric, meaning business measures come before learning measures.) Immediately below the organizational goal is the learning outcome measure, which is "impact of learning on sales." This is the Phillips Level 4 isolated impact of training, which the goal owner and L&D program manager have agreed upon. In this case, both are comfortable with a plan for the learning to contribute 2 percent higher sales, assuming the content is properly designed, developed, communicated, delivered, and reinforced.

Notice that the learning plan contains informal learning (community of practice and content available on the employee portal) as well as formal.

Below the outcome measures are the key learning programs and their associated efficiency and effectiveness measures, which L&D and the goal owner will manage monthly to deliver the planned result of 2 percent higher sales. The first program is new product features training, which L&D will develop and deliver. The second program is consultative selling skills, which L&D must also develop and deliver. Key efficiency measures for both programs are the completion dates for development and delivery, unique and total participants, and completion rates. L&D will also capture cost for both programs combined. Key effectiveness measures for both programs are Levels 1–3. Note that the Level 4 isolated impact (2 percent higher sales due to learning) already appears as the outcome measure for the impact of both programs together at the top of the report. Likewise, Level 5 net benefit and ROI measures are at the bottom showing the impact of both programs combined.

A roles and responsibilities document should complete the plan. We have provided an example in appendix B.

Table 9-3. Learning Plan for Achieving an Organizational Goal for Sales

Goal Owner: Kronenburg, SVP of Sales	Unit of Measure	2020 Actual	2021 Plan
Enterprise Goal: Increase sales	%	8%	10%
Impact of Learning on Sales: 20% contribution to goal	%	N/A	2%
Programs to Increase Sales			
Product Features Training			
Efficiency measures			
Unique participants	Number	55	100
Total participants	Number	81	200
Develop two courses by January 31	% complete	N/A	100%
Deliver both by February 28	% complete	N/A	100%
Completion rate	%	95%	100%
Community of practice usage	Number of unique users	34	100
Effectiveness measures			
Level 1 participant reaction to formal learning	% favorable	70%	80%
Level 1 participant reaction to informal learning	% favorable	45%	80%
Level 2 learning	% first-time pass rate	86%	90%
Level 3 intent to apply	% of content	53%	95%
Level 3 actual application	% of content	39%	90%
Consultative Selling Skills Training			
Efficiency measures			
Unique participants	Number	N/A	100
Total participants	Number	N/A	300
Develop three courses by February 28	% complete	N/A	100%
Deliver all three courses by April 30	% complete	N/A	100%
Completion rate	%	N/A	100%
Selling skills content accessed by participants	Number of total documents	N/A	400
Content usage by participants	Number of unique users	N/A	100
Effectiveness measures			
Level 1 participant reaction to formal learning	% favorable	N/A	80%
Level 1 participant reaction to informal learning	% favorable	N/A	80%
Level 2 learning	% first-time pass rate	N/A	90%
Level 3 intent to apply	% of content	N/A	90%
Level 3 actual application	% of content	N/A	80%
Total			
Efficiency measures			
Unique participants	Number	55	100
Total participants	Number	81	500
Total cost	Dollars, thousands	$41	$76
Effectiveness measures			
Level 5 net benefit	Dollars, thousands	$14	$44
Level 5 ROI	%	34%	58%

Ideally, L&D should work with the goal owner to complete the plan and have the business approve it before the design and development begin. For programs that need to start early in the year, the plan should be completed and approved before the new year begins.

> **Note**
>
> The larger the agreed-upon impact from learning, the earlier in the year L&D must deploy the programs to have sufficient time in the fiscal year to deliver results. A program deployed in the fourth quarter of the fiscal year cannot have much impact in that year. Also, the larger the agreed-upon impact from learning, the greater the effort must be from both L&D and the goal owner's organization, especially the supervisors.

Disciplined Execution

The second part of running learning like a business is disciplined execution of the plan, and this is where management reporting comes in. Disciplined execution requires the active, ongoing management of learning to deliver planned results. No matter how good the plan is, it will not implement itself. Furthermore, there will usually be unforeseen challenges and problems that L&D and the business must address to deliver the planned results. The only way to successfully execute a program is to continually manage it by comparing YTD results to plan and forecasting how the year is likely to end without any additional, unplanned effort.

Once the year is underway, there are only two questions a leader should be asking:

- Are we on plan year to date?
- Are we going to make plan for the year?

The leader should ask both questions for each measure. Start with the outcome measure if reliable YTD information is available. Typically, it will be available for an organizational outcome measure like sales but not always for the learning outcome measure. In this case, proceed directly to the efficiency and effectiveness measures. By employing a chain of evidence approach, if all these measures are on plan, we may be more confident that the outcome measure must be as well. Typically, some measures will be on plan, some will be exceeding plan, and some will be behind plan. Management attention should first focus on any measures that are behind plan.

It is possible, however, to be on plan YTD but still miss plan by year-end. Conversely, sometimes the programs take longer to launch than planned so measures are behind plan YTD; however, they are expected to still end the year on plan. This is why the forecast is so important. It represents the team's best thinking of how the measure is likely to end the year, which in turn will dictate whether leaders need to take corrective action now. We illustrate the possibilities in Table 9-4.

Table 9-4. Disciplined Action

YTD Results	Forecast	
	Below Plan	**On or Ahead of Plan**
Behind plan	Take action	No action required
On plan	Take action	No action required
Ahead of plan	Take action	No action required

There are three cases that warrant action, and all three are where the forecast indicates results will fall short of plan. The first step to take is typically an analysis to better understand the reason why the forecast is falling short of plan. Upon further examination, the leadership team may be comfortable waiting for further information or may change the forecast to be on plan. If leaders deem they need to act, the next step is to identify how to achieve plan for the year. The leadership team will have to evaluate the cost of implementing these steps and find the required additional resources, which may need to come from another program. This is the real work of active management: analyzing the issue, generating ideas to address it, identifying required resources, and reallocating resources from another program (if necessary) to get this program back on track, entailing trade-offs and opportunity costs.

As shown in Table 9-1, the measures for strategic programs are captured in the TDRp Program Report, which is explored in detail in the next section.

Non-Strategic Programs

Non-strategic programs are important, often enterprise-wide initiatives to address key organizational needs like onboarding, basic skills training, and compliance. Typically, neither the CEO nor head of HR will have a high-level goal for these. Nonetheless, they are very important to the organization's success, and the learning department is usually tasked with them. In addition, non-strategic programs encompass other courses or programs that may not have the same high-level of visibility, but nonetheless are important and need to be managed. Examples might include courses for business acumen, communication, and innovation. Of course, many other courses will be offered, but our focus here is on just those that L&D and the business need to actively manage (set plans for all critical measures and a monthly review of progress against plan).

The Plan

The plan to address these needs will be similar to that for the strategic goals. The CEO or head of HR may have raised the need for learning's support in the discussions about strategic goals. More often, learning has been responsible for these needs for years, so it is simply a matter of confirming next year's plans with the program owner, who may be the head of HR, the chief operating officer (COO), or some other high-level leader. For some programs, the CLO may be the owner. Table 9-5 lists some of these types of organizational needs.

Table 9-5. Important Organizational Needs

Item	Important Needs	Program Owner
A	Provide basic training for new employees	COO: Goh
B	Onboard new employees	SVP HR: Wang
C	Provide compliance training	COO: Goh
D	Diversity and inclusion	SVP: Wang
E	Business acumen	CFO: Davis
F	Communication	CLO: Parks
G	Innovation	Chief Engineer: D'Agoto

While the next step for strategic programs is for the CLO to meet with the goal owners to determine if L&D has a role to play, here we generally already know that it does and is expected to meet the need. (If this is not the case, then L&D should conduct a needs analysis and discuss with the owner the appropriate role of learning.) The next step is to discuss whether L&D should change the program and whether the business has emerging or new requirements (for example, new compliance training). Even if the business requires no changes to the program, L&D may need to make changes based on the size or location of the target audience or the manner in which learners want to consume the content.

After the program owner and L&D agree on the program for the coming year, L&D will need to establish plans for each key effectiveness and efficiency measure, just like for strategic programs. For most non-strategic programs, however, there will not be an outcome measure. L&D and the program owner may chose an effectiveness or efficiency measure as a headline measure of success to appear at the top of the report.

Table 9-6 is an example of a learning plan for onboarding.

Table 9-6. Learning Plan for Onboarding

Program Owner: Wang, SVP HR			
Enterprise Need: Provide onboarding for new employees			
Measures of Success	**Unit of Measure**	**2020 Actual**	**2021 Plan**
Number onboarded	Number	548	700
Leader satisfaction with onboarding	% favorable	67%	80%
Efficiency Measures			
Develop two courses by January 31	% complete, date	N/A	100%
Start using by February 28	% complete, date	N/A	100%
Hire five new instructors	Number	N/A	5
Portal onboarding content accessed by new employees	Number of documents	N/A	3,500
Portal general content accessed by new employees	Number of documents	N/A	1,400
Unique portal usage by new employees	Number of unique users	N/A	700
Provide facilitator training to new instructors in their first month	% complete	N/A	100%
Provide refresher training to select instructors	Number	7	12
Program duration	Days	61	50
Cost	Dollars, thousands	$657	$800
Effectiveness Measures			
Level 1 participant reaction to formal learning	% favorable	70%	80%
Level 1 participant reaction to informal learning	% favorable	N/A	80%
Level 1 program owner satisfaction	5-point scale	3.7	4.5
Level 2 learning	% first-time pass rate	86%	90%

There is no outcome measure shown in Table 9-6 because it is not showing a strategic program. The goal here is to deliver the training as efficiently and effectively as possible. However, we do show two measures of success: number onboarded and leader satisfaction with the onboarding (the leaders receiving the onboarded employees). Note that the first is an efficiency measure and the second is an effectiveness measure. The program owner and L&D have decided to highlight these measures as the "headline" measures of success. The plan includes informal learning (content on the employee portal) as well as formal learning.

Table 9-7 shows a second example to illustrate the flexibility in creating a good business plan. In this case, the need is to increase the business acumen of leaders and associates throughout the enterprise. CFO Davis (the program owner) and L&D have chosen not to highlight any measures of success, but they have crafted a plan showing detail by program, with the first program focused on business acumen for leaders and the second focused on associates. Notice that the program includes efficiency and effectiveness measures for informal learning (performance support).

Disciplined Execution

Leaders should execute the plan for non-strategic learning just like the plan for strategic learning. Once the year is underway, leaders need monthly reports to compare YTD progress against plan and to compare forecast against plan. Whenever the forecast indicates that plan may not be achieved, learning leaders need to analyze the root causes, identify potential solutions, cost them out, and decide what action, if any, to take. The only difference is that with non-strategic programs, leaders will not be managing an outcome measure.

Non-strategic programs should be managed through the TDRp program report, just as strategic programs are. While there won't be an outcome measure, an efficiency or effectiveness measure may be highlighted as a headline measure of success. Some organization leaders prefer to use owner satisfaction or leader satisfaction (both effectiveness measures) as measures of success in place of an outcome measure. If the program owner has a goal to reduce the duration of the program, duration may be used as a measure of success. For non-strategic programs it is possible to have multiple headline measures (like goal owner satisfaction and duration).

Department Initiatives

The purpose of department initiatives is to improve the efficiency and effectiveness of processes and systems (like informal learning, the LMS, or a help desk) or to improve efficiency and effectiveness measures across all programs (like the utilization rate of classrooms or e-learning, or Levels 1 and 3). While the management approach is different than that for strategic and non-strategic programs, department initiatives still require a plan and disciplined execution for success.

Table 9-7. Learning Plan to Increase Business Acumen

Programs to Increase Business Acumen	Unit of Measure	2020 Actual	2021 Plan
Business Acumen for Leaders			
Efficiency Measures			
Unique participants	Number	N/A	100
Total participants	Number	81	200
Develop two courses by March 31	% complete, date	N/A	100%
Deliver first by April 30	% complete, date	N/A	100%
Deliver second by May 31	% complete, date	N/A	100%
Completion rate for both courses	%	N/A	100%
Usage of performance support tools	Number of tools	N/A	10
Users of performance support tools	Number of unique users	N/A	100
Effectiveness Measures			
Level 1 participant reaction to formal learning	% favorable	N/A	80%
Level 1 participant reaction to informal learning	% favorable	N/A	80%
Level 2 learning	% first-time pass rate	N/A	90%
Level 3 intent to apply	% of content applied	N/A	90%
Level 3 actual application	% of content applied	N/A	80%
Business Acumen for Associates			
Efficiency Measures			
Unique participants	Number	N/A	10,000
Develop one course by May 31	% complete, date	N/A	5/31
Deliver by September 30	% complete	N/A	100%
Completion rate	%	N/A	100%
Usage of performance support tools	Number of tools	N/A	5
Users of performance support tools	Number of unique users	N/A	5,000
Effectiveness Measures			
Level 1 participant reaction to formal learning	% favorable	N/A	80%
Level 1 participant reaction to informal learning	% favorable	N/A	80%
Level 2 learning	% first-time pass rate	N/A	90%
Level 3 intent to apply	% of content applied	N/A	70%
Total			
Efficiency Measures			
Unique participants	Number	N/A	10,100
Total cost	Dollars, thousands	N/A	$300
Effectiveness Measures			
Level 5 net benefit	Dollars, thousands	N/A	$200
Level 5 ROI	%	N/A	67%

The Plan

At the department level, the CLO and leadership team will decide what efficiency or effectiveness improvements to make in processes or systems, or in all programs. These will be tactical rather than strategic decisions and are usually left up to the CLO. In other words, unlike the plan for strategic programs, the CLO does not need to start by asking the CEO for input, and the initiatives will not be aligned to organizational goals unless the CEO has a goal for increasing productivity. And, unlike strategic programs, there will be no outcome measures and no need to talk with goal owners. The focus here is on improvements internal to the L&D department or to aggregate efficiency and effectiveness measures.

To begin the planning process, the CLO simply needs to articulate what is targeted for improvement, perhaps after getting feedback from staff. If there are too many suggestions, the CLO will need to prioritize them.

The next step is to flesh out the initiatives so learning leadership has a clear picture of what they can accomplish, at what cost, and with what potential impact. This usually leads to some reprioritizing and eventually a short list of initiatives to include in the department plan for the coming year. A director, program manager, or staff person will be assigned responsibility to lead or at least coordinate the effort. Each department initiative should have specific, measurable goals to improve the primary measure and all important complementary and ancillary measures. (See chapter 7 for a discussion of primary, complementary, and ancillary measures.)

Table 9-8 shows a sample plan for department process and system improvement initiatives. This plan reflects the CLO's desire to dramatically increase the use of three types of informal learning: communities of practice, portal content, and performance support. The CLO also wants much better performance metrics for the help desk and plans to provide additional training to four help desk employees. To improve the LMS, the IT function plans an upgrade at mid-year, which will require additional training for staff. As a result of both initiatives, L&D expects a significant improvement in user satisfaction.

This plan is organized by initiative, but it could also be organized just by efficiency and effectiveness measures.

While Table 9-8 focused on specific process and system improvements, the CLO also might choose to implement initiatives to improve efficiency or effectiveness measures across all programs. Table 9-9 shows a sample plan for achieving or improving key efficiency and effectiveness measures for all programs.

In this example, L&D has targeted five efficiency measures and three effectiveness measures for improvement in 2021. The CLO wants to significantly increase both unique and total participants and also wants to dramatically improve the on-time completion rates for development and delivery. L&D plans a small increase in reach as well. For the effectiveness measures, L&D has planned significant improvements at all three levels.

Table 9-8. Sample Department Plan for Process and System Improvements

Informal Learning Initiatives	Unit of Measure	2020 Actual	2021 Plan
Communities of Practice			
Efficiency Measures			
Number of active communities	Number	29	50
Number of unique users	Number	312	750
Number of total users	Number	1,968	7,500
Effectiveness Measures			
User satisfaction	% favorable	67%	80%
Content on Portal			
Efficiency Measures			
Number of documents	Number	51	100
Number of unique users	Number	2,301	5,000
Number of total users	Number	3,590	7,500
Effectiveness Measures			
User satisfaction	% favorable	37%	60%
Performance Support			
Efficiency Measures			
Number of tools	Number	N/A	20
Number of unique users	Number	N/A	5,000
Number of total users	Number	N/A	10,000
Effectiveness Measures			
User satisfaction	% favorable	45%	70%
Help Desk Initiatives			
Efficiency Measures			
Number of associates trained	Number	1	4
Completion date for training	Date	N/A	3/31
Hold time	Minutes	2.5	0.5
Dropped calls	Number	564	100
Effectiveness Measures			
User satisfaction	% favorable	47%	80%
Quality metric (accuracy)	5-point scale	4.1	4.5
LMS Initiatives			
Efficiency Measures			
Number of associates trained	Number	N/A	20
Go live date	Date	N/A	8/1
Completion date for training	Date	N/A	7/31
Effectiveness Measures			
User satisfaction	% favorable	62%	70%
Staff satisfaction	% favorable	75%	90%

Table 9-9. Sample Department Plan to Improve Efficiency and Effectiveness Measures for All Programs

	Unit of Measure	2020 Actual	2021 Plan
Efficiency Measures			
Total participants	Number	7,689	9,000
Total unique participants	Number	24,567	36,000
Percentage of courses meeting deadline for development	%	68%	90%
Percentage of courses meeting deadline for delivery	%	59%	90%
Reach (percent of employees reached by L&D)	%	85%	88%
Effectiveness Measures			
Level 1 participant reaction (all programs)			
Quality of content	% favorable	76%	80%
Quality of instructor	% favorable	80%	85%
Relevance	% favorable	72%	78%
Recommend to others	% favorable	68%	75%
Total for Level 1	Average of measures	74%	80%
Level 2 learning (select programs)	Score	78%	85%
Level 3 application rate (select programs)			
Intent to apply (from post-event survey at the end of the course)	% content applied	70%	75%
Actual application (from the follow-up survey after three months)	% content applied	51%	65%

Disciplined Execution

As with strategic programs, the success for department initiatives depends on disciplined execution as well as a good plan. The philosophy for disciplined execution is the same and requires reporting both YTD results and forecast so the initiatives can be managed to success. The CLO and department leaders each month must answer the same two questions:

- Are we on plan?
- Are we going to end the year on plan?

Inevitably, some, if not most, of the initiatives will show measures falling short of plan throughout the year. Leadership will then have to employ the same steps to decide whether to act:

1. Analyze the issue to determine the cause.
2. Identify possible solutions.
3. Identify the resources required to implement solutions.
4. Decide on action steps and re-allocate resources as needed.
5. Implement actions.

Measures to improve the efficiency and effectiveness through learning department initiatives are captured in the TDRp Operations Report, which is explored in detail in the next section.

The TDRp Management Reporting Framework

With this background on running learning like a business, we are now ready to examine the TDRp management reporting framework in greater detail. The three TDRp reports were specifically designed to provide leaders with the measures and information they need to execute with discipline. Each report includes the measures at the appropriate level of aggregation and the following information about each measure:

- unit of measure
- last year's results (if available)
- plan for this year
- YTD results for this year
- comparison of YTD results to plan
- forecast for this year (optional but strongly recommended)
- comparison of forecast to plan.

Some practitioners may wish to add YTD plan and a comparison to YTD results to make it easier to determine if a measure is on plan. Management reports sometimes also include results for the most current month and plan for the month. (All four of these require seasonal adjustments to the data, which is covered in chapter 11.)

While all three reports are designed for the purpose of management, each has a different use and audience as well as other characteristics. Table 9-10 presents an overview of the TDRp management reports.

Table 9-10. Comparison of the Three TDRp Management Reports

Report	User	Purpose	Frequency	Types of Measures
Program	• Program manager • CLO • Goal or program owner	Manage programs to meet organizational goals and needs	Monthly	• Outcome for strategic programs • Efficiency • Effectiveness
Operations	• CLO • Initiative leaders	Manage department initiatives to improve efficiency and effectiveness	Monthly	• Efficiency • Effectiveness
Summary	• CEO, CFO, SVP HR, CLO • Governing body • L&D employees • Other interested parties	Manage expectations of senior leaders and demonstrate alignment and impact	Quarterly	• Outcome • Efficiency • Effectiveness

The program report is designed to help the program manager and CLO manage the programs in support of a particular organizational goal or need. For example, if learning can support the goal to increase sales, there should be a program report to manage that effort. The operations report is designed to help the CLO and senior L&D leaders as well as designated leads manage improvement initiatives. The operations report will include only those measures to be managed—not monitored or used to inform. Last, the summary report is intended to share high-level, aggregate data for key measures with senior organization leaders as well as employees. It also shows the strategic alignment of programs to organization goals.

With this background, we revisit the TDRp management reporting framework first shared in chapter 1 (Figure 9-1).

Figure 9-1. TDRp Management Reporting Framework

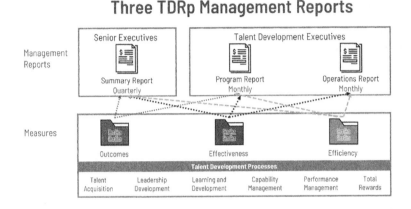

The summary report is at the top left with all three types of measures feeding it. It will be at an enterprise level with aggregated data and no learning jargon. The program and operations reports are to the right with a narrower audience. All three types of measures feed the program report, but the operations report contains only efficiency and effectiveness measures.

We are now ready to examine each TDRp management report in detail, beginning with the program report.

Program Reports

Program reports apply to both strategic and non-strategic programs. The template is the same except that most non-strategic programs will not have an outcome measure. We start with the strategic program report and then move to the non-strategic report.

- Strategic program report:
  - Simple strategic program report
  - Complex strategic program report
  - Creating the strategic program report
- Non-strategic program report:
  - Simple non-strategic program report
  - Creating the non-strategic program report

Strategic Program Report

The program report is a natural place to start since nearly every L&D department has at least one organizational goal it can support or one important need to address through training. The program report brings together all the data for the key programs and key measures in support of one goal. A department should have one program report for each organizational goal supported by learning. L&D should generate reports monthly and provide them to the program managers, their teams, the CLO, the goal owners, and the goal owner's staff to manage the programs.

A program report should include the organizational goal supported by learning, the goal owner's name, and the outcome measure for learning—all at the top of the report. The programs to achieve the learning outcome are shown next. Each program will typically have at least one efficiency measure and one effectiveness measure. Usually, there will be several of each and the most common for strategic programs include:

- Efficiency measures
  - Unique participants
  - Total participants
  - Completion date
  - Completion rate
  - Cost
- Effectiveness measures
  - Participant reaction (Level 1)
  - Goal owner reaction (Level 1)
  - Learning (Level 2)
  - Intent to apply (Level 3)
  - Actual application (Level 3)
  - Net benefit and ROI (Level 5).

Note

Level 4, impact, is the outcome measure for learning. It appears at the top of the report and is almost always reported for all the programs combined in support of the goal rather than for each program.

The program report needs to include all the key measures that must be actively managed to deliver the learning outcome, which is why the list of measures is so important. It is hard to imagine how programs could be managed without these measures.

Simple Strategic Program Report

A simple program report is displayed in Table 9-11. Following the philosophy of running learning like a business, the organizational goal is front and center at the top of the report. In this case, the goal owner, Swilthe, and L&D have agreed that training should help reduce injuries. The organizational goal or outcome measure is to reduce injuries by 25 percent, a significant increase over the 8 percent reduction made last year. Both parties (Swilthe and L&D) have agreed that it would be reasonable to plan for a high impact from the learning, assuming it is properly designed, developed, communicated, delivered, and reinforced. High impact is a qualitative outcome measure, meaning the learning will be responsible for most of the 25 percent reduction in injuries. (Note in the report that "impact of learning on injuries" in row 3 is the learning outcome measure and that there is usually just one learning outcome measure per program report.)

Table 9-11. Example of a Simple Program Report

Results Through March							
					2021		
Goal Owner: Swilthe, VP of Manufacturing	**Unit of Measure**	**2020 Actual**	**Plan**	**YTD Results**	**YTD Results Compared to Plan**	**Forecast**	**Forecast Compared to Plan**
Enterprise Goal: Reduce injuries	%	8%	25%	10%	Below plan	22%	3% below
Impact of Learning on Injuries: High impact for 2021*	H/M/L	High	High		Below plan		Near plan
Develop Two Courses							
Efficiency Measure							
Development complete by January 31†	Number	N/A	2	2	100%	2	100%
Deliver Two Courses							
Efficiency Measures							
Unique participants‡	Number	452	3,000	2,800	93%	3,200	107%
Total participants	Number	858	6,000	5,542	92%	6,300	105%
Completion date, rate§	Date, rate	N/A	3/31	92%	Behind plan	4/22	22 days late
Effectiveness Measures							
Level 1 participant reaction△	% favorable	70%	80%	85%	5% above	82%	2% above
Level 2 learning#	% first-time pass rate	86%	90%	95%	5% above	92%	2% above
Level 3 intent to apply**	% of content applied	53%	95%	75%	20% below	90%	5% below
Actual application††	% of content applied	39%	90%	67%	23% below	85%	5% below
Deploy Performance Support							
Efficiency Measures							
Number of performance support tools	Number	N/A	20	18	90%	22	110%
Unique users	Number	N/A	3,000	2,756	92%	3,000	100%
Effectiveness Measures							
Level 1 participant reaction‡‡	% favorable	N/A	80%	73%	7% below	75%	5% below

* YTD and forecast contribution based on Level 1 and 3 results and ongoing discussions with sponsor
† Both completed on January 29
‡ Manufacturing leaders responsible for attendance
§ 100% completion planned on April 22
△ YTD sample size = 1,872
YTD sample size = 3,848
** YTD sample size = 2,567. Reinforcement plan in place
†† YTD sample size = 2,145. Reinforcement plan in place
‡‡ YTD sample size = 823

The programs to reduce injuries come next, along with their key efficiency and effectiveness measures. In this simple example, there are just two programs, with the first consisting of two courses. First, the two courses must be developed with a completion date (efficiency measure) of January 31. Second, the two courses must be delivered to 3,000 unique participants and 6,000 total participants (each unique participant will take two courses, so 3,000 × 2 = 6,000) by March 31. Furthermore, the two courses must be very effective to have a high impact on injuries. Specifically, 80 percent of participants should rate them favorably, 90 percent should pass the knowledge test on the first attempt, and most importantly, 95 percent should indicate they will apply it and 90 percent actually should apply it.

The effort also calls for performance support tools to be developed, deployed, and used. The plan is for 20 tools to be deployed, and all 3,000 unique employees are expected to use at least one tool. The plan calls for an 80 percent favorable rating.

These plans or targets for each measure represent the best thinking of both parties about what will be required for training to have high impact and significantly reduce injuries. If the training is not deployed to the entire target audience, if it is deployed later in the year, or if it is not applied at a very high rate, the learning will likely not have a high impact, and both parties as well as the CEO will be disappointed. Since this is a strategic program in support of one of the CEO's top goals, both parties will need to actively manage the program for success.

The program report contains the information they need to do just that. In this case, the learning outcome measure is not directly observable, so there is no YTD result for it. However, we can look at the key efficiency and effectiveness measures to get a sense for whether the outcome measure is on plan. The two courses were developed on time, and by March 31, 92 percent of the total participants had completed the courses, falling just short of the March 31 deadline. Participants have reacted very favorably to the courses, exceeding plan by five points. And they have had a higher than anticipated first-time pass rate at 95 percent, five points above plan. Use of performance support tools is also on plan. So far, so good. The bad news, however, is that intent to apply rate is only 75 percent (20 percentage points below plan), and the actual application rate is only 67 percent (23 percentage points below plan). Without higher applications rates, the training will not have its intended impact, and thus the YTD comparison to plan for the outcome measure is "below plan." Furthermore, since the training was planned to be the dominant driver of reduced injuries, the organization is behind plan YTD with only a 10 percent reduction.

These results are for March, and it would have been apparent earlier in the year that application was below plan. Consequently, both parties would have already implemented additional steps to reinforce the learning and address any other causes of low application. The all-important forecast column shows that both parties are cautiously optimistic that the training may still deliver a reduction in injuries near plan (a 22 percent reduction, which would be only 3 percentage points below plan). The application rates are forecast to improve considerably, to 90 percent for intent and 85 percent for actual application, both 5 percentage points below plan but a big improvement from March. Swilthe has also identified an additional 200 employees for the training (for a total of 3,200 unique participants), which will help make up for the slow start.

So, if it had been done in February or March, the program report would have alerted both parties that the completion rate was a little slow, and more importantly, that the application rate was way below plan and likely to result in the organizational goal not being achieved. The report shows sample size, so the leaders would have known when the application rate became statistically significant and management action was required. (The March sample sizes allow a very high level of confidence about all effectiveness measures. In other words, the actual application rate may not be exactly the 67 percent reported from the sample, but since the sample is 2,145 out of 2,800, the error margin around 67 percent would be very small and likely less than 1 percent.)

Complex Strategic Program Report

Program reports often need to be more complex to contain all the important programs and measures. The format is the same but typically there will be multiple programs and more activities that need to be managed. More complex program reports also benefit from a summary at the bottom, which provides totals of some key measures as well as those like cost, net benefit, and ROI, which are best presented in total rather than by program.

A more complex program report with three programs and more measures is shown in Table 9-12.

Table 9-12. Example of a More Complex Program Report

Results Through August					2021		
Goal Owner: Swilthe, VP of Manufacturing	**Unit of Measure**	**2020 Actual**	**Plan**	**YTD Results**	**YTD Results Compared to Plan**	**Forecast**	**Forecast Compared to Plan**
Enterprise Goal: Reduce injuries	%	12%	20%	13%	7% below	20%	On plan
Impact of Learning on Injuries: 70% contribution planned for 2021*	% reduction in injuries	N/A	14%	9%	5% below	14%	On plan
Program A (Deliver Existing Two Courses to Factory A)							
Efficiency Measure							
Unique participants†	Number	452	3,000	3,078	103%	3,200	107%
Total participants	Number	858	6,000	6,067	101%	6,300	105%
Completion rate (100% by March 31)‡	% complete, date	N/A	3/31	101%		105%	Above plan
Effectiveness Measures							
Level 1 participant reaction§	% favorable	70%	80%	85%	5% above	82%	2% above
Level 1 goal owner reaction	5-point scale	3.8	4.5	4.3	0.2 below	4.3	0.2 below
Level 2 learning△	% first-time pass rate	86%	90%	95%	5% above	92%	2% above
Level 3 intent to apply#	% content applied	53%	95%	87%	7% below	95%	On plan
Level 3 actual application**	% content applied	39%	90%	87%	3% below	90%	On plan
Program B (Design and Deliver Three New Courses to Factory B)							
Design New Courses							
Efficiency Measure: Complete by 3/31	Number	N/A	3	3	100%	3	100%
Effectiveness Measure: Goal owner reaction	5-point scale	4.0	4.5	4.5	On plan	4.5	On plan

Table 9-12. Example of a More Complex Program Report (cont.)

			2021				
	Unit of Measure	2020 Actual	Plan	YTD Results	YTD Results Compared to Plan	Forecast	Forecast Compared to Plan
Deliver New Courses							
Efficiency Measures							
Unique participants††	Number	N/A	1,000	1,023	102%	1,100	110%
Total participants	Number	N/A	3,000	2,940	98%	3,200	107%
Completion rate (100% by July 31)‡‡	% complete, date	N/A	7/31	98%	Below plan	9/30	100%
Effectiveness Measures							
Level 1 participant reaction§§	% favorable	N/A	80%	80%	On plan	82%	2% above
Level 1 goal owner reaction	5-point scale	3.8	4.5	4.1	0.4 below	4.3	0.2 below
Level 2 learning ΔΔ	% first-time pass rate	N/A	90%	92%	2% above	90%	On plan
Level 3 intent to apply##	% content applied	N/A	95%	91%	4% below	95%	On plan
Level 3 actual application***	% content applied	39%	90%	82%	8% below	87%	3% below
Program C (Deploy Performance Support to Both Factories)							
Efficiency Measures							
Number of performance support tools	Number	N/A	30	26	87%	33	110%
Unique users	Number	N/A	4,000	3,562	89%	4,000	100%
Effectiveness Measures							
Level 1 participant reaction	% favorable	N/A	80%	73%	7% below	75%	5% below
Summary							
Total							
Courses developed	Number	1	3	3	100%	3	100%
Unique participants	Number	452	4,000	4,101	103%	4,300	108%
Total participants	Number	858	9,000	9,007	100%	9,500	106%
Cost (including opportunity cost)	Dollars, thousands	$37	$250	$178	71%	$255	Near plan
Net benefit	Dollars, thousands	N/A	$150	$65	43%	$170	Above plan
ROI	%	N/A	60%	37%	on plan	67%	Above plan

*YTD and forecast impacts based on participant estimates
†Manufacturing leaders responsible for attendance
‡Completion rate at March 31 was 96% (100% achieved April 25)
§YTD sample size = 1,872
ΔYTD sample size = 3,848
#YTD sample size = 2,567 (Reinforcement plan in place)
**YTD sample size = 1,765 (Reinforcement plan in place)
††Manufacturing leaders responsible for attendance
‡‡Completion rate at August 30 was 98%
§§YTD sample size = 939
ΔΔYTD sample size = 1,001
##YTD sample size = 792 (Reinforcement plan in place)
***YTD sample size = 276 (Reinforcement plan in place)

In this example, the goal is to reduce injuries by 20 percent. Once again, Swilthe is the goal owner and both parties have agreed that learning will play a significant role in achieving the goal. This time, however, they agree on a quantitative outcome measure for learning; namely, that learning will contribute 70 percent to the reduction in injuries (Level 4 isolated impact), which translates to a 14 percent reduction in injuries due to learning alone (70% × 20% = 14%). Two formal learning programs are planned along with an informal learning program. The first is to deploy two existing courses to factory A. The second is to develop and deploy three different courses to factory B. Each program is designed to address the unique causes of injuries in the factories. Third, performance support tools will be developed and deployed in both factories to help reduce injuries.

Since Program A is already developed, there are no development measures. The efficiency measures for delivery focus on unique and total participants and completion date with a plan to be 100 percent complete by March 31. Effectiveness measures include participant and goal owner reaction, learning, and application. Program B has efficiency and effectiveness measures for both development and delivery. For development, the efficiency measure is the deadline of March 31 for all three courses and the effectiveness measure is goal owner reaction of 4.5 out of 5.0. For delivery, the plan calls for the same efficiency and effectiveness measures as Program A with similar plans for each except completion date, which for Program B is 100 percent by July 31. Program C to deploy performance support has two efficiency measures and one effectiveness measure. The efficiency measures focus on the number of performance support tools and the unique users.

The summary at the bottom captures the total number of courses developed as well as the total number of unique and total participants. The summary also shows the cost, net benefit, and ROI for both programs combined. Some program reports might also show one measure for goal owner satisfaction in the summary rather than for each program.

Unlike the case in the simple program report, the YTD results look good, except for application, which is slightly behind plan. The new courses were developed on time, participation rates are close to plan, and Levels 1 and 2 are near or better than plan. Given the YTD results for key efficiency and effectiveness measures, we would expect the outcome measure for learning to be close to plan. If no reliable data were available, we would probably characterize the YTD impact of learning as slightly below plan just due to the application rate. However, assume in this example, that reliable data do exist for learning outcome as a result of a question about impact being asked in the post-event and follow-up surveys. The confidence-adjusted isolated impact from participants so far is running at 73 percent, which multiplied by the observable 13 percent reduction in injuries yields a 9 percent YTD reduction in injuries due just to learning.

The forecast reflects that both Swilthe and L&D are confident the year will end on plan. Swilthe believes injuries will decline by 20 percent, and both parties agree that learning will contribute about 70 percent of the total or a 14 percent reduction in injuries due just to learning. They have based their forecast for outcomes on the YTD results for impact as well as the forecasts for all key program measures, which show being near plan. In this case, some actions were taken earlier in the year to address the application issue, but all other measures were on track without any special action. The summary shows that cost will be near plan, but net benefit will exceed plan, resulting in a slightly higher than plan ROI.

Creating the Strategic Program Report

Create the program report by working closely with the goal owner, as shown in Figure 9-2. The starting point, of course, is step 1, discuss with the goal owner (like the head of sales) whether learning has a role to play. If it appears that it does, then learning professionals can work with goal owner's staff to develop a recommendation for learning programs to help achieve the goal. At this point, you should share the recommendation with the goal owner for feedback and modification, and this may take several iterations before everyone is comfortable. In step 2, reach agreement on the measures to use. Step 3 focuses on reaching agreement on a plan (a number) for the learning outcome measure as well as the key effectiveness and efficiency measures required to achieve the planned outcome. For example, how many participants must complete the training, by when, and with what level of application, if learning is to have the planned impact?

Figure 9-2. Eight Steps to Create a Strategic Program Report

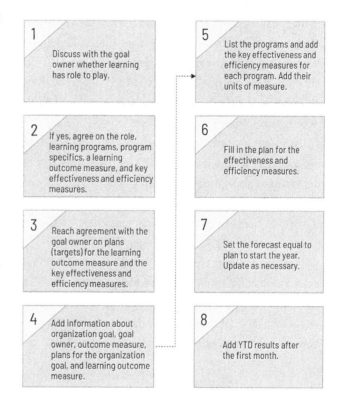

After you complete the first three steps, you can create the report. Start at the top and work your way down. In step 4, fill in the goal, the goal owner name, and the learning outcome measure (this is the impact of learning). Next, add last year's actuals if they are available and the plans for organizational goal (like a 10 percent increase in sales) and the learning outcome measure (like 2 percent higher sales due to learning).

With the top portion complete, in step 5, add the names of the programs and the effectiveness and efficiency measures associated with each, along with their units of measure. Next, in step 6, add the plan numbers for each effectiveness and efficiency measure.

If there is a summary section at the bottom, complete it. In step 7, for all rows in the report, set the forecast column to equal plan to start. So, at the start of the year, the report will show forecast being on plan. You can update the forecast for a measure whenever you have new information that leads you to believe the existing forecast is no longer the best guess about how the year is likely to end.

Once you have the first month's results, fill in the YTD column in step 8. Data on the organizational goal will come from a company system or from the goal owner. Data on the learning outcome measure will come from post-event or follow-up surveys if a question was asked about estimated impact. If not, learning professionals and the goal owner can make an educated guess about whether the programs are on track to deliver planned outcome by looking at the effectiveness and efficiency measures. If they are all on plan, the assumption may be made that the outcome measure is also on track.

Non-Strategic Program Report

The non-strategic program report is just like the strategic report except that the program will address an important need rather than a high-level goal; consequently, there typically will not be an outcome measure. Instead of "goal owner," the person with ultimate responsibility for the program's success is the "program owner." Generally, this will be a senior leader like the COO, head of manufacturing, or CFO, but in some cases may be the CLO. The program owner should not be the program director or manager within L&D.

Just like the strategic program report, the non-strategic program report is designed to bring together all the data for the key programs and key measures in support of the need. A department should have one program report for each organizational need supported by learning if the intent is to actively manage it. L&D would generate the reports monthly and provide them to program managers, their teams, the CLO, the program owners, and the program owner's staff to manage the programs.

A program report should include the organizational need supported by learning and the program owner's name—all at the top of the report. The programs to address the need are shown next. Each program will typically have several efficiency measures and several effectiveness measures. If there is only one program or course, the report may move immediately to the key effectiveness and efficiency measures. The most common include:

- Efficiency measures
  - Unique participants
  - Total participants
  - Completion date
  - Completion rate
  - Cost
- Effectiveness measures
  - Participant reaction (Level 1)
  - Goal owner reaction (Level 1)
  - Learning (Level 2)
  - Intent to apply (Level 3)
  - Actual application (Level 3).

The program report needs to include all the key measures, which leaders must actively manage to meet the need effectively and efficiently.

Simple Non-Strategic Program Reports

Next we show a simple non-strategic program report for onboarding (Table 9-13). In this example, the report highlights two headline measures of success: number successfully onboarded and an increase in the satisfaction of the business unit leaders with the onboarding. YTD results are available through June.

Table 9-13. Simple Non-Strategic Program Report for Onboarding

| Results Through June | | | | | 2021 | | |
Program Owner: Wang, SVP HR Enterprise Need: Provide onboarding for new employees	Unit of Measure	2020 Actual	Plan	YTD Results	YTD Results Compared to Plan	Forecast	Forecast Compared to Plan
Measures of Success							
Number onboarded	Number	548	700	321	46%	700	100%
Leader satisfaction with onboarding*	% favorable	67%	80%	75%	5% below	80%	On plan
Efficiency Measures							
Develop two courses by January 31†	% complete, date	N/A	100%	1/29	2 days early	100%	On plan
Start using by February 28‡	% complete, date	N/A	100%	2/18	10 days early	100%	On plan
Hire five new instructors§	Number	N/A	5	3	2 behind plan	5	On plan
Portal onboarding content accessed by new employees	Number of documents	N/A	3,500	2,154	62%	3,800	109%
Portal general content accessed by new employees	Number of documents	N/A	1,400	597	43%	1,400	100%
Unique portal usage by new employees	Number of unique users	N/A	700	700	100%	700	100%
Provide facilitator training to new instructors in their first month	% complete	N/A	100%	100%	On plan	100%	On plan
Provide refresher training to select instructors△	Number	7	12	12	100%	15	125%
Program duration#	Days	61	50	50	100%	50	On plan
Cost	Dollars, thousands	$657	$800	$393	49%	$800	On plan
Effectiveness Measures							
Level 1 participant reaction to formal learning**	% favorable	70%	80%	73%	7% below	75%	5% below
Level 1 participant reaction to informal learning††	% favorable	N/A	80%	81%	1% above	80%	On plan
Level 1 program owner satisfaction	5-point scale	3.7	4.5	4.2	0.3 below	4.5	On plan
Level 2 learning	% first-time pass rate	86%	90%	88%	2% below	90%	On plan

* YTD and forecast contribution based on Level 1 and 3 results and ongoing discussions with the sponsor
† First done January 26, second January 29
‡ Started using February 18
§ The last two are expected to be hired in July

△ Three additional instructors identified
Shorter duration achieved with first cohort
** YTD sample size = 254
†† YTD sample size = 560

In this example, the need is to onboard 700 employees, an increase over the previous year. Wang, SVP of HR, is the onboarding process owner. Wang and L&D have agreed to use the number onboarded (an efficiency measure) and the satisfaction of the leaders of the new employees (an effectiveness measure) as the "headline" measures of success.

Both parties agree that two new courses must be developed by January 31 and in use by February 28 to provide important new content. These will replace three older courses and help achieve the plan of reducing the program's duration by 11 days. Five new instructors will have to be hired and trained, and existing instructors will need to be updated. Furthermore, the plan calls for content on the portal to play an important role in onboarding and three efficiency measures have been identified to manage that. A cost target has also been agreed upon.

For effectiveness measures, both Wang and L&D believe it is possible to increase the participant reaction score by 10 points and to increase the first-time pass rate by four points. L&D hopes all these actions will lead to higher satisfaction on the part of the SVP of HR.

June YTD results show that 46 percent of planned participants have been onboarded and forecast shows everything is on plan to onboard all 700 by December 31. Receiving unit leaders are already much happier with the newly onboarded employees (75 percent favorable versus 67 percent last year), and forecast shows the year should end at 80 percent favorable, on plan. The two new courses were deployed ahead of plan, but L&D is having difficulty hiring new instructors. Nonetheless, the forecast shows that the remaining two are expected to be hired. New facilitator training and refresher training for existing facilitators is all on plan. The program has already met the 50-day target for duration, and cost is in line with plan.

The participant reaction measure indicates that this year's participants are slightly more satisfied than last year's (75 percent versus 70 percent) but greater improvement has been targeted and the forecast indicates the effort will fall short for the year by 5 points. This may be caused by larger than planned class size due to the delays in hiring staff or there may be other issues the program manager needs to investigate to see what can be done to get closer to plan in the second half. Level 2 has made good progress in the first six months and is on target to reach plan by year-end. Program owner Wang is happy with the progress made so far this year (4.2 versus 3.9 in December), and L&D is still hoping to get a 4.5 rating at year-end.

The example in Table 9-14 shows a business acumen course. Note that no headline measures of success are featured, but two courses are shown, each with their own effectiveness and efficiency measures. Since there are no headline measures, the need and program owner are centered. YTD results are available through April, which in this example means that results are not available (N/A) for numerous measures.

Table 9-14. Sample Non-strategic Program Report for Business Acumen

Enterprise Need: Increase Business Acumen for All Employees Program Owner: Davis, CFO Programs to Increase Business Acumen	Unit of Measure	2020 Actual	Plan	YTD Results	**2021** YTD Results Compared to Plan	Forecast	Forecast Compared to Plan
Business Acumen for Leaders							
Efficiency Measures							
Unique participants*	Number	N/A	100	85	85%	105	105%
Total participants	Number	81	200	85	43%	210	105%
Develop two courses by March 31	% complete, date	N/A	100%	3/24	7 days early	3/24	7 days early
Deliver first by April 30	% complete, date	N/A	100%	4/8	2 days early	4/8	2 days early
Deliver second by May 31	% complete, date	N/A	100%	80%	On plan	5/31	On plan
Completion rate for both courses	%	N/A	100%	0%	On plan	100%	On plan
Usage of performance support tools	Number of tools	N/A	10	6	60%	10	100%
Users of performance support tools	Number of unique users	N/A	100	43	43%	105	105%
Effectiveness Measures							
Level 1 participant reaction to formal learning†	% favorable	N/A	80%	84%	4% above	85%	5% above
Level 1 participant reaction to informal learning‡	% favorable	N/A	80%	87%	7% above	85%	5% above
Level 2 learning	% first-time pass rate	N/A	90%	85%	5% below	87%	3% below
Level 3 intent to apply§	% of content	N/A	90%	84%	6% below	87%	3% below
Level 3 actual application△	% of content	N/A	80%	N/A	N/A	75%	5% below
Business Acumen for Associates							
Efficiency Measures							
Unique participants#	Number	N/A	10,000	0	N/A	10,000	On plan
Develop one course by May 31	% complete, date	N/A	5/31	80%	On plan	5/31	On plan
Deliver by September 30	% complete	N/A	100%	N/A	N/A	9/30	On plan
Completion rate	%	N/A	100%	N/A	N/A	100%	On plan
Usage of performance support tools	Number of tools	N/A	5	2	40%	5	100%
Users of performance support tools	Number of unique users	N/A	5,000	569	11%	5000	100%
Effectiveness Measures							
Level 1 participant reaction to formal learning	% favorable	N/A	80%	N/A	N/A	80%	On plan
Level 1 participant reaction to informal learning	% favorable	N/A	80%	N/A	N/A	80%	On plan
Level 2 learning	% first-time pass rate	N/A	90%	N/A	N/A	90%	On plan
Level 3 intent to apply	% of content	N/A	70%	N/A	N/A	70%	On plan

Table 9-14. Sample Non-Strategic Program Report for Business Acumen (cont.)

	Unit of Measure	2020 Actual	Plan	YTD Results	2021 YTD Results Compared to Plan	Forecast	Forecast Compared to Plan
Total							
Efficiency Measures							
Unique participants	Number	N/A	10,100	85	1%	10,105	100%
Total cost	Dollars, thousands	N/A	$300	$95	32%	$300	100%
Effectiveness Measures							
Level 5 Net Benefit	Dollars, thousands	N/A	$200	N/A	N/A	$200	100%
Level 5 ROI	%	N/A	67%	N/A	N/A	67%	On plan

* Decision made to put five additional leaders through
† Sample size for Levels 1 and 3 = 78
† Sample size for Levels 1 and 3 = 78

§ Developing additional plans for reinforcement
△ Plan of 80% may have been optimistic
Too early to deviate from forecast

In this example, program owner and CFO Davis has asked for L&D's help to increase the business acumen of all employees. The two parties agree that learning has a role to play and that different programs should be deployed for leaders and employees. The plan is to deploy to leaders first, conveying both content and guidance on how to coach their employees and reinforce their learning. Once the leaders are ready, their employees will take a course. Performance support tools are also planned to provide help at the time of need. No measures have been singled out as "headline" measures of success.

Plans call for developing and delivering two courses to 100 leaders by May 31. All leaders are expected to complete the two courses, and CFO Davis will ensure that they do. There is no history to guide plan setting for the effectiveness measures, but similar courses have achieved 80 percent favorable ratings from participants with initial pass rates of 90 percent on the knowledge tests. A 90 percent intent to apply is very high but possible given CFO Davis's commitment and the leader-first model. It is hoped that after 90 days, 80 percent will have displayed some business acumen from the training.

One course has to be developed for the associates by April 30; it needs to be tested and approved for production by May 31 when the leaders complete their two courses. Deployment to all 10,000 associates is planned by September 30, which will require a lot of coordination. All associates are also expected to complete the program. Total cost, including opportunity cost, is expected to be $300,000, with a net benefit of $200,000, resulting in a high ROI of 67 percent.

April YTD results show that 85 of the 100 leaders have completed the first course and forecast indicates that all will complete on plan plus an additional five. Expectations are that the second course will also be delivered and completed on time by all 100 leaders. Level 1 for the leaders is running four points above plan and should end the year slightly above plan. (The sample size is large enough to confirm YTD results are truly above plan.)

First-time pass rates aren't meeting expectations, but there are plans in place to improve these slightly by year-end. Intent to apply is 6 points below plan, and L&D believes it is unlikely that plan of 90 percent can be achieved for the year. In hindsight, the plan may have been too aggressive, and the forecast for both the intended and actual application rates have been lowered to reflect that.

The performance support tools are still being deployed so YTD usage is low, but the forecast indicates they are on plan for the year.

Data for the associates reflects that this portion of the program has not yet been deployed. Forecasts for this section of the report indicate that L&D and CFO Davis continue to believe the plan is achievable. The same goes for the summary at the bottom.

Creating the Non-Strategic Program Report

L&D creates the non-strategic program report by working with the program owner, which in some cases may be the CLO (Figure 9-3). Step 1 is always to meet with the program owner to review expectations for the year. Even when the program has been conducted for many years, there will likely be some change required for the coming year if only in the number of participants. Often L&D will need to update course content or add new modules to keep the training current and relevant.

Step 2 is to agree on the programs and courses for the coming year, including program specifics (such as objectives, modality, duration, and audience), key effectiveness and efficiency measures, and roles and responsibilities. Both parties might also choose to select one or two effectiveness or efficiency measures to use as headline measures of success, elevating them in importance over the rest of the measures.

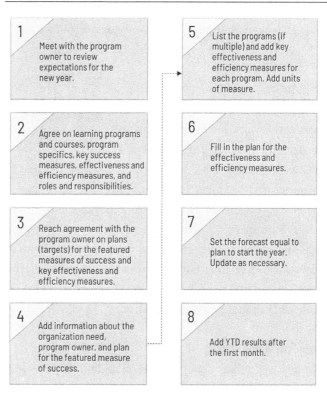

Figure 9-3. Steps to Create a Program Report for Non-Strategic Programs

1. Meet with the program owner to review expectations for the new year.

2. Agree on learning programs and courses, program specifics, key success measures, effectiveness and efficiency measures, and roles and responsibilities.

3. Reach agreement with the program owner on plans (targets) for the featured measures of success and key effectiveness and efficiency measures.

4. Add information about the organization need, program owner, and plan for the featured measure of success.

5. List the programs (if multiple) and add key effectiveness and efficiency measures for each program. Add units of measure.

6. Fill in the plan for the effectiveness and efficiency measures.

7. Set the forecast equal to plan to start the year. Update as necessary.

8. Add YTD results after the first month.

These measures will appear at the top of the report, where the outcome measure for strategic programs would normally appear. For example, L&D and the program owners might choose the number of participants or some measure of satisfaction for the program headline measures of success. In an existing relationship, the discussion is likely to focus on any changes that need to be made. If it is a new program or new owner, more discussion will be required and it may take several meetings before agreement is reached on all items.

Step 3 is to reach agreement on plans for the effectiveness and efficiency measures, including the headline measures. Once the first three steps have been completed, the report itself can be created. Start at the top and work your way down. In step 4, fill in the need, program owner name, and the headline measures if there are any. Next, add last year's actuals if they are available and the plans for the headline measures, such as a 10 percent increase in number of participants or a 3 point increase in the program owner or senior leader satisfaction with the program.

With the top portion complete, in step 5, add the names of the programs (if there are multiple programs) as well as the effectiveness and efficiency measures associated with each and their units of measure. Next, in step 6, add the plan numbers for each effectiveness and efficiency measure.

For all rows in the report, in step 7, set the forecast column to equal plan to start. So, at the start of the year, the report will show the forecast being on plan. You can update the forecast for a measure whenever you have new information that leads you to believe the existing forecast is no longer the best guess about how the year is likely to end.

Once you have the first month's results, fill in the YTD column in step 8.

Operations Report

The operations report is the next report most users are likely to create. The primary users of this report are the CLO and senior L&D leaders who manage efforts to improve efficiency

or effectiveness measures across all programs as well as manage initiatives to improve the efficiency and effectiveness of department processes and systems. The operations report includes both efficiency and effectiveness measures but no outcome measures because department initiatives are not aligned directly to a top-level organization goal. There will be just one operations report, which L&D should generate monthly.

Simple Operations Report

A simple operations report might include efficiency and effectiveness measures for only improvement efforts aimed at all programs or for improvement efforts aimed at learning processes and systems. It might also include a few measures from each type of improvement initiative. A more complex operations report would typically include more measures, such as measures from each type of improvement effort.

We begin with a simple operations report for program initiatives (Table 9-15). In this example, all the initiatives are directed at improving efficiency and effectiveness measures across all programs.

Table 9-15. Simple Operations Report for Program Initiatives

			2021			
	Unit of Measure	2020 Actual	Plan	YTD Results	YTD Results Compared to Plan	Forecast	Forecast Compared to Plan
Efficiency Measures							
Total participants	Number	7,689	9,000	4,390	49%	9,000	100%
Total unique participants	Number	24,567	36,000	15,467	43%	34,000	94%
Percentage of courses meeting deadline for development	%	68%	90%	78%	12% below	85%	5% below
Percentage of courses meeting deadline for delivery	%	59%	90%	72%	18% below	82%	8% below
Reach (percent of employees reached by L&D)	%	85%	88%	72%	16% below	88%	On plan
Effectiveness Measures							
Level 1 participant reaction (all programs)							
Quality of content	% favorable	76%	80%	79%	1% below	79%	1% below
Quality of instructor	% favorable	80%	85%	86%	1% above	85%	On plan
Relevance	% favorable	72%	78%	73%	5% below	75%	3% below
Recommend to others	% favorable	68%	75%	69%	6% below	71%	4% below
Total for Level 1	Average of measures	74%	80%	77%	3% below	78%	2% below
Level 1 goal owner reaction (select programs)	% favorable	66%	80%	68%	12% below	75%	5% below
Level 2 learning (select programs)	Score	78%	85%	83%	2% below	85%	On plan
Level 3 application rate (select programs)							
Intent to apply (from post-event survey at end of course)	% content applied	70%	75%	70%	5% below	72%	3% below
Actual application (from follow-up survey after three months)	% content applied	51%	65%	55%	10% below	63%	2% below

This example contains five efficiency measures and three high-level effectiveness measures (Levels 1, 2, and 3). The plan is to provide learning to more unique participants and to increase the average number of courses taken by each unique participant so that the number of total participants rises even more. The CLO also wants to significantly improve on-time course development and delivery and slightly improve the percentage of employees reached by learning. For effectiveness measures, the CLO wants to improve all three levels.

The operations report shows mixed YTD results for the efficiency measures. Depending on historic norms at this time of year, 49 percent of plan for unique participants may indicate the measure is on plan and likewise for total participants at 43 percent. Let's say the CLO asked what these percentages have been the last few years and was told 47 percent and 41 percent, respectively. In that case, the measures appear to be on plan and a forecast showing the year ending near plan makes sense. The same analysis is needed to judge whether reach is on plan and likely to make plan by year-end. In this case, history shows reach is normally about 72 percent at this time of year, so it's on plan and likely to make plan by year-end.

The two measures for percentage on-time are more problematic. While each has made good progress since last year, both are still considerably below plan, and it seems unlikely plan will be achieved. Consequently, forecast shows both measures falling short of plan, which may indicate the plan was too aggressive or simply turned out to be much harder to achieve than anticipated.

The report shows good YTD progress for Levels 1 (participant) and 2, but application rates are significantly below plan with little improvement over last year. Forecast indicates that all effectiveness measures are likely to end the year below plan except for Level 2 learning.

The next simple example explores department process initiatives. In this case, the department is seeking to improve its informal learning, help desk, and LMS. Table 9-16 shows the operations report.

The plans for these initiatives were shared in Table 9-7. For the informal learning initiative, three efficiency measures and one effectiveness measure have been identified for each component. For the help desk initiative, L&D identified four efficiency and two effectiveness measures. Three efficiency and two effectiveness measures are planned for the LMS initiative.

The operations report indicates that the informal learning initiative is making good progress for the communities of practice and portal content, and most measures are expected to make plan by year-end. The performance support initiative is struggling, however, and likely to end the year below plan for all measures except number of tools, where it should exceed plan. Further analysis is warranted here.

The help desk initiative is on plan YTD with training completed about a week ahead of schedule and for one more person than planned. Hold time has already dropped by about half, and dropped calls are running significantly below last year's pace. User satisfaction has also improved dramatically, and the quality metric is halfway to plan (0.2 point improvement out of 0.4 point planned improvement). Forecasts for these key measures indicate ending the year very close to plan for hold time and dropped calls, and on plan for both effectiveness measures.

The LMS initiative also appears to be on plan. The upgrade has not yet occurred (planned for August 1), but the YTD and forecast columns shows that the project leader believes everything is on plan. The effectiveness measures have not shown any improvement yet and have actually deteriorated slightly, but the training has not yet been completed and the upgrade is still a month away from going live.

Table 9-16. Simple Operations Report for Department Process and System Improvements

	Unit of Measure	2020 Actual	2021 Plan	YTD Results	YTD Results Compared to Plan	Forecast	Forecast Compared to Plan
Informal Learning Initiatives							
Communities of Practice							
Efficiency Measures							
Number of active communities	Number	29	50	43	86%	50	100%
Number of unique users	Number	312	750	512	68%	750	100%
Number of total users	Number	1,968	7,500	3,968	53%	7,000	93%
Effectiveness Measures							
User satisfaction	% favorable	67%	80%	75%	5% below	80%	On plan
Content on Portal							
Efficiency Measures							
Number of documents	Number	51	100	82	82%	100	100%
Number of unique users	Number	2,301	5,000	4,023	80%	6,000	120%
Number of total users	Number	3,590	7,500	5,423	72%	7,500	100%
Effectiveness Measures							
User satisfaction	% favorable	37%	60%	56%	4% below	60%	On plan
Performance Support							
Efficiency Measures							
Number of tools	Number	N/A	20	18	90%	25	125%
Number of unique users	Number	N/A	5,000	3,000	60%	4,000	80%
Number of total users	Number	N/A	10,000	4,600	46%	6,000	60%
Effectiveness Measures							
User satisfaction	% favorable	45%	70%	59%	11% below	60%	10% below
Help Desk Initiatives							
Efficiency Measures							
Number of associates trained	Number	1	4	5	1 above	6	2 above
Completion date for training	Date	N/A	3/31	3/25	On plan	7/31	On plan
Hold time	Minutes	2.5	0.5	1.2	0.7 above	0.6	0.2 above
Dropped calls	Number	564	100	63	37 below	110	10 above
Effectiveness Measures							
User satisfaction	% favorable	47%	80%	75%	5% below	80%	On plan
Quality metric (accuracy)	5-point scale	4.1	4.5	4.3	0.2 below	4.5	On plan
LMS Initiatives							
Efficiency Measures							
Number of associates trained	Number	N/A	20	15	5 below	20	On plan
Go live date	Date	N/A	8/1		On plan	8/1	On plan
Completion date for training	Date	N/A	7/31		On plan	7/31	On plan
Effectiveness Measures							
User satisfaction	% favorable	62%	70%	61%	N/A	70%	On plan
Staff satisfaction	% favorable	75%	90%	73%	N/A	90%	On plan

Complex Operations Report

A more complex operations report would have a greater number of initiatives and may contain measures for both program and process and system improvements. Due to the complexity of planning and executing so many initiatives, this level of effort is usually reserved for the very mature L&D departments with more staff and budget. Table 9-17 includes numerous program measures as well as the process and system improvement measures from Table 9-16.

Table 9-17. Complex Operations Report

Initiatives to Improve All Programs					2021		
	Unit of Measure	2020 Actual	Plan	YTD Results	YTD Results Compared to Plan	Forecast	Forecast Compared to Plan
Efficiency Measures							
Total participants	Number	7,689	9,000	4,390	49%	9,000	100%
Total unique participants	Number	24,567	36,000	15,467	43%	34,000	94%
Percentage of courses meeting deadline for development	%	68%	90%	78%	12% below	85%	5% below
Percentage of courses meeting deadline for delivery	%	59%	90%	72%	18% below	82%	8% below
Reach (% of employees reached by L&D)	%	85%	88%	72%	16% below	88%	On plan
Effectiveness Measures							
Level 1 participant reaction (all programs)							
Quality of content	% favorable	76%	80%	79%	1% below	79%	1% below
Quality of instructor	% favorable	80%	85%	86%	1% above	85%	On plan
Relevance	% favorable	72%	78%	73%	5% below	75%	3% below
Recommend to others	% favorable	68%	75%	69%	6% below	71%	4% below
Total for Level 1	Avg of measures	74%	80%	77%	3% below	78%	2% below
Level 1 goal owner reaction (select programs)	% favorable	66%	80%	68%	12% below	75%	5% below
Level 2 learning (select programs)	Score	78%	85%	83%	2% below	85%	On plan
Level 3 application rate (select programs)							
Intent to apply (from post-event survey at the end of the course)	% content applied	70%	75%	70%	5% below	72%	3% below
Actual application (from the follow-up survey after three months)	% content applied	51%	65%	55%	10% below	63%	2% below
Level 4 impact (select programs)							
Initial estimate by participants (post-event survey)	% contribution to goal	19%	50%	47%	3% below	50%	On plan
Final estimate (follow-up survey)	% contribution to goal	14%	30%	28%	2% below	30%	On plan
Level 5 ROI (select programs)							
Net benefits	Dollars, thousands	$254	$380	$140	37%	$400	105%
ROI	Dollars, thousands	30%	40%	30%	10% below	43%	3% above

Initiatives to Improve Processes and Systems			2021				
	Unit of Measure	2020 Actual	Plan	YTD Results	YTD Results Compared to Plan	Forecast	Forecast Compared to Plan
Informal Learning Initiatives							
Communities of Practice							
Efficiency Measures							
Number of active communities	Number	29	50	43	86%	50	100%
Number of unique users	Number	312	750	512	68%	750	100%
Number of total users	Number	1,968	7,500	3,968	53%	7,000	93%
Effectiveness Measures							
User satisfaction	% favorable	67%	80%	75%	5% below	80%	On plan
Content on Portal							
Efficiency Measures							
Number of documents	Number	51	100	82	82%	100	100%
Number of unique users	Number	2,301	5,000	4,023	80%	6,000	120%
Number of total users	Number	3,590	7,500	5,423	72%	7,500	100%
Effectiveness Measures							
User satisfaction	% favorable	37%	60%	56%	4% below	60%	On plan
Performance Support							
Efficiency Measures							
Number of tools	Number	N/A	20	18	90%	25	125%
Number of unique users	Number	N/A	5,000	3,000	60%	4,000	80%
Number of total users	Number	N/A	10,000	4,600	46%	6,000	60%
Effectiveness Measures							
User satisfaction	% favorable	45%	70%	59%	11% below	60%	10% below
Help Desk Initiatives							
Efficiency Measures							
Number of associates trained	Number	1	4	5	1 above	6	2 above
Completion date for training	Date	N/A	3/31	3/25	On plan	7/31	On plan
Hold time	Minutes	2.5	0.5	1.2	0.7 above	0.6	0.2 above
Dropped calls	Number	564	100	63	37 below	110	10 above
Effectiveness Measures							
User satisfaction	% favorable	47%	80%	75%	5% below	80%	On plan
Quality metric (accuracy)	5-point scale	4.1	4.5	4.3	0.2 below	4.5	On plan
LMS Initiatives							
Efficiency Measures							
Number of associates trained	Number	N/A	20	15	5 below	20	On plan
Go live date	Date	N/A	8/1		On plan	8/1	On plan
Completion date for training	Date	N/A	7/31		On plan	7/31	On plan
Effectiveness Measures							
User satisfaction	% favorable	62%	70%	61%	N/A	70%	On plan
Staff satisfaction	% favorable	75%	90%	73%	N/A	90%	On plan

Notice that the top section for effectiveness measures now includes both measures for impact (Level 4) and both measures for ROI (Level 5) in contrast to the simple report, which ended with application. The bottom portion is just the simple operations report for department process and system improvements.

The report indicates that most of the effectiveness initiatives for programs are behind plan YTD but are forecast to improve significantly in the second half, and end the year near plan. Goal owner satisfaction is expected to fall short of plan by 5 points but still show improvement over 2020. In contrast, unique participants are on plan and forecast to end the year on plan, while total participants are forecast to fall 6 percentage points short of plan. On-time completion measures are much improved YTD but forecast to fall short of plan with reach expected to end the year on plan.

As discussed previously, the initiatives to improve communities of practice, portal content, the help desk, and LMS appear to be on plan and are forecast to end the year near plan. Consequently, no special action is necessary for these initiatives while performance support is struggling.

Creating the Operations Report

L&D creates the operations report through close collaboration between the CLO and senior learning leaders in the department. The report should capture measures for all the important initiatives planned for the coming year since it will be used monthly to manage these initiatives toward successful completion. The steps to create the operations report are shown in Figure 9-4.

Figure 9-4. Steps to Create the Operations Report

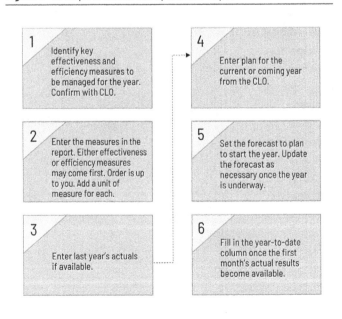

Step 1 of the process is identifying next year's key efficiency and effectiveness measures (or this year's measures if you are implementing partway through the year). These come from the CLO and senior learning leaders in the department. Typically, these leaders will have measures in mind to improve for next year or targets for particular measures (like number of participants or courses). So, the analyst simply needs to ask and then confirm with the CLO once the list of measures is complete. If it is a long list, the CLO will need to prioritize.

In step 2, list the measures as rows in the report. The CLO can decide whether to start with effectiveness or efficiency measures, but the measures should be grouped by type. Each measure should also have a unit of measure. In step 3, enter last year's actual results if available for each measure.

In step 4, add the all-important plan numbers for each measure. These will come from the CLO and senior leaders who are responsible for the initiatives. The CLO should approve all the plan numbers. In step 5, set the forecast equal to plan at the start of the year, then update as necessary throughout the year. Last, in step 6, fill in the YTD column after the first month's results are in.

So, the creation of the report itself is straightforward. The work is identifying the measures to be managed for the coming year and creating a plan value for each measure. Also, L&D will need to update the forecast periodically during the year as YTD results come in and as new information about the rest of the year becomes available. Chapter 11 provides guidance on creating plan and forecast values.

Summary Report

The last TDRp report is the summary report, which draws from both the program and operations reports. It contains all three types of measures and serves to brief senior leaders such as the CEO and CFO as well as govern-

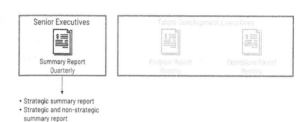

ing bodies and the SVP of HR. The summary report is also excellent for briefing employees in the L&D function at monthly all-employee meetings and to use in presentations to other groups.

The summary report provides high-level, aggregate data on the most important outcome, effectiveness, and efficiency measures. It also depicts the alignment of learning to the organization's most important goals. Given these target audiences, the report should not contain any learning or HR jargon. L&D should also produce the report at least quarterly.

In addition to being a briefing, the report helps the CLO manage expectations, reprioritize when necessary, and occasionally make the case for an increase in resources during the year. While the day-to-day management of L&D takes place through the program and operations reports, the summary report is the tool used by the CLO to manage at the highest level with the CEO, CFO, and governing bodies.

Format

In keeping with the TDRp philosophy to run learning like a business, the summary report has a business-centric format, meaning that the information most important to the senior business leaders (the key users) comes first. Consequently, the report begins with the organizational goals in the CEO's priority order. If the goal owner agreed that learning could help achieve the goal, the planned learning program is aligned or listed below the goal. This clearly shows the strategic alignment of learning to the organization's top goals.

Next, the report lists HR and other important goals supported by learning along with the agreed-upon learning programs. Learning can usually support planned improvements in employee engagement, leadership, turnover, and diversity. Moreover, in some organizations learning also plays a very important tactical role in meeting important organizational needs like basic skills training for large numbers of employees. This is the case in retail, restaurants, and the military. Other important needs may be onboarding, compliance training, and advanced skills training. While there may not be a high-level goal to provide this training, it is understood that this is critical to the organization's success and that L&D is responsible. In these cases, any need addressed by L&D should be added. And if meeting these more tactical needs is the primary mission of L&D, then put them at the top of the report.

Last, the summary report includes a few key efficiency and effectiveness measures from the operations report. This shows senior leaders that L&D is not only closely aligned to the goals of the organization, but that L&D is always working to improve its own efficiency and effectiveness.

Since the format includes the standard columns for last year's results, this year's plan, YTD results, and forecast, the report also clearly demonstrates that specific, measurable plans have been set for each measure and the CLO is willing to be held accountable for delivering the planned results. The report shows that learning will be managed like any other department with plans and disciplined execution.

Strategic Summary Report

First, we examine a sample summary report for an L&D department that has responsibility primarily for strategic goals (Table 9-18). By "strategic" we mean the CEO's or senior leader's business goals for the year. These would have been approved by the board of directors or by the CEO for business units. In either case, the CEO or business unit leader is accountable for delivering these goals and will suffer in terms of pay, bonus, or promotion if the goals are not attained. In this model, business units provide the more tactical training for new hires and others in need of upskilling or reskilling.

As you can see, there are four high-level goals for the CEO:

· Increase revenue by 20 percent.
· Reduce injuries by 20 percent.
· Reduce operating costs by 15 percent.
· Improve quality by 4 points.

The CLO or program managers would have met with the goal owners and decided if learning had a role to play. If it did, both parties would agree on the type of learning and all the specifics associated with the training, including the cost, planned impact, and their mutual roles and responsibilities.

In this example, learning content is planned for all four goals, and the agreed-upon learning programs are listed beneath each goal (shown in italics). A quantitative outcome measure has been agreed upon for the first goal, with learning expected to contribute about 25 percent toward the goal of a 20 percent increase in revenue. In other words, learning should increase revenue by about 5 percent (25% × 20% = 5%).

For the next two goals, a qualitative outcome measure has been chosen to define expectations. Both parties believe training will be the major contributor to a reduction in injuries and thus the "high" impact. A "medium" impact is planned on operating costs, meaning that training, while very important, by itself will not likely be responsible for most of the cost reduction.

Last, learning is also planned to improve quality, but the two parties could not reach agreement on an outcome measure. So, they settled on the next-best measure, application (Level 3), on which they could agree to a plan. A high application rate may not always lead to impact, but it usually does, and we know for sure that there will be no impact without application.

Table 9-18. Sample Summary Report With Focus on Strategic Goals

Results Through June				2021			
	Unit of Measure	2020 Actual	Plan	YTD Results	YTD Results Compared to Plan	Forecast	Forecast Compared to Plan
Business Goals and Supporting L&D Programs							
Revenue: Increase Sales by 20%							
Corporate goal or actual	%	10%	20%	20%	On plan	25%	5% above
Impact of Learning on Sales: 25% contribution to goal for 2021	%	1%	5%		On plan		Above
New product features training *Consultative selling skills*							
Safety: Reduce Injuries by 20%							
Corporate goal or actual	%	10%	20%	15%	5% below	20%	On plan
Impact of Learning on Injuries: High impact on goal for 2021	H/M/L	Medium	High		Below		On plan
Safety programs to address top five causes of injuries							
Costs: Reduce Operating Expenses by 15%							
Corporate goal or actual	%	5%	15%	7%	8% below	12%	3% below
Impact of Learning on Expenses: Medium impact on goal for 2021	H/M/L	Low	Medium		Below		Below
Training for purchasing agents *Training for all employees on reducing costs* *Training for department heads to meet 15% goal*							
Quality: Improve Quality Score by 4 Points to 80%							
Corporate goal or actual	Points	1.6 pts	4 pts	2.9 pts	1.1 below	3.5 pts	100%
Application rate	% content applied	84%	95%	80%	15% below	92%	Near
Design skills for engineers to improve manufacturability *Sourcing training for purchasing to reduce purchased defects* *Cell leader training to ensure manufacturing to specifications*							

Table 9-18. Sample Summary Report With Focus on Strategic Goals (cont.)

			2021				
	Unit of Measure	2020 Actual	Plan	YTD Results	YTD Results Compared to Plan	Forecast	Forecast Compared to Plan
HR Goals and Supporting L&D Programs							
Engagement: Increase Engagement Score by 3 Points to 69.4%							
Corporate goal or actual	Points	1 pt	3 pts	1.9 pts	1.1 below	3 pts	On plan
Impact of Learning on Engagement: Low impact on goal for 2021	H/M/L	Low	Low		Below		On plan
IDP for each employee to include some training *Increase use of online learning for general development*							
Leadership: Improve Score by 4 Points to 75%							
Corporate goal or actual	Points	1 pt	4 pts	2.2 pts	1.8 below	4 pts	On plan
Impact of Learning on Leadership: High impact on goal for 2021	H/M/L	Medium	High		Below		On plan
Intro to Supervision *Leadership for managers* *Advanced leadership for department heads*							
Retention: Improve Retention of Top Performers by 5 Points to 90%							
Corporate goal or actual	Points	-3 pts	5 pts	2 pts	3 below	4 pts	Near
No training identified							
Effectiveness Measures							
Participant reaction to formal learning	% favorable	74%	80%	80%	On plan	84%	4% above
Participant reaction to informal learning	% favorable	N/A	80%	83%	3% above	85%	5% above
Goal owner reaction	% favorable	N/A	80%	68%	12% below	75%	5% below
Learning	Score	78%	85%	85%	On plan	85%	On plan
Actual application rate	% content applied	51%	65%	55%	10% below	63%	2% below
Efficiency Measures							
Percentage of employees reached by L&D	%	85%	88%	72%	16% below	88%	On plan
Percentage of employees with development plan	%	82%	85%	85%	On plan	90%	5% above
Percentage of courses developed on time	%	73%	92%	67%	25% below	78%	14% below
Participants in all programs							
Total participants	Number	109,618	147,500	67,357	46%	145,000	98%
Unique participants	Number	40,729	45,300	36,998	82%	44,000	97%
Unique informal learning users	Number	19,345	50,000	43,258	87%	50,000	100%

> **Note**
>
> This report is an example of a summary report with mixed outcome measures, meaning more than one type is used. Alternatively, a summary report might contain only quantitative or only qualitative outcome measures.

The next section of the report includes the three goals of the SVP of HR:

- Increase employee engagement by 3 points.
- Improve the leadership score by 4 points.
- Improve retention of top performers by 5 points.

The SVP of HR and the CLO agree that learning can contribute to the first two but not to the third. They agree on qualitative outcome measures with a "low" contribution of learning planned for employee engagement, but a "high" contribution planned for leadership.

Agreement on the value of the outcome measure is a critical part of the planning process because it will directly influence decisions about the level of resources required to achieve the goal (higher impact requires more resources), timing of the program (higher impact requires an earlier deployment), and goal owner commitment (higher impact requires greater commitment by the goal owner).

The top two sections, then, show the alignment of learning to the CEO's and SVP of HR's goals. The bottom section completes the report by sharing five important effectiveness measures and five important efficiency measures. These will be aggregated across all programs for which data are available and show the commitment of the CLO to improvements in both areas. The CLO might also include measures showing planned improvement in department processes and systems.

The summary report shows that learning is on plan YTD for revenue impact but forecasted to exceed plan by year-end, contributing to higher than planned revenue. Learning is behind plan YTD with its impact on injuries but is expected to make plan for the year, so no further special action is necessary. Learning to reduce operating costs, however, is significantly behind plan YTD and expected to fall short of plan by year-end. In other words, the lost ground in the first six months cannot be made up without special action, and the organization is likely to miss plan for the year unless something changes, in part due to a smaller contribution from learning than planned. This is an example of where the CLO, program manager, and goal owner need to understand the reasons for lagging performance, identify options, and decide what special action to take to get back on plan. In contrast to operating expenses, the quality initiative appears to be on plan YTD and should end the year just slightly below plan, so no special action is necessary.

Looking at the next section of the report for HR goals, learning appears to be on plan and the organization is forecasting that both goals supported by learning will be achieved.

The last section includes 10 important effectiveness and efficiency measures, highlighting efforts by the department to improve these measures across all programs. These measures are mixed:

- learning is on plan and forecast to end the year on or near plan
- the percentage of employees reached by learning is behind plan but forecast to catch up
- actual application rate, unique participants, total participants, and unique informal learning users are behind plan but expected to end the year near plan
- goal owner reaction and percentage of courses developed on time are behind plan and not expected to catch up
- participant reaction to formal learning, participant reaction to informal learning, and percentage with development plan are above plan YTD and forecast to end the year above plan.

The CLO and senior L&D leaders may consider special action for those not forecast to end the year on plan or may simply explain to the CEO that the plans were too aggressive or unforeseen issues developed that will take longer to address.

Strategic and Non-Strategic Summary Report

We can now build on the strategic summary report in the last section by adding some non-strategic programs. Most L&D departments will have at least one or two strategic goals as well as HR goals they can support, so the strategic and HR goal sections remain. Many L&D departments, however, spend the majority of their resources on basic training of new employees or skill enhancement for advancing employees. The example in Table 9-19 provides several programs of this type, which are not directly aligned to the CEO's or SVP of HR's goals but are critical nonetheless to the organization's ongoing operations and long-term success.

Table 9-19 shows a summary report for an organization in the fast food industry where thousands of new and advancing employees need to be trained. In this report, the non-strategic programs are shown first because they represent most of the L&D group's efforts. The plan calls for providing basic skills training to 9,000 employees, a significant increase from 2020. The program owner also wants the duration shortened by two days while increasing the satisfaction of the receiving managers from 78 percent to 85 percent. The plan also focuses on the leadership training provided to new and existing leaders. For 2021, 600 leaders will need to be trained with a manager satisfaction score of 85 percent. The three measures (number trained, duration, and manager satisfaction) are the agreed-upon or headline measures of success for these two important programs. Since these are not strategic programs, there are no outcome measures.

Table 9-19. Sample Summary Report With a Focus on Non-Strategic Programs

Results Through June

| | | | 2021 | | | |
	Unit of Measure	2020 Actual	Plan	YTD Results	YTD Results Compared to Plan	Forecast	Forecast Compared to Plan
Important Organizational Goals							
Basic Skills							
Number trained	Number	6589	9000	3785	42%	10,000	111%
Program duration	Days	14	12	12	On plan	12	On plan
Receiving manager satisfaction	% favorable	78%	85%	82%	3% below	85%	On plan
Restaurant Leadership							
Number trained	Number	420	600	321	54%	650	108%
Receiving manager satisfaction	% favorable	82%	85%	85%	On plan	85%	On plan
Business Goals and Supporting L&D Programs							
Revenue: Increase Sales by 20%							
Corporate goal or actual	%	10%	20%	20%	On plan	25%	5% above
Impact of Learning on Sales: 25% contribution to goal for 2021	%	1%	5%		On plan		Above
New product features training _Consultative selling skills_							
Safety: Reduce Injuries by 20%							
Corporate goal or actual	%	10%	20%	15%	5% below	20%	On plan
Impact of Learning on Injuries: High impact on goal for 2021	H/M/L	Medium	High		Below		On plan
Safety programs to address top five causes of injuries							
Costs: Reduce Operating Expenses by 15%							
Corporate goal or actual	%	5%	15%	7%	8% below	12%	3% below
Impact of Learning on Expenses: Medium impact on goal for 2021	H/M/L	Low	Medium		Below		Below
Training for purchasing agents _Training for all employees on reducing costs_ _Training for department heads to meet 15% goal_							
Quality: Improve Quality Score by 4 Points to 80%							
Corporate goal or actual	Points	1.6 pts	4 pts	2.9 pts	1.1 below	3.5 pts	100%
Application rate	% content applied	84%	95%	80%	15% below	92%	Near
Design skills for engineers to improve manufacturability _Sourcing training for purchasing to reduce purchased defects_ _Cell leader training to ensure manufacturing to specifications_							

Table 9-19. Sample Summary Report With a Focus on Non-Strategic Programs (cont.)

			2021				
	Unit of Measure	2020 Actual	Plan	YTD Results	YTD Results Compared to Plan	Forecast	Forecast Compared to Plan
HR Goals and Supporting L&D Programs							
Engagement: Increase Engagement Score by 3 Points to 69.4%							
Corporate goal or actual	Points	1 pt	3 pts	1.9 pts	1.1 below	3 pts	On plan
Impact of Learning on Engagement: Low impact on goal for 2021	H/M/L	Low	Low		Below		On plan
IDP for each employee to include some training *Increase use of online learning for general development*							
Leadership: Improve Score by 4 Points to 75%							
Corporate goal or actual	Points	1 pt	4 pts	2.2 pts	1.8 below	4 pts	On plan
Impact of Learning on Leadership: High impact on goal for 2021	H/M/L	Medium	High		Below		On plan
Intro to Supervision *Leadership for managers* *Advanced leadership for department heads*							
Retention: Improve Retention of Top Performers by 5 Points to 90%							
Corporate goal or actual	Points	-3 pts	5 pts	2 pts	3 below	4 pts	Near
No training identified							
Effectiveness Measures							
Participant reaction to formal learning	% favorable	74%	80%	80%	On plan	84%	4% above
Participant reaction to informal learning	% favorable	N/A	80%	83%	3% above	85%	5% above
Goal owner reaction	% favorable	N/A	80%	68%	12% below	75%	5% below
Learning	Score	78%	85%	85%	On plan	85%	On plan
Actual application rate	% content applied	51%	65%	55%	10% below	63%	2% below
Efficiency Measures							
Percentage of employees reached by L&D	%	85%	88%	72%	16% below	88%	On plan
Percentage of employees with a development plan	%	82%	85%	85%	On plan	90%	5% above
Percentage of courses developed on time	%	73%	92%	67%	25% below	78%	14% below
Participants in all programs							
Total participants	Number	109,618	147,500	67,357	46%	145,000	98%
Unique participants	Number	40,729	45,300	36,998	82%	44,000	97%
Unique informal learning users	Number	19,345	50,000	43,258	87%	50,000	100%

While the YTD results for employees are only 42 percent of plan, forecast shows that not only will plan be reached by year-end, but an additional 1,000 employees will be trained, exceeding plan by 11 percent. The plan to reduce the program by two days has been achieved, and manager satisfaction is forecast to average 85 percent for the year. Leadership training is ahead of plan YTD, and forecast shows an additional 50 leaders will be trained by year-end. The planned level of manager satisfaction has also been achieved and is expected to hold for the remainder of the year.

The business, HR, efficiency goals, effectiveness goals, YTD results, and forecast are from Table 9-17. You can refer to that section for explanation and analysis.

How to Create a Summary Report

Create the summary report by leveraging the program reports and the operations report. If you have already created these reports, you should not require any new information—simply transfer the information to the summary report. If you have not yet completed the program and operations report, you can create the summary report from scratch. Refer to the steps shown in Figure 9-5.

For step 1, enter the CEO's top goals for the coming year. These need to come from the CEO and should be in priority order. Along with the goal (such as increase sales by 10 percent), enter the unit of measure and last year's actual results if available. Typically, a CEO has four to seven key goals that have been approved by the board of directors. The CEO will be evaluated by the board on these goals.

In step 2, enter the learning

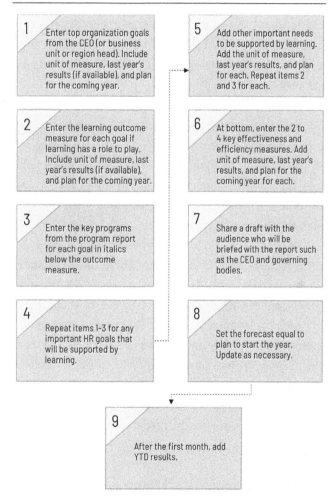

Figure 9-5. Steps to Create a Summary Report

1. Enter top organization goals from the CEO (or business unit or region head). Include unit of measure, last year's results (if available), and plan for the coming year.

2. Enter the learning outcome measure for each goal if learning has a role to play. Include unit of measure, last year's results (if available), and plan for the coming year.

3. Enter the key programs from the program report for each goal in italics below the outcome measure.

4. Repeat items 1-3 for any important HR goals that will be supported by learning.

5. Add other important needs to be supported by learning. Add the unit of measure, last year's results, and plan for each. Repeat items 2 and 3 for each.

6. At bottom, enter the 2 to 4 key effectiveness and efficiency measures. Add unit of measure, last year's results, and plan for the coming year for each.

7. Share a draft with the audience who will be briefed with the report such as the CEO and governing bodies.

8. Set the forecast equal to plan to start the year. Update as necessary.

9. After the first month, add YTD results.

outcome measure for each goal where the goal owner and CLO have agreed that learning has a role to play. The learning outcome measure will usually be the impact of learning on the goal but sometimes it's a next-best measure, such as the application rate, instead. The goal owner and CLO need to agree on the measure and the plan value for the measure. If impact is used, state the percentage contribution from learning next to the learning outcome measure and the resulting impact in the plan column. For example, if learning is expected to contribute 20 percent toward achieving the goal of a 10 percent increase in sales, state the 20 percent planned impact next to "impact of learning" and place 2 percent (20% × 10%) in the plan column. The percentage contribution and the resulting impact should be agreed upon by the goal owner and the CLO.

For step 3, add the names of the programs planned to support the goal under the outcome measure for each goal. Use italics to make the report more readable. This shows the direct alignment of programs to the CEO's top goals. The information for this step and the prior step can be found in the program reports if they have been created. If not, the information comes from the CLO and program manager working closely with each goal owner.

In step 4, repeat the same basic process for HR goals that will be supported by learning. The CLO will get the HR goals from the head of HR and, if both parties agree that learning has a role to play, show the goal, the agreed-upon learning outcome measure, units of measure, and last year's results.

To complete the alignment portion of the summary report, in step 5, list other important needs supported by learning. These might include compliance training and onboarding if they're not already included under HR goals, and may also include basic or advance skills training. In some organizations the bulk of the training effort is directed toward new hires so it is important to capture this activity. Add the need and whatever measures of success have been agreed upon along with the unit of measure, last year's results, and plan for the coming year.

In step 6, add two to four key effectiveness measures and two to four key efficiency measures at the bottom of the report. These should be stated in plain language with no learning jargon. Add the unit of measure, last year's results, and plan for the coming year. These will come from the operations report if it exists. If not, they will come from the CLO.

Step 7 is best practice—share the summary report draft with your CEO and governing bodies to see if they have any questions or would like to see any additional information. Given that the purpose of the summary report is to share results with senior leaders and manage their expectations, it is important that they are comfortable with it and that it meets their needs.

In step 8, you set forecast values equal to plan to start the year and then finish with step 9, adding YTD results after the first month's results are available.

Conclusion

This chapter focused on the three management reports as well as the concept of running learning like a business. A management report is the highest-level and most complex type of report. Consequently, it will contain only those measures to be managed, requiring a plan, YTD results, and forecast for each measure. This information answers two fundamental questions each month: "Are we on plan year to date? Are we going to end the year on plan?" Answers to these questions often require analysis, which in turn may lead to more analysis to determine root causes and potential solutions.

Each management report serves a different purpose, and we recommend using all three in a learning department. The program report enables the program manager, CLO, goal owner, and staff in the goal owner's organization to manage learning programs to deliver the impact agreed upon by the goal owner and CLO. L&D should generate and share the report monthly, showing the latest YTD results and forecast. A program report should be created for each top CEO goal, HR goal, and any other important goal or need supported by learning. A mature organization would typically have five to 10 program reports.

The operations report provides the CLO and senior learning leaders with information monthly to manage planned improvements in efficiency or effectiveness measures or to achieve planned targets (like number of participants). Unlike the program reports, which focus on specific programs, the operations report contains data aggregated across the enterprise. Along with the program report, this is how the CLO runs learning like a business. Specifically, the CLO has set measurable goals and allocated resources, and the learning leadership team is executing them with discipline using monthly reports to ensure that the plan numbers are achieved.

The actual management of the function occurs using the program reports and the operations report; the summary report serves a different purpose and audience. The summary report briefs senior leaders, governing boards, learning department employees, and other groups interested in learning. The report clearly and simply demonstrates the alignment of learning to the goals and needs of the organization. It shows that the learning department worked closely with goal owners to agree on the role of learning and the planned impact of learning on the goal. In addition, it shows that the CLO is working to improve effectiveness and efficiency across all programs and internally within the department as well. In short, the summary report shows that the CLO is running the learning function with business-like discipline, just the same as sales, manufacturing, and other departments.

Now that we have a good understanding of the five general types of reports from chapter 8, coupled with the in-depth examination of the three types of management reports from this chapter, we are ready to create our reporting strategy.

CHAPTER 10
Creating Your Reporting Strategy

We are now ready to employ what we have learned about measures in chapters 2–7 and reports in chapters 8 and 9 to create a reporting strategy. Just like the measurement strategy, we start by identifying the elements of a reporting strategy and then move on to the heart of the strategy—selecting the right reports based on the user's needs.

Elements of a Measurement and Reporting Strategy

As we discussed in chapter 6, it's not enough to select a suite of measures and start reporting. Rather, you need to have an overarching strategy both for measurement and reporting:

1. a clear articulation of the reasons for measuring
2. the users, why they want the measures, when they need the data and how they want to see it reported
3. the measures overall, with specific measures identified for important programs or department initiatives
4. how you plan to collect the data, including the use of sampling and expected response rates
5. the types of reports you will use to communicate to stakeholders
6. how you plan to share the data
7. the resources you require to execute and sustain measurement and reporting over time.

Having a strategy signals to the business and L&D stakeholders that you are purposeful in your measurement efforts and that their engagement matters.

In most cases, L&D organizations craft an integrated measurement and reporting strategy because the two are so closely linked (see appendix C for an example). However, in this book, we have separated the two so that we can create the building blocks for each section. At this point, we assume the practitioner has already created their measurement strategy (items 1–4 discussed in chapter 6). Now we'll focus on items 5–7, which address the reporting side of the strategy as well as the resources required.

At this point, we know who our users are, why they want measures, and how they intend to use them. We also know the required frequency (monthly, quarterly, annually) and the specific measures. If the reason for measuring is to answer a simple question (for example, how many unique participants took a course last year?) or to determine if a trend exists in the data, a report may not be necessary. However, if the reason is to answer a more complex question involving multiple time periods or measures, or to monitor, evaluate, analyze, or manage, then you will need to create a report to display and share the data.

Consequently, an integrated measurement and reporting strategy needs to include several additional elements. First, we need to add a discussion of report types and formats (item 5). We also identify how we will produce and distribute the reports (item 6). Last, we need identify the required resources to maintain and sustain our measurement and reporting strategy over time (item 7).

In the rest of this chapter, we discuss items 5–7 in detail, giving the most attention to selecting the right report for a given user and purpose.

Report Types and Formats

An integrated measurement and reporting strategy should include a list of recommended reports, identifying the user for each as well as the frequency. This section will help you select the right report, and is followed by a short discussion of formats to help you understand the layout options for reports.

The recommended report type for the user should follow directly from their intended use. This is why the measurement framework introduced in chapter 1 is so important. Dashboards and scorecards are appropriate for both informing and monitoring as they can provide information on specific measures or trends as well as depict threshold or breakpoints for measures. Program evaluation reports, which provide detailed results on a specific solution or learning initiative, are commonly used for evaluation. When analysis is the purpose, custom reporting is typically warranted given the disparate needs that trigger an analysis effort. Finally, management reports are essential for managing because they provide essential information not simply about the plan but also the YTD results and the forecast for end of period performance.

The implications of the reasons for measuring on report selection are captured in Table 10-1. Our recommendations for selecting the right report follow.

Scorecard

If the reason for measuring is to inform—for example, to answer a complex question about the data and the user needs to see detail—we recommend using a scorecard. The scorecard (or a graph or chart based on it) is also recommended for identifying trends. The report will be in tabular form with rows typically containing the measures and the columns showing the time periods (month, quarter, YTD, or year). The cells in the table should provide the answers the user seeks. The scorecard only contains the history (actual results) because the user's question was about the past (last month, last quarter, last year). A scorecard may also be used to monitor if a threshold is included. (See chapter 8 for sample scorecards.)

Table 10-1. Measurement Requirements at Each Maturity Level

Measurement Purpose	Primary Use	Level of Analysis	Measurement Frequency	Key Elements	Shared In
Manage	• Identify if the program is delivering planned results and where adjustments are needed to meet goals.	High	• Monthly	• Plan • YTD results • Forecast for measures being managed	• Management reports
Evaluate and analyze	• Analyze program and non-program data. • Explore relationships among measures. • Predict outcomes.	Medium to high	• Based on business need	• Analytical methods (e.g. regression analysis, predictive modeling)	• Custom analysis reports
	• Evaluate the efficiency, effectiveness, or impact of a learning program.		• End of program or pilot	• Six levels of evaluation (Level 0 to Level 5)	• Program evaluation reports
Monitor	• Determine if measure meets threshold or is within acceptable range.	Low	• Monthly or quarterly	• Threshold or breakpoints for measures	• Dashboards • Scorecards
Inform	• Answer questions, identify key trends, and share activity.	Low	• As needed	• Specific measures or trends	• Dashboards • Scorecards

Copyright applied for by Center for Talent Reporting (2020). Used with permission.

(Measurement Maturity — vertical axis label)

Dashboard

If the reason for measuring is to inform and the user wants a visual display combined with summary measures (versus the detailed data in a scorecard), we recommend using a dashboard. Dashboards are particularly well suited for sharing information with higher-level leaders who are interested in summary measures rather than detail and who appreciate the visual displays.

We also recommend a dashboard with thresholds if the reason for measuring is to monitor and the user also wants some visualization or interactivity. In this case, the dashboard is typically color-coded. The report must include the threshold specified by the user, which will determine if the measure is in the green (meeting expectations), yellow (not quite meeting expectations), or red (not meeting expectations). Like a scorecard, the dashboard will contain only history, since the user is looking to ensure that the measure's past performance has been acceptable.

If the reason is to either inform or monitor, and the user wants the ability to drill down into the data, we recommend using a dynamic dashboard with drill down capability. Typically, the user will be able to click on a cell and change the measure or time period or see the components of a measure. (See chapter 8 for examples of dashboard types.)

Program Evaluation Report

If the reason for measuring is to evaluate a program's efficiency, effectiveness, and outcome, we recommend using a program evaluation report. The program evaluation report may be a written document or a PowerPoint presentation, with the format and length determined by the user. A three- to five-slide PowerPoint may be all that is required for a 15- to 30-minute briefing. Likewise, a short two-page memo may suffice if an in-person briefing is not possible. However, a much longer PowerPoint or memo would be required for a go or no-go decision after the pilot for a large, expensive program as well as for a final or year-end review of a large, expensive program. The program evaluation report should include the following elements:

- the goal or need addressed by the program (like a goal to increase sales by 10 percent)
- the plan to achieve the impact or meet expectations
- results of the implementation
- results for the business outcome measure (like a 9 percent increase in sales)
- the ROI on the program (if the Phillips approach is used)
- lessons learned.

(Chapter 8 has a more detailed list of elements to include in a program evaluation report; see the example in Figure 8-5.)

Custom Analysis Report

If the reason for measuring is to analyze the relationships among several measures (such as whether the amount or type of training has an impact on employee engagement or retention), we recommend using a custom analysis report. Like the program evaluation report, the type and length of a custom report will depend on the user's needs. A short PowerPoint or memo may suffice, or you may require a longer PowerPoint presentation or memo, depending on the decision to be made and the commitment of resources involved. A custom analysis report typically includes the following elements:

- question to answer (for example, is there a relationship between amount of learning and employee retention?)
- brief description of the analysis
  - methodology
  - data
  - problems encountered
- results
- opportunities for additional research.

(See chapter 8 for a more detailed discussion and the example in Figure 8-6.)

A custom analysis report is also recommended to share the results of a department initiative to improve efficiency or effectiveness across all programs or to improve processes or systems. The format, though, would be different.

The Three Management Reports

If the reason for measuring is to manage a program or measure to an agreed-upon plan level, we recommend using a management report. In contrast to the reasons for measuring discussed in the previous sections, which all focus on history (actual results), management implies a focus on the future. Recall the two questions any good manager should ask:

- Are we on plan year-to-date?
- Are we going to end the year on plan?

Providing answers to these two questions for management users requires a special type of report. It is the same type used by our colleagues who manage other departments like sales and manufacturing. All management reports contain the same basic elements in addition to the measures themselves:

- last year's results (if available)
- plan or target for this year
- YTD results for this year
- comparison of YTD results and plan
- forecast for how this year will end if no unplanned, special action is taken
- comparison of forecast to plan.

We suggest using a program, operations, or summary management report, with the recommended report depending on the user and purpose (Table 10-2).

Table 10-2. The Three Management Reports

Report	User	Purpose	Frequency	Types of Measures
Program	• Program manager • CLO • Goal or program owner	Manage programs to meet organizational goals and needs	• Monthly	• Outcome for strategic programs • Efficiency • Effectiveness
Operations	• CLO • Initiative leaders	Manage department initiatives to improve efficiency and effectiveness	• Monthly	• Efficiency • Effectiveness
Summary	• CEO, CFO, SVP HR, CLO • Governing body • L&D employees • Other interested parties	Manage expectations of senior leaders and demonstrate alignment and impact	• Quarterly	• Outcome • Efficiency • Effectiveness

Program Report

When the CLO and program manager (or a goal owner) want to actively manage a program to meet a specific organizational goal or need, we recommend using the program report. For example, organizations typically have goals to improve sales, increase productivity, reduce injuries, increase employee engagement, improve leadership, increase business acumen, or improve teamwork and communications. The typical users of a program report include the program manager, CLO, and the goal or program owner. In this case, the users want to actively manage the effectiveness and efficiency measures, and the outcome measure if present, to meet the plan or target set for each at the start of the year.

The program report identifies the goal or need and the owner as well as the planned contribution from learning if it is a strategic program (aligned directly to the goal). The report includes all the key effectiveness and efficiency measures and their plans (targets) for the year. Since it is a management report, it also includes the YTD results and forecast for each measure.

L&D should generate the program report monthly as long as the program is active.

Operations Report

If the CLO wants to actively manage department initiatives, we recommend using the operations report. Typical uses include managing initiatives to improve the effectiveness or efficiency measures across all programs (like a higher application rate or improved on-time delivery) and initiatives to improve internal L&D department measures of effectiveness and efficiency (like improved user satisfaction with the LMS or LMS uptime).

The operations report lists all the measures selected by the CLO for improvement, and the measures are grouped by category (efficiency or effectiveness). The order of the categories is up to the CLO. The CLO or other senior L&D leaders set a plan or target for each measure. Once the year is underway, there will be YTD results and a forecast for each measure. There are no outcome measures in an operations report.

L&D should generate the operations report monthly.

Summary Report

The summary report is appropriate for a high-level user like the CEO, CFO, SVP of HR, or a governing board. Since the actual management of programs and initiatives is accomplished using the program and operations reports, the purpose of the summary report is to show:

- alignment of learning to organizational goals and needs
- planned and actual impact (the outcome measure)
- progress throughout the year (comparison of YTD results to plan)
- how the year is likely to end absent any unplanned effort (comparison of forecast to plan)
- plans, progress, and forecast for key department initiatives to improve effectiveness and efficiency.

While this may sound like a "show and tell" exercise, in practice it is much more. The report demonstrates that the learning leaders are disciplined (setting specific, measurable plans and managing monthly to achieve them) and accountable. Furthermore, the summary report helps the CLO manage senior leader expectations throughout the year so there are no surprises at year end.

The summary report is also excellent for sharing at monthly L&D all-employee meetings and for making presentations to others about L&D. It immediately conveys the strategic focus of L&D, highlights all the important programs and initiatives, and reinforces that L&D leaders are running learning like a business with discipline and accountability.

The report lists all the important organization goals or needs, the learning programs aligned to them, and the agreed-upon impact of learning for each. This represents the organization's best thinking by the CLO, program managers, goal and program owners, and stakeholders. The report also includes plans for the improvement of internal effectiveness and efficiency measures. Once the year is underway, you can add the YTD results and update the forecast.

You would typically generate a high-level report like the summary report quarterly because the meetings with the CEO, where it is used, typically happen on a quarterly basis. However, you can also generate it monthly, especially if a stakeholder uses the information in monthly employee meetings.

Sharing Report Types in Your Strategy

In your measurement and reporting strategy, it is important to identify the types of reports you plan to use, the users of those reports, and the distribution frequency. Table 10-3, on the next page, shows an example report list. Note that most reports will have multiple users. The program manager, CLO, and L&D leaders are the most common users, but senior organization leaders will be important users, too, including a governing body (if you have one) like the board of governors.

Formats

The format of these reports may be altered to some degree to accommodate the needs of the user as long as the required elements remain present. The examples shared in chapters 8 and 9 are the most common formats for scorecards and management reports. The users can decide what order of measures best meets their need with the exception of the program report, where the organizational goal or need and the outcome measure must be at the top, and the summary report, where the goals and needs should come before the department initiatives to improve effectiveness and efficiency.

Dashboards, as you can tell from our discussion, do not have a single format or a common look. Some will be tabular with no visual elements. Some will have a table plus visual elements, and either the table or the visual elements may dominate. So, there is tremendous flexibility in designing the dashboard's format.

Program evaluation reports and custom analysis reports, by definition, are designed to meet the needs of the user so they may also take many forms. That said, if the purpose is to share program evaluation or research results, then the formats suggested for the sequence of elements make the most sense.

Table 10-3. Sample Report List With User and Frequency

Reports	User 1	User 2	User 3	Frequency
Program				
Strategic (aligned to goals)				
Sales	Program Mgr	CLO	VP Sales	Monthly
Safety	Program Mgr	CLO	VP Mfg	Monthly
Quality	Program Mgr	CLO	VP Quality	Monthly
Employee engagement	Program Mgr	CLO	VP HR	Monthly
Leadership	Program Mgr	CLO	CEO	Monthly
Diversity and inclusion	Program Mgr	CLO	VP HR	Monthly
Non-strategic				
Basic skills	Program Mgr	CLO	COO	Monthly
Onboarding	Program Mgr	CLO	VP HR	Monthly
Compliance	Program Mgr	CLO	Risk Officer	Monthly
Reskilling	Program Mgr	CLO	COO	Monthly
Business acumen	Program Mgr	CLO	CFO	Monthly
Communications	Program Mgr	CLO	Bd Governors	Monthly
Operations Report	CLO	Sr L&D Ldrs	Initiative Ldrs	Monthly
Summary Report	CEO, CFO, COO	Bd Governors	CLO	Quarterly
Program Evaluation Reports				
Sales	Program Mgr	VP Sales		Pilot, end-of-year
Quality	Program Mgr	VP Quality		End-of-year
Business acumen	Program Mgr	CFO		Pilot, end
Custom Analysis Reports				
Relationship between training and key HR measures	Initiative Ldr	CLO	VP HR	One time only
Dashboards				
Customer satisfaction	CLO			Monthly
Level 1 participant reaction	CLO	L&D Ldrs		Monthly
LMS uptime	CLO	L&D Ldrs		Weekly
L&D help desk satisfaction	CLO	L&D Ldrs		Weekly
Scorecards				
Courses by modality	CLO	L&D Ldrs		Monthly
Participants by modality	CLO	L&D Ldrs		Monthly

Plans to Generate and Distribute the Reports

After you have selected the appropriate reports, you need to develop a strategy for when to generate and distribute them.

Report Generation

The strategy should include the name of the person responsible for generating each report as well as the report owner within L&D. In some cases, this may be the same person. For example, the program manager may generate the program report each month, which in turn is used to talk with staff, discuss with the goal owner, and share with the CLO. In other cases, a central measurement group may be responsible for generating all the reports.

The strategy should also include the frequency with which L&D generates each report. You generate most reports monthly, but some may be quarterly and a few may be generated annually. (Some of our L&D clients generate a "state of L&D annual report" that is distributed to business leaders and made available to company employees.)

Users often prefer to establish a cadence of production reports that automatically run monthly or quarterly. Production reports continue to run until someone intervenes to stop or edit them and are generated each period. Many organizations automate some parts of their scorecards, dashboards, program reports, operations reports, and summary reports, typically the YTD data. Because program evaluation and custom analysis reports are unique to the specific situation, they are almost always created manually.

The reporting strategy might also include a list or discussion of who (or what system) needs to provide data to produce the report. Does the data come from a system such as an LMS or the organization's HR information system? Are there manual feeds for certain data elements that L&D needs to extract each month to get the data? Or, does a person within or outside L&D produce, manipulate, and transform the data before sending it along to L&D? The reporting strategy needs to clarify the data source and what data are available directly from a system or what data requires some manual intervention. The strategy might also indicate when the previous month's data will be available.

With these considerations in mind, you can expand the report to provide a more comprehensive list of factors. Your report would now include the report owner, generation process (manual or automated), and day of month for generation (Table 10-4).

Table 10-4. Sample Report List Including Generation

Reports	User 1	User 2	User 3	Frequency	Report Owner	Generation Process	Day
Program							
Strategic (aligned to goals)							
Sales	Program Mgr	CLO	VP Sales	Monthly	Program Mgr	Manual	5
Safety	Program Mgr	CLO	VP Mfg	Monthly	Program Mgr	Manual	5
Quality	Program Mgr	CLO	VP Quality	Monthly	Program Mgr	Manual	5
Employee engagement	Program Mgr	CLO	VP HR	Monthly	Program Mgr	Manual	5
Leadership	Program Mgr	CLO	CEO	Monthly	Program Mgr	Manual	5
Diversity & inclusion	Program Mgr	CLO	VP HR	Monthly	Program Mgr	Manual	5
Non-Strategic							
Basic skills	Program Mgr	CLO	COO	Monthly	Program Mgr	Manual	5
Onboarding	Program Mgr	CLO	VP HR	Monthly	Program Mgr	Manual	5
Compliance	Program Mgr	CLO	Risk Officer	Monthly	Program Mgr	Manual	5
Reskilling	Program Mgr	CLO	COO	Monthly	Program Mgr	Manual	5
Business acumen	Program Mgr	CLO	CFO	Monthly	Program Mgr	Manual	5
Communications	Program Mgr	CLO	Bd Governors	Monthly	Program Mgr	Manual	5
Operations Report	CLO	Sr L&D Ldrs	Initiative Ldrs	Monthly	Measurement Mgr	Automated	5
Summary Report	CEO, CFO, COO	Bd Governors	CLO	Quarterly	Measurement Mgr	Manual	5
Program Evaluation Reports							
Sales	Program Mgr	VP Sales		Pilot, end-of-year	Program Mgr	Manual	N/A
Quality	Program Mgr	VP Quality		End-of-year	Program Mgr	Manual	N/A
Business acumen	Program Mgr	CFO		Pilot, end	Program Mgr	Manual	N/A
Custom Analysis Reports							
Relationship between training and key HR measures	Initiative Ldr	CLO	VP HR	One time only	Initiative Ldr	Manual	N/A
Dashboards							
Customer satisfaction	CLO			Monthly	Measurement Mgr	Automated	10
Level 1 participant reaction	CLO	L&D Ldrs		Monthly	Measurement Mgr	Automated	3
LMS uptime	CLO	L&D Ldrs		Weekly	Measurement Mgr	Automated	3
L&D help desk satisfaction	CLO	L&D Ldrs		Weekly	Measurement Mgr	Automated	3
Scorecards							
Courses by modality	CLO	L&D Ldrs		Monthly	Measurement Mgr	Automated	3
Participants by modality	CLO	L&D Ldrs		Monthly	Measurement Mgr	Automated	3

Report Distribution

Once you have generated the reports, you need to provide them to the intended audience. Some organizations have the capability to fully automate the generation and distribution process so the system sends the report electronically to the user as soon as it is available. In other organizations, a person must intervene to pull and organize the data before sending or delivering the report to the user.

You should be cautious about sending reports automatically to users. For most of our clients, we have found that the administrators generating L&D reports assume their users know how to read and interpret the information in them. While this assumption is probably valid for the CLO and other senior L&D leaders, it's often not for other report recipients (including both L&D and non-L&D audiences). In our discussions with report users, we have found that even L&D audiences can find the reports challenging to interpret. They become overwhelmed with the amount of data and are uncertain how to find the story in it. They also tell us that they often won't ask for assistance because they don't want to admit they don't understand the reports.

As a result of our ad hoc discussions with clients, we strongly recommend at a minimum, that you brief non-L&D users in person (and L&D users if you suspect they don't understand the reports). In-person meetings provide an excellent opportunity to discuss how to review the report, interpret the findings, and identify next steps, including further research into root cause or creating an action plan for improvement. If you have a lot of users who need this type of coaching, you may need to consider meetings with several users to review the reports in a group, such as "data parties."

For example, a best practice is for the program manager and goal owner to meet each month to review the program report. If you are meeting in person, we recommend that you do not send the report in advance of the meeting so that you can discuss it first and provide context for what is in the report. If an in-person review of the report is not possible, you should include a short memo with the report summarizing the key points and focusing the user's attention on just a few key measures that may require action.

Data Parties

After all the work to clarify the reasons for measuring, create a measurement and reporting strategy, select measures, and generate reports, measurement and evaluation practitioners want to see their stakeholders engage with and use the results.

With the exception of managing, reports generated for informing, monitoring, and evaluation and analysis often are underused or even unused. To address this underutilization, evaluation practitioners are increasingly using more engaging means of reviewing data with their stakeholders. Instead of formal presentations, some have embraced the concept of "data parties."

A data party is a facilitated discussion among stakeholders to explore the findings and understand the results. The purpose of the party is to enable the "data consumers" to interact with the draft findings and contribute to the final conclusions and recommendations.

A key outcome of the data party should not only be agreement on the most important findings but also an action plan with assigned accountabilities and timelines.

The key point here is that reports do not speak for themselves, so don't just send them to goal owners or senior leaders like the CFO, CEO, or board of governors. Brief them in person so you can interpret the report for them and answer their questions immediately. Left on their own, it is too easy for them to misinterpret the data and draw incorrect conclusions, which can quickly (within hours) lead to serious problems for the CLO and learning department.

The strategy should also include information about how you will distribute the reports. You might accomplish this by adding a column to show whether distribution will be automated or manual (see the last column in Table 10-5).

Table 10-5. Report List Including Generation and Distribution

Reports	User 1	User 2	User 3	Frequency	Report Owner	Generation Process	Day	Distribution
Program								
Strategic (Aligned to Goals)								
Sales	Program Mgr	CLO	VP Sales	Monthly	Program Mgr	Manual	5	Manual-meeting
Safety	Program Mgr	CLO	VP Mfg	Monthly	Program Mgr	Manual	5	Manual-meeting
Quality	Program Mgr	CLO	VP Quality	Monthly	Program Mgr	Manual	5	Manual-meeting
Employee engagement	Program Mgr	CLO	VP HR	Monthly	Program Mgr	Manual	5	Manual-meeting
Leadership	Program Mgr	CLO	CEO	Monthly	Program Mgr	Manual	5	Manual-meeting
Diversity and inclusion	Program Mgr	CLO	VP HR	Monthly	Program Mgr	Manual	5	Manual-meeting
Non-Strategic								
Basic skills	Program Mgr	CLO	COO	Monthly	Program Mgr	Manual	5	Manual-meeting
Onboarding	Program Mgr	CLO	VP HR	Monthly	Program Mgr	Manual	5	Manual-meeting
Compliance	Program Mgr	CLO	Risk Officer	Monthly	Program Mgr	Manual	5	Manual-meeting
Reskilling	Program Mgr	CLO	COO	Monthly	Program Mgr	Manual	5	Manual-meeting
Business acumen	Program Mgr	CLO	CFO	Monthly	Program Mgr	Manual	5	Manual-meeting
Communications	Program Mgr	CLO	Bd Governors	Monthly	Program Mgr	Manual	5	Manual-meeting

Table 10-5. Report List Including Generation and Distribution (cont.)

Reports	User 1	User 2	User 3	Frequency	Report Owner	Process	Day	Distribution
						Generation		
Operations Report	CLO	Sr L&D Ldrs	Initiative Ldrs	Monthly	Measurement Mgr	Automated	5	Auto-email
Summary Report	CEO, CFO, COO	Bd Governors	CLO	Quarterly	Measurement Mgr	Manual	5	Manual-email
Program Evaluation Reports								
Sales	Program Mgr	VP Sales		Pilot, end-of-year	Program Mgr	Manual	N/A	Manual-meeting
Quality	Program Mgr	VP Quality		End-of-year	Program Mgr	Manual	N/A	Manual-meeting
Business acumen	Program Mgr	CFO		Pilot, end	Program Mgr	Manual	N/A	Manual-meeting
Custom Analysis Reports								
Relationship between training and key HR measures	Initiative Ldr	CLO	VP HR	One time only	Initiative Ldr	Manual	N/A	N/A
Dashboards								
Customer satisfaction	CLO			Monthly	Measurement Mgr	Automated	10	Auto-email
Level 1 participant reaction	CLO	L&D Ldrs		Monthly	Measurement Mgr	Automated	3	Auto-email
LMS uptime	CLO	L&D Ldrs		Weekly	Measurement Mgr	Automated	3	Auto-email
L&D help desk satisfaction	CLO	L&D Ldrs		Weekly	Measurement Mgr	Automated	3	Auto-email
Scorecards								
Courses by modality	CLO	L&D Ldrs		Monthly	Measurement Mgr	Automated	3	Auto-email
Participants by modality	CLO	L&D Ldrs		Monthly	Measurement Mgr	Automated	3	Auto-email

Resources Required for Reporting

Just as with the measurement strategy, the reporting strategy will require resources in terms of both staff and budget. The more complex the reporting strategy, the more resources you will need.

There often is a trade-off between the automated and manual process for the generation and distribution of reports. An automated system requires setup time by staff to put the reports in production, but once in production, little additional staff time is required. And if you can distribute the reports within L&D automatically upon generation, little to no additional staff time will be required. Automated generation and distribution, however, may require IT assistance, which in some organizations will be charged to L&D.

In contrast, a manual system for report generation will typically rely on Excel spreadsheets, so you won't need special coding or IT assistance. You may have some minimal setup time to create templates for recurring reports (like the program and operations reports) and the majority of the time each month will be spent collecting and inputting the data. The report generator typically would access a database or data warehouse and extract the latest month's values and then manually input them into the template. You would then send the completed report as an email attachment to other users within L&D or use it to brief the CLO.

The resources required to fulfill a one-time request for a report depend on the maturity of the measurement and reporting effort. If the L&D department has an easy-to-use data warehouse and if the report generators are skilled in accessing it, you may be able to generate special reports fairly quickly, especially if the software includes a custom report generator (where you can specify not only rows and columns, but also filter for categories and time periods). However, if your organization does not have a data warehouse or you can't access it easily, L&D may need to dedicate considerable resources to extract the data and create the report. The data may even have to be printed out on paper for someone else to then input into an Excel spreadsheet. In this case, even a simple-sounding request could take three to four hours to complete.

Conclusion

In many ways, the measurement and reporting strategy represents the culmination of all the work in chapters 1–9. The strategy will guide you to select the right measures and reports to meet the needs of many different users. A good strategy will ensure that users receive the measures they need in the most appropriate report with the best format.

There is also much to be said for the discipline required to create this strategy. It compels you to answer basic questions about why you measure, which measures you should select, how you will use the measures, and how you can best report them. In the end, the process to create the strategy will be just as valuable as the completed strategy itself. And few organizations have a well-thought-out measurement and reporting strategy, so this is tremendous opportunity for improvement.

While the strategy takes time to create, the payoff comes during the year and will contribute to improving the efficiency and effectiveness of the function. L&D staff will have clarity about the measures to be collected, the users and the purpose of the measures, and the reports containing the measures. Moreover, the strategy document ensures business continuity; when staff leave the L&D department, new employees can consult the strategy and get answers to the practical questions about what they need to measure, what reports to generate, and how to distribute them.

In the next chapter, we will discuss how to create plans for the selected measures, which are an essential part of running training like a business.

CHAPTER 11
Creating Plans

The management reports in chapters 8 and 9 contained columns for plans, YTD results, and forecasts. In this chapter and the next we explore where these numbers come from. Of course, plans, YTD results, and forecasts may be used independently of the three management reports, and the discussion in this chapter will prepare you for that as well. Scorecards and dashboards may also include YTD values for measures, but they typically do not contain plans or forecasts. While you can create a measurement and reporting strategy without the information in this chapter, you will not be able to implement it, generate reports, or use them without knowing how to create plans, report results, and make forecasts. This book includes more than 40 figures to illustrate the concepts and show number placement in the reports.

In this chapter we focus on creating plans or target numbers for the year, which is the hardest of the three activities. Then, in chapter 12, we explore reporting YTD results, which is the easiest, and making forecasts. Within each discussion we cover all three types of measures (efficiency, effectiveness, and outcomes).

Creating plans, reporting YTD results, and making forecasts are all essential for running learning like a business. In short, plans are set at the start of the year and represent a best guess about what is achievable. YTD results become available after the first month and are reported monthly throughout the year. YTD results are compared to plan each month, and if actual YTD results are not available, an estimate may be used in their place. Finally, once the year is underway, a forecast is made for how the measure is likely to end the year. This will also be compared to plan on a monthly basis. The sequence is shown in Figure 11-1 on the next page.

Plans for measures are the defining element in management reports and, along with forecasts, distinguish a management report from a scorecard or dashboard. Furthermore, plans are essential to running learning like a business. A plan for a measure is nothing more than a target or best guess for the value of the measure for a time period (like a year). It should be specific, measurable, and actionable. The plan should also be reasonable and achievable, but it will almost always be made in the face of uncertainties about the future. There is no guarantee that the plan value will be realized. In fact, you can usually assume just the opposite: It will not be achieved exactly. At the end of the period, the value is likely to be above or below the plan. The good news is that you will have the opportunity to influence the result and take actions to end the period as near plan as possible.

Figure 11-1. Cycle of Creating Plans, Reporting Results, and Forecasting Year-End

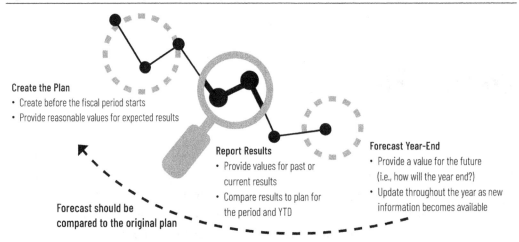

Create the Plan
- Create before the fiscal period starts
- Provide reasonable values for expected results

Forecast should be compared to the original plan

Report Results
- Provide values for past or current results
- Compare results to plan for the period and YTD

Forecast Year-End
- Provide a value for the future (i.e., how will the year end?)
- Update throughout the year as new information becomes available

Why are plans so important? First, the act of creating a plan or target for a measure will force you to think critically about how much improvement is possible and what will be required to achieve it. Second, the process will force you to reflect on history as a guide for what is possible in the future and hopefully glean some lessons from the past. Third, a plan will allow you to manage better throughout the year because you will be able to compare plan to YTD results and to forecast so that you can take corrective action if it appears you may not make plan. Bottomline, you will be a better and more successful manager if you set plans and actively manage to deliver them.

The plan number or value may come from a goal owner, CLO, or program manager, and often will be the result of discussion by several parties. The plan for an organization outcome (goal) like 5 percent higher sales or a 3 point increase in employee engagement will come from the goal owner (head of sales and HR, respectively). The plan for the learning outcome measure will come from a discussion among the goal owner, the CLO, and program manager. The plans for efficiency and effectiveness measures will come from the CLO and goal owner for programs, and from the CLO and senior L&D leaders for department initiatives to improve efficiency and effectiveness. The key parties involved in creating plans are shown in Table 11-1.

Table 11-1. Parties Involved in Creating Plans

Type of Measure	Parties Involved
Outcome	
With goal owner	• Goal owner (and goal owner staff) • CLO • Program manager
Without goal owner	• CLO • Senior L&D leaders • Program manager
Efficiency and Effectiveness	
Programs	• Goal owner (and goal owner staff) • CLO • Program manager
Department initiatives	• CLO • Senior L&D leaders • Initiative managers

Creating Plans for Outcome Measures

We start by creating plans for outcome measures, which are typically the hardest and most challenging aspect of plan setting. Before describing in detail how to create plans for outcome measures, we want to first highlight three reasons for doing so. Then, we quickly review some key concepts from chapters 5 and 9 on outcome measures, management reports, and running learning like a business. Last, we set you up for the discussion with the goal owner, which will be used to reach agreement on plan for both qualitative and quantitative outcome measures.

In our experience, creating plans for outcome measures is viewed by most as one of the most difficult aspects of TDRp and running learning like a business. However, it is also one of the most important if L&D is to be a true strategic business partner delivering bottom-line value to the organization. The goal owner and L&D must find agreement on:

- level of effort (staff hours and budget) required to deliver the planned outcome (high impact requires greater effort)
- timing of the program (high impact requires early deployment in the fiscal year)
- roles and responsibilities of both parties (high impact requires much greater involvement from the goal owner).

If they cannot agree on these basic elements, L&D will fail to meet expectations, resulting in departments taking training away from L&D and deciding to do it on their own.

Outcome measures are used in both the program and summary reports.

Two Approaches and Two Types of Outcome Measures

There are two basic approaches to creating plans for outcome measures. First, the CLO and program manager could create the plan themselves. This is easy but lacks credibility and goal owner buy-in. Second, L&D can work with the goal owner to reach agreement on the outcome measure. This requires much more work but is worth it in terms of credibility and strategic partnership with the goal owner. We explore the second approach first since the thought process behind it can be used to create plans without goal owner involvement.

There are two types of outcome measures: quantitative and qualitative. Ideally, the outcome measure is the isolated impact of learning on the organization's results (Phillips Level 4 impact), which is the quantitative measure, meaning it is expressed as a number. In this case, both parties need to agree on the percentage contribution of learning to achieve the goal, like a 20 percent contribution toward the organizational goal to increase sales by 10 percent, which would result in a 2 percent increase in sales due just to learning.

> **Note**
>
> We attribute the 2 percent increase in sales due to learning, not L&D. Neither party alone can deliver that increase. Instead, sales and L&D must work together to boost sales by 2 percent through learning. L&D brings professional knowledge of learning. The goal owner brings professional knowledge of the discipline and the power to ensure employees apply the content.

If either party is uncomfortable pursuing a quantitative outcome measure, then it may be possible to reach agreement on a qualitative outcome measure. In this case, both parties would agree on some adjective to describe the planned impact of learning, and more importantly, on all that will be required to deliver that planned impact, regardless of the adjective chosen.

Last, if there is resistance to both quantitative and qualitative outcome measures, the two parties should at least agree on the Level 3 application rate. For example, the goal owner and L&D might agree on an 80 percent application rate (either intended or actual) and then agree on all that will be required to achieve it. This approach, while not as robust as Level 4 isolated impact, still forces the two parties to think critically about level of effort, timing, roles and responsibilities, and the plan values for all the key efficiency and effectiveness measures.

Regardless of which type of outcome measure is chosen, this should be thought of as a business planning exercise where the two parties who know best (the goal owner and L&D) come together and reach agreement on reasonable and achievable values for plans. As we noted, there is no guarantee that the plan numbers will be correct. In fact, they seldom are, and business plans are usually outdated within a month of their creation. We still create them, however, because we will perform better and accomplish more with them than without them.

Note

It will be easier to discuss and agree on outcome measures if the organizational goal (outcome measure) is expressed as the change, or delta, in percentage. The delta is simply the change from the year ending to the plan year. For example, if sales are expected to end 2020 at $10 million and plan for 2021 is $11 million, the delta is an increase of $1 million for a percentage increase of 10% ($1 million ÷ $10 million). In many organizations, goals are already expressed this way, but it is easy to calculate the delta if they are not. This allows us to focus on the contribution of learning to the change from one year to the next rather than on the level. For example, we can more easily discuss the impact of learning on a $1 million increase in sales than on the $11 million level of sales for 2021.

Steps to Reach Agreement on Program Plans

Reaching agreement on outcome measures is just part of the planning process described in chapter 9 on how to run learning like a business. The key elements for agreeing on a program plan are shown in Table 11-2.

The first step is to meet with the goal owner, who is the highest-level leader responsible for the goal. For example, this would be the SVP of sales for a sales goal, SVP of manufacturing for a production or safety-related goal, and the SVP of HR for an employee engagement goal. Typically, these senior leaders report directly to the CEO or to a direct report to the CEO. The CLO and program manager will represent L&D. The goal owner usually has several staff present as well. The meeting should be scheduled for 30–60 minutes, and the discussion and length will depend largely on whether L&D has worked with the goal owner before. Often, organizational goals carry over from one year to another and only the plan value for the goal changes (such as a 5 percent increase in sales versus a 4 percent increase last year). If L&D already is providing programs to meet a need, the discussion will be shorter. If the goal owner is new or the goal is new, the discussion will take longer as both parties get to know each other.

Table 11-2. Steps to Reach Agreement With Goal Owner on Program Plans

1	Meet with goal owner to determine if learning might have a role in meeting the organization goal.
2	If it appears learning might have a role, staff from both parties meet to explore further and agree on a recommendation.
3	Present recommendation for a learning program to goal owner. Note that finalizing the program will typically require follow-up work.
4	Make final recommendation to goal owner. Reach agreement on plan for outcome measure and for all key efficiency and effectiveness measures as well as on level of effort, timing, and roles and responsibilities. Discussion may result in modifications to recommendation to achieve higher impact or reduce level of effort.
5	Reach final agreement between goal owner and L&D on programs, plan numbers, effort, timing, and roles and responsibilities.

In the second step, if it appears that learning may have a role to play, staff from both parties will begin to meet to perform at least a high-level needs analysis and develop recommendations about a learning program, audience, objectives, and so forth. This may take several meetings and span several weeks.

The third step is to share the preliminary recommendation with the goal owner. Often the goal owner will raise questions or make suggestions requiring the parties to refine the recommendation. There may be several iterations.

The fourth step is to share the revised recommendation. At this point, the two parties are ready to discuss and reach agreement on the plan for the outcome measure (such as "high" impact or a 20 percent contribution to the goal) and on plans for all the key efficiency and effectiveness measures required to achieve the planned outcome. These might be viewed as the links in a compelling chain of evidence or as Levels 0–3 on the left-hand planning side of the Phillips "V" (Figure 11-2).

Figure 11-2. Phillips "V" Diagram for Planning

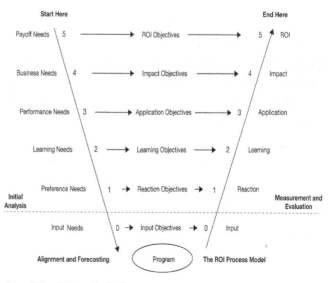

Source: Phillips, Phillips, and Ray (2020)

The outcome discussion may result in directions for staff to modify the recommendation to get higher (or lower) planned impact.

The fifth and final step is for the goal owner and L&D to agree on the final recommendation along with plans for the outcome measure, all efficiency and effectiveness measures, level of effort, cost, timing, and roles and responsibilities.

For purposes of reaching agreement on the outcome measure, the fourth and fifth steps are the most important. The meeting for the fourth step might begin with the program manager saying to the goal owner:

Thank you for your time today.

We agreed several weeks ago that learning could help achieve your goal of increasing sales by 10 percent. We have been working with your staff and today we would like to share our recommendation with you. If we decide to move forward, we will also need to agree on planned impact and what it will take to achieve it.

We recommend _____ . *(Share the details of the program.)*

If this sounds reasonable, let's discuss the impact this initiative could have on your goal to increase sales by 10 percent if we work together. Our goal is to agree on a reasonable impact and identify what each of us must do to deliver the planned outcome. The agreed-upon outcome will also drive our work effort and the timing of the initiative.

Here is how we can determine a reasonable impact _____ .

Note

The rest of the explanation depends on whether the outcome measure will qualitative or quantitative. The next sections describes the approach for each.

With this jumping-off point, we are now ready to explore the fourth step in detail to create outcome measures by working with the goal owner. We start with qualitative outcome measures and then proceed to quantitative measures. We end with a discussion of using the application rate instead of impact and a discussion about creating the plan without goal owner involvement.

Creating Plans With Goal Owner Involvement

The best way to create a plan for the learning outcome measure is to work with the goal owner. Each party brings expertise to the discussion and the outcome measure should reflect that. Moreover, working with the goal owner to create the plan will increase their buy-in, improve your partnership, and boost the chances of program success.

Qualitative Outcome Measures

A qualitative outcome measure is expressed as an adjective to convey the planned impact of learning or any other factor on an organizational goal. This approach does require a scale, but the actual scale is left to the user. Typically, high/medium/low (H/M/L) is employed, but it could just as easily be significant/very important/important. The adjectives are not as important as the discussion and the agreement on particulars that come out of the discussion. In other words, any scale will get you there.

That said, for this approach to work there does need to be some discipline around the use of a scale. The selected adjectives need to have meaning. For example, we suggest the interpretations for a H/M/L scale outlined in Table 11-3.

Table 11-3. Interpretations of High/Medium/Low for Qualitative Outcomes

Adjective	Impact of Learning on Organization Goal
High	Learning is the primary driver in achieving the goal and by itself is expected to be responsible for at least 50% of the goal.
Medium	Learning is one of several important drivers and is expected to contribute 20–50% of the goal. It may be the primary driver but due to other important drivers, it is not expected to contribute more than 50%.
Low	Learning is important but not a key or primary factor in achieving the goal. Learning is expected to contribute less than 20% to achieving the goal.

We are now ready for the methodology itself. Unless the goal owner is experienced in this methodology, it will not work to simply ask what planned impact sounds reasonable. The goal owner will simply not have any context to provide a good answer. Instead, the CLO or program manager needs to walk the goal owner through a few questions and then discuss the results. We've summarized the steps here:

- Ask the goal owner to list all the factors or drivers contributing to achievement of the goal.
- Ask the goal owner to prioritize the factors.
- Use the ranking to discuss relative importance.

If one factor is dominant (more important than all the other factors combined), label it "high" impact. If no factor is dominant, but one or two are very important and considerably more important than the others, label them "medium" impact. Label all the other factors "low" impact. A forced ranking is helpful here, where there can be no more than one "high" and two "medium" impacts.

Remember that this is primarily a business discussion to help L&D and the goal owner allocate the right level of resources, agree on the timing of the initiative, set good plans for the key efficiency and effectiveness measures (especially the application rate), and agree on roles and responsibilities. There is no "right" answer.

As an example of this process, for an organization goal of increasing sales by 10 percent, the goal owner provided six factors or drivers to achieve the goal. The order is not important in step 1; top of mind responses are fine (Table 11-4).

Table 11-4. Qualitative Outcome Plan Example: Step 1

Drivers to increase sales by 10%:	
• Hiring five new salespeople	• New advertising campaign
• Growth in the economy	• New products
• New salesperson incentive system	• Consultative sales and products features training

Next, the goal owner is asked to prioritize the six factors or drivers (Table 11-5).

Table 11-5. Qualitative Outcome Plan Example: Step 2

Prioritized drivers to increase sales by 10%:	
1. Growth in the economy	4. New salesperson incentive system
2. Consultative sales and product features training	5. Hiring five new salespeople
3. New products	6. New advertising campaign

Step 3 requires the CLO or program manager to use the relative rankings to suggest an adjective for each. Since there are only three buckets, it is not as hard as it may seem. Not surprisingly for a sales goal, the economy ranks first, so the CLO asks how the economy compares in importance to the other factors. In this example, the goal owner says it is the dominant factor and more important than all the rest combined. Mark it "high." Next, the CLO asks how training compares to new products. The goal owner says about the same. Ties are allowed, so the next question is how factors 2 and 3 compare to factors 4–6. The goal owner responds by saying that while all six factors are important, factors 2 and 3 are more important than factors 4–6. That is all we needed to hear. Mark training and new products as "medium" and factors 4–6 as "low" (Table 11-6).

We are most interested in the relative contribution for training, which is medium. This is the plan for the learning outcome measure. At this point, we know the six factors the goal owner will rely on to achieve 10 percent higher sales. The

Table 11-6. Qualitative Outcome Plan Example: Step 3

Prioritized Drivers to Increase Sales by 10%	Relative Contribution
1. Growth in the economy	High
2. Consultative sales and product features training	Medium
3. New products	Medium
4. New salesperson incentive system	Low
5. Hiring five new salespeople	Low
6. New advertising campaign	Low

goal owner cannot control the economy, so that puts extra pressure on the other five to deliver results. In this example, training is tied with new products for second place and top of the list for factors that the organization can control. So, this training program is going to be very important and a key contributor to achieving the organizational goal. With this perspective in mind, the parties now need to agree on effort, timing, and plans for all the key efficiency and effectiveness measures required to achieve this (medium) level of impact.

We enter the qualitative outcome measure under the plan column as high, medium, or low (or whatever adjectives have been chosen). The name of the outcome measure is simply impact of learning on sales or whatever the goal is. Also enter the planned impact right after the outcome measure—for example, medium for 2021 plan. The plans for the three goals are shown at the top of a summary report (Table 11-7), and placement is similar in the program report (Table 11-8). Notice that in both examples there are no YTD results since the year has not yet begun, and the forecast is set equal to plan to start the year.

Table 11-7. Placement of Plans for Qualitative Outcome Measures in a Summary Report

Priority	Business Goals and Supporting L&D Programs	Unit of Measure	2020 Actual	2021 Plan	YTD Results	YTD Results Compared to Plan	Forecast	Forecast Compared to Plan
1.	Revenue: Increase Sales by 10%							
	Corporate goal or actual	%	7%	10%			10%	
	Impact of Learning on Sales: Medium for 2021 Plan	H/M/L	Low	Medium			Medium	
	New product features training *Consultative selling skills*							
2.	Safety: Reduce Injuries by 20%							
	Corporate goal or actual	%	10%	20%			20%	
	Impact of Learning on Injuries: High for 2021 Plan	H/M/L	Medium	High			High	
	Safety programs to address the top five causes of injuries							
3.	Costs: Reduce Operating Expenses by 15%							
	Corporate goal or actual	%	5%	15%			15%	
	Impact of Learning on Expenses: Medium for 2021 Plan	H/M/L	Low	Medium			Medium	
	Training for purchasing agents *Training for all employees on reducing costs* *Training for department heads to meet 15% goal*							

Table 11-8. Placement of Plans for Qualitative Outcome Measures in a Program Report

Goal Owner: Swilthe, VP of Manufacturing	Unit of Measure	2020 Actual	2021 Plan	YTD Results	YTD Results Compared to Plan	Forecast	Forecast Compared to Plan
Enterprise Goal: Reduce Injuries	%	10%	20%			20%	
Impact of Learning on Sales: Medium for 2021 Plan	H/M/L	Medium	High			High	

Quantitative Outcome Measures

The approach to reach agreement on a quantitative outcome measure is the same as that for a qualitative measure except that in step 3 we ask the goal owner for a percentage contribution for each factor or driver:

- Ask the goal owner to list all the factors or drivers contributing to achievement of the goal.
- Ask the goal owner to prioritize the factors.
- Ask the goal owner to attribute a percentage contribution to each factor.

The goal owner may require a few iterations until the percentage contribution for all factors adds up to 100 percent. In Table 11-9, we show step 3 (steps 1 and 2 are unchanged), where the goal owner assigned a 50 percent contribution to the economy, explaining that the economy is the dominant factor. In other words, if the economy does not grow as expected, it is highly unlikely that sales will grow 10 percent. The goal owner attributed a 20 percent contribution to consultative sales and product features training and 15 percent to new products. Like in the qualitative example, these two factors are viewed as hav-

Table 11-9. Quantitative Outcome Plan Example: Step 3

Prioritized Drivers to Increase Sales by 10%	Percentage Contribution
1. Growth in the economy	50%
2. Consultative sales and product features training	20%
3. New products	15%
4. New salesperson incentive system	5%
5. Hiring five new salespeople	5%
6. New advertising campaign	5%

ing almost the same impact. The last three factors are tied at 5 percent—still important, but considerably less important than the first three. Given that this a planning exercise, the recommendation is to use increments of 5 percent.

We are most interested in the percentage contribution from the learning program, which is 20 percent. This 20 percent is the planned isolated impact from learning (Phillips Level 4). If the organizational goal is in delta form and expressed as a percentage, we can use the 20 percent contribution to calculate the resulting plan for the outcome measure, which will be a 2 percent increase in sales due just to learning. By formula:

Quantitative outcome plan = Organizational goal × Percentage contribution from learning
= 10% increase in sales × 20% contribution from learning
= 2% increase in sales due to learning.

In other words, both the head of sales and L&D believe it is reasonable to plan for a 20 percent contribution from learning to result in a 2 percent increase in sales due just to learning if the content is well conceived, designed, delivered, and reinforced, and if both parties fulfill their mutually agreed-upon roles and responsibilities. Once the goal owner and L&D have agreed on the plan for the outcome measure, both parties need to agree on plans for the key efficiency and effectiveness measures that will be required to achieve the 20 percent contribution from learning. We will discuss these plans in the next section.

While the 20 percent came from the goal owner, it is important that L&D is comfortable with it as well. Sometimes, goal owners will assume that learning can contribute more than is reasonable and in these cases the CLO or program manager will need to counsel them to be more conservative.

The percentage contribution (such as 20 percent) comes right after the name of the learning outcome measure, which is impact of learning on sales (or whatever the goal is). The plan for the learning outcome measure is entered under the plan column as 2 percent. The placement of the terms at the top of a summary report is shown in Table 11-10, as well as placement of plans for the first goal in a program report in Table 11-11. You should always create the plan before the year begins, which means that there are no YTD results and the forecast is set equal to plan.

Table 11-10. Placement of Plans for Quantitative Outcome Measures in a Summary Report

Priority	Business Goals and Supporting L&D Programs	Unit of Measure	2020 Actual	Plan	YTD Results	YTD Results Compared to Plan	Forecast	Forecast Compared to Plan
				2021				
1.	Revenue: Increase Sales by 10%							
	Corporate goal or actual	%	6%	10%			10%	
	Impact of Learning on Sales: 20% contribution to goal for 2021 plan	% increase in sales	1%	2%			2%	
	New product features training *Consultative selling skills*							
2.	Safety: Reduce Injuries by 20%							
	Corporate goal or actual	%	10%	20%			20%	
	Impact of Learning on Injuries: 70% contribution to goal for 2021 plan	% decrease in injuries	3%	14%			14%	
	Safety programs to address top five causes of injuries							
3.	Costs: Reduce Operating Expenses by 15%							
	Corporate goal or actual	%	5%	15%			15%	
	Impact of Learning on Expenses: 30% contribution to goal for 2021 plan	% decrease in expenses	0%	5%			5%	
	Training for purchasing agents *Training for all employees on reducing costs* *Training for department heads to meet 15% goal*							

Table 11-11. Placement of Plans for a Quantitative Outcome Measure in a Program Report

Goal Owner: Chen, VP of Sales	Unit of Measure	2020 Actual	Plan	YTD Results	YTD Results Compared to Plan	Forecast	Forecast Compared to Plan
			2021				
Enterprise Goal: Reduce Injuries	%	6%	10%			10%	
Impact of Learning on Injuries: 20% contribution planned for 2021	%	1%	2%			2%	

Of course, it is unlikely that at the end of the year learning will have contributed exactly 20 percent. It is just a plan, and all we know for sure about plans is that they are wrong. Perhaps it will be 16 percent or 23 percent, but the hope is that the 20 percent will be close enough to drive the right resource allocation and make the right decisions about plans for the key efficiency and effectiveness measures. It will be interesting to use one of the Phillips methodologies to determine the actual contribution at year-end and compare it to the plan of 20 percent. There are always lessons we can learn from the variance between plan and actual. It may be that the plan was good, but the execution was poor. Or, it may turn out that the plan was too pessimistic or optimistic. In any case, the variance is your teacher and reflecting on it will improve your ability to set good plans in the future.

In the previous example, we assumed that the organization had specific, measurable goals that would allow the calculation of the delta. Unfortunately, a surprising number of organizations do not. Instead, they have focus areas or pillars for next year like increase sales, enhance customer satisfaction, and improve the culture. This is disappointing, but not a reason to give up. You can still use the methodology to agree on the percentage contribution from learning (or an adjective for qualitative) and have the rich discussion on all that will have to be done to deliver that contribution. In this case, show the percentage contribution for the outcome measure (Table 11-12).

Table 11-12. Case 1: Placement of Plans for Quantitative Outcome Measures When No Plan Is Available for Organizational Outcome

| Priority | Business Goals and Supporting L&D Programs | Unit of Measure | 2020 Actual | 2021 | | | | |
				Plan	YTD Results	YTD Results Compared to Plan	Forecast	Forecast Compared to Plan
1.	Revenue: Increase Sales							
	Corporate goal or actual	%	6%					
	Impact of Learning on Sales: 20% contribution for 2021	% contribution	1%	20%			20%	
	New product features training *Consultative selling skills*							
2.	Safety: Reduce Injuries							
	Corporate goal or actual	%	10%					
	Impact of Learning on Injuries: 70% contribution for 2021	% contribution	3%	70%			70%	
	Safety programs to address top five causes of injuries							
3.	Costs: Reduce Operating Expenses							
	Corporate goal or actual	%	5%					
	Impact of Learning on Expenses: 30% contribution for 2021	% contribution	0%	30%			30%	
	Training for purchasing agents *Training for all employees on reducing costs* *Training for department heads to meet 15% goal*							

Another alternative is to eliminate all three steps and directly determine the plan for learning. For example, both parties could agree that it would be reasonable to plan for a 3 percent increase in sales due just to learning. This approach skips the percentage contribution and also does not rely on a specific, measurable organizational goal (Table 11-13).

Table 11-13. Case 2: Placement of Plans for Quantitative Outcome Measures When No Plan Is Available for Organization Outcome

						2021			
Priority	Business Goals and Supporting L&D Programs	Unit of Measure	2020 Actual	Plan	YTD Results	YTD Results Compared to Plan		Forecast	Forecast Compared to Plan
1.	Revenue: Increase Sales								
	Corporate goal or actual	%	6%						
	Impact of Learning on Sales: 3% increase in sales planned for 2021	% increase	1%	3%				3%	
	New product features training *Consultative selling skills*								
2.	Safety: Reduce Injuries								
	Corporate goal or actual	%	10%						
	Impact of Learning on Injuries: 15% reduction in injuries planned for 2021	% reduction	3%	15%				15%	
	Safety programs to address top five causes of injuries								
3.	Costs: Reduce Operating Expenses								
	Corporate goal or actual	%	5%						
	Impact of Learning on Expenses: 2% reduction in expenses planned for 2021	% reduction	0%	2%				2%	
	Training for purchasing agents *Training for all employees on reducing costs* *Training for department heads to meet 15% goal*								

This concludes our discussion of reaching agreement on qualitative and quantitative outcome measures. We hope you agree that conceptually the approach is not too difficult. We do understand, though, that these types of discussions are new not only for the goal owners but also for L&D, and thus there will be some discomfort and resistance. Next, we discuss an easier alternative.

Use of the Application Rate Instead of the Outcome Measure

There may be times when the goal owner (or even the CLO or program manager) is not comfortable with either the qualitative or quantitative approach to reaching agreement on an outcome measure. In these cases, our recommendation is to use the application rate as the next-best measure of success. It is highly correlated with Level 4 impact and is a leading indicator of Level 4. Everyone would agree that if there is no application, there can be no impact. While it is true that we could have application and still have no impact, it is usually the case that application will result in at least some impact. So, the two levels are correlated, meaning they move together. And application precedes impact, so it is a leading indicator of impact. Either intent to apply or actual application may be used for Level 3.

> **Note**
>
> Levels 1 and 2 should never be used as next-best measures for Level 4 outcome. They are not correlated with Level 4 and are not leading indicators. The learning profession is full of examples of programs that received high marks for Levels 1 and 2 but had no impact.

The use of Level 3 application as a next-best measure for outcome has the added advantage of being easier to understand and measure. The goal owner likely is already familiar with the concept of application whereas they may not have been familiar with isolated impact. In addition, many organizations already measure and report application rates. If not, online survey tools make it easy for any organization to start.

The section on setting plans for effectiveness measures provides guidance on setting Level 3 plans, so we will not repeat that here. It is important, though, for the goal owner and L&D to agree on the definition for application: intent to apply or actual application or both? Will the measure be percent of content applied or percent or audience applying it? Once the two parties have agreed on definitions, they need to agree on a value for the plan. Then, they need to agree on level of effort, timing, resources, and roles and responsibilities, as well as plans for the other key effectiveness and efficiency measures.

Use of the application rate as a next-best measure will provide many, but not all, of the benefits of using isolated impact from a planning perspective. Setting a plan for Level 3 will still force the goal owner and L&D to have a good discussion about level of effort, timing, resources required, and roles and responsibilities. The two parties must still agree on plans for the other effectiveness and efficiency measures. The discussions will not be quite as rich as those intended to isolate impact and there will be no impact plan, but the use of application is still a good alternative and much better than not reaching agreement with the goal owner on any measure of success.

When application is used as a next-best measure for outcome, it should appear in the program and summary report on the row for outcome measure. Replace "impact of learning: xx% contribution" with "application rate: xx% planned for xxxx." The plan for the application rate appears in the same row under the plan column heading. Refer to Table 11-14 for an example of placement in a summary report for the first goal.

Table 11-14. Placement of Plan for Application Rate as a Next-Best Measure for Outcome

Priority	Business Goals and Supporting L&D Programs	Unit of Measure	2020 Actual	2021 Plan	2021 YTD Results	2021 YTD Results Compared to Plan	2021 Forecast	2021 Forecast Compared to Plan
1.	Revenue: Increase Sales by 10%							
	Corporate goal or actual	%	6%	10%			10%	
	Application Rate: 80% planned for 2021	Application rate	71%	80%			80%	
	New product features training *Consultative selling skills*							
2.	Safety: Reduce Injuries by 20%							
	Corporate goal or actual	%	10%	20%			20%	
	Impact of Learning on Injuries: 70% contribution to goal for 2021	% decrease in injuries	3%	14%			14%	
	Safety programs to address top five causes of injuries							
3.	Costs: Reduce Operating Expenses by 15%							
	Corporate goal or actual	%	5%	15%			15%	
	Impact of Learning on Expenses: 30% contribution to goal for 2021	% decrease in expenses	0%	5%			5%	
	Training for purchasing agents *Training for all employees on reducing costs* *Training for department heads to meet 15% goal*							

In a program report, if there are multiple programs with different application rates, the highlighted application rate should be the weighted average of the application rates for the multiple programs. Use the number of participants as the weight. Plans for the application rates for individual programs can be shown under each program. Table 11-15 is an example where an 80 percent application rate is planned for the first program and a 70 percent application rate planned for the second program.

The weighted average of 87 percent for planned application rate is found using total participants as weights: 6,000 for Program A and 3,000 for Program B:

Weighted Average Plan for Application Rate
= (Rate for Program A × Weight for Program A) + (Rate for Program B × Weight for Program B)
= (90% × 6000 ÷ 9000) + (80% × 3000 ÷ 9000)
= (90% × 0.67) + (80% × 0.33)
= 60.3% + 26.4%
= 87%

Table 11-15. Use of Weighted Average Application Rate in a Program Report

Goal Owner: Swilthe, VP of Manufacturing	Metric	2020 Actual	2021				
			Plan	YTD Results	YTD Results Compared to Plan	Forecast	Forecast Compared to Plan
Enterprise Goal: Reduce Injuries	%	12%	20%			20%	
Application Rate Used as a Next-Best Measure for Impact of Learning	%	N/A	87%			87%	
Program A (Deliver Existing Two Courses to Factory A)							
Efficiency Measure							
Unique participants	Number	452	3,000			3,000	
Total participants	Number	858	6,000			6,000	
Completion rate (100% by March 31)	% complete, date	N/A	3/31			3/31	
Effectiveness Measures							
Level 1 participant reaction	% favorable	70%	80%			80%	
Level 2 learning	% first-time pass rate	86%	90%			90%	
Level 3 intent to apply	% content applied	53%	90%			90%	
Program B (Design and Deliver Three New Courses to Factory B)							
Design New Courses							
Efficiency Measure: Complete by 3/31	Number	N/A	3			3	
Effectiveness Measure: Goal Owner reaction	5-point scale	4.0	4.5			4.5	
Deliver New Courses							
Efficiency Measures							
Unique participants	Number	N/A	1,000			1,000	
Total participants	Number	N/A	3,000			3,000	
Completion rate (100% by July 31)	% complete, date	N/A	7/31			7/31	
Effectiveness Measures							
Level 1 participant reaction	% favorable	N/A	80%			80%	
Level 2 learning	% first-time pass rate	N/A	90%			90%	
Level 3 intent to apply	% content applied	N/A	80%			80%	

Creating Plans for Outcome Measures Without Goal Owner Involvement

There are cases where it may be impossible to engage with a goal owner. For example, there may not be an identified goal owner or there may be a committee that cannot agree among themselves. The goal owner may simply not want to participate in the exercises to isolate impact. Even when the CLO can identify a single goal owner, they may decide the learning team is not ready to engage with senior leaders about either isolated impact or the use of the application rate. In any of these cases, it will be better for L&D to unilaterally set the plan for outcome measures than not to have a plan at all.

The recommendation is to use a team approach within L&D to discuss a reasonable qualitative plan (such as H/M/L) or a reasonable percentage contribution for the quantitative approach. If those in L&D know enough about the goal, they might try to use the same methodologies described in the previous sections to list and prioritize the factors and then assign an adjective or percentage contribution to each. If that is not feasible, then just use your best thinking to assign a plan to each outcome measure, remembering it should be reasonable and achievable. We might add in this case, that it should also be conservative since L&D is setting the plan unilaterally. Next, share the plans and your assumptions with the goal owners to see if they will engage or at least provide feedback. If they still won't, share with other senior leaders (governing board if you have one, CFO, or CEO) and ask for their feedback. Explain that you are trying to run learning like a business by setting specific, measurable plans, which you believe will enable greater efficiency, effectiveness, and impact. Incorporate their comments.

Since this approach is new for most organizations, some CLOs want to practice for the first year without sharing the plans outside L&D. This makes perfect sense from a change management point of view and provides a safe environment for the team to learn together. The CLO may also want to tell program managers that they will not be judged on the accuracy of their plans for the first year since setting plans is new to everyone. These steps will go a long way to reducing resistance and will allow for a whole year to practice setting plans and using reports.

Recommendation

It is very important to get started, even in practice mode. Managers will not become comfortable planning or running learning like business without actually doing it. Reading books or articles and attending webinars or workshops will provide basic knowledge but will not overcome the natural fears about being wrong or falling short of plan. The only way to get better at setting plans and managing programs is to do it, which will entail making mistakes. Just remember that you learn the most from mistakes and from the variance between plan and actual results. If you never set plans, you will never learn how to do it.

This concludes our discussion of creating plans for outcome measures—a key element in running learning like a business. The process of reaching agreement with goal owners is invaluable in setting both parties up for success. The pros and cons of the different approaches are summarized in Table 11-16.

The process is certainly subjective, but remember that is true of the entire business planning process. Senior leaders simply want the best thinking from you and the goal owner. The questions is, "What can the two of you, and your organizations, make happen if you work together?" Like any other planning number, the agreed-upon plan for the outcome measure will not be perfect, but with some effort, it can be reasonable and achievable.

Table 11-16. Pros and Cons of Each Method to Create Outcome Measures

By Measure Type	Pros	Cons
Qualitative	• Easier to reach agreement	• More subjective • May be difficult to agree on adjectives and their definitions
Quantitative	• Fosters the most joint accountability between the goal owner and L&D • Identifies the planned isolated impact of the learner	• Can be difficult to agree on or assign the percentage of contribution from learning, especially when there are many factors
Application rate as a next-best measure	• More familiar to the goal owner • Easier to reach agreement • Simplifies data collection	• Does not demonstrate a tight link between learning and the goal • No plan for isolated impact
By Approach	**Pros**	**Cons**
With goal owner	• Increases credibility and accuracy • Fosters strategic partnership • Greater buy-in from the goal owner	• Time consuming • Many in L&D are uncomfortable having these types of discussions with senior leaders
Without goal owner	• Faster and less stressful	• Deprives L&D of the opportunity to partner strategically with the goal owner

This wraps up our discussion of creating plan numbers for outcome measures and brings us to creating plans for efficiency and effectiveness measures.

Creating Plans for Efficiency and Effectiveness Measures

Our next task is to set plans for efficiency and effectiveness measures. We use these plans both for strategic and non-strategic programs (contained in program reports) as well as for department initiatives to improve efficiency and effectiveness (contained in the operations and summary reports). For strategic and non-strategic programs, the goal or program owner and staff in the owner's organization should be involved in setting these plans since they will be responsible in some cases for achieving them (for example, number of participants and application rate). For department initiatives, the CLO and senior learning leaders will be the ones setting plans.

The methodology differs depending on whether you will use the measures in a program report or in the operations report. In a program report, plans for the efficiency and effectiveness measures must support the plan for the outcome measure. In an operations report, plans should simply be reasonable and achievable and in line with the CLO's expectations.

We begin with plans in support of an outcome measure found in a program report.

Plans in a Program Report in Support of an Outcome Measure

The plan for the outcome measure must be set first, and options to do this were discussed in the previous section. Now our question is, "What must the plans be for the key efficiency and effectiveness measures to achieve the planned outcome?"

The guidance is straightforward:

- Higher impact will require higher values for all efficiency and effectiveness measures and will require completion dates early in the fiscal year.
- The resulting plans must be reasonable and achievable.

The first consideration is just common sense, and one of the reasons that it is so important to begin by reaching agreement on an outcome. The planned value for each efficiency and effectiveness measure will depend on individual circumstances, reflecting how hard the outcome will be to achieve as well as any history available on what level of outcome was achieved with different levels of efficiency and effectiveness measures. So, you will simply have to use whatever information you have and your best professional judgment. The good news is that your judgment and ability to plan will improve with practice.

That said, Table 11-17 is a conceptual framework for planning.

Table 11-17. Conceptual Framework for Planning in a Program Report

	Low Impact	High Impact
Efficiency Measures		
Participants	Small number Less than the entire audience	100% of target audience
Completion date	Later in the year	Early in the year
Completion rate	Less than 100%	100%
Effectiveness Measures		
Level 1 participant	Lower % favorable	Higher % favorable
Level 2	Lower score or pass rate	High score or pass rate
Level 3	Lower application rate	Higher application rate

In most organizations, high impact (high, or a large percentage contribution) will require the entire target audience to take and complete the training early in the fiscal year. In addition, the application rate will have to be high and ideally, Level 1 and 2 scores are also high. High for Levels 1–3 would typically be above 80 percent, but again this depends on the organization, program, and other factors.

At this point you might be thinking that you will simply plan on very high values for all these key measures. The constraint, of course, is the second factor mentioned earlier;

namely, that they must be reasonable and achievable. Budget and time are usually the two limiting factors. It often takes considerable effort and budget to get application rates above 80 percent and to reach everyone in a large audience early in the year. While you might aspire to high plans for all your program efficiency and effectiveness measures, it is simply not realistic. L&D and the goal owners might be able to dedicate the requisite resources for one or two programs but probably not all of them. This in turn will limit how many programs can have a high plan for outcome.

We have provided two scenarios to help illustrate the point. Table 11-18 shows high plan values for efficiency and effectiveness measures in support of a plan for high impact; Table 11-19 shows more moderate values in support of a plan for low impact. The potential target audience in each case is 3,000, and the fiscal year runs from January 1 to December 31.

Notice that in the first case the entire target audience is targeted, the completion date is earlier, and the completion rate higher than in the second case. Also, the plan values for effectiveness measures are considerably higher than in the second case.

Bottom line: The plans for efficiency and effectiveness measures in a program report need to support the plan for the outcome measure.

Table 11-18. Plans for Efficiency and Effectiveness Measures in Support of High Impact

Goal Owner: Swilthe, VP of Manufacturing	Metric	2020 Actual	2021 Plan	YTD Results	YTD Results Compared to Plan	Forecast	Forecast Compared to Plan
Enterprise Goal: Reduce Injuries	%	8%	25%			25%	
Impact of Learning on Injuries: High Impact for 2021	H/M/L	High	High			High	
Develop Two Courses							
Efficiency Measure: Development complete by January 31	Number	N/A	2			2	
Deliver Two Courses							
Efficiency Measures							
Unique participants	Number	452	3,000			3,000	
Total participants	Number	858	6,000			6,000	
Completion date, rate	Date, rate	N/A	3/31			3/31	
Effectiveness Measures							
Level 1 participant reaction	% favorable	70%	80%			80%	
Level 2 learning	% first-time pass rate	86%	90%			90%	
Level 3 intent to apply	% of content applied	53%	95%			95%	
Level 3 actual application	% of content applied	39%	90%			90%	

Table 11-19. Plans for Efficiency and Effectiveness Measures in Support of Low Impact

Goal Owner: Swilthe, VP of Manufacturing	Metric	2020 Actual	2021				
			Plan	YTD Results	YTD Results Compared to Plan	Forecast	Forecast Compared to Plan
Enterprise Goal: Reduce Injuries	%	8%	10%			10%	
Impact of Learning on Injuries: High Impact for 2021	H/M/L	N/A	Low			Low	
Develop Two Courses							
Efficiency Measure: Development complete by June 30	Number	N/A	2			2	
Deliver Two Courses							
Efficiency Measures							
Unique participants	Number	N/A	1,000			1,000	
Total participants	Number	N/A	2,000			2,000	
Completion date	Date	N/A	9/30			9/30	
Completion rate	%	N/A	50%			50%	
Effectiveness Measures							
Level 1 participant reaction	% favorable	N/A	60%			60%	
Level 2 learning	% first-time pass rate	N/A	60%			60%	
Level 3 intent to apply	% of content applied	N/A	50%			50%	
Level 3 actual application	% of content applied	N/A	40%			40%	

Plans in an Operations Report

Unlike the efficiency and effectiveness measures found in a program report, those in an operations report are aggregated across all programs or represent measures used for internal process improvements. So, the approach to create plans for them will be different. In this case, plans for efficiency and effectiveness measures come from the professional judgment of those setting the plans. Your professional judgment, in turn, will be informed by your organization's history, by other organizations' history and benchmarks, and by experience. The last part (experience) means you simply need to start setting plans and you will get better with experience. That said, we can offer the following guidance if you believe the future will be shaped by the same forces that shaped the past:

1. Look at the history for the measure.
2. Can you explain the history?
3. What effort are you planning?
4. Will external factors play a role?
5. Are there benchmarks available?

As long as you believe that history may offer some insights, it is the natural place to begin. Even if you are not sure whether the history will provide insights, it is still a good starting point. First, graph the last five years of data if you have it and see if there is a trend. If yes, is the trend smooth or erratic? Is it up or down? Accelerating or not?

Second, can you explain the history? If there is a trend in the data, do you know why? Were plans for improvement set, and if so, how did results compare to the plan? Were there concerted efforts to improve or did the improvement happen by accident? Are there people who have been in the organization for the last several years who can tell you whether the movement in the measure was intentional or not. Were there any one-time-only events that resulted in abnormally high or low values for the measure?

Third, what effort are you planning and how does that compare to the effort put in for the past several years? If an effort had been made the last several years to improve a measure, how much effort did that take and can you put the same amount or perhaps even more effort in next year? If so, you may be able to bend the curve (trend line) up.

Fourth, were external factors responsible for any movement in the data? How much of an impact did they have? Are any likely to be present this coming year? How do they compare to what has happened before?

Fifth, are there any benchmarks for this measure to help you set a reasonable plan? A benchmark can let you know what average and best-in-class organizations are doing. For example, it may be unreasonable to set a plan for a measure that is higher than that achieved by the best-in-class organizations. Benchmarks were identified in chapters 3 and 4 for numerous measures.

All these factors will help you understand what has happened in the past and what a reasonable plan for improvement would be going ahead. In the absence of better information, it is not illogical to assume that a trend will continue, but it is far more reassuring to understand what has driven the history. If we have some level of understanding about the past, we will be more confident in setting plans for the coming year, especially if we want to bend the curve up or down.

An example will help. Suppose you are interested in setting a plan for Level 1 participant reaction for the year 2020. You have data on the measure for the last five years as shown in Figure 11-3.

Figure 11-3. Case Study 1: Level 1 History for Last Five Years

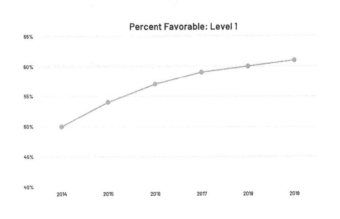

There is clearly a smooth trend to the data. However, the improvement has been decelerating, meaning that each year's gain is a little less than the year before. So, we have a positively sloped trend that is slowing. In the absence of any other information, what would a reasonable plan be for 2020? If the recent trend of improving one point per year continues, a good plan would be 62 percent, which is 1 percent higher than 2019. However, it is possible the improvement is flattening out, so it may settle at 61 percent. So, either 61 percent or 62 percent would be reasonable in the absence of any other information.

Now, let's assume that we can get more information about the case from people who were present the last five years. In case 1, we find that there had been efforts to improve Level 1, but L&D expended less effort recently. We conclude that the amount of effort does make a difference so if we invest more next year, we should be able to bend the curve up. Further, benchmarks indicate that 80 percent favorable is possible, but gains of more than 5 points per year are unlikely. Given this additional information and our intention to invest considerably more than the last several years, it would be reasonable to set plan at 64 percent or 65 percent, in effect bending the curve up. We recognize that this is 2 to 3 percent above trend and will take considerable effort to achieve.

Contrast Figure 11-4 with Figure 11-3. This figure shows much more erratic data, which more likely resembles what you would see in the real world.

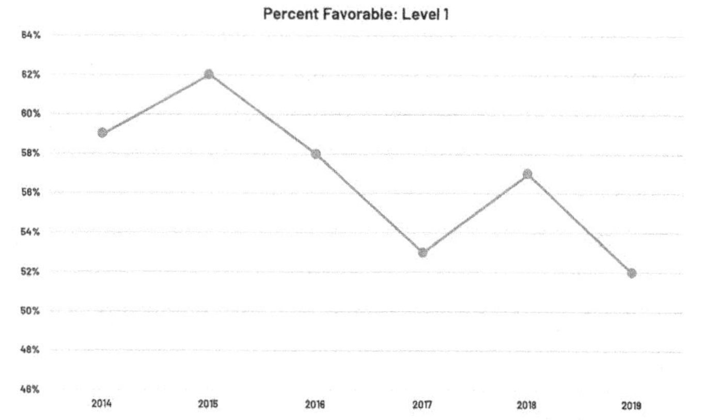

There does appear to be a downward trend in Figure 11-4, but it is very uneven and it is unclear if the trend is accelerating. In the absence of any other information, what would a reasonable plan be for 2020? In this case, it is very hard to say. We really need to understand what has been happening.

Let's assume we can find out what was going on these last five years. We discover that the swings in Level 1 were due to several factors. First, in 2015, the department invested to improve Level 1. However, in 2016, the department laid off staff experienced in design and development and outsourced those services to the lowest cost bidder. Not surprisingly, the quality of the programs suffered. In 2018, due to service-level agreements, the outsourcing company improved their scores somewhat. However, the department made additional budget cuts in 2019, which once again affected

Figure 11-4. Case Study 2: Level 1 History for the Last Five Years

satisfaction levels. Furthermore, the 2016 layoffs included some of the staff responsible for data collection and measurement, resulting in less reliable reporting.

With this additional information, we now understand why Level 1 turned up in 2015 and then fell in 2016 and 2017 before turning back in 2018. It seems that Level 1 is responsive to the effort invested in it, so it would be reasonable to assume that L&D can positively affect the results with additional focus. However, given the erratic history, the downward trend in 2019, and the issues with data collection, a reasonable plan for 2020 may be to stabilize the department in the first half of the year and begin to make progress in the second half. This is likely to result in an average Level 1 for the year of about 52 or 53 percent. Then, good progress should be possible in 2021, returning to 56–57 percent.

We hope these examples provide guidance on how to use the criteria prompted by our questions. We showed you an example of a department initiative to improve an effectiveness measure across all programs, and the guidance would be the same for department initiatives to improve internal processes. As always when it comes to plans, there is a large subjective element involved in setting a plan number. The good news is that it gets easier with practice. The bad news is that you will never be good at it if you don't do it. So, you just have to jump in and start setting plans!

Now that you have created plans for efficiency and effectiveness measures, they need to be placed in the operations report. Table 11-20 illustrates their placement before the year starts. Notice that there are no YTD results yet and forecast is set equal to plan.

It should go without saying that the department will need action plans to achieve these planned improvements. Simply putting a plan number in the operations report will not make it happen. There will need to be an owner for the improvement effort (a leader within L&D) and an action plan with specific steps. The CLO will have to hold the owner accountable for making plan.

Conclusion

You have now concluded one of the most difficult chapters in the book, where you learned how to create plans for all three types of measures. We know that some of these concepts may seem difficult, but creating plans gets easier with practice. Like everything that is worth doing, after a year you will wonder what all the fuss was about. The next chapter provides detailed guidance on reporting YTD results and making forecasts.

Table 11-20. Plans for Effectiveness and Efficiency Measures

	Metric	2020 Actual	Plan	YTD Results	YTD Results Compared to Plan	Forecast	Forecast Compared to Plan
Effectiveness Measures							
Level 1 participant reaction (all programs)							
Quality of content	% favorable	76%	80%			80%	
Quality of instructor	% favorable	80%	85%			85%	
Relevance	% favorable	72%	78%			78%	
Recommend to others	% favorable	68%	75%			75%	
Total for Level 1	Average of measures	74%	80%			80%	
Level 1 goal owner reaction (select programs)	% favorable	66%	80%			80%	
Level 2 learning (select programs)	Score	78%	85%			85%	
Level 3 application rate (select programs)							
Intent to apply (from the post-event survey at end of course)	% content applied	70%	75%			75%	
Actual application (from the follow-up survey after three months)	% content applied	51%	65%			65%	
Efficiency Measures							
Total participants	Number	109,618	147,500			147,500	
Total unique participants	Number	40,729	45,313			45,313	
Courses Taken by Type of Learning							
ILT only	% of total	56%	25%			25%	
vILT only	% of total	3%	12%			12%	
E-learning only	% of total	35%	48%			48%	
Blended only	% of total	6%	15%			15%	
Total courses	% of total	100%	100%			100%	
Use of E-Learning Courses							
Available	Number	60	74			74	
Taken by more than 20	Number	50	70			70	
Percent taken by more than 20	%	83%	95%			95%	

CHAPTER 12

Reporting Year-to-Date Results and Making Forecasts

Like creating plans, reporting year-to-date (YTD) results and making forecasts play a very important role in running learning like a business. Recall the two key questions a manager must answer each month if they are executing the plan with discipline: 1) Are we on plan year-to-date? and 2) Will we make plan for the year? A comparison of YTD results to plan answers the first question, and a comparison of forecast to plan answers the second.

Consequently, reporting the comparison to plan is just as important as reporting the YTD results or forecasts themselves, which is why the management reports in chapter 9 contain columns for all four: YTD results, YTD results compared to plan, forecast, and forecast compared to plan. Note that you can make the comparison numerically (for example, 5 percent below plan) or characterize it simply as above plan, on plan, or below plan.

Furthermore, while we recommend you make the comparison of YTD results directly against plan, some may prefer to make it against YTD plan. Most organizations do not create YTD plans (which require a plan for each month of the year), so the comparison is against where you think you should be at this time of the year. For example, suppose the plan is for a 4 percent increase in sales due to learning and June YTD results show a 2 percent increase due to learning. If you compare to the annual plan increase of 4 percent, you are 2 percentage points below plan. On the other hand, you might conclude that you are making good progress toward achieving the 4 percent. In fact, you are halfway to the planned increase of 4 percent by the end of June, so in that sense you may be "on plan." Either type of YTD comparison is fine as long as it is clear to the reader (user) which method is being employed. We will make our comparisons to the annual plan but factor in the progress against annual plan when making the forecast. So, for this example, we would characterize YTD results as 2 points below plan but characterize the forecast as being on plan since we are making good progress YTD.

We include YTD results and forecasts in all three management reports for all three types of measures. You may also choose to include YTD results in scorecards and dashboards, although there will be no comparison to plan. Scorecards and dashboards seldom include forecasts.

We begin with a discussion of reporting YTD results.

Reporting YTD Results

Our discussion starts with reporting YTD results for outcome, which are the most complex of the three types of measures. Then we will explore reporting YTD results for efficiency and effectiveness measures.

Reporting YTD Results for Outcome Measures

We examine reporting YTD results separately for quantitative and qualitative measures. It will also be helpful to explore quantitative measures when outcome data are and are not available. The scenarios we examine are shown in Table 12-1.

Table 12-1. Plan for Exploring the Creation of Outcome Measures

	Are Outcome Data Available?	
Type of Outcome Measure	Yes	No
Quantitative	X	X
Qualitative		X

When outcome data are available, we generally do not use qualitative outcome measures, as shown by the empty cell in Table 12-1.

Quantitative Outcome Measures

Unlike efficiency and effectiveness measures, YTD results for outcome measures generally won't be found in any corporate system unless the organization has automated collection of survey results that include a question on isolated impact. Alternatively, you may use a manual system to generate the results, which will simply be saved in a spreadsheet. Otherwise, there will be no "hard data" on outcomes. Consequently, you may have to estimate the YTD values for outcome measures.

We start by examining the case where the organization collects outcome data and then explore the more frequent case where no outcome data exist.

Outcome Data Are Available

In chapter 4 we discussed how outcome data could be collected by survey in an automated process. This requires the addition of at least one question in the post-event survey or follow-up survey. If asked in the post-event survey, the question will be about the expected isolated impact of learning on their performance, referred to as the initial estimate for Level 4. (This is the percentage contribution learning is expected to make on their performance.) If asked during the follow-up survey, the question will be about the isolated impact from learning on their performance as a result of the course, referred to as the final estimate for Level 4. In either case, an 11-point decile scale should be used, with choices ranging from 0 to 100 percent in 10 percent increments. A standard confidence factor such as 50 percent could be applied to all answers to calculate the confidence-adjusted isolated impact from learning, or you could add a question about the confidence of the answer for isolated impact. This would also have an 11-point decile scale from 0 percent to 100 percent. The system would have to be able to multiply the two factors (percentage contribution from learning and the confidence in that estimate) for each respondent.

Modern survey tools make it very easy to obtain at least the estimate of isolated impact since it requires adding just one question. And most organizations today already administer a post-event survey, so simply add the question for your initial estimate. If the organization also has the ability to ask about confidence and multiply the two together, then add the confidence question. If not, simply apply a standard confidence factor of 50 percent to the average for the isolated impact. If the organization does follow-up surveys two to three months after the training, add at least the question on impact.

Even if the questions are not embedded in the post-event or follow-up surveys, they could be asked of a sample group of at least 30 participants.

The YTD data will be organized by program and used in both the program and summary reports. The YTD results for the outcome measure will simply be the average confidence-adjusted isolated impact from the surveys multiplied by the YTD results for the organizational goal (also called the organization outcome), for instance, sales. The organization outcome YTD results will be readily available from a corporate system or from the goal owner. By formula, the YTD results for the learning outcome measure are:

YTD Results for Learning Outcome: Average confidence-adjusted isolated impact × YTD results for organizational outcome (goal).

For example, if the average confidence-adjusted isolated impact from the survey is 30 percent and YTD sales are up 6 percent, the YTD results for learning outcome would be $0.3 \times 6\% = 1.8\%$. This means that learning, by itself, contributed about 1.8 percent higher sales so far this year. The 1.8 percent is entered in the YTD results column for the learning outcome measure.

As mentioned, it is also important to characterize the YTD results compared to plan for the user of the report. In this case, that can be done by adding a note below the YTD results or in the right-hand margin comparing the average confidence-adjusted isolated impact (such as 30 percent) to the planned isolated impact, which is provided after the colon in the outcome measure. If the plan called for a 20 percent isolated impact, then the YTD results of 30 percent are above plan, so note that the 30 percent is above plan. If the YTD results are close to plan (plus or minus about 5 points), characterize it as on plan. If the YTD contribution is less than plan by 5 percent or more, characterize it as below plan in the note. Placement of the YTD results are shown in Table 12-2. The notes could also appear in a notes column on the right-side of the report or at the bottom of the report denoted with symbols.

Table 12-2. YTD Results for Organizational and Learning Outcome Measures When Learning Outcome Data Are Available

Priority	Business Goals and Supporting L&D Programs	Unit of Measure	2020 Actual	2021				
				Plan	YTD Results	YTD Results Compared to Plan	Forecast	Forecast Compared to Plan
1.	Revenue: Increase Sales by 10%							
	Corporate goal or actual	%	6%	10%	5.8%	4.2% below	10%	On plan
	Impact of Learning on Sales: 20% contribution planned for 2021	% increase in sales	1%	2%	1.8%	0.2% below	3%	1% above
	New product features training *Consultative selling skills*				*Note: YTD contribution is 30%, which is above plan*			
2.	Safety: Reduce Injuries by 20%							
	Corporate goal or actual	%	10%	20%	15%	5% below	20%	On plan
	Impact of Learning on Injuries: 70% planned for 2021	% decrease in injuries	3%	14%	9%	5% below	14%	On plan
	Safety programs to address top five causes of injuries				*Note: YTD contribution is 60%, which is below plan*			
3.	Costs: Reduce Operating Expenses by 15%							
	Corporate goal or actual	%	5%	15%	10%	5% below	18%	3% above
	Impact of Learning on Expenses: 30% contribution planned for 2021	% decrease in expenses	0%	5%	3%	2% below	6%	1% above
	Training for purchasing agents *Training for all employees on reducing costs* *Training for department heads to meet 15% goal*				*Note: YTD contribution is 27%, which is close to plan*			

Results Through June

Outcome Data Are Not Available

Although it's not difficult with current survey tools, most organizations are not yet collecting outcome data. Without outcome data, we cannot be as precise, but we can nonetheless at least characterize YTD results compared to plan, which is what leaders most want to know. And, in some cases, we can estimate YTD results for the outcome measure.

Let's start with the former case, where we don't have an estimate for YTD results. The best approach here is to follow a chain-of-evidence methodology. Ideally, L&D and the goal owner agreed on expectations for all the key efficiency and effectiveness measures before the program was launched, and you will have actual YTD results for these measures. (All captured in the program report.) If these measures, such as number of participants, completion dates, participant reaction, learning, and application rate are on or near plan, and if the organizational goal (outcome) is on plan, then it would be reasonable to assume that the isolated impact of learning is also on plan. So, enter "on plan" under the YTD results compared to plan column, or since we don't have any actual YTD results for the outcome measure, center "on plan" between both columns (Table 12-3).

Table 12-3. Example 1: YTD Results for Organizational and Learning Outcome Measures When Learning Outcome Data Are Not Available

Priority	Business Goals and Supporting L&D Programs	Unit of Measure	2020 Actual	Plan	YTD Results	YTD Results Compared to Plan*	Forecast	Forecast Compared to Plan
	Results Through June				**2021**			
1.	Revenue: Increase Sales by 10%							
	Corporate goal or actual	%	6%	10%	5.8%	On plan	10%	On plan
	Impact of Learning on Sales: 20% contribution planned for 2021	% increase in sales	1%	2%		On plan	2%	On plan
	New product features training Consultative selling skills							
2.	Safety: Reduce Injuries by 20%							
	Corporate goal or actual	%	10%	20%	7%	Below plan	17%	Below plan
	Impact of Learning on Injuries: 70% planned for 2021	% decrease in injuries	3%	14%		Below plan	10%	Below plan
	Safety programs to address the top five causes of injuries							
3.	Costs: Reduce Operating Expenses by 15%							
	Corporate goal or actual	%	5%	15%	10%	Above plan	18%	3% above
	Impact of Learning on Expenses: 30% contribution planned for 2021	% decrease in expenses	0%	5%		Above plan	6%	1% above
	Training for purchasing agents Training for all employees on reducing costs Training for department heads to meet 15% goal							

* Comparison of YTD results to plan reflects whether the outcome measures are on track to make plan for the year.

In this case, we are really comparing the learning outcome measure to our expectations for how it should be performing, rather than to any measured YTD results. For consistency and to avoid confusion, make the comparison of the organization outcome measure the same way. In other words, for each outcome measure, answer the question, "Are we on track to make plan for the year?" And add a note at the bottom to tell the reader this is what the YTD results compared to plan characterization means.

If YTD results for most or all efficiency and effectiveness measures are below plan, enter "below plan" for the outcome measure. If the key efficiency and effectiveness measures are above plan and if the organization outcome is above plan as well, you might enter "above plan" for the outcome measure (or you might be conservative and just enter "on plan"). Of course, it is possible that the situation is less clear cut, in which case you will have to use your judgment. Our advice is to be conservative and discuss it with the goal owner.

The second case involves estimating and showing YTD results for the learning outcome measure. The thought process is the same as the first case; namely, compare the YTD results for the efficiency and effectiveness measures to plan. In this case, though, we use the results of the comparison to estimate the YTD value for the outcome measure. If the efficiency and effectiveness measures are on plan, and if the organizational outcome is on plan, assume that the isolated impact is also on plan and simply multiply the YTD results for the organization outcome by the planned isolated impact. By formula:

> **YTD Results for Learning Outcome:** Planned isolated impact × YTD results for organization goal.

For example, suppose the planned isolated impact is 20 percent and YTD sales are up 6 percent. If the other key learning measures are on plan, and if sales are on plan, multiply the 6 percent by 20 percent for a 1.2 percent YTD increase in sales due just to learning. In this case you would enter 1.2 percent in the YTD results column and "on plan" in the YTD results compared to plan column. If the other learning measures are below plan, then work with the goal owner to agree on a reasonable isolated impact to use that will be less than plan. Likewise, if the learning measures are above plan and the organizational outcome is above plan, you might agree on an isolated impact greater than plan. Add a note for each one providing the estimated contribution (see Table 12-4 for an example).

Table 12-4. Example 2: YTD Results for Organizational and Learning Outcome Measures When Learning Outcome Data Are Not Available

						2021		
Results Through June								
Priority	Business Goals and Supporting L&D Programs	Unit of Measure	2020 Actual	Plan	YTD Results	YTD Results Compared to Plan*	Forecast	Forecast Compared to Plan
1.	Revenue: Increase Sales by 10%							
	Corporate goal or actual	%	6%	10%	6%	On plan	10%	On plan
	Impact of Learning on Sales: 20% contribution planned for 2021	% increase in sales	1%	2%	1.2%	On plan	2%	On plan
	New product features training Consultative selling skills					*Note: YTD contribution is estimated to be 20%*		
2.	Safety: Reduce Injuries by 20%							
	Corporate goal or actual	%	10%	20%	7%	Below plan	18%	2% below
	Impact of Learning on Injuries: 70% planned for 2021	% decrease in injuries	3%	14%	3.5%	Below plan	9%	5% below
	Safety programs to address the top five causes of injuries					*Note: YTD contribution is estimated to be 50%*		
3.	Costs: Reduce Operating Expenses by 15%							
	Corporate goal or actual	%	5%	15%	10%	Above plan	18%	3% above
	Impact of Learning on Expenses: 30% contribution planned for 2021	% decrease in expenses	0%	5%	4%	Above plan	6%	1% above
	Training for purchasing agents Training for all employees on reducing costs Training for department heads to meet 15% goal					*Note: YTD contribution is estimated to be 40%*		

* Comparison of YTD results to plan reflects whether the outcome measures are on track to make plan for the year.

In both cases, when outcome data are not available, it is best not to show YTD results for the learning outcome measure if they exceed those for the organizational outcome measure. For example, if sales are on plan YTD, it would be best not to show the learning outcome YTD results as above plan. Likewise, if sales are below plan, be cautious in showing YTD results for the learning outcome measure as on or above plan. It may well be the case that learning is contributing as expected and the poor performance of the organizational outcome is due to other factors, but it would be best to make sure the goal owner is on board with this characterization before sharing widely with others.

Qualitative Outcome Measures and Outcome Data Not Available

Generally, qualitative outcome measures are employed when outcome data are not available, so we will assume outcome data are not available.

In this case, the goal owner and L&D leaders have decided to use a qualitative outcome measure like H/M/L. As there is no outcome data available to help create a YTD estimate, we rely on a chain of evidence methodology, which calls for looking at results for the outcome measure and results for Levels 0–3. First, are the YTD results for the organizational outcome measure (such as sales or injuries) showing improvement? Does it appear to be on plan? If so, how do the YTD results for Levels 0–3 compare with plan? If the organizational outcome is on plan and the key learning efficiency and effectiveness measures are on plan, we may assume that learning is also on plan. Of course, this should be discussed with the goal owner, who may have a different opinion. Assuming the goal owner and L&D both agree that goal owner expectations are being met, enter the plan for the learning outcome measure (such as H/M/L) in the YTD results column and enter "on plan" in the YTD results compared to plan column.

If the organizational outcome is not meeting expectations or the goal owner is not happy with the role training is playing, or if Levels 0–3 are not on plan, the goal owner and L&D need to agree on how to characterize YTD results. Perhaps they will agree that learning is below plan in impact and that a plan for medium impact should be downgraded to low impact (or high to medium). If so, make the appropriate entries. Conversely, if both parties agree that learning is exceeding expectations, mark the column for YTD results compared to plan as "above plan" and raise the YTD results column from "low" to "medium" or "medium" to "high."

Some of the possibilities from a summary report are shown in Table 12-5. For the first goal, learning is having the expected impact but other factors (perhaps the economy) are driving sales higher than planned. For the second goal, learning is contributing less than planned, resulting in the organizational outcome being below plan. For the third goal, learning is also having the planned impact, but other factors are preventing the organization from achieving its planned impact.

We are now ready to examine the relatively simpler cases of reporting YTD results for efficiency and effectiveness measures.

Table 12-5. YTD Results for Qualitative Outcome Measures

| Results Through June | | | | 2021 | | | | |
Priority	Business Goals and Supporting L&D Programs	Unit of Measure	2020 Actual	Plan	YTD Results	YTD Results Compared to Plan*	Forecast	Forecast Compared to Plan
1.	Revenue: Increase Sales by 20%							
	Corporate goal or actual	%	7%	10%	11%	1% above	11%	On plan
	Impact of Learning on Sales: Medium for 2021	H/M/L	Low	Medium	Medium	On plan	Medium	On plan
	New product features training *Consultative selling skills*							
2.	Safety: Reduce Injuries by 20%							
	Corporate goal or actual	%	10%	20%	15%	5% below	20%	On plan
	Impact of Learning on Injuries: High for 2021 Plan	H/M/L	Medium	High	Medium	Below plan	High	On plan
	Safety programs to address top five causes of injuries							
3.	Costs: Reduce Operating Expenses by 15%							
	Corporate goal or actual	%	5%	15%	9%	6% below	10%	5% below
	Impact of Learning on Expenses: Medium for 2021 plan	H/M/L	Low	Medium	Medium	On plan	Medium	On plan
	Training for purchasing agents *Training for all employees on reducing costs* *Training for department heads to meet 15% goal*							

* Comparison of YTD results to plan reflects whether the outcome measures are on track to make plan for the year.

Reporting YTD Results for Efficiency Measures

Unlike outcome measures, YTD data should always be available for the key efficiency measures, so we do not need to estimate them. Data on number of participants, courses, hours, and types (modalities) as well as performance support are usually available in an LMS, while data for other efficiency measures like percentage on-time completion, cycle times, and costs may be kept in spreadsheets or data warehouses. Content-related data (like time spent on task) may be found in an LMS or a system specially designed for the purpose. Likewise, data on communities of practice or performance support tools may also be on a dedicated platform or integrated into other platforms.

Bottomline, the data exist so you will have actual YTD results. There may be a challenge to extract it and manipulate at scale, but you don't have to create it or estimate it. Simply enter it into the YTD results column.

The numerical comparison to plan is also straightforward, but we suggest some standard practices to make the comparisons more user friendly:

- If the measure is a number, express the comparison to plan as a percentage of plan. For example, if plan is 1,000 unique participants and there have been 650 YTD, enter 65 percent in the column for YTD compared to plan. This tells the reader that 65 percent of plan has been achieved. When the measure is a number, readers are used to this type of comparison.
- If the measure is a percentage, express its comparison to plan in terms of the difference in percentage points. For example, if plan is for 80 percent utilization and YTD utilization is 76 percent, enter "4% below plan" or "4% below" in the YTD compared to plan column. This saves the reader the effort of doing the math. We recommend this approach rather than showing the percentage of plan (76% ÷ 80% = 95%) because most readers find percentages of percentages to be confusing. It is easy to lose track of whether the percentage is the measure itself or a comparison of the measure to something else.

Table 12-6 is an example of an operations report showing the two ways of expressing the comparison of YTD results to plan.

Table 12-6. Case 1: Two Ways to Express YTD Comparison for Efficiency Measures

Efficiency Measures	Unit of Measure	2020 Actual	Plan	2021				
				June YTD Results	YTD Results Compared to Plan	Forecast	Forecast Compared to Plan
Total participants	Number	109,618	147,500	67,357	46%	145,000	98%
Total unique participants	Number	40,729	45,313	36,998	82%	44,000	97%
Courses taken by type of learning							
ILT only	% of total	56%	25%	40%	15% below	33%	8% below
vILT only	% of total	3%	12%	9%	3% below	10%	2% below
E-learning only	% of total	35%	48%	39%	9% below	42%	6% below
Blended only	% of total	6%	15%	12%	3% below	15%	On plan
Total courses	% of total	100%	100%	100%		100%	
Utilization of e-learning courses							
Available	Number	60	74	65	88%	70	95%
Taken by more than 20 participants	Number	50	70	19	27%	55	79%
Percent taken by more than 20 participants	%	83%	95%	29%	66% below	79%	16% below
Reach							
Percentage of employees reached by L&D	%	85%	88%	72%	16% below	88%	On plan
Percentage of employees with development plans	%	82%	85%	84%	1% below	90%	5% above

While the numerical comparison to plan is straightforward, the characterization of being on, above, or below plan can be nuanced. Recall the discussion at the start of the Reporting YTD Results section about comparing to annual plan or YTD plan. All the comparisons in

Table 12-6 are to the annual plan. Alternatively, you could try to answer the question: "Are we about where we expected to be at this point in the year?" Since there is no actual YTD plan for comparison, the answer is subjective. For example, suppose plan for the year is to have 1,000 total participants take courses. YTD through June, there have been 400 total participants, which is 40 percent of plan. Would you say this measure is on plan or not? Clearly, plan for the year has not been achieved, but that is to be expected. Usually there are no YTD plans to compare with the YTD results, so the analyst is left to determine if 40 percent is in line with plan.

For measures like participants that increase throughout the year, the best approach is to look up the YTD results compared to plan percentage for the last several years at the same point in time. If for the past several years, the measure has been close to 40 percent at the end of June, then we could say that we are where we expected to be or we are on plan. If the percentage is typically 50 percent by this point, then this year is running behind plan. This method will work for any efficiency measure that accumulates through the year; for example, number of participants, hours, courses, and costs. If you choose to take this approach to compare YTD results to plan, include a note telling the reader you are comparing progress against where you expected to be at this time of the year. See the example in Table 12-7.

Table 12-7. Case 2: Two Ways of Expressing YTD Comparison for Efficiency Measures

Efficiency Measures	Unit of Measure	2020 Actual	2021				
			Plan	June YTD Results	YTD Results Compared to Plan	Forecast	Forecast Compared to Plan
Total participants	Number	109,618	147,500	67,357	On plan	145,000	98%
Total unique participants	Number	40,729	45,313	36,998	On plan	44,000	97%
Courses taken by type of learning							
ILT only	% of total	56%	25%	40%	15% below	33%	8% below
vILT only	% of total	3%	12%	9%	3% below	10%	2% below
E-Learning only	% of total	35%	48%	39%	9% below	42%	6% below
Blended only	% of total	6%	15%	12%	3% below	15%	On plan
Total courses	% of total	100%	100%	100%		100%	
Utilization of e-learning courses							
Available	Number	60	74	65	On plan	70	95%
Taken by more than 20 participants	Number	50	70	19	Below plan	55	79%
Percent taken by more than 20 participants	%	83%	95%	29%	66% below	79%	16% below
Reach							
Percentage of employees reached by L&D	%	85%	88%	72%	On plan	88%	On plan
Percentage of employees with development plans	%	82%	85%	84%	On plan	90%	5% above

Note: Comparison of YTD results to plan for participants and reach reflect whether the efficiency measures are on track to make plan for the year given historical trends.

Reporting YTD Results for Effectiveness Measures

Like efficiency measures, YTD data should be available for effectiveness measures so there is no need to estimate them. In most organizations the data will be stored in a data warehouse or on spreadsheets. If the organization uses a partner to collect and store the data, it will be in their database. So, the good news is that YTD results should be readily accessible.

The bad news is that effectiveness measures for Levels 1, 3, and 4 are typically gathered through surveys, which means that the data represent a sample rather than the entire population. Whenever a sample is involved, the user of the report will need to know the sample size or the level of confidence to decide whether to take action based on the sample or wait for more data. We discussed this issue at length in chapter 4 and will not repeat it here. However, we reiterate the importance of conveying the statistical significance of the sample data so the user can make an informed decision. Options include listing the sample size or level of confidence for each measure in the notes column, under the effectiveness measures, or at the bottom of the report.

Alternatively, any YTD results that are not statistically significant could be designated as "NSS" for "not statistically significant" or color coded perhaps in yellow, indicating they should not be used for decision making yet. (Note that efficiency measures generally do not have this same issue since they typically represent the entire population—participants, hours, dollars, and so forth.) An example is shown in Table 12-8 using the NSS approach. Typically, this is only required early in the year or in program deployment for programs with large target audiences, but it may always pose an issue for programs with small target audiences.

In Table 12-8, the first course received only 13 responses, so the average is not statistically significant and marked "NSS." The follow-up survey has not been administered yet, so there are no data and thus the "N/A" comment for actual application. Likewise, no impact data have been collected so "N/A" is entered in the YTD outcome measure column. The Level 2 measure for learning represents results from all 56 people who have completed the first course, so there is no issue of statistical significance.

Table 12-8. Insufficient Sample Size in a Program Report

Results Through February					2021		
Goal Owner: Swilthe, VP of Manufacturing	Unit of Measure	2020 Actual	Plan	YTD Results	YTD Results Compared to Plan	Forecast	Forecast Compared to Plan
Enterprise Goal: Reduce Injuries	%	8%	25%	10%	Below plan	25%	On plan
Impact of Learning on Injuries: High Impact for 2021	H/M/L	High	High	N/A			On plan

Table 12-8. Example Showing Insufficient Sample Size in a Program Report (cont.)

	Unit of Measure	2020 Actual	Plan	YTD Results	YTD Results Compared to Plan	Forecast	Forecast Compared to Plan
				2021			
Develop Two Courses							
Efficiency Measure: Development complete by January 31	Number	N/A	2	2	100%	2	100%
Deliver Two Courses							
Efficiency Measures							
Unique participants	Number	452	3,000	56	2%	3,200	107%
Total participants	Number	858	6,000	56	1%	6,300	105%
Completion date, rate	Date, rate	N/A	5/31	1%	On plan	5/31	On plan
Effectiveness Measures							
Level 1 participant reaction	% favorable	70%	80%	NSS		82%	2% above
Level 2 learning	% first-time pass rate	86%	90%	95%	5% above	92%	2% above
Level 3 intent to apply	% of content applied	53%	95%	NSS		90%	5% below
Level 3 actual application	% of content applied	39%	90%	N/A		90%	On plan
				Note: Sample size is 13 for post-event survey and 0 for follow-up survey			

We offer the same general guidance as previously for efficiency measures when expressing the comparison to plan for measures where the unit of measure is a percentage. For example, if plan calls for an 80 percent application rate and YTD results are 77 percent, enter "3% below" in the YTD Compared to Plan column. The guidance is similar if the unit of measure is the Likert scale (a number). In this case, express the comparison in terms of points above or below the plan. In other words, do not calculate a percentage by dividing YTD results by plan. For example, if plan is 4.5 on a 5-point Likert scale and YTD results are 4.3, enter "0.2 points below plan" or "0.2 below" in the YTD compared to plan column. If the measure is in units (like cost), divide the YTD results by plan and express as a percentage. The next example from an operations report shows all three approaches (Table 12-9).

This concludes our examination of reporting YTD results for all three types of measures, leaving the creation of forecasts as the last section in this chapter.

Making Forecasts

Unlike reporting YTD estimates for efficiency and effectiveness measures, you will have to make forecasts. While you can use programs with formulas to automatically create a forecast, a manager or analyst should always review them and make the final determination.

Table 12-9. Three Ways of Expressing the YTD Comparison for Effectiveness Measures

Results Through June					2021		
Effectiveness Measures	Metric	2020 Actual	Plan	YTD Results	YTD Results Compared to Plan	Forecast	Forecast Compared to Plan
Level 1 participant reaction (all programs)							
Quality of content	5-point scale	3.7	4.0	3.9	0.1 below	3.9	0.1 below
Quality of instructor	5-point scale	4.0	4.5	4.2	0.3 below	4.5	On plan
Relevance	5-point scale	3.8	4.0	3.6	0.4 below	3.9	0.1 below
Recommend to others	5-point scale	3.5	4.0	4.1	0.1 above	4.1	0.1 above
Total for Level 1	Average of measures	3.8	4.1	4.0	0.1 below	4.1	0.1 above
Level 1 goal owner reaction (select programs)	% favorable	66%	80%	68%	12% below	75%	5% below
Level 2 learning (select programs)	Score	78%	85%	83%	2% below	85%	On plan
Level 3 application rate (select programs)							
Intent to apply (from post-event survey at end of course)	% content applied	70%	75%	70%	5% below	72%	3% below
Actual application (from follow-up survey after three months)	% content applied	51%	65%	55%	10% below	63%	2% below
Level 4 impact (select programs)							
Initial estimate by participants (post-event survey)	% contribution to goal	19%	50%	47%	3% below	50%	On plan
Final estimate (follow-up survey)	% contribution to goal	14%	30%	28%	2% below	30%	On plan
Level 5 ROI (select programs)							
Net benefits	Dollars, thousands	$254	$380	$140	37%	$400	105%
ROI	%	30%	40%	30%	10% below	43%	3% above

A forecast answers the second question a manager should always ask when presented with YTD results: "Will we make plan by the end of the year?" which really means, "Will we make plan without taking any unplanned or special actions?" In other words, if things continue to go as they have gone so far this year, and if we do just what we are already planning on doing for the remainder of the year, is that enough for us to end the year on plan? In many cases, the answer is no, meaning that the leadership team will have to come up with options, cost them out, and decide what to implement (if anything) during the remainder of the year.

The forecast is important because it answers this question. If forecast is the same as plan, no special actions are required and things can continue as planned. If forecast is better than plan, that means management can focus their attention elsewhere for the time being. If forecast is worse than plan, management may need to take action to address the performance gap.

The good news about forecasts is that L&D can influence how the year turns out. If the application rate is below plan through June, there is still time to take action to get back on plan by year end. Contrast that with economic forecasts where the forecaster has no influence over the measure. If interest rates are forecast to be below plan, there is nothing an economist can do about it. There is almost always something we can do in our profession to influence the measure.

Conceptually, a forecast is composed of two parts. It starts with YTD results and then factors in what is expected to happen in the remainder of the year. So:

Forecast for the Period: YTD results + Forecast for the remainder of the year.

Since YTD results are either already known or estimated, the hard part is the forecast for the rest of the year. The following three factors provide general guidance:

1. What have you learned from the YTD results?
2. What new information do you have about the rest of the year?
3. (For outcome measures) What are the forecasts for the key efficiency and effectiveness measures?

Typically, as the year goes on you learn more about how easy or hard it is to achieve the planned results. For example, you may learn that it is far more difficult than anticipated to deliver high impact. In essence, you have learned that the original plan was too optimistic. This challenge is likely to persist throughout the rest of the year, so the forecast for the remainder of the year should be below plan.

The second factor is new information that was not available when you set the plan. New information almost always becomes available, which is why plans can become dated just a few months after they are finished. For example, you might discover that facilitators planned for the second half will not be available or are not as qualified as you were led to believe. You may discover that some of the planned target audience should not receive the training, diminishing its overall impact. You might discover some managers no longer can dedicate the planned time to reinforcement. Any of these factors would lead you to conclude that the forecast for the rest of the year should be below plan. Alternatively, everything may be on plan YTD with no surprises and no new information about the rest of the year. In this case the forecast for the rest of the year should be on plan. And, yes, sometimes, there are pleasant surprises where you learn that something is going to be easier to achieve than you thought. Or, perhaps, you learn that more participants are going to go through the program than planned or that those not yet through it have much more supportive supervisors, a circumstance that should result in higher levels of application. Any of these should lead to an above plan forecast for the remainder of the year.

Third, pertaining only to forecasting outcome measures and following the chain of evidence philosophy, how do the forecasts for the key efficiency and effectiveness measures compare to plan for the remainder of the year? If they are forecast to be below plan, then the outcome may also be below plan. Likewise, if they are forecast to be above plan, perhaps the outcome will be as well. Through experience you will increase your professional judgment in considering these three factors, and they will become much easier to use.

With this as general introduction to forecasting, we now explore forecasting by type of measure. We begin with forecasts for outcome measures, which are more straightforward but less rigorous than forecasts for efficiency and effectiveness measures, where some additional forecasting techniques are available. We recommend creating forecasts for all three types of measures contained in the three types of TDRp management reports.

Making Forecasts for Outcome Measures

For outcome measures, we recommend two forecasts: organizational outcome and learning outcome. The forecast for an organizational outcome like sales will come from the head of sales. L&D may be able to access it through a corporate database or it may need to come directly from the sales organization, but it almost always exists. The forecast for the learning outcome, however, will have to be made, and ideally L&D will work with the goal owner to make it or at least get goal owner approval before it is shared.

As previously discussed, the starting point for the forecast is YTD results. If outcome data are available, there will be an actual YTD result. If outcome data are not available, L&D will have an estimated YTD result (a number) or simply characterize it as being above, below, or on plan. In any case, thought has already been given to the YTD result. So, our attention will now turn to what is likely to happen in the remainder of the year.

All three factors are relevant when forecasting. The program manager should be meeting with the goal owner regularly to discuss YTD results and prospects for the remainder of the year. An important part of this discussion is factors 1 and 2. As the year progresses, both parties should be learning lessons and receiving new information so together they should be a good position to make a forecast for the rest of the year, especially in the second half of the year (for a year-long deployment). They may also be able to employ factor 3 to help make the forecast.

There is no automated process for generating forecasts for outcome measures. You must use subjective, professional judgment, which all managers have to do as part of their job. Organizations always want to know how the year is going to end, especially for strategic programs in support of important goals.

Like the YTD results discussion, we examine three different scenarios:

1. Quantitative outcome measures when outcome data are available
2. Quantitative outcome measures when outcome data aren't available
3. Qualitative outcome measures when outcome data aren't available.

We begin with quantitative measures, which are more complex than qualitative measures.

Quantitative Outcome Measures

First, we will examine making forecasts for outcome measures when YTD outcome data are available. Then we will explore our options when YTD outcome data are not available.

Outcome Data Are Available

If outcome data are available for YTD results, then begin with the YTD percentage contribution. How does it compare to plan? Do you understand why it is higher or lower? It may simply be a matter of timing, meaning that participants have not yet had time to apply what they learned.

Discuss with the goal owner to see if you can come to agreement on what to use for the year (or the remainder of the year). Then multiply it by the goal owner's forecast for the organizational outcome measure. Suppose the planned percentage contribution was 20 percent, but

YTD results are 15 percent. Decide whether to use 15 percent for the entire year or assume that it will rise for the remainder of the year. If you agree to use the 15 percent and the goal owner is now forecasting a 9 percent increase in sales, the forecast for the learning outcome measure is 15 percent × 9 percent = 1.35 percent, which is less than the planned 2 percent. Rounding, enter "1.4%" under the forecast column and "0.6% below plan" for the forecast compared to plan column, since the 15 percent is less than the planned 20 percent contribution (and since 1.4 percent is less than 2.0 percent). See the example in Table 12-10.

Table 12-10. Quantitative Outcome Measure Forecasts When YTD Outcome Data Are Available

						2021			
Priority	Business Goals and Supporting L&D Programs	Unit of Measure	2020 Actual	Plan	June YTD Results	YTD Results Compared to Plan	Forecast	Forecast Compared to Plan
1.	Revenue: Increase Sales by 10%							
	Corporate goal or actual	%	6%	10%	4.3%	5.7% below	9%	On plan
	Impact of Learning on Sales: 20% contribution planned for 2021	% increase in sales	1%	2%	0.7%	1.3% below	1.4%	0.6% below
	New product features training *Consultative selling skills*					*Note: YTD contribution is 15%, which is below plan* *Forecast contribution is expected to be 15%*		
2.	Safety: Reduce Injuries by 20%							
	Corporate goal or actual	%	10%	20%	11%	5% below	20%	On plan
	Impact of Learning on Injuries: 70% contribution planned for 2021	% decrease in injuries	3%	14%	8%	5% below	14%	On plan
	Safety programs to address top five causes of injuries					*Note: YTD contribution is 70%, which is on plan* *Forecast contribution is expected to be 70%*		
3.	Costs: Reduce Operating Expenses by 15%							
	Corporate goal or actual	%	5%	15%	10%	5% below	18%	3% above
	Impact of Learning on Expenses: 30% contribution planned for 2021	% decrease in expenses	0%	5%	3%	2% below	5%	On plan
	Training for purchasing agents *Training for all employees on reducing costs* *Training for department heads to meet 15% goal*					*Note: YTD contribution is 27%, which is close to plan* *Forecast contribution is expected to be 30%*		

Outcome Data Are Not Available

If outcome data are not available, begin with the estimate for YTD results. This has already been characterized as on plan, below plan, or above plan and perhaps a number has been estimated. Apply the three factors to learn from the YTD results, consider new information about the remainder of the year, and following a chain of evidence methodology, compare the forecasts for key efficiency and effectiveness measures to plan. If YTD results are on plan, no issues have arisen, no new information is available, and the key measures are forecast to be on plan for the rest of the year, then the forecast may be on plan for the remainder of the year and for the full year. In this case, assume the originally agreed-upon percentage contribution from learning is still on plan and multiply by the goal owner's forecast for the full year. Enter this number for impact of learning under the forecast column and characterize it as "on plan" in the forecast compared to plan column.

If you expect the rest of the year to be under plan, the goal owner and L&D need to agree on a new, lower percentage contribution from learning for the year. This will be subjective (since no outcome data are available) but directionally correct. Perhaps the plan was for learning to contribute 70 percent toward achieving the goal and now it appears that 50 percent is a better forecast. Multiply the goal owner's estimate for the full-year organizational outcome by the new percentage and enter under the forecast column. Change the forecast compared to plan column to "below plan."

It is also possible that YTD results are better than plan or the rest of the year looks considerably better than planned. In this case, the goal owner and L&D should agree on a higher (but still conservative) percentage contribution from learning to multiply by the goal owner's estimate for outcome. Enter the new percentage under the forecast column and enter "above plan" in the forecast compared to plan column. See examples of these three cases in Table 12-11.

Table 12-11. Example 1: Quantitative Outcome Measure Forecasts When Outcome Data Are Not Available

| | | | | | 2021 | | | |
Priority	Business Goals and Supporting L&D Programs	Unit of Measure	2020 Actual	Plan	June YTD Results	YTD Results Compared to Plan*	Forecast	Forecast Compared to Plan
1.	Revenue: Increase Sales by 10%							
	Corporate goal or actual	%	6%	10%	6.0%	On plan	10%	On plan
	Impact of Learning on Sales: 20% contribution planned for 2021	% increase in sales	1%	2%	1.2%	On plan	2%	On plan
	New product features training Consultative selling skills				*Note: 20% contribution still seems reasonable*			
2.	Safety: Reduce Injuries by 20%							
	Corporate goal or actual	%	10%	20%	7%	Below plan	14%	Below plan
	Impact of Learning on Injuries: 70% contribution planned for 2021	% decrease in injuries	3%	14%	4%	Below plan	7%	Below plan
	Safety programs to address top five causes of injuries				*Note: 50% contribution now seems more likely*			
3.	Costs: Reduce Operating Expenses by 15%							
	Corporate goal or actual	%	5%	15%	10%	Above plan	18%	Above plan
	Impact of Learning on Expenses: 30% contribution planned for 2021	% decrease in expenses	0%	5%	4%	Above plan	7%	Above plan
	Training for purchasing agents Training for all employees on reducing costs Training for department heads to meet 15% goal				*Note: 40% contribution now seems more likely*			

* *Comparison of YTD results to plan reflects whether the outcome measures are on track to make plan for the year.*

Another approach is to not enter the new learning outcome measure in the forecast column and simply characterize it versus plan, which was also an option explored for YTD results. You might take this approach if you have little confidence in creating a numeric outcome measure. See examples of these scenarios from a summary report in Table 12-12.

Table 12-12. Example 2: Quantitative Outcome Measure Forecasts When Outcome Data Are Not Available

Priority	Business Goals and Supporting L&D Programs	Unit of Measure	2020 Actual	2021 Plan	June YTD Results	YTD Results Compared to Plan*	Forecast	Forecast Compared to Plan
1.	Revenue: Increase Sales by 10%							
	Corporate goal or actual	%	6%	10%	6.0%	On plan	10%	On plan
	Impact of Learning on Sales: 20% contribution planned for 2021	% increase in sales	1%	2%		On plan		On plan
	New product features training Consultative selling skills				*Note: 20% contribution still seems reasonable*			
2.	Safety: Reduce Injuries by 20%							
	Corporate goal or actual	%	10%	20%	7%	Below plan	14%	Below plan
	Impact of Learning on Injuries: 70% contribution planned for 2021	% decrease in injuries	3%	14%		Below plan		Below plan
	Safety programs to address top five causes of injuries				*Note: 50% contribution now seems more likely*			
3.	Costs: Reduce Operating Expenses by 15%							
	Corporate goal or actual	%	5%	15%	10%	Above plan	18%	Above plan
	Impact of Learning on Expenses: 30% contribution planned for 2021	% decrease in expenses	0%	5%		Above plan		Above plan
	Training for purchasing agents Training for all employees on reducing costs Training for department heads to meet 15% goal				*Note: 40% contribution now seems more likely*			

Qualitative Outcome Measures (When No Outcome Data Are Available)

If outcome data are not available, then begin with the qualitative comparison of YTD results to plan. Consider the three factors and discuss with the goal owner. Given what both of you have learned so far this year and any new information you now have about the rest of the year, and given the forecasts for the underlying efficiency and effectiveness measures, what is your best thinking about the rest of the year? Is it likely to be better, the same, or worse than YTD or plan? If the remainder of the year is expected to be the same as the YTD results, the forecast is simply the same as YTD results (either below plan, on plan, or above plan). Forecasting the outcome for the entire year is more interesting when the remainder is expected to be different. Table 12-13 shows the thought framework for forecasting.

The forecast for the entire year depends on the weighting of the YTD results and the remainder of the year. If it is early in the year or deployment, you can assign more weight to the remainder of the year. For example, if the outcome measure is running below plan YTD but most of the deployment is yet to come, and the forecast for the remainder of the year is expected to be on plan, the forecast for entire year would also be on plan. If plan had been for medium impact, then enter "medium" in the forecast column and "on plan" in the forecast compared to plan column. If it is later in the year or deployment cycle, you may not have enough time left in the fiscal year to offset below-plan performance in the first part of the year. Table 12-14 shows an example from a summary report with various possibilities.

Table 12-13. Thought Framework for Forecasting When Outcome Data Is Not Available

YTD Results	Forecasts for the Rest of the Year	Forecast for the Entire Year
Below plan	• Below plan • On plan • Above plan	• Below plan • Below or on plan • Depends on time below and above
On plan	• Below plan • On plan • Above plan	• On or below plan • On plan • On or above plan
Above plan	• Below plan • On plan • Above plan	• Depends on time above or below • Above or on plan • Above plan

Table 12-14. Example Showing Qualitative Outcome Measure Forecasts (When Outcome Data Isn't Available)

Priority	Business Goals and Supporting L&D Programs	Unit of Measure	2020 Actual	Plan	YTD Results	YTD Results Compared to Plan*	Forecast	Forecast Compared to Plan
1.	Revenue: Increase Sales by 20%							
	Corporate goal or actual	%	7%	10%	6%	Below plan	10%	On plan
	Impact of Learning on Sales: Medium for 2021 Plan	H/M/L	Low	Medium		Below plan	Medium	On plan
	New product features training *Consultative selling skills*							
2.	Safety: Reduce Injuries by 20%							
	Corporate goal or actual	%	10%	20%	15%	On plan	20%	On plan
	Impact of Learning on Injuries: High for 2021 Plan	H/M/L	Medium	High		On plan	High	On plan
	Safety programs to address top five causes of injuries							
3.	Costs: Reduce Operating Expenses by 15%							
	Corporate goal or actual	%	5%	15%	2%	13% below	7%	8% below
	Impact of Learning on Expenses: Medium for 2021 Plan	H/M/L	Low	Medium		Below plan	Low	Below plan
	Training for purchasing agents *Training for all employees on reducing costs* *Training for department heads to meet 15% goal*							

Results Through June / 2021

Given all these variables, our advice is to be conservative and check a proposed forecast against the organizational outcome for reasonableness. If the goal owner is forecasting sales to double by year end, do you really want to forecast the outcome measure for learning to triple? Considering all the factors, what would a safe characterization be for the forecast?

This concludes the discussion of creating forecasts for outcome measures. Last, we tackle forecasts for efficiency and effectiveness measures.

Making Forecasts for Efficiency Measures

Forecasting efficiency measures is much simpler than forecasting outcome measures. The starting point, of course, is the YTD results, which will always be available. Use the first two factors presented earlier—What have you learned from the YTD results? What new information do you have about the rest of the year?—to think about how the remainder of the year will likely compare to plan or to the first part of the year. Unlike outcome measures, the forecast for some efficiency measures can be automated.

We start by recognizing there are two basic types of efficiency measures. As noted in the YTD results section, the value of some efficiency measures accumulates or increases throughout the year. Examples are number of participants, number of courses, number of hours, and costs. Each starts at 0 for the year and may continue to increase until the end of the year (or program). For this type of measure, we can employ a simple formula to annualize or forecast the value for the entire year (all 12 months) based on the YTD value. The formula for annualization of partial-year data is:

Annualized Value: YTD value × (12 ÷ Current month).

For example, if 500 employees took the training through May, which is the fifth month of the fiscal year, the formula forecasts 1,200 will participate by December 31. By formula:

Annualized Value: 500 × (12 ÷ 5) = 1,200.

This simple formula, which can easily automate to calculate the value for the forecast column, assumes that the rest of the year will be exactly like the YTD period. In other words, the monthly rate will not change. In our example, the monthly rate is 100 participants. The formula projects that same rate for every month remaining in the year. This assumption is good for some measures but not for others. So, before using it, you need to check for something called *seasonality*, which is simply a predictable pattern in the data based on month or season. For example, most retailers have a seasonal sales pattern where sales in the last three months of the year vastly exceed sales in any other three-month period. Moreover, the same pattern repeats every year.

We can apply this same concept to learning (Table 12-15). It is not uncommon for people to put off some learning until the last quarter, when they rush to complete it. This could lead to a repeatable pattern in the data, in which case seasonality exists. Our recommendation is to calculate the average monthly values for the measure in question for at least the last five years. Then examine the data. Are the monthly values essentially the same? If so, there is no seasonality and the simple formula will work to create a forecast. If they are not the same, is there a pattern? Are some months consistently higher than others? If yes, then seasonality is present, and a different but still simple formula must be used.

It is clear that the amount of training done in the last four months in Table 12-15 is much higher than the other months, so seasonality is definitely present. The table also shows the percentage by month (Each month's value ÷ Total) and the cumulative percentage (Current month's percentage + Sum of all previous months). We need the cumulative percentage for the next formula, which should be used whenever seasonality is present:

Table 12-15. Example of Seasonality in the Number of Total Participants

Month	Averages for 2015–2019	% of Total	Cumulative % of Total	2020 YTD
Jan	550	5%	5%	650
Feb	600	6%	11%	700
Mar	650	6%	17%	750
Apr	700	6%	23%	800
May	750	7%	30%	800
Jun	750	7%	37%	850
Jul	600	6%	42%	900
Aug	500	5%	47%	1,000
Sep	1,200	11%	58%	
Oct	1,450	13%	71%	
Nov	1,850	17%	88%	
Dec	1,250	12%	100%	
Total	10,850	100%		6,450

Annualized Value: YTD value ÷ Cumulative percentage.

Suppose we have YTD results through August, which show 6,450 participants, and we want to use the formula to annualize that number. The row for August shows the cumulative percentage to be 47 percent, meaning that on average 47 percent of the total year's participants have gone through by the end of August. By formula:

Annualized Value: $6,450 ÷ 0.47 = 13,723$.

So, taking the typical seasonal pattern into account, our forecast is 13,723 participants, which is much higher than we would have gotten using the first formula ($6,450 × [12 ÷ 8] = 9,675$). This makes sense because we know many employees don't take the training until the last four months.

Now you have a simple formula that is appropriate for the efficiency measures that accumulate throughout the year. How about other types of efficiency measures that do not accumulate? For example, measures like utilization rates, cycle times, percentage of learning by modality, and percentage on-time completions. For these, we resort to our basic formula for the full-year forecast:

Full-Year Forecast: YTD results + Forecast for the remainder of the year.

Since YTD results are available, we will need to make a forecast for the rest of the year and add the two together. The forecast for the rest of the year will be made starting with YTD results and considering our first two factors (What have you learned from the YTD results? What new information do you have about the rest of the year?)

Once the forecast is made for the rest of the year, we can use a weighted average to combine the two to get the forecast for the full year. Weights are generally just the number of months. So, the weight for YTD results would be the number of months for which you have data (m) divided by 12, and the weight for the remainder of the year is (12–m) divided by 12. By formula:

Full-Year Forecast: (YTD results × [m ÷ 12]) + (Forecast for remainder of year × [12 – m] ÷ 12).

For example, suppose the utilization rate for a suite of online courses is 40 percent for the first four months. The forecast for the last eight months is 70 percent, given the marketing campaign that is planned and the new employee portal that is scheduled to go live next month. By formula:

Full-Year Forecast:
= (40% × [4 ÷ 12]) + (70% × [12 – 4] ÷ 12)
= (40% × [4 ÷ 12]) + (70% × [8 ÷ 12])
= 13.33% + 46.67%
= 60%

So, the full year forecast for the utilization rate is 60 percent. This formula can be partially automated but does require the forecast for the remainder of the year.

The inclusion of forecasts and comparisons to plan for efficiency measures is illustrated in Table 12-16.

Table 12-16. Forecasts for Efficiency Measures in an Operations Report

Efficiency Measures	Unit of Measure	2020 Actual	Plan	June YTD Results	YTD Results Compared to Plan	Forecast	Forecast Compared to Plan
					2021		
Total participants	Number	109,618	147,500	67,357	46%	145,000	98%
Total unique participants	Number	40,729	45,313	36,998	82%	44,000	97%
Courses taken by type of learning							
ILT only	% of total	56%	25%	40%	15% below	33%	8% below
vILT only	% of total	3%	12%	9%	3% below	10%	2% below
E-learning only	% of total	35%	48%	39%	9% below	42%	6% below
Blended only	% of total	6%	15%	12%	3% below	15%	On plan
Total courses	% of total	100%	100%	100%		100%	
Utilization of e-learning courses							
Available	Number	60	74	65	88%	70	95%
Taken by more than 20 participants	Number	50	70	19	27%	55	79%
Percent taken by more than 20 participants	%	83%	95%	29%	66% below	79%	16% below
Reach							
Percentage of employees reached by L&D	%	85%	88%	72%	16% below	88%	On plan
Percentage of employees with development plans	%	82%	85%	84%	1% below	90%	5% above

Making Forecasts for Effectiveness Measures

Forecasting effectiveness measures is much like forecasting efficiency measures. The starting point is the YTD results, which will always be available, although in this case it may not always be statistically significant. Use the first two factors to think about how the remainder of the year will likely compare to plan or to the first part of the year. Unlike some efficiency measures, the forecast for effectiveness measures cannot be fully automated, but we can use formulas for weighted average to calculate the full-year forecast.

Unlike some efficiency measures, most effectiveness measures do not accumulate through the year and should not display any seasonal pattern. (Net benefits would be the exception but don't use an annualization formula for them.) Instead, a forecast must be made for the remainder of the year based on YTD results and the two factors, and then this forecast must be added to the YTD results. In this case we can use the formula for weighted averages, but the weights will not be months. Instead, the number of participants is used. The weight for YTD results is the YTD number of participants divided by the total planned for the full year, and the weight for the remainder of the year is the number of participants planned for the remainder of the year divided by the number of participants planned for the full year. By formula:

Full-Year Forecast:
[YTD results × (YTD number of participants ÷ Forecasted number of participants for the year)] + [Forecast for remainder of year × (Planned remaining participants ÷ Forecasted number of participants for the year)].

For example, suppose the Level 3 application rate is 50 percent for the first seven months, but there are plans in place to increase reinforcement, so the forecast for the last five months is 80 percent. If 400 participants have completed the training so far and an additional 600 are scheduled for the last five months, the forecasted total for the year will be 1,000. By formula:

Full-Year Forecast for Application Rate:
$$= [50\% \times (400 \div 1{,}000)] + [80\% \times (600 \div 1{,}000)]$$
$$= [50\% \times 0.4] + [80\% \times 0.6]$$
$$= 20\% + 48\%$$
$$= 68\%$$

So, the full-year forecast is for a 68 percent application rate.

This methodology will work for Levels 1–4. For ROI, we recommend a simple average of the programs completed so far plus the forecasted ROI for programs to be completed by year end. Typically, ROI is calculated or forecasted for a small number of projects, so it is easy to find the average, which will be the forecast for the full year. For example, suppose we have ROI for three completed programs of 15 percent, 30 percent, and 50 percent, and we are forecasting ROI of 25 percent and 80 percent for two more. The simple average of the five programs is 40 percent. If weighting is desired because some programs are much larger than others, weight them by total cost. Table 12-17 shows how to include forecasts and comparisons to plan for effectiveness measures.

Table 12-17. Forecasts for Effectiveness Measures in an Operations Report

Effectiveness Measures	Unit of Measure	2020 Actual	Plan	June YTD Results	2021 YTD Results Compared to Plan	Forecast	Forecast Compared to Plan
Level 1 participant reaction (all programs)							
Quality of content	% favorable	76%	80%	79%	1% below	79%	1% below
Quality of instructor	% favorable	80%	85%	86%	1% above	85%	On plan
Relevance	% favorable	72%	78%	73%	5% below	75%	3% below
Recommend to others	% favorable	68%	75%	69%	6% below	71%	4% below
Total for Level 1	Average of measures	74%	80%	77%	3% below	78%	2% below
Level 1 goal owner reaction (select programs)	% favorable	66%	80%	68%	12% below	75%	5% below
Level 2 learning (select programs)	Score	78%	85%	83%	2% below	85%	On plan
Level 3 application rate (select programs)							
Intent to apply (from post-event survey at end of course)	% content applied	70%	75%	70%	5% below	72%	3% below
Actual application (from follow-up survey after three months)	% content applied	51%	65%	55%	10% below	63%	2% below
Level 4 impact (select programs)							
Initial estimate by participants (post-event survey)	% contribution to goal	19%	50%	47%	3% below	50%	On plan
Final estimate (follow-up survey)	% contribution to goal	14%	30%	28%	2% below	30%	On plan
Level 5 ROI (select programs)							
Net benefits	Dollars, thousands	$254	$380	$140	37%	$400	105%
ROI	%	30%	40%	30%	10% below	43%	3% above

Conclusion

Congratulations! You have completed the two most difficult chapters in the book. We have shared a lot of technical guidance on how to create and use plans, report YTD results, and make forecasts. The good news is that you will not need any of this to begin your measurement and reporting journey. However, you will need it if you progress to creating and using management reports, so we wanted to provide it for you. No need to memorize anything—just remember that it's here in chapters 11 and 12 waiting for you when the need arises.

Next, we turn to how you and your organization can implement the shift to what we call a management mindset, in chapter 13.

PART IV

Putting It
All Together

CHAPTER 13
Implementing Measurement and Reporting

O ver the past five years, L&D organizations increasingly have embraced measurement and analytics. They have replaced static scorecards with interactive dashboards to ensure they uncover the underlying causes of underperforming programs. They have also begun to monitor key results to determine if measures are meeting agreed-upon thresholds.

Despite the creation of more attractive and user-friendly reports, however, much of the measurement work still focuses on informing and monitoring progress, which are the two lowest rungs on the measurement maturity curve.

The good news is that an increasing number of our clients are now conducting impact studies to determine if their most strategic programs are affecting business outcomes. More ambitious functions are moving their measurement resources under a talent analytics team to integrate learning and HR analytics and uncover drivers of engagement, retention, and high performance. These organizations are also building data literacy within their teams to ensure that L&D practitioners and business leaders act on the findings from analytics and reporting.

These organizations are engaged in Shift 1 (Figure 13-1), making the move from simply monitoring their results to evaluating and analyzing their data. We applaud these shifts and are heartened as more organizations embrace this change.

But that still leaves the final shift to manage. While we have spent a large portion of this book providing tactical details about measuring and reporting, at its heart, *Measurement Demystified* is about learning how to manage, or what might be called building a "management mindset." As we stated in chapter 1, management is the highest-level reason for measuring programs, initiatives, processes, resources, and the overall function. Managing requires that leaders first establish plans or targets for critical measures and then use monthly reported measures to determine if the program is on target to achieve the planned results. If not, managers need to take corrective action to get the program back on track.

Figure 13-1. Shift 1: From Monitor to Evaluate and Analyze

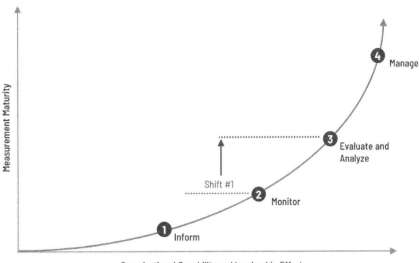

Management is the most intensive use of measurement and requires the greatest skill and effort. As you can see, as you embrace Shift 2 and move up the curve from evaluate and analyze, the trajectory gets noticeably steeper and requires more commitment and a new approach for managing the learning function (Figure 13-2). At the same time, this shift also delivers the biggest payoff.

Figure 13-2. Shift 2: From Evaluate and Analyze to Manage

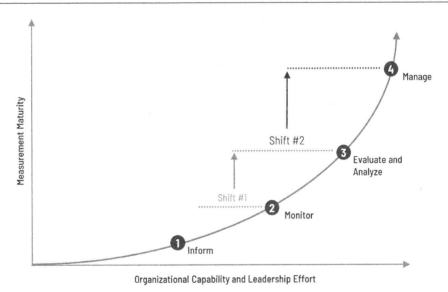

As we also noted, while management seems like the obvious and logical level that leaders should aspire to achieve, in our opinion, many organizations have not fully embraced it. The practice of setting plans and comparing results to plan monthly requires a level of business acumen, analysis, and discipline that many organizations simply don't have or desire to acquire. Management also requires a tolerance for uncertainty and a willingness to be accountable. We believe that enabling L&D not just to monitor and analyze but to manage the function is absolutely critical.

This chapter is focused on how to navigate this shift, including the critical success factors and key elements you must address to achieve a "management mindset."

L&D's Opportunity

Successful change requires that you have a clear picture of your current state and, once you know that, you are committed to making the move to the future state. If your organization is at the bottom of the maturity curve, for example, only using data to inform or monitor, then you may not be fully ready to embrace Shift 2. You may instead need to start more slowly and address the fundamentals of measurement to build a strong foundation before moving aggressively to managing.

Table 13-1 provides a short diagnostic to help you assess your readiness to make the transition to managing. For each statement, indicate if these actions occur never, rarely, sometimes, often, or always.

Table 13-1. Assessment: Are You Ready for Management?

	Never	Rarely	Sometimes	Often	Always
Strategic Alignment Senior L&D leaders have a defined and consistently executed process to align the learning organization's priorities to business requirements.	☐	☐	☐	☐	☐
Goal Setting and Standards Senior L&D leaders set goals for efficiency, effectiveness, and outcome metrics.	☐	☐	☐	☐	☐
Data Collection The L&D organization uses consistent methods to gather talent activity, cost, effectiveness, and outcome data.	☐	☐	☐	☐	☐
Reporting Methods The L&D organization has consistent methods for reporting results both to senior executives within the business and to L&D leaders.	☐	☐	☐	☐	☐
Analysis and Use The talent organization uses results and recommendations to improve the overall effectiveness, efficiency, and impact of the function on business results.	☐	☐	☐	☐	☐
Technology L&D has data reporting tools that enable scalable reporting for senior business and talent leaders.	☐	☐	☐	☐	☐

If most of your answers are "never" or "rarely," you will need to work on the foundational aspects of measurement. If your answers are "often" or "always," your organization is ready to embrace an approach that focuses on managing, not simply analyzing, monitoring, or informing.

What's Changing?

The journey up the measurement maturity curve is a change effort. Unless your organization is already mature, it will require a suite of changes, which can be segmented into three dimensions: people, process, and technology (Figure 13-3). People changes focus on the role of leaders and how they work with their business colleagues and ensure that L&D focuses on managing the function like a business. People changes also address roles, accountabilities, skills, capabilities, and resourcing. Process changes encompass the alignment of L&D priorities to business goals. They also address

Figure 13-3. Three Dimensions of Change

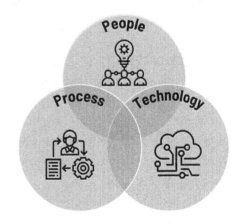

goal setting, data management, gathering, and reporting. Technology changes may involve the implementation of new systems and tools, but most often require better integration of existing systems across disparate platforms.

We discuss each of these dimensions in detail, starting with the people changes, as they are often the most challenging.

People Changes

The most significant type of change that organizations face with the shift to managing is with their people. This dimension includes four major areas (Figure 13-4):

- leadership and governance of the function
- clear accountabilities for leaders and practitioners
- skills and capabilities of L&D staff and often business partners
- resources and commitments to ensure the change sticks.

Figure 13-4. People Changes

Leadership and Governance

A critical success factor for adoption of a management mindset is that senior L&D leaders embrace the opportunity to run L&D like a business. Regardless of your level of measurement maturity, if senior L&D leaders are not on board, you won't be successful in making this shift.

Leaders need to be open and willing to change and model new behaviors within their own organization and with their business colleagues. Many L&D leaders may already have the skills to drive this change. For those who do not, they will need to commit to developing them and seek feedback on their progress. Beyond supporting the effort, focusing on managing requires that L&D leaders:

- Have a deep understanding of the business and where L&D can contribute.
- Develop strong relationships with senior business leaders that promote candid and meaningful dialogue about current and emerging needs.
- Embrace joint accountability for results. Joint accountability implies that L&D is willing to commit to plans and targets that contribute to business outcomes.
- Communicate consistently and educate key stakeholders on why this change is important, your progress to date, challenges, and how stakeholders can contribute.
- Establish a governance board comprising senior business leaders. A governance board creates strategic engagement and ensures that leadership confirms and revisits priorities for resources and action.

If senior L&D leaders in your organization are already doing these things, you can focus your energies on the other people dimensions we discuss next. If they are not, the first step is to ensure they understand their role in this process and the required actions to create the foundation for success.

Roles and Accountabilities

When an organization makes the shift to managing (versus monitoring, evaluating, or analyzing), accountabilities need to shift as well. Managing implies two key elements:

1. Leaders have clearly delineated to their staff and business partners their accountability for success.
2. The accountable persons understand and agree to the necessary actions required to achieve that success

For example, an organization with which we worked recently implemented a new learning experience portal (LXP). In past projects, such portals started out strong but usage declined as content aged and was not replaced with updated or new information. The portal program leader determined that domain owners needed to manage the freshness of content on the site. This entailed not simply archiving old content, but also soliciting new content based on user feedback. Moreover, domain owners needed to determine if low activity resulted from content that didn't meet user needs or if it was because users didn't know existed due to inadequate tagging, placement, or poor search engine optimization. Each domain owner had a defined role, clear expectations for action, a well-defined measure of success (freshness), a goal, and regular updates of performance against the plan. This project was a microcosm of the broader organization. Without clear accountabilities, everyone would have assumed that the work was everyone's job, which means it's no one's job and nothing gets done.

Skill and Capabilities

The shift to managing requires new skills and capabilities for L&D practitioners. Program managers and directors must now identify what measures to manage (versus analyze or monitor), recommend a plan (target) for the measure, as well as a plan to achieve it, and over time, forecast end-of-year results. These are new activities for many L&D employees. While they may know how to manage a program (from a business needs assessment to design, development, and implementation), they have not learned how to establish measures of success or how to develop specific plans to achieve them.

Moreover, establishing clear success measures requires understanding the goal owner's expectations and how the business operates. For example, consider an organization that has a low client retention rate. In the discussion with the goal owner, the L&D practitioner might assume that the only relevant success indicator is the client retention rate. By going deeper, the practitioner uncovers that the organization tracks client flight risk using a rubric that includes multiple risk factors (for example, share of wallet over time, the quality of C-suite relationships, client complaints, and NPS scores). The goal owner and practitioner agree that instead of focusing the learning on improving client retention, the organization would get more value from reducing client flight risk. As this example shows, the L&D practitioner needs the skills to ask the right questions, grounded in the knowledge of the business.

In addition, when the organization shifts to a management mindset, the L&D practitioner needs to think about how to uncover root causes of poor performance. Let's use our client flight risk example. L&D reports on the impact of training on risk reduction. The reports reveal that flight risk declined in Europe, but not in the United States. What data might uncover why the program worked in one region but not another? L&D needed to think about these data requirements at the outset of the measurement process to ensure that the data would be available if needed. In this case, L&D learned that Europe had a more mature "client success" process and staff. The Europe team embraced the change and quickly applied the learning. Without additional data about team tenure, the client may have assumed that the differences were cultural, putting in place corrective action that would have yielded no benefits.

Resources and Commitments

In the early stages, moving to managing from monitoring will require incremental effort. In the first year, organizations find they need to allocate at least one FTE to oversee the tactical effort in terms of data gathering, analysis, and reporting. Over time, as they automate or streamline the process, leaders reintegrate these resources back into the organization. But in the early stages, be prepared to dedicate additional staff to the end-to-end process.

Process Changes

The next largest area of change relates to process. In particular, organizations must ensure they have a robust alignment, planning, and goal-setting process. Moreover, if your organization doesn't have a data warehouse, you will likely need to address how you gather and manage your data for management reporting. Finally, you will need to reconsider how you engage with leaders, not only at the front end of the process (during alignment) but also at the back end (during reporting; Figure 13-5).

Figure 13-5. Process Changes

Alignment and Planning

One of the biggest process shifts required for organizations moving to a management mindset is in the area of alignment. As we talk to organizations, mature L&D functions have a fairly robust business alignment in place. Senior L&D leaders meet with the business at least annually to identify fiscal year priorities and where they should allocate their resources. This is a good start, but L&D needs to go a step further. The conversation is not just about priorities, but also:

- Does L&D have a role to play for each priority, and if so, in what way?
- If L&D can contribute to strategic priorities, how much of a contribution is L&D expected to make?
- And given that contribution, how much should L&D invest to contribute to the strategic outcomes.

As we work with L&D leaders, we observe that, in general, they are doing a better job of moving from an order taker role to a trusted business partner. CLOs and their staff work with the business to ensure that training is indeed a solution to the observed business problem.

However, at this point, the process gets a bit "squishy." For example, L&D and the business agree that training in consultative selling is important. But no one wants to commit how much the training will contribute to sales in the coming year, even qualitatively (that is, high, medium, or low). L&D develops a plan for design, development, and implementation, without any sense of whether they are spending more than is justified based on their contribution to the business. They base their budget simply on what it will cost, not based on what is reasonable given their contribution.

This shift from cost-based budgeting to value-based budgeting is one of the most significant changes and hurdles organizations face as they embrace Shift 2.

Goal Setting

Another significant change for many L&D functions is the creation of specific goals for each measure leaders intend to manage. Today, we observe one of four behaviors in L&D functions:

- L&D leaders do not set goals for any measure beyond cost. Reports show the variability of activity (usage) or effectiveness (Levels 1–4) scores from one period to the next without any clear indication of what good looks like.
- L&D uses preestablished benchmarks instead of goals. These organizations typically review their progress against benchmarks and may use more aggressive benchmarks over time to drive improved performance. When asked what their goals are, they answer, "The benchmark."
- Some L&D organizations set thresholds that are often the same across all courses and delivery types (for example, scrap rates of 25 percent or less for all courses). They may use color coding (see chapter 8) to show when results are above, at or under the threshold.
- L&D sets goals for efficiency, effectiveness, and outcomes that are appropriate for the measures and organizational priorities.

Earlier in this chapter, we discussed the importance of clarifying roles and accountability for specific measures of success. Clearly, accountability requires at least some goal, threshold, or benchmark to clarify what constitutes success. However, organizations often adopt a one-size-fits-all approach regardless of the type of program, its past history, or its maturity. For example, scrap rates for compliance programs are often higher than for strategic programs, simply because compliance programs are not designed for immediate application. If the goal for scrap is the same regardless of the type of program, managers of compliance programs will cease to review the results, knowing full well that the goal is meaningless.

Goal setting is crucial, but the goals must be meaningful so that program owners can adjust their action plans to achieve them.

Data Gathering and Management

Organizations that are beginning their journey toward managing over monitoring often find that their data management processes are lacking. Due to mergers, acquisitions, restructuring, or divestment, organizations may code the same field in different ways or use the same data name to mean different things in different parts of the organization. Some departments may gather the same data field daily, while others collect it monthly or even quarterly. Inconsistent data and data gathering can not only complicate the process of populating the reports but also result in data that is not credible or meaningful.

Organizations that are implementing a robust measurement and reporting framework need to determine how current data gathering and management practices will impact success. Addressing data gathering and management can be a major effort on its own. We recommend finding approaches to mitigate the impact rather than defer implementation.

Leadership Engagement

Increasing measurement maturity requires a fundamental shift in how organizations report their data to senior leaders and how senior leaders engage with the data in those reports. For many organizations, reporting is a single act, not a process. A system or person generates a report and then sends it to the recipient. Done. No further action required.

If a question arises, the onus is on the recipient to contact the report generator or even research the question to answer it on their own. More often, the recipient glances at the report, and if nothing appears amiss, that's the end of the review.

As we discussed in chapter 8 on reporting, even for monitoring, we don't recommend a cursory review of the data. Summary results can mask issues that hide in the details and without a deeper look, leaders can miss issues as they emerge.

When leaders are managing versus simply monitoring, it's important they review monthly reports in detail and understand the nuances in the details. L&D has an important role to play in helping leaders understand these nuances. As the generators of the data, L&D needs to explore the data and discuss the results with the leaders on a regular cadence.

Technology Changes

As with any change, technology is often a key enabler to manage the new approach both efficiently and effectively (Figure 13-6).

Figure 13-6. Technology Changes

Data Collection and Aggregation Tools

It is the rare L&D function that has a completely integrated suite of data gathering tools. Organizations are continually upgrading their LMS or implementing new learning measurement systems to streamline data collection. Some are creating stronger connections between their HR information system (HRIS) and learning data. While you may eventually need more robust tools to manage versus monitor, we recommend you avoid automation in the early stages of your journey. Develop your initial reports manually, using data extracts from your existing systems to populate your reports. As you review these reports with stakeholders, you will inevitably change them and identify ways to streamline their creation. Once you have a solid set of reports that you will develop monthly or quarterly, then you can identify how best to automate the process and the systems and tools you require.

Analytics and Reporting Tools

In addition to data collection and aggregation tools, increased measurement maturity may require more robust analytics and reporting tools. Increasingly, software is providing automated analysis and text analytics. Dashboards are common and provide robust capability for analysis. Also, as we've seen, most dashboards don't display the data in a way that enables management. If you are going to increase your measurement maturity, you will likely need more robust software than most reporting tools provide.

As with data gathering tools, you need to understand your users' needs for analytics and reporting before you make significant decisions about the format and content of the reports. The question is not, "What analysis and reports do you need?" but rather, "What decisions will you make, and what data (in what form) will enable you to make these decisions and manage your operation?"

You may find, however, that users often can't answer these questions at the outset. As leaders shift to a management mindset, they will likely learn as they go. In that case, clarify their requirements as best you can, but recognize that you may need to produce the reports and share them before they (and you) can finalize the most effective way to display the data.

Managing the Change

At this point, you might be thinking that this shift is just too big to tackle. Too much change, too many issues to address. We recognize that after you conduct the inventory of what's changing, the effort might seem too daunting.

It doesn't need to be. After you review the changes at a high level, use a matrix such as the one in Table 13-2. For each change, identify two to four areas needed for success. Assign a "high," "medium," or "low" rating to each area to reflect the level of change required.

Next, think about the implementation in stages. You will not shift organizational behavior overnight, so consider where you can make progress and build confidence in the process and its benefits. In our example, we show three implementation waves. Wave 1 focuses on the L&D function and doesn't yet engage business leaders in the process. The rationale is that L&D must put its own house in order before it shifts its engagement with business leaders. Wave 2 focuses on key business initiatives in which L&D already plays a role. Wave 3 focuses on enterprise business alignment and builds processes and relationship for ongoing business engagement.

Actions that involve a high degree of change may not be suited to Wave 1 simply because you need to build capability and credibility with your business colleagues.

When you complete this activity, review your assessment with senior L&D leaders and trusted business partners. Adjust your assessment of the degree of change and implementation priority (wave) based on this input. After you have solidified the assessment, you can now create a high-level approach for implementing TDRp as shown in Figure 13-7.

Table 13-2. Change Assessment Matrix

Change Area	What Changes Should We Make?	Change Level	Wave
People			
Leadership and governance	• Establish an advisory board • Build leadership advocacy skills or governing body	• Medium • High	• 1 • 2
Skills and capabilities	• Adopt common measurement language • Build skills in goal setting or forecasting • Develop data literacy skills	• Medium • High • Medium	• 1 • 1 • 2
Roles and accountabilities	• Establish role level accountability	• Medium	• 2
Resources and commitments	• Reallocate resources	• Low	• 1
Process			
Alignment and planning	• Develop or execute strategic alignment process • Identify key business initiatives • Identify business outcomes; agree on L&D's contribution	• Medium • Medium • High	• 3 • 2 • 3
Measurement	• Identify measures to manage (efficiency and effectiveness) • Develop a measures library	• Medium • Medium	• 1 • 1
Goal setting	• Develop a goal-setting process • Set goals for key measures	• High • High	• 1 • 1
Data gathering and management	• Streamline data gathering for outcome data • Improve data quality of cost and activity data	• High • Medium	• 3 • 2
Leadership engagement	• Enhance interaction with business leaders during the end-to-end process	• High	• 3
Technology			
Data collection tools	• Implement a new LMS. • Implement a data warehouse	• Medium • High	• 3 • 3
Analysis and reporting tools	• Automate analysis and reporting tools	• Medium	• 3

Figure 13-7. High-Level Implementation Approach

Wave 1: Internal L&D

• Adopt a common measurement language
• Identify effectiveness and efficiency measures to manage
• Build a measures library
• Reallocate resources
• Build skills in goal setting and planning
• Develop a goal-setting process
• Set goals for key measures
• Improve scorecards and dashboard for informing and monitoring

Develop Operations Report

Wave 2: Business Programs

• Identify key business initiatives
• Identify business outcomes
• Agree on L&D's contribution
• Develop program reports

• Build leadership advocacy skills
• Develop data literacy skills
• Establish role-level accountability
• Improve cost and activity data quality
• Improve program evaluation and custom analysis reports for evaluation and analysis

Develop Program Report

Wave 3: Strategic Priorities

• Establish an advisory board
• Develop and execute a strategic alignment process
• Enhance interaction with business leaders on the end-to-end process
• Develop a summary report

• Streamline data gathering for impact and outcome data
• Improve LMS reporting
• Implement a data warehouse
• Automate any analysis and reporting tools

Develop Summary Report

Select a Change Management Model

Once you have identified what's changing and your change priorities, you need to identify how you will manage the change. We recommend that you employ a change management approach to guide your efforts. There are several approaches (some of which we have listed here), any of which will be useful. If your organization has a preferred model, use that.

- Kurt Lewin's change model
- Kotter's change management theory (eight step model)
- Prosci's ADKAR approach
- William Bridges' change transition model.

A change management model will provide a road map for navigating the change. Adoption of a management mindset requires a change of behavior in L&D leaders, practitioners, and even in some cases, business leaders. It's not sufficient to sell leaders on the benefits; they have to want to change ("desire" in ADKAR) and then have the knowledge, skill, and ability to make that change stick. Change management models will provide the steps, tools, techniques, and guidelines for your journey.

Recognize that change is rarely smooth. A common challenge with change initiatives is illustrated in Figure 13-8. After some initial skepticism, leaders get on board. They announce the change effort with great fanfare. However, transformative change is not easy. As we said earlier, when the change requires a lot of new behaviors, the road can get rocky. At this point, leaders and practitioners alike often complain that it's taking too long or we can't yet see the results. The downward slide from optimism to pessimism puts change efforts at risk. When the project hits the "dark night of the innovator," many organizations decide that it's not worth it and scrap the project, or worse, abandon support and let it limp along.

Figure 13-8. Anatomy of Change

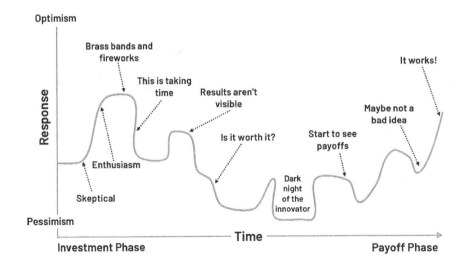

If you have done your homework upfront, and have secured the right support, started small and built on your successes, you can likely avoid this fate.

Sources of Resistance and How to Address Them

Having worked with dozens of organizations in their transformation to a management mindset, we also recognize that you will encounter resistance and pushback along the way. The most common challenges are dealing with resistance from within the L&D organization itself and creating a process that L&D practitioners and business partners can sustain over time. We share some of the most common questions or objections raised and our suggestions on how to handle them in Table 13-3.

Table 13-3. Resistance and How to Address It

Objection	Response	How to Address It
Our CLO is not on board with this approach. How should we proceed?	It's critical that the CLO or your head of learning owns this change effort. You won't be successful otherwise.	• Discuss the benefits of shifting to a management mindset. • Identify what factors may be inhibiting the CLO from moving forward. • Determine if a pilot might be worth undertaking to demonstrates the value of this transformation.
We have never set goals for measures beyond adhering to a financial budget. Where do we start?	You are not alone. Budget accountability is often the sole measure for L&D.	• Lead with a small number (5–6) of critical, balanced measures (see chapter 2), starting with L&D efficiency and effectiveness measures (see chapters 3 and 4). • Gain agreement from L&D leadership that these measures are critical to manage. • Use chapter 11 to guide you on how to set plans and forecasts for these critical few measures.
L&D practitioners are resistant to being held accountable for goals.	We hear this a lot. If practitioners have never been held accountable for results, this is a huge shift.	• Acknowledge the fear and concern. • Make the first year a period to learn. What works? What doesn't? How can they create better plans and forecasts? How can they influence results? • As the team learns and gets more comfortable with the approach, they should build their goals into their annual development plan.
Business leaders were engaged in the beginning but now they don't seem to care about the reports or results.	You need to appeal to your CLO or sponsor for this effort in L&D.	• The shift to managing over monitoring will not happen overnight. • Early engagement is often the "brass bands" and fireworks stage for everyone. • If business leaders are not engaged, explore why. Are the reports meaningful? Are you discussing the results with them and exploring areas for improvement? • Identify approaches that will appeal to what they care about: their business results.
Our systems are old and don't provide us with the data we need. Should we wait until we implement new systems?	No! Don't wait. Start with what you have.	• For the critical measures you identified, determine how you can gather the data in a relatively efficient way. • This may be manual at first if your systems don't provide what you need.
We've generated the management reports, but they take too much time to create. We don't have the capacity to produce them monthly or even quarterly.	In the early phases, you may find that the reports take more time to generate, particularly if you don't have systems that generate the source data.	• Focus on one report first, perhaps the operations report. • Most organizations have the data available either in their LMS or learning evaluation system (if separate) and can extract this data for the operations report. • If you are creating the report manually in Excel, hire a person to write macros that can populate the report. • Ensure you aren't trying to gather too much data and stay focused initially on the critical few measures.

Change Management Tips

To avoid falling too deeply into the dark night of the innovator, we suggest six remedies (Figure 13-9). None of these are new or rocket science, but it's surprising how many change leaders fail to pay heed to them.

Figure 13-9. Managing the Change

- **Build support and sponsorship early and often.** A project of this type requires sponsorship at multiple levels. First, the CLO must fully support the work. But beyond the CLO, business partners must also support the effort, since this shift will affect them as well. Don't assume that everyone will get on board. As we discuss later in this chapter, you need to know who will help, who will resist, and who will just go along. Find the friendlies and start there. The resistors usually come along later after you get to the "It Works!" stage.
- **Communicate and educate early and often.** Remember that building support can take time. In the early stages, you need to build awareness. Engage with your peers and business colleagues as well as key influencers. As you communicate, find the likely early adopters, those who want to be part of the journey. Before you go too far, develop a communication plan that includes messaging about why this change is important, what it entails, its benefits to the organization, and the old standby, WIIFM or "What's in it for me?" (We won't provide a communication plan template in this book, but Google the term and you will find dozens of sites with downloadable templates.) As you communicate, engage other enthusiastic peers to broaden the message and show that support is spreading.
- **Get regular feedback.** Communication must be two-way. Find out what's working and what isn't. Determine if the issues are substantive or simply part of the

adjustment process. If you need to shift your approach, do so. But take care to stay focused on the goal.

· **Don't try to tackle everything at once; be purposeful about how you will start.** For most organizations, it makes sense to start within L&D. As you build capability and confidence in the process, L&D practitioners can become ambassadors for the process with their business partners.

· **Treat your implementation as a project by allocating resources and developing a project plan.** In our experience, L&D leaders underestimate the effort required to build a management mindset. They expect that somehow this shift will happen by communicating or talking about it with the business. Treat this shift as a project and resource it appropriately.

· **Make the process developmental not punitive.** In the early stages of the effort, employees, particularly L&D practitioners, are apt to be worried about the impact of the change in the process. "What if I don't meet my goals? What if I can't get good data? What if my business partners won't cooperate?" As we indicated in chapter 11, you will only get better at this approach if you try. And you will likely have some successes as well as failures. Use the failures to learn, not punish. We recommend that L&D leaders treat the first year as a learning year, where staff are not penalized for failing to achieve goals. This approach tends to reduce the anxiety and can generate excitement about learning a new skill.

Tools and Templates

In this section, we provide three tools that will simplify your change management efforts. The first is the project charter document to get your effort off to a solid start. The second is the stakeholder analysis tool to assess the level of support for the effort. The third is a detailed implementation plan template that enables you to envision the implementation journey.

Project Charter Document

As we have mentioned, you should view the implementation of a management mindset as a project with a well-defined project plan and with a project charter document that defines the scope, objectives, and participants of your effort. A charter document ensures that everyone involved in the effort is aware of its purpose and objectives. It provides a preliminary delineation of roles and responsibilities, outlines the project objectives, identifies the main stakeholders, and defines the authority of the project manager. The project manager should update it periodically to reflect changes in project scope, key players, and resources available. It provides an ongoing record of the agreements about the project between the project manager, the primary sponsor, and key stakeholders. To help you visualize this process, the charter structure we describe is shown in greater detail in Figure 13-10, and we also provide a subset of a charter we developed with a client (Table 13-4).

Figure 13-10. Structure of a Project Charter Document

Project Charter								
Project Overview		Project Details				Resource Requirements		Signatures
Project Objectives	Project Scope	Milestones	Critical Success Factors	Constraints and Impacts	Assumptions and Risks	Roles and Responsibilities	Other Resources	Customer, Sponsors, and Project Manager

Project overview
- **Project objectives:** Explain the specific objectives of the implementing a robust measurement and reporting framework. What value does this project add to the organization? How does this project align with the strategic priorities of the organization? What results do you expect? What are the deliverables? What benefits will the organization realize? What problems will this effort address?
- **Project scope:** The project scope establishes the boundaries of the project. It identifies the limits of the project and defines the deliverables. You should also delineate what is not in scope of this project.

Project details
- **Milestones:** List the major milestones and deliverables of the project.
- **Critical success factors:** Identify the business and organizational factors that are critical to the success of this project. (In other words, what must go right for this project to succeed?)
- **Project constraints:** What constraints has the business imposed on this project? For example, have business sponsors limited the scope of the project or the resources they will provide?
- **Impact statement:** What impact might this project have on existing systems or departments? For example, will this project require additional resources to clean or organize data?
- **Assumptions and risks:** List and describe the assumptions made in the decision to charter this project. Identify the high-level project risks and the strategies to mitigate them.

Resource requirements
- **Roles and responsibilities:** Describe the roles and responsibilities of project team members. They include:
  - **Sponsor:** As mentioned earlier, implementing a management mindset requires that the CLO takes on the role of project sponsor. The CLO provides overall direction on the project. Responsibilities include:
    » Approve the project charter and plan.
    » Secure resources for the project, not only within L&D, but perhaps in IT (if you require technical resources) and finance personnel, HRIS resources, and business partners.
    » Confirm the project's goals and objectives; keep abreast of major project activities; make decisions on escalated issues; and assist in the resolution of roadblocks.
  - **Project manager:** As we've discussed, making the transition to managing versus monitoring will not happen by itself. The project needs a designated project manager who will lead the planning and development of the project and manages

the project to scope. The duties are identical to what a project manager would do on any major effort including:

» Develop the project plan and identify project deliverables along with risk and risk mitigation plans.

» Direct the project resources (team members).

» Manage the scope; oversee quality assurance of the project management process; maintain all documentation including the project plan.

» Report and forecast project status; resolve conflicts within the project or between cross-functional teams.

» Ensure that the project's product meets the business objectives; communicate project status to stakeholders.

◦ **Team member:** This shift requires team members of several types:

» Business partners who can provide input on business priorities and the expectations of senior leaders.

» L&D practitioners who can provide subject matter expertise on L&D and HR priorities.

» Technology specialists who are conversant in the data residing in relevant systems and how to extract the data for easy input into L&D management reports.

◦ **Internal stakeholders:** The persons or departments you will partner with on the key deliverables (these may be HR partners or business stakeholders depending on the scope of your implementation). Responsibilities include:

» Provide input to the project charter.

» Provide a clear definition of the business objective.

» Sign off on project deliverables.

◦ **SME:** Provides expertise on a specific subject. Responsibilities include:

» Maintain up-to-date experience and knowledge on the subject matter.

» Provide advice on what is critical to the performance of a project task and what is nice-to-know.

· **Other resources:** Identify the initial funding, personnel, and other resources committed to this project by the project sponsor.

Signatures

· Ensure that each major stakeholder signs off on the charter document including:

◦ The CLO as project sponsor.

◦ The key stakeholders—a senior HR or business leader who will work with L&D in the initial stages.

◦ The project manager—this person will likely come from L&D.

To bring the charter document to life, we include an example from an organization we worked with (Table 13-4). We masked the names but pulled this information from their initial charter document.

Table 13-4. Project Charter Example

Project Overview	Description
Project objectives	• The purpose of the Talent Management (TM) Talent Development Reporting principles (TDRp) Implementation Project is to improve TM capability to report efficiency, effectiveness, and outcome measures of key TM projects • This will provide visibility into TM alignment to institutional strategy and impact on institutional goals • We will achieve this by using TDRp processes, measures, statements, and reports in our TM operations • By incorporating TDRp, TM will be better able to create forecasts and plans aligned to institutional strategic drivers, manage projects and programs to these plans, and capture business impact

Project scope	• In scope:
	  ○ Select and gain approval from stakeholders on enterprise programs to track using TDRp program reports
	  ○ Create and manage a TM measures library in accordance with TDRp standards approved by TM leadership and stakeholders
	  ○ Create and manage efficiency, effectiveness, and outcome statements for key TM initiatives, which will include data from the measures library as selected by stakeholders
	• Out of scope:
	  ○ Adopting measures, statements, or reports not recommended in the TDRp process guidelines
	  ○ Incorporating TDRp into other HR functions outside TM

Project Details	
Milestones	• Educate senior TM leaders on the TDRp process • Identify a pilot business unit for implementation, including the engagement of a senior business leader • Identify one to two programs to shift to management • Engage with goal owners to identify key measures of success • Develop a measures library • Produce the initial program report
Critical success factors	• Leadership: Talent leaders engage in ongoing dialogue with senior business leaders and team using TDRp reports to drive decisions and manage toward institutional goals • Talent business planning: TM initiatives are driven by business priorities, and planning for those initiatives involves customer stakeholders with whom TM identifies efficiency, effectiveness, and outcome measures with SMART goals
Constraints	• Time: Competing priorities and short-term deliverables will continue to take up time needed to build the TDRp implementation process and culture
Assumptions	• Primary purpose of human capital initiatives and processes: Build capability that enables the organization to achieve its goals or achieve its goals more quickly or at lower cost • Human capital initiatives and processes should align strategically to the goals of the organization • Business environment characterized by significant uncertainty; we make plans with the best information available—waiting for absolute certainty and perfection is not an option • We will use recommended reports; the underlying data will be used appropriately by competent, experienced leaders to manage the function to meet agreed-upon goals and continuously improve
Risks	• Poor data quality: Inconsistent definitions and calculations, untrusted sources of data, and delayed report delivery may affect trust in reports and adoption of TDRp • Resource expertise: Lack of familiarity with how to create, interpret, or apply TDRp reports may affect adoption • Low adoption: Culture, competing priorities, and change overload may dampen enthusiasm and focus on adopting TDRp
Resource Requirements	
Roles and responsibilities	• This project will primarily be managed by Jane Smith, the talent analytics consultant • Senior TM leadership will be closely involved with the project in the planning, championing, and adopting capacity • The talent consulting team and program managers will be involved early and often
Other resources	None at this time
Signatures	Head of Talent

Stakeholder Analysis Tool

Successful projects require support from a variety of stakeholders, be they business leaders or members of your own organization. It's always wise to assess the readiness of your stakeholders to engage and commit to the effort and resources required for success.

A stakeholder readiness assessment can reveal important insights about your stakeholders:
- potential resisters who may place organizational or financial roadblocks in your way
- early adopters or hidden supporters who want to engage with you and make change happen
- neutral parties who are not likely to engage but will not block your effort.

The assessment can also uncover other inflight projects that could either bolster your efforts or perhaps conflict with your work. Finally, a well-executed stakeholder assessment can generate excitement in the organization about your initiative and a desire to get involved.

How to Conduct the Assessment

You can conduct a readiness assessment in several ways:
- **Stakeholder interviews:** We recommend conducting brief interviews with stakeholders whom you are likely to involve or who will be critical to your success. The purpose of the interview is twofold: first, to communicate about the project and why it's important to the organization; second, to assess the level of commitment of this stakeholder to measurement in general and the shift to a management mindset.
- **Discussions with stakeholder influencers:** If you can't get access to the stakeholder, the next best method is to meet with influencers of the stakeholder. The influencer might be a trusted staff member or may be a peer who has insight in the stakeholder's perspective on a project of this sort.
- **Surveys:** If you have a large number of stakeholders to engage, you might consider developing a very short survey (five to seven questions) to identify specific pain points in the organization that the implementation will address. Findings from this survey can inform your communications and how you engage these individuals in the future.

Information to Include in the Assessment

After you gather data through interviews or a survey, you need to document your findings. We recommend using an Excel spreadsheet that contains the following:
- **Stakeholder information:**
  - Stakeholder name
  - Department or BU
  - Job title or role
  - Location

- **Current view of the initiative:** We recommend that you categorize how each stakeholder currently views the initiative using a predefined rating scale such as:
  - Committed: The stakeholder has demonstrated their commitment to managing over monitoring the effort by engaging in the implementation and committing resources and funds to the effort.
  - Supportive: The stakeholder has communicated or demonstrated support or advocacy toward your approach.
  - Positive perception: The stakeholder has expressed a positive perception toward the effort and is interested in learning more.
  - Neutral: The stakeholder is aware of and understands the reason for the shift to measurement and reporting and in particular to managing the business, but is neither supportive nor resistant.
  - Resistant: The stakeholder is aware of and understands what you plan to achieve but has communicated or demonstrated resistance.
- **Desired view of initiative:** Next, you should identify what view you need from each stakeholder. You will never get everyone to be equally enthusiastic about your work. Some stakeholders may see it as a threat, others may simply not have the energy to engage. We recommend that you identify the lowest level of support you need from each stakeholder this project to be successful.

Example

Inez Gomez leads a large business unit in the organization. You have met with her, and she is interested in what you are doing but is noncommittal. While you would like to include her business unit in your implementation, you have uncovered other, more supportive leaders who will participate. Her current view is "neutral" and you can live with that. So you would indicate that the desired view is also neutral. Over time, you may want to move her to "positive perception" so that you can introduce measurement and reporting into her business unit, but for now, neutral is sufficient.

On the other hand, you interviewed Vijay Patel about the project. Vijay heads up talent analytics and he was very negative about your work. He perceived that the effort would consume a lot of time from his staff and would provide minimal benefits to him or his department. Given his role in the organization, you will need to move him from resistant to at least supportive to ensure you can get the necessary data to generate your management reports.

- **Influence:** This dimension provides insights into how much influence the stakeholder wields in the organization. We suggest using a simple three category assignment:
  - High: The stakeholder can influence others and significantly impact the success of the initiative.

- ◦ Medium: The stakeholder might influence the success of the initiative depending on the scope of the effort.
  - ◦ Low: The stakeholder will be impacted by the initiative but is not likely to influence others.
  - ◦ Note that the level of influence of the stakeholder should also affect the desired view of the work. High influence stakeholders will need to be more supportive of your work.
- · **Issues and actions:** What this stakeholder needs and the challenges you need to address based on your findings. This section should also specify the actions you will take to move the stakeholder from their current to desired perception.
- · **Relationship owner:** Identify who will work with this stakeholder to keep them informed and positively impact their perspective.

Table 13-5 is an example of a stakeholder assessment.

Table 13-5. Example of a Completed Stakeholder Assessment

Stakeholder Analysis	Organization:							
	Leader							
	Exec Sponsor:							
Stakeholder Information							**Issue Identification and Resolution**	
Department or Business Unit and Stakeholder	Job Title or Role Location	Comments	Current View of Initiative	Desired View of Initiative	Influence		Issues and Actions	Relationship Owner
Organization Name								
Alison Lockwood	SVP of HR	Alison is a strong believer in TDRp and has been an advocate across the organization.	Committed	Committed	High		None at present. It is important to set Alison up for success.	Jason
Rand Jackson	BU VP	Rand has indicated that he is in favor of a more financially driven HR reporting approach. However, he is concerned that he may have to devote too much time to his new process.	Positive perception	Supportive	Medium		It is critical that Rand support TDRp as his involvement and role modeling will be key. We need to identify how to engage him without him feeling like it is taking up too much of his time.	Jennifer
Cory Jones	HR Director	Cory is not supportive of TDRp. He believes the approach is too difficult to execute and doesn't see the benefits. Cory works closely with Rand.	Resistant	Positive perception	Medium		Work with Cory to get him at least to a neutral position.	Ariana
Kristine Walker	HR Director	Kristine is a potential supporter but she will not be involved right now	Neutral	Neutral	Medium		Keep in contact with Kristine so that she stays at neutral at a minimum.	Ariana

Final Thoughts About the Assessment

Stakeholder assessments needn't take a lot of time; most organizations can complete them within a week or two. If you are pressed for resources and time, consider how you can streamline the effort. Identify the key stakeholders with whom you must engage and focus your attention there. If and when your implementation expands, simply add to your assessment, and identify how each new stakeholder fits within the project. In some cases, you can assess groups of stakeholders, for example a department or team. By grouping stakeholders, you can minimize the number of interviews or data you must collect.

Regardless of your approach, we highly recommend that you spend the time upfront to understand the perspectives, influence, and interest of your key stakeholders. You will greatly simplify the downstream effort to gain support and adoption.

Implementation Plan Template

The final tool is the implementation plan template. The implementation plan contains the following elements:

- The major stages of the plan:
  - Startup
  - Planning
  - Implementation: Waves 1, 2, and 3
- Detailed tasks (numbered) that show:
  - Start and end dates
  - Duration (time to complete the task)
  - Dependencies (what precedes the task and what follows it)
  - The individuals responsible for executing each task (not shown in Table 13-6)
- Milestones delineated by the delta (Δ). A milestone is a task with zero duration that identifies the completion of a body of work.

The partial plan shown in Table 13-6 follows the high-level implementation approach to managing change in Figure 13-7. It divides the major areas into specific tasks required to provide the deliverable of each phase. (Appendix D provides the full set of tasks for this plan.)

Conclusion

Making the shift to a management mindset won't happen simply by wishing it into existence. This shift requires a level of discipline and multi-year commitment to being more purposeful about how you manage the business, measure your programs, report on progress, and ensure continuous improvement based on your reporting and feedback systems.

Table 13-6. Implementation Plan (partial)

		TDRp Implementation Plan					
Milestone	Task #	Task Name	Duration	Start	Finish	Predecessors	Successors
	1	Begin Project	0 days	Mon 1/4	Mon 1/4		5, 4
	2						
	3	Startup	32 days	Mon 1/4	Tue 2/16		
	4	Agree on commitment to TDRp, goals, and resources	5 days	Mon 1/4	Fri 1/8	1	6
	5	Stakeholder analysis	8 days	Mon 1/11	Wed 1/20	1	
	6	Conduct stakeholder analysis	5 days	Mon 1/11	Fri 1/15	4	7
	7	Synthesize findings	3 days	Mon 1/18	Wed 1/20	6	8
Δ	8	Initial stakeholder assessment complete	0 days	Wed 1/20	Wed 1/20	7	10
	9	Change assessment	17 days	Thu 1/21	Fri 2/12		
	10	Conduct change assessment	5 days	Thu 1/21	Wed 1/27	8	11
	11	Develop implementation approach	5 days	Thu 1/28	Wed 2/3	10	12
	12	Review recommendations with key stakeholders	5 days	Thu 2/4	Wed 2/10	11	13
	13	Modify implementation approach based on feedback	2 days	Thu 2/11	Fri 2/12	12	14
Δ	14	High-level approach complete	0 days	Fri 2/12	Fri 2/12	13	15
	15	Complete sponsor commitment plan	2 days	Mon 2/15	Tue 2/16	14	16
Δ	16	Startup complete	0 days	Tue 2/16	Tue 2/16	15	20
	17						
	18	Planning	30 days	Wed 2/17	Tue 3/30		
	19	Implementation Planning	15 days	Wed 2/17	Tue 3/9		
	20	Develop tactical plan with team	10 days	Wed 2/17	Tue 3/2	16	21
	21	Develop high-level change and communications plan	5 days	Wed 3/3	Tue 3/9	20	22
	22	Identify resource requirements	5 days	Wed 3/3	Tue 3/9	21	23
	23	Review implementation and change plan with key resources	5 days	Wed 3/10	Tue 3/16	22	24
	24	Finalize implementation plan	5 days	Wed 3/17	Tue 3/23	23	25
	25	Senior leader review and signoff	5 days	Wed 3/24	Tue 3/30	24	26
Δ	26	Planning complete	0 days	Tue 3/30	Tue 3/30	25	30

We recommend that you embrace both project management and change management discipline for your transformation. You will experience resistance and, at times, you may find that the journey challenging. Not everyone in your current organization will be able to adapt. But over time, you will be able to grow the skills of your team and hire other practitioners who have the needed skills and can model them for others.

In our experience, this shift is not an easy one. But organizations that make the transition realize numerous benefits including enhanced credibility with the business, more clarity on where they add value and where they don't, and finally, enhanced impact on the business with more predictable performance. We believe it's worth it.

CHAPTER 14
Pulling It All Together

Our goal in writing this book is to provide the foundation, tools, and practical guidance to create a meaningful measurement and reporting strategy. We hope we have accomplished that goal by sharing the TDRp framework with guidance on four broad reasons to measure, three types of measures, and five general types of reports, along with recommendations on how to select the appropriate measures and reports.

Key Takeaways

While we hope we have provided many good ideas that you can apply, here are some basic tips:

1. Always start by asking questions.

This is the natural starting point to answer any specific request for measurement or to create a measurement and reporting strategy. Begin by asking:

- Why do you want to measure?
- Who will use it?
- For what purpose?
- How often is it needed?

Answers to these questions will determine the purpose of measuring, which in turn will inform the selection of measures, frequency of reporting, audience, type of report, and level of analysis. All of these considerations are captured in the measurement hierarchy first shared in chapter 1 and shown in Table 14-1.

2. Understand the difference between informing, monitoring, and managing.

There are four basic reasons for measuring, and it is vitally important to understand the differences between informing, monitoring, and managing. Informing is simply answering a question or providing historical data. No action is required. Monitoring means that thresholds have been set for each measure, and if the value falls outside the threshold, action may need to be taken. Managing is the highest-level use of measurement. It requires that a plan be established for each measure and that monthly management reports be used to deliver that plan by year end. Create plans for measures when you want to drive a change in the value of a measure. Use thresholds when you want to ensure that a measure's value remains in an existing and acceptable range. In other words, if you are happy with the current level of performance, use a threshold. If you want to move the needle to a higher or lower value, create a plan reflecting the new desired state.

Table 14-1. Measurement Hierarchy

Measurement Purpose	Primary Use	Level of Analysis	Measurement Frequency	Key Elements
Manage	• Identify if the program is delivering planned results and where adjustments are needed to meet goals.	High	Monthly	• Plan • YTD results • Forecast for measures being managed
Evaluate and analyze	• Analyze program and non-program data. • Explore relationships among measures. • Predict outcomes.	Medium to high	Based on business need	• Analytical methods (e.g., regression analysis, predictive modeling)
	• Evaluate the efficiency, effectiveness, or impact of a learning program.		End of program or pilot	• Six levels of evaluation (Level 0 to Level 5)
Monitor	• Determine if measure meets threshold or is within acceptable range.	Low	Monthly or quarterly	• Threshold or breakpoints for measures
Inform	• Answer questions, identify key trends, and share activity.	Low	As needed	• Specific measures or trends

Copyright applied for by Center for Talent Reporting (2020). Used with permission.

(Left margin arrow label: Measurement Maturity)

3. Understand the difference between scorecards, dashboards, and management reports.

This follows directly from understanding the different types of measures. If the purpose is simply to inform, use a scorecard or dashboard without thresholds or plans—just historical results. If the purpose is to monitor to ensure a measure remains in an historically acceptable range, use a scorecard or dashboard with thresholds. If the purpose is to manage to move a measure higher or lower, use management reports, which contain plan, YTD results, and forecast—all the tools needed to manage successful delivery of the plan.

4. Follow a disciplined, thoughtful process. Never measure just to measure.

The process should begin by asking the questions at the beginning of this chapter. Also, be sure to review all the measures currently being reported and answer the following questions:

- Do we need all our current measures?
- Is someone still using them or has the original user moved to another position?
- Could we use better measures to answer questions from the users?
- Could we identify better reports to help us monitor or manage?

A best practice would be to interview users of measures and reports at least annually. Retire reports that no one uses. Understand the reasons why and provide more meaningful reports or displays that stakeholders will use.

5. Use frameworks to simplify language and communication and ensure selection of appropriate measures and reports.

We recommend the TDRp framework, first shared in chapter 1, which comprises four reasons to measure, three types of measures, and five types of reports (Figure 14-1). We have identified more than 170 measures for L&D alone and more than 700 for HR in total. With this many measures, a framework makes life easier for the profession. The framework builds on the work of Trolley, Boudreau, Kirkpatrick, and Phillips.

Figure 14-1. TDRp Framework for Measurement and Reporting

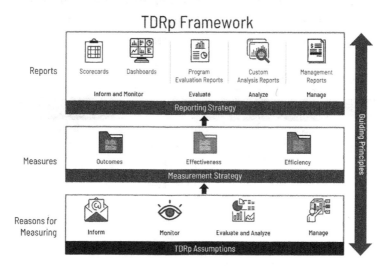

Copyright applied for by Center for Talent Reporting (2020). Used with permission.

The TDRp framework provides a holistic view of the entire measurement and reporting process incorporating the reasons to measure, the types of measures, and the types of reports.

6. Create a holistic measurement strategy, which should always include at least some efficiency and some effectiveness measures. If the program supports a strategic goal, your strategy should also include an outcome measure.

The recommended measures for any program or initiative should always include at least one efficiency and one effectiveness measure. Typically, you will have multiples of each. Very importantly, if the program serves a high-level organization goal set by the CEO or senior leadership team, you should identify an outcome measure for learning, which ideally will be the impact of learning on achieving the organizational goal.

7. The reason to measure should dictate which type of report you should use to share the data.

We identified five types of reports, and each has its own purpose. Consequently, once you have answered the key questions about the reasons for measuring, be sure to use the right report to share the data.

8. Management is the highest-level use of measurement and analytics, and three special TDRp management reports are dedicated to this use. Management reports are characterized by plan and forecast for each measure.

While some in the profession believe analysis is the highest-level use of measurement, we believe it is the active management of strategic and non-strategic programs as well as department initiatives. This active management requires considerable effort and skill to create good plans for the key measures and then execute the plans to come as close as possible to delivering agreed-upon results. This requires the analysis of YTD results and regular forecasting. We recommend three TDRp management reports, each designed specifically to manage at either the program, department, or enterprise level (Table 14-2).

Table 14-2. The TDRp Management Reports

Report	Level	Audience	Measures
Program	Program	• Program manager • Goal owner • Department head	• Outcome • Efficiency • Effectiveness
Operations	Department	• Department head	• Efficiency • Effectiveness
Summary	Enterprise	• CEO, CFO • Governing body • Department head	• Outcome • Efficiency • Effectiveness

9. Run the learning function with business discipline.

This means that programs in support of strategic goals should have specific, measurable plans. It also means that L&D needs to generate reports monthly showing YTD results compared to plan and forecast compared to plan. Your colleagues in sales, manufacturing, and other disciplines run their departments this way. L&D should too.

10. L&D professionals, like any other professionals, must make plans and decisions in the face of uncertainty.

The only guarantee is that plans and decisions will be wrong. Nonetheless, you will accomplish more if you create solid plans and execute them, with discipline, allowing for midcourse corrections to come as close as possible to plan by year-end.

11. You will need a change management plan.

Implementing many of the recommendations in this book will require new skills and new ways of thinking. This is true even with respect to the four reasons to measure, three types of measures, and five types of reports. We can almost guarantee that you will need to address change management to run learning like a business and create plans for key measures. You will likely experience some resistance, so a change management plan is essential for success.

Opportunities

From a maturity point of view, L&D is still a young profession. This means that we don't yet agree on language, terms, definitions, and conceptual frameworks. The good news is that there are a lot of very smart, dedicated people working to advance the profession, and we are making progress every day. It also means that there is room for improvement and new ideas. Here are the greatest opportunities we see for the profession in the areas of measurement, analytics, and reporting.

Adopt a common language and framework.

We recommend the TDRp framework with a limited number of reasons to measure, types of measures, and types of reports, but you could imagine others. We believe that a successful framework contains five or fewer high-level categories because it is simply too hard to remember more. It would represent a major step forward if everyone just adopted the three types of measures (efficiency, effectiveness, and outcomes) or the five basic types of reports (scorecard, dashboard, program evaluation, custom analysis, and management).

Be more disciplined. Stop taking orders from the business.

Ask questions when a stakeholder asks you to provide a measure or report. Determine what the stakeholder truly needs and which measures and reports will best meet those needs. The stakeholder may not need something new at all or perhaps they need something different than requested. Review all the reports you currently generate to see what you can eliminate. If you haven't reviewed your reporting recently, you can probably find several to discontinue.

Move up the maturity curve.

We shared a measurement maturity model in chapter 1 with management as the highest use of measurement.

Most measurement and reporting today is to inform. This is foundational and the logical starting point, but it should not be the ending point. While dashboards with elements of interactivity or visualization are becoming increasingly common, a big opportunity lies in using scorecards and dashboards to monitor, which requires thresholds. Perhaps the single biggest opportunity for the profession is to actively manage learning, which means setting plans for key measures and then using management reports monthly to determine if programs are on plan or not, and if not, taking corrective action early.

Be accountable.

As you move up the maturity curve, you will need to take on greater levels of accountability. Sadly, many in L&D and HR in general do not want to be accountable. They are frightened by the need to set plans and manage programs to plan in a world full of uncertainties. After all, they may be wrong! And active management takes much more work than the traditional passive approach of simply providing YTD results and making the occasional comparison to history or benchmark.

Measure more at Levels 3, 4, and 5.

Moving up the maturity curve also requires that you measure beyond reaction and learning. If the reason to measure is evaluation, analysis, or management, you can only address this reason through higher levels of evaluation. After the need to manage, this probably represents the next greatest opportunity for the profession. Jack Phillips showed in his research of CEOs who said that what they most wanted to see from L&D was impact, followed by ROI, and application. In other words, they want to see Levels 3, 4, and 5!

The profession made good progress from 2000 to 2010, especially with regard to application. Since 2010, however, we don't appear to have made significant gains. Modern survey tools make it easier than ever to get this data. Virtually all organizations today administer a post-event survey, so just add a question on intent to apply and a question on impact. That will get you started and then you can consider doing a follow-up survey two to three months later for your most important strategic programs to ask about actual application and a final estimate for impact. You might also try using a control group, trendline, or regression to estimate the isolated impact for your most important programs.

Create a written strategy for measurement, analytics, and reporting.

The process of creating the strategy will be as valuable as the final product. It is a great way to get the L&D team on the same page and reinforces the need to use a common language. It also provides excellent guidance for someone new to the measurement effort or to a new measurement leader or CLO. The strategy should contain all three types of measures and indicate measures to be employed for each program or group of courses. The strategy should also identify the reports by user.

Create a measures library.

This will be your single source of truth regarding measures. Your selected measures are the rows, and important information about the measures is contained in the columns. Typical columns include type of measure, definition, and formula, at a minimum.

Leverage the ISO Human Capital Reporting standards to increase your measurement and reporting efforts.

Compare your current reporting to the ISO recommendations. Be sure you can meet their recommended public and internal reporting standards. Moreover, consider how your measures for public reporting are likely to compare to other organizations. Once some organizations begin to publicly disclose key training and HR-related measures, investment analysts as well as employees are going to start asking why your organization is not disclosing. They will assume that your measures are not favorable. Act now to ensure your reporting is robust and that your measures are favorable.

Closing Thoughts

Measurement, analytics, and reporting are very exciting areas these days. You might say others are finally beginning to appreciate their importance, something we have known for some time. New tools, processes, and systems allow us to collect and report more data than ever before, and the pace of change is only going to accelerate. So, it is all the more important to have a solid foundation on which to build and disciplined processes in place for guidance. We hope this book provides that foundation and guidance in addition to answering specific questions about measures, analysis, and reports.

The road to improved measurement and reporting is a journey. This is true at both the individual and organizational level. No one person or organization has all the answers, and even if they did, the world is continually evolving so there will always be new issues. Resolve to improve through time and plan to make steady progress each year. Use the frameworks and discipline described in this book to help you on your journey.

We wish you the very best.

Appendixes

APPENDIX A
History of the TDRp Approach

The Talent Development Reporting principles (TDRp) framework is the result of a two-year effort begun in September 2010 by a group of industry thought leaders and leading practitioners to create a framework of measures and reports much like accountants have in their Generally Accepted Accounting Principles (GAAP). Your authors served as the principal investigators and writers, and the contributors are listed in Table A-1.

Table A-1. TDRp Contributors

Thought Leaders	Leading Practitioners
• Kent Barnett, KnowledgeAdvisors	• Tamar Elkeles, Qualcomm
• Kendall Kerekes, KnowledgeAdvisors	• Carrie Beckstrom, ADP
• Jac Fitz-enz, Human Capital Source	• Sandy Shaw, Sodexo
• Josh Bersin, Bersin & Associates	• Terry Bickham, Deloitte
• Laurie Bassi, McBassi & Company	• Karen Kocher, CIGNA
• Jack Phillips, ROI Institute	• Marilyn Figlar, Lockheed Martin
• Rob Brinkerhoff, Western Michigan University	• Sundar Nagarathnam, Net App
• Frank Anderson, Defense Acquisition University	• Don Shoultz, BP
• Jeff Higgins, HCMI	• Tom Simon, CNA Insurance
• Kevin Oakes, i4cp	• Cedric Coco, Lowes
• Peggy Parskey, Parskey Consulting	• Kevin Jones, PWC
• Dave Vance, Manage Learning	• David Kuhl, First Data
	• Claudia Rodriguez, Motorola Solutions
	• David Sylvester, Booz Allen Hamilton
	• Lou Tedrick, Verizon Wireless
	• Deb Tees, Lockheed Martin

Note: The companies listed show where the contributors were working during the initial TDRp efforts.

The working group focused initially on L&D but quickly extended the principles to all core talent processes, defined as those processes that directly contribute to achieving high-level organizational outcomes. By mid-2012, we had expanded TDRp to include talent acquisition, performance management, leadership development, capability development, and total rewards:

- **Talent acquisition.** The process of recruiting, evaluating candidates, selecting, and onboarding employees into the organization.
- **Leadership development.** The process of identifying, assessing, reviewing, and planning for leadership bench strength at the most senior levels in the organization to enhance the overall breadth, depth, and quality of leadership within the organization.

- **Learning and development.** The processes of building skills and knowledge in the workforce to improve individual, team, and organizational performance.
- **Capability management.** The processes to build organizational competency and capability in the organization, typically below the senior leadership levels.
- **Performance management.** The process of setting aligned performance goals, creating individual development plans, monitoring goals, and evaluating progress to create accountability.
- **Total rewards.** The process of allocating compensation (including bonuses) and benefits to the workforce to reward them for performance.

Figure A-1. Extension of TDRp Beyond Learning

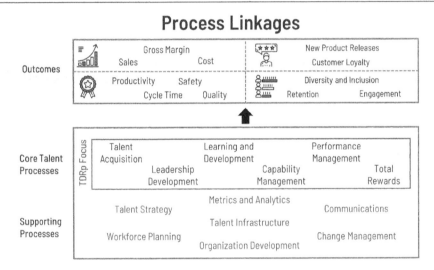

The working group identified measures and created sample reports for each core process or discipline. Supporting processes also play an important role in an organization's success by enabling the core processes, but the focus of TDRp was on the measurement and reporting of measures for the six identified core processes.

Sample Roles and Responsibilities Agreement

This is a sample description of roles and responsibilities for the goal owner and the L&D department.

Purpose

This document provides an example of roles and responsibilities that an L&D department can share with a goal owner during the initial planning discussions. These role descriptions enable the L&D department head and the business goal owner to gain clarity and agreement on the roles and accountabilities of each party to deliver the agreed-upon impact from the L&D initiative. Some organizations will ask each party to sign their agreement at the bottom. (This example contains a sign line but that may not be necessary in your organization.)

L&D Introductory Script

"We have found that an understanding and acceptance of the following roles and responsibilities is critical to the success of our learning initiatives. Each party has a very important role to play. If either party believes they may be unable to fulfill their responsibilities, serious consideration should be given to postponing the initiative until a more appropriate time."

Source: The Center for Talent Reporting website: CenterforTalentReporting.org

Roles and Responsibilities for the L&D Department and the Goal Owner

L&D Department Roles and Responsibilities

- Work with you (the goal owner) to determine if L&D can help achieve your goal and, if it can, recommend an appropriate program or initiative.
- Collaboratively agree on the appropriate target audience, approach, and timing of the training.
- Collaboratively agree on an appropriate measurement and reporting strategy to meet the needs of both parties.
- Discuss your role as goal owner and change manager. Recommend steps you can take to ensure successful deployment. Discuss your plans to reinforce the learning.
- Reach agreement with you on the planned impact of the program. Reach agreement on plans for the key effectiveness and efficiency measures required to achieve the planned impact. These will constitute our joint success measures for this initiative.
- Design, develop (or procure), and deliver the program, including performance support tools, according to the agreed-upon timetable. Create any agreed-upon communities of practice or facilitate other informal learning opportunities.
- Meet with you regularly during development and implementation to share progress, discuss issues, and manage the program to a successful conclusion. Provide reports with agreed-upon measures. Provide a list of those who completed (or did not complete) the program by the required dates.
- Conduct a project close-out review upon completion to review results and identify opportunities for improvement and lessons learned.

Business Goal Owner Roles and Responsibilities

- Be available for discussions about your goal, how you plan to achieve it, and whether L&D has a role to play. If you agree it does, then make resources available in your organization to work with the L&D department on an appropriate program and target audience.
- Meet with the L&D department to review and approve the recommended program, target audience, and timing. Discuss and agree on the planned impact of this initiative on your goal. Agree on other key measures of success. Discuss what will be required to achieve these goals. Agree on an appropriate measurement and reporting strategy, including frequency of reporting.
- Discuss and agree on your role as goal owner and change leader. In particular, agree on steps you will perform to kick off this initiative, how you will manage it through your direct reports, how you and your leaders will reinforce it, and what positive and negative consequences are planned to ensure completion and application.

- Ensure subject matter experts (SMEs) and others in your organization are available to the L&D department. Communicate the importance of providing the required assistance per the agreed-upon timetable. Follow up with them if necessary.
- Meet with the L&D department regularly through development and deployment to review progress and resolve issues. Review agreed-upon reports on a monthly basis to identify where year-to-date progress or forecast is falling short of plan. Eliminate roadblocks. Let the L&D department know what else you need from them.
- Take required action with your leaders to ensure the target audience has completed the learning program by the agreed-upon dates. The L&D department will provide lists of those who have (or have not completed) the training.
- Establish accountability (and consequences) for employees in your organization to achieve the desired application and impact. (Note: The L&D department can provide suggestions and guidance for creating accountability, but only you and those in your organization can ensure that your employees apply the learned behaviors and knowledge.)
- Meet with the L&D department at the completion of the program to review results and identify opportunities for improvement and lessons learned.

Agreed to on_____

Regarding the program or initiative to_____

By _____

_____   _____
Printed Name of L&D Representative   Signature of L&D Representative

_____   _____
Printed Name of Goal Owner   Signature of Goal Owner

APPENDIX C

Sample Measurement and Reporting Strategy

Appendix C contains a sample measurement and reporting strategy to help you understand how to apply the recommendations in chapters 6 and 10 on creating a measurement and reporting strategy in practice.

The sample, which also includes an introduction and conclusion, follows the seven critical elements identified in the two chapters:

1. a clear articulation of the reasons for measuring
2. the users, why they want the measures, when they need the data, and how they want to see it reported
3. the measures overall, with specific measures identified for important programs or department initiatives
4. how you plan to collect the data, including the use of sampling and expected response rates
5. the types of reports you will use to communicate to stakeholders
6. how you plan to share the data
7. the resources you require to execute and sustain measurement and reporting over time.

Your strategy may be shorter or longer than this sample, depending on the complexity and needs of your organization.

2021
Learning Measurement and Reporting Strategy for

[Company Name]

Prepared by

[Company Name]

Learning and Development Department

For the Fiscal Year January 1–December 31, 2021

Approved December 17, 2020

by the

Board of Governors

Contents

Introduction

The 2021 Measurement and Reporting Strategy describes all the essential elements for our measurement and reporting efforts for the coming year. This is the first time a written strategy has been prepared, and we hope it will provide excellent guidance throughout the year as well as a foundation upon which to build in the future. Although effort is required to create a written plan, we believe there is tremendous value in committing a strategy to writing. In particular, it forces us to be very clear about our plans and helps ensure greater internal consistency. Review of a written plan by others will also help identify any omitted items or opportunities for improvement.

A measurement and reporting strategy has other benefits as well (Figure 1). It signals to the business and L&D stakeholders that we are purposeful in our measurement efforts and that their engagement matters. It also ensures that we and the business are aligned on what success looks like for any given program or suite of programs.

The strategy creates ownership and accountability for success. If the measurement plan requires observational feedback or reinforcement from the managers of participants, then the program goal owner must ensure that

Figure 1. Benefits of a Measurement and Reporting Strategy

the managers understand the expectations and are committed to meeting them. The strategy also identifies the budget and resources required for execution. Being clear on what's required is essential to the strategy's success.

Finally, the measurement and reporting strategy provides guidance and ensures continuity over time. A good strategy provides a clear road map for the department to follow and is invaluable when there is staff turnover. With this document, a new person can come into a measurement position and easily understand the plan for the year, the key users, what they want, and the agreed-upon measures.

We strongly believe that measurement and reporting are absolutely critical to set achievable plans and to execute those plans successfully throughout the year. Without measurement and reporting, we cannot identify opportunities for improvement, determine the impact of our programs, or forecast how the year is likely to end. Without measurement and reporting, we cannot deliver value, ensure an acceptable return on investment (ROI), or continuously improve. Bottomline, measurement and reporting are necessary to run L&D with business discipline and will be integrated into all we do.

Our strategy for the year starts with a discussion of the reasons for measuring, followed by a description of the users. With this foundation in place, we turn to the recommended measures, both at a high level and at a program-specific level. Next, we discuss the reports that will convey the measures to the users, and we include examples since some will be new. A discussion of data collection follows, including plans for the use of sampling. Last, we discuss how the reports will be shared and the resources required for this effort.

Reasons for Measuring

The starting point for any measurement strategy is a discussion of the reasons to measure, which will dictate the selection of measures as well as the frequency and type of reporting. We will employ the Talent Development Reporting principles (TDRp) framework developed by the Center for Talent Reporting, which is a nonprofit focused on improving measurement and reporting in the human capital field. According to the TDRp framework, there are four broad categories of reasons to measure: inform, monitor, evaluate, and manage (Figure 2). In 2021 we will measure for all four reasons.

Figure 2. TDRp Framework for Measurement and Reporting

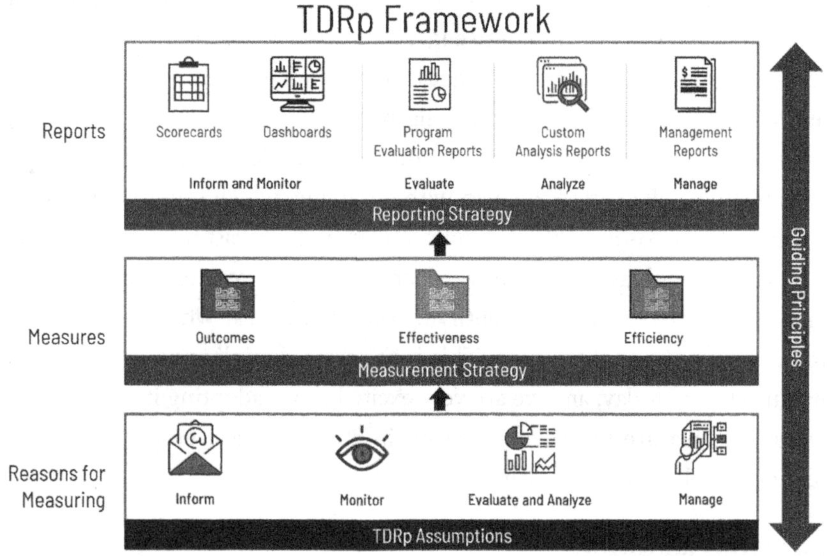

Copyright applied for by Center for Talent Reporting (2020). Used with permission.

The first reason, inform, is the most foundational. It simply means that measurement is undertaken to answer questions and identify trends. Much of our current measurement activity is undertaken precisely for this purpose. Many people want to know basic information like how many employees receive training, how many courses and hours are offered, and how much programs cost. People also want to know about trends, like whether e-learning, mobile, virtual, and informal learning are gaining in popularity. Informing will remain an important reason to measure in 2021 because it provides a basic and foundational level of data. However, we can do a better job ensuring that users receive exactly what they need to answer their questions or identify trends, and we can eliminate some reports that are no longer needed.

The second reason, monitor, is relatively new to us although some monitoring has always gone on. Monitoring is done to ensure that a measure remains in an acceptable range. For example, we will monitor our participant reaction data to ensure that the percentage favorable score remains above 80 percent, where it has been for the last two years. We do not plan to expend any effort to improve it because we believe it is good enough at its current level. We just want to make sure it stays at an acceptable level throughout the year. We plan to monitor participant and goal owner reaction, first-time pass rates, LMS uptime, utilization rates for instructors and classrooms, and class cancellation rates in 2021.

The third reason, evaluate and analyze, is important to us and an area in which we plan to devote more resources in 2021. Program evaluation entails measuring the application rate of the learning content back on the job, determining its impact on business goals, and calculating its ROI. This analysis allows us to determine if the program was effective and impactful—in essence, whether it was worthwhile. In 2020 we measured the application rate for several programs and the impact for one program. For 2021 we plan to measure application for all important programs, impact for all strategic programs, and ROI for three programs (sales, safety, productivity). In 2021, we will also conduct a statistical analysis to determine if the amount of and type of learning is related to employee engagement and retention.

The fourth reason, manage, is our biggest opportunity for improvement in 2021. This means that we intend to start running learning with business discipline, which requires that plans be created at the start of year with specific, measurable goals. Once the year is underway, it means that we will execute the plan with discipline, which requires the use of monthly reports to compare year-to-date (YTD) results to plan and forecast to plan. This discipline will allow us to create better plans upfront, more clearly identify action items and roles and responsibilities, and deliver better results by identifying early in the year when corrective action must be taken to get a program back on plan. This is the same discipline used by our colleagues in sales and manufacturing today, and we are very excited about adopting it in L&D.

So, we plan to measure for all four reasons in 2021 with less emphasis on measuring to inform and more emphasis on measuring to evaluate and manage.

Users and Their Needs

The list of users will expand in 2021 as we focus more on the management of key programs that necessarily involves the goal owners and the stakeholders in their organization. The list for 2021 will also include the CEO, CFO, and SVP of HR who will begin to receive a high-level summary report. Users internal to L&D will continue to be the CLO, directors, program managers, and staff.

The needs of each user were identified through structured discussions that took place in September and October. In some cases, the measures were identified in the initial discussion, while follow-up meetings were required in others. All users except the company's senior leaders plan to use measures to inform, monitor, evaluate, and manage. Senior leaders will use measures to inform and manage only. The results of these discussions are summarized in Table 1.

Specific measures to meet these needs are identified in the next section, while the reports containing the measures are described in a later section.

Table 1. Users and Their Needs

User	Needs
CLO	• Know what the department is accomplishing • Answer questions and identify trends • Monitor select measures to ensure their acceptability • Determine if programs are efficient, effective, and producing desired results • Identify opportunities for improvement and optimization • Plan and manage programs and initiatives to successful completion
Directors	• Plan and manage department initiatives to deliver planned results • Evaluate the efficiency and effectiveness of department initiatives • Identify opportunities for improvement and optimization
Program managers	• Plan and manage programs to deliver planned results • Ensure planned outcomes are delivered • Evaluate the efficiency and effectiveness of the program • Analyze issues and decide on corrective actions • Identify opportunities for improvement and optimization
Program staff	• Produce reports, answer questions, and identify trends • Analyze issues and recommend corrective actions • Evaluate the efficiency and effectiveness of the program
Goal owners and their staff	• Plan and manage programs to deliver planned results • Ensure planned outcomes are delivered • Identify opportunities for improvement and optimization
CEO, CFO, and SVP HR	• Know what the department is accomplishing • Determine if programs are efficient, effective, and producing desired results

Note

Programs are defined as learning efforts in support of business and HR goals or important needs. Initiatives are defined as learning in support of department efforts to either improve the efficiency or effectiveness of L&D systems or processes or improve the efficiency and effectiveness of all programs.

Measures

This section represents the heart of the measurement and reporting strategy. We will first identify and discuss the types of measures to be collected. Second, we will identify the measures for each program and initiative.

For 2021 we plan to measure all three types of measures: efficiency, effectiveness, and outcomes. Efficiency measures deal with quantity, activity, or volume and are sometimes referred to as Level 0. Examples include the number of participants, courses, hours, communities of practice, documents accessed, or performance support tools used; utilization rates; cost; and percentage of on-time completions. Effectiveness measures are measures of quality and include participant reaction to the learning content (Level 1), goal owner satisfaction with L&D (Level 1), learning (Level 2), application on the job (Level 3), and ROI (Level 5). Outcome measures show the impact of learning on business or HR goals (Level 4).

Our measurement efforts in previous years focused on Levels 0, 1, and 2. In 2021 we will devote more resources to the higher-level measures (Levels 3–5). Strategic programs, defined as those that contribute directly to the achievement of our CEO's or SVP of HR's goals, will be measured more intensely than non-strategic programs or L&D department initiatives. We will also use statistics to explore the relationship between learning (amount and type) and the key HR measures of employee engagement and retention. A summary of our key 2021 programs, initiatives, and research is provided in Table 2.

Table 2. 2021 Programs and Initiatives for L&D

Strategic programs	• Help achieve 10% increase in sales • Help achieve 20% reduction in injuries • Help achieve 5% increase in productivity • Help achieve a 3 point improvement in leadership • Help achieve a 4 point increase in employee engagement
Non-strategic programs	• Onboarding new employees • Basic skills training • Compliance • Reskilling
Initiatives to improve efficiency and effectiveness across all programs	• Increase application rate • Increase reach
Initiatives to increase process, systems, and tools	• Increase use of informal learning • Improve satisfaction with the help desk
Research topic	• Explore the relationship between learning (amount and type) and employee engagement and retention

Note

A program typically consists of more than one course and often includes different types of formal learning (instructor-led, e-learning, virtual instructor-led, and mobile) as well as some elements of informal learning (such as a community of practice, performance support, content accessed from our portal, and coaching).

In addition to the programs identified in Table 2, numerous individual courses are offered. These courses are not part of strategic or non-strategic programs and have been developed by L&D or purchased from vendors. These non-program-related or general interest courses may be taken at the discretion of the employee or suggested by a leader.

Table 3 provides a summary by type and name of measure for the same five categories of programs, non-program courses, and initiatives described in Table 2. A "Yes" indicates that the measure will be used for at least one program or initiative. The table clearly shows, even at this high level, how the measurement strategy differs depending on the type of program or initiative.

Table 3. Summary of Measures by Type, Program, and Initiative

Type and Name of Measure	Unit of Measure	Program Level		Non-Program Courses	Improvement Initiatives	
		Strategic	Non-Strategic		For All Programs	Processes, Systems, and Tools
Efficiency Measures						
Formal Learning						
Unique participants	Number	Y	Y	Y	Y	N
Total participants	Number	Y	Y	Y	N	N
Completion rate	%	Y	Y	Y	N	N
Percentage of on-time completion						
Development	%	Y	Y	N	N	N
Delivery	%	Y	Y	N	N	N
Cost						
Direct	Dollars	Y	Y	Y	Y	N
Total	Dollars	Y	N	N	N	N
Class cancellation rate	Number	N	N	Y	N	N
Hours available	Number	Y	Y	Y	N	N
Hours used	Number	Y	Y	Y	N	N
Number of courses	Number	Y	Y	Y	N	N
Utilization rates for instructors and classrooms	%	Y	Y	Y	N	N
Reach	%	Y	Y	Y	Y	N
Percentage of learning by modality	%	N	N	Y	N	N

Table 3. Summary of Measures by Type, Program, and Initiative (cont.)

Type and Name of Measure	Unit of Measure	Program Level		Non-Program Courses	Improvement Initiatives	
		Strategic	Non-Strategic		For All Programs	Processes, Systems, and Tools
Informal Learning						
Number of active communities of practice (CoP)	Number	N	N	N/A	N	Y
Number of unique CoP users	Number	Y	N	N/A	N	Y
Number of total CoP users	Number	Y	N	N/A	N	Y
Number of documents available	Number	Y	Y	N/A	N	Y
Number of unique documents used	Number	Y	Y	N/A	N	Y
Number of total documents used	Number	Y	Y	N/A	N	Y
Percentage of documents used	%	Y	Y	N/A	N	Y
Number of unique document users	Number	Y	Y	N/A	N	Y
Number of total document users	Number	Y	Y	N/A	N	Y
Number of performance support (PS) tools available	Number	Y	Y		Y	Y
Number of unique PS tools used	Number	Y	Y	N/A	Y	Y
Percentage of PS tools used	%	Y	Y	N/A	Y	Y
Number of unique PS users	Number	Y	Y	N/A	Y	Y
Number of total PS users	Number	Y	Y	N/A	Y	Y
Effectiveness Measures						
Formal Learning						
Participant reaction (Level 1)	5-pt scale	Y	Y	Y	N	N
Goal owner satisfaction (Level 1)	5-pt scale	Y	N	N	N	N
Learning (Level 2)						
Score	Score	Y	Y	N	N	N
First-time pass rate	%	Y	Y	N	N	N
Application rate (Level 3)						
Intent to apply	% of content applied	Y	Y	N	Y	N
Actual application	% of content applied	Y	N	N	Y	N
ROI (Level 5)	%	Y	N	N	N	N
Informal Learning						
Participant reaction (Level 1)	5-pt scale	Y	Y	N/A	Y	Y
Leader satisfaction (Level 1)	5-pt scale	N	Y	N/A	Y	Y
Outcome Measures						
Impact (Level 4)						
Actual (using control group)	Same as supported goal	Y	N	N	N	N
Estimate from regression	Same as supported goal	Y	N	N	N	N
Initial estimate	Same as supported goal	Y	N	N	N	N
Final estimate	Same as supported goal	Y	N	N	N	N

While Table 3 provides a good high-level summary of our strategy, more detail is needed to provide direction at the specific program or initiative level. This greater level of specificity is shown in Tables 4, 5, and 6:

- Table 4 shows the measures for each program, which will be used to manage and will be contained in program reports.
- Table 5 shows the measures for each initiative, which will also be managed but will be included in the operations report.
- Table 6 shows the measures to be aggregated across all programs, which will be included in the operations report and used to inform, monitor, evaluate, and manage.

Table 4. Specific Measures by Program

Strategic and Non-Strategic Programs	
All Measures to Be Managed in Program Reports	
Strategic Programs	Non-Strategic Programs
1. Help achieve a 10% increase in sales	**1. Onboarding**
Unique and total participants	Unique participants
Percentage of on-time completion	Percentage of on-time completion
Development and delivery	Development and delivery
Completion rate	Direct cost
Direct and total cost	Number of portal documents accessed
Number of sales community of practice users	Number of portal content users
Percentage of performance support tools for sales used	Duration
Level 1 participant and goal owner	Level 1 participant, goal owner, and leaders
Level 2 score	**2. Basic Skills Training**
Level 3 intent and actual	Unique and total participants
Level 4 impact estimated by regression	Percentage of on-time completion
Level 5 ROI	Development and delivery
2. Help achieve a 20% reduction in injuries	Completion rate
Unique and total participants	Direct cost
Percentage of on-time completion	Number of portal documents accessed
Development and delivery	Number of portal content users
Completion rate	Percentage of performance support tools for basic skills used
Direct and total cost	Level 1 participant and goal owner
Percentage of performance support tools for sales used	Level 2 score
Level 1 participant and goal owner	Level 3 intent and actual
Level 2 score	
Level 3 intent and actual	
Level 4 impact (initial and final estimates)	
Level 5 ROI	

Table 4. Specific Measures by Program (cont.)

Strategic and Non-Strategic Programs All Measures to Be Managed in Program Reports	
Strategic Programs	**Non-Strategic Programs**
3. Help achieve a 5% increase in productivity	**3. Reskilling**
Unique participants (only 1 course)	Number of courses and modules offered
Percentage of on-time completion	Unique and total participants
Development and delivery	Completion rate
Completion rate	Number of portal documents accessed
Direct and total cost	Number of portal content users
Number of productivity community of practice users	Percentage of performance support tools for reskilling used
Number of portal documents accessed	Direct cost
Level 1 participant and goal owner	Level 1 participant and goal owner
Level 2 score	Level 2 score
Level 3 intent and actual	Level 3 intent and actual
Level 4 impact from control group	**4. Compliance**
Level 5 ROI	Unique and total participants
4. Help achieve a 3-point increase in leadership	Percentage of on-time completion
Unique participants (only 1 course)	Development and delivery
Percentage of on-time completion	Completion rate
Development and delivery	Direct cost
Direct cost	Level 1 participant and goal owner
Number of leadership community of practice users	Level 2 score, first-time pass rate
Number of portal documents accessed	Level 3 intent to apply
Level 1 participant and goal owner	
Level 3 intent and actual	
Level 4 impact (initial and final estimates)	
5. Help achieve a 4-point increase in employee engagement	
Number of discretionary courses taken	
Unique and total participants for above	
Direct cost	
Number of portal documents accessed	
Number of unique and total portal users	
Level 1 participant and user reaction	
Level 4 impact (initial and final)	

Notice that the lists of measures for strategic programs are similar but not identical. For example, no ROI study is planned for leadership. There is more diversity in the lists for non-strategic programs. Application measures are repeated in the lists for initiatives to improve efficiency and effectiveness measures across all programs.

Table 5. Specific Measures by Initiative

Strategic and Non-Strategic Programs	
All Measures to Be Managed in Program Reports	
Improve Efficiency and Effectiveness Across All Programs	**Improve Processes, Systems, and Tools**
1. Increase application rate	**1. Increase informal learning**
Aggregate Level 3 intent	Communities of practice
Aggregate Level 3 actual (if available)	Number of active communities
Goal owner satisfaction with L&D efforts to improve application	Number of unique users
Level 1 user for Applic PS (every 3 months)	Number of total users
2. Increase reach	Level 1 user (every 6 months)
Number of unique participants	Content on portal
Reach	Number of documents
	Percentage of documents accessed
	Number of unique users
	Number of total users
	Level 1 user (every 3 months)
	Performance support
	Number of tools available
	Percentage of tools used
	Number of unique users
	Number of total users
	Level 1 user (every 6 months)
	2. Satisfaction with help desk
	Level 1 user
	Quality metric
	Number of associates trained
	Completion date for training
	Hold time
	Dropped calls
	Number of tickets

The measures in Table 4 for strategic programs and all the measures in Table 5 will be aggregated across all programs. In addition, there are other measures the CLO would like to see that have not yet been identified. These are all contained in Table 6. Measures to be managed will appear in the operations report while measures to inform or monitor will appear in scorecards or dashboards.

Table 6. Additional Measures to Be Aggregated Across All Programs and Courses

Measures to Be Managed in the Operations Report	Measures to Be Monitored in a Dashboard	Measures to Inform in a Dashboard	Measures to Inform in a Scorecard
• Total participants • Percentage of on-time completion ◦ Development and delivery • Direct cost	• Level 1 participant and goal owner reaction • Level 2 first-time pass rate • LMS uptime • Utilization rate for instructors and classrooms • Class cancellation rate	• Percentage of learning by modality • Course usage by area or business unit	• Unique and total participants by modality • Total participants by business unit • Hours available and used • Number of courses

Tables 4–6 should provide the details that analysts, managers, and stakeholders will need to know exactly what to measure.

Reports

Reports provide the data that users need in the most appropriate format based on their reasons for measuring. We have adopted the TDRp reporting framework, which was summarized and aligned to the reasons for measuring in Figure 2. A high-level summary is illustrated in Table 7.

Table 7. Reporting Framework for 2021

Reason for Measuring	Type of Report
Inform	Scorecards or dashboards
Monitor	Scorecards or dashboards with thresholds
Evaluate and analyze	Program evaluation reports and Custom analysis report
Manage	Three management reports

Note: A scorecard is typically shown in tabular form and consists primarily of data. In contrast, a dashboard typically has a more visual display, more summary measures, and less data.

Following this framework, we will employ scorecards where the need is to share history for a number of measures by month or quarter. If a more visual presentation is appropriate, we will use dashboards for sharing summaries. If the reason for measuring is to monitor to ensure that a measure's value remains in an acceptable range, we will employ either a scorecard or dashboard with thresholds. When the purpose is to share program, initiative, or research results, we will create a PowerPoint program evaluation or custom analysis report.

If the primary purpose of measuring is to manage a measure to deliver its planned value, then we will employ either a program or operations report. The program report focuses on the strategic or non-strategic programs to help achieve a high-level goal or need. A strategic program report will include all three types of measures while a non-strategic program report will contain only efficiency and effectiveness measures. The operations report will contain all the efficiency and effectiveness measures the CLO has targeted to be managed for improvement. Last, the summary report is used to share information with the CEO, CFO, SVP of HR, and board of governors. It shows the alignment of our programs to high-level company goals and L&D's progress in delivering planned impact. It also shows our plans and progress to improve efficiency and effectiveness measures across all programs and to improve the systems, processes, and tools we use.

Since we have not used management reports before, a sample of each is included in the appendix. The measures and plan values represent our current thinking for 2021 but we have made up YTD data to show what the report would look like midyear.

With this background, our plan is to generate all five broad types of reports. Some will be created on a monthly basis, others on an as-needed basis. A program report will be generated monthly for each strategic and non-strategic program, containing the measures identified in Table 4. One operations report will be generated each month with the measures identified in Table 5 for L&D initiatives to improve efficiency and effectiveness measures across all programs and to improve processes, systems, and tools. (The operations report will also include a few additional measures from Table 6 to be managed that were not part of an initiative.) A summary report will be generated quarterly with the outcome measures for each strategic program, headline measures for the non-strategic programs, and the key efficiency and effectiveness measures for improvement. Only measures to be managed will be included in these three management reports.

Program evaluation reports will be generated at the end of each strategic program and at the end of the year for the non-strategic programs. A custom analysis report will also be prepared to show the results of the research to help determine if learning is correlated with higher employee engagement and retention.

Scorecards and dashboards will be created monthly or on an ad hoc basis to meet the needs of informing and monitoring, including the measures identified in Table 6. Only measures to be monitored will be included in the five dashboards with thresholds.

Plans to create and distribute regular production (non-ad hoc) reports are shown in Table 8. In addition to outlining the primary users of each report, this table also shows the frequency, report owner, nature of the generation process (manual or automated), the day of the month it is generated, and the nature of the distribution process (manual or automated).

Table 8. Plans to Create and Distribute Regular Reports

Reports	User 1	User 2	User 3	Frequency	Report Owner	Generation Process	Day	Distribution
Program								
Strategic (Aligned to Goals)								
Sales	Program Manager	CLO	VP Sales	Monthly	Program Manager	Manual	5	Manual-meeting
Safety	Program Manager	CLO	VP Mfg	Monthly	Program Manager	Manual	5	Manual-meeting
Productivity	Program Manager	CLO	VP Quality	Monthly	Program Manager	Manual	5	Manual-meeting
Employee engagement	Program Manager	CLO	SVP HR	Monthly	Program Manager	Manual	5	Manual-meeting
Leadership	Program Manager	CLO	CEO	Monthly	Program Manager	Manual	5	Manual-meeting
Non-Strategic								
Onboarding	Program Manager	CLO	SVP HR	Monthly	Program Manager	Manual	5	Manual-meeting
Basic skills	Program Manager	CLO	COO	Monthly	Program Manager	Manual	5	Manual-meeting
Compliance	Program Manager	CLO	CRO	Monthly	Program Manager	Manual	5	Manual-meeting
Reskilling	Program Manager	CLO	COO	Monthly	Program Manager	Manual	5	Manual-meeting
Operations	CLO	Sr. L&D Leaders	Initiative Leaders	Monthly	Measurement Manager	Automated	5	Automated-email
Summary Report	CEO, CFO, COO, SVP HR	Board of Governors	CLO	Quarterly	Measurement Manager	Manual	5	Manual-meeting
Project Evaluation Reports								
Sales	Program Manager	VP Sales		Pilot, End of Year	Program Manager	Manual	N/A	Manual-meeting
Safety	Program Manager	VP Mfg		End of Year	Program Manager	Manual	N/A	Manual-meeting
Productivity	Program Manager	VP Quality		End of Year	Program Manager	Manual	N/A	Manual-meeting
Employee engagement	Program Manager	SVP HR		End of Year	Program Manager	Manual	N/A	Manual-meeting
Leadership	Program Manager	CEO		End of Year	Program Manager	Manual	N/A	Manual-meeting
Custom Analysis Reports								
Relationship between training and key HR measures	Initiative Leader	CLO	SVP HR	Project End	Initiative Leader	Manual	N/A	Manual-meeting

Table 8. Plans to Create and Distribute Regular Reports (cont.)

Reports	User 1	User 2	User 3	Frequency	Report Owner	Generation Process	Day	Distribution
Dashboards With Thresholds								
Level 1 participant and goal owner reaction	CLO	L&D Leaders		Monthly	Measurement Manager	Automated	3	Automated-email
Level 2 first-time pass rate	CLO	L&D Leaders		Monthly	Measurement Manager	Automated	3	Automated-email
LMS uptime	CLO	L&D Leaders		Weekly	Measurement Manager	Automated	3	Automated-email
Utilization rate for instructors and classrooms	CLO	L&D Leaders		Weekly	Measurement Manager	Automated	3	Automated-email
Class cancellation rate	CLO	L&D Leaders		Monthly	Measurement Manager	Automated	3	Automated-email
Dashboards Without Thresholds								
Percentage of learning by modality	CLO	L&D Leaders		Monthly	Measurement Manager	Automated	3	Automated-email
Course usage by area and business unit	CLO	L&D Leaders	Business Leaders	Monthly	Measurement Manager	Automated	3	Automated-email
Scorecards								
Unique and total participants by modality	CLO	L&D Leaders		Monthly	Measurement Manager	Automated	3	Automated-email
Total participants by business unit	CLO	L&D Leaders	Business Leaders	Monthly	Measurement Manager	Automated	3	Automated-email
Hours available and used	CLO	L&D Leaders		Monthly	Measurement Manager	Automated	3	Automated-email
Number of courses	CLO	L&D Leaders		Monthly	Measurement Manager	Automated	3	Automated-email

Note that the completed program report, the summary report, program evaluation report, and custom analysis report are likely to be shared for the first time in a meeting where they will be discussed. This is particularly important for any briefing of a senior leader, who should never receive a report by itself in the email. If an in-person briefing of the report to a senior leader is not possible, we will write a summary to accompany it highlighting any major points and action items. Reports internal to L&D may be distributed by email because the receiving parties will know how to read them.

Additional reports will be generated as needed throughout the year. These will typically be scorecards generated on an ad-hoc basis.

Data Collection

There are two important aspects of data collection: sources and use of sampling and response rates. We describe the data sources first.

Data Sources

Data sources for the measures are listed in Table 9. Most efficiency measures come from the LMS, knowledge sharing platform, portal analytics (for content), or the performance support platform. The outcome measures and most effectiveness measures come from our vendor and our data warehouse. `

Table 9. Sources for the Measures

Type and Name of Measure	Source
Efficiency Measures	
Formal Learning	
Unique participants	LMS
Total participants	LMS
Completion rate	LMS
Percentage of on-time completion	
Development	Spreadsheet
Delivery	Spreadsheet
Cost	
Direct	Spreadsheet
Total	Spreadsheet
Class cancellation rate	LMS
Reach	LMS, spreadsheet
Percentage of learning by modality	LMS
Informal Learning	
Number of communities of practice (CoP)	KS platform
Number of CoP users	KS platform
Number of documents available	Portal analytics
Number of documents used	Portal analytics
Percentage of documents used	Portal analytics
Number of document users	Portal analytics
Number of performance support (PS) tools available	PS platform
Number of PS tools used	PS platform
Percentage of PS tools used	PS platform
Number of PS users	PS platform

Table 9. Sources for the Measures (cont.)

Type and Name of Measure	Source
Effectiveness Measures	
Formal Learning	
Participant reaction (Level 1)	Vendor, data warehouse
Goal owner satisfaction (Level 1)	Internal survey, spreadsheet
Learning (Level 2)	
Score	LMS
First-time pass rate	LMS
Application rate (Level 3)	
Intent to apply	Vendor, data warehouse
Actual application	Vendor, data warehouse
ROI (Level 5)	Spreadsheet
Informal Learning	
Participant reaction (Level 1)	Vendor, data warehouse
Leader satisfaction (Level 1)	Vendor, data warehouse
Outcome Measures	
Impact (Level 4)	
Initial estimate	Vendor, data warehouse
Final estimate	Vendor, data warehouse

Use of Sampling and Expected Response Rates

Sampling and response rates are not an issue for efficiency measures that have complete data. For example, we can easily find out the total number of participants or courses. Most effectiveness measures (Levels 1, 3, and 4), however, rely on surveys of the participants, which raises two issues. First, over-surveying can cause survey fatigue, which diminishes the accuracy of the responses. In these cases, we will use a sample, which is a subset of the population. Second, 100 percent of the participants seldom complete the survey, meaning that we will use a sample instead of the entire population who took the course.

The average obtained from a sample will be close, statistically speaking, to the average we would calculate from the entire population as long as two conditions are met:

1. The sample must be large enough to make the results statistically significant. In practice, we would like a sample size greater than 30—the larger the sample, the more accurate the sample average will be. If the course has less than 30 participants, we need a high response rate (like 70 percent) before we can act on the sample average.
2. The population for small sample size should be normally distributed if we are to trust the results. We will assume our small samples are normally distributed, but will be careful when acting on the results.

Our sampling and surveying strategy is summarized in Table 10 for the various categories of programs and initiatives as well as for non-program (general interest) courses.

Table 10. Sampling and Surveying Strategy

Strategic Programs	Population Size	Sampling and Surveying Strategy
Strategic Programs		
1. Help achieve a 10% increase in sales	Small	Survey all participants; follow up to achieve >70% response rate
2. Help achieve a 20% reduction in injuries	Large	Survey all participants; expected response rate is 30%
3. Help achieve a 5% increase in productivity	Large	Survey all participants; expected response rate is 30%
4. Help achieve a 3-point improvement in leadership	Medium	Survey all participants; expected response rate is 80%
5. Help achieve a 4-point increase in employee engagement	Large	Survey a sample quarterly; expected response rate is 50%
Non-Strategic Programs		
1. Onboarding new employees	Large	Survey all participants; expected response rate is 80%
2. Basic skills training	Large	Survey all participants; expected response rate is 50%
3. Compliance	Large	Survey a sample quarterly; expected response rate is 30%
4. Reskilling	Large	Survey all participants; expected response rate is 30%
Initiatives to Improve Efficiency and Effectiveness Across All Programs		
1. Increase the application rate	Large	Survey all participants; expected response rate is 30%
2. Increase reach	N/A	
Initiatives to Improve Processes, Systems, and Tools		
1. Increase the use of informal learning	Large	Survey a sample quarterly; expected response rate is 30%
2. Improve satisfaction with the help desk	Large	Survey all participants; expected response rate is 30%
Research Topics		
Explore the relationship between L&D (amount and type) and employee engagement and retention	N/A	
Non-Program (General Interest) Courses		
Non-program (general interest) Courses	Large	Survey a sample quarterly; expected response rate is 30%

Resources for Measurement and Reporting

A modest increase in resources is budgeted for 2021, which will allow us to measure more programs at higher levels (Levels 3–5) and generate management reports for the five strategic and four non-strategic programs. These expanded efforts are required if we are to deliver greater impact and make the best use of our resources (Table 11).

The FY2021 staffing plan includes an additional part-time resource, which will add 0.6 FTE. The budget includes the cost of the additional part-time employee as well as $20,000 more for our vendor to conduct surveying for the higher-level measures (Levels 3 and 4) for all strategic and non-strategic programs. (Staff costs are calculated at fully burdened labor and related rates.) In total, the budget calls for an additional $71,000 to enable us to take measurement and reporting to the next level.

Table 11. Resource Requirements for FY2021

	FY20 Plan	FY20 Estimated Actual	FY21 Plan	Change	Percent Increase
Staff					
FTE	1.5	1.4	2.0	0.6	43%
Full-time	1.0	1.0	1.0	0.0	0%
Part-time	1.0	1.0	2.0	1.0	100%
Budget					
Staff	$165.000	$159,245	$210,000	$50,755	32%
Vendors	$50,000	$49,632	$70,000	$20,368	41%
Total	$215,000	$208,877	$280,000	$71,123	34%

Conclusion

This measurement and reporting strategy details our plans for FY2021 to significantly enhance our capabilities and deliver increased value to the company. We will shift our focus to higher level measurements and management reporting, which will allow us to better evaluate and manage the effectiveness of our key programs. At the same time, we will rationalize our reporting to reduce the number of reports generated and to improve the utility of those we do produce. Our written strategy ensures that we have a consistent, purposeful plan throughout the year, even if there is turnover among the measurement staff or leadership.

Appendix

The appendix contains four examples of management reports. The first two are program reports, the third is an operations report, and the fourth is a summary report. The reports reflect the strategy discussed in the measurement and reporting strategy. Each report contains made-up YTD results through June and forecasts for year-end to illustrate what they will look like once the year is under way.

Appendix Figure 1. Sample Report for a Strategic Program

| Results Through June | | | | | 2021 | | |
Goal Owner: Swilthe, VP of Manufacturing	Metric	2020 Actual	Plan	YTD Results	YTD Results Compared to Plan	Forecast	Forecast Compared to Plan
Enterprise Goal: Reduce injuries	% reduction in injuries	12%	20%	11%	9% below	20%	On plan
Impact of Learning on Injuries: 70 percent contribution planned for 2021*	% reduction in injuries	N/A	14%	8%	6% below	14%	On plan
Program A (Deliver Existing Two Courses to Factory A)							
Efficiency Measure							
Unique participants†	Number	452	3,000	3,078	103%	3,200	107%
Total participants‡	Number	858	6,000	6,067	101%	6,300	105%
Completion rate (100% by March 31)§	%, date	N/A	3/31	101%	1% above	105%	Above plan
Percentage of performance support tools used	%	N/A	100%	93%	7% below	93%	7% below
Effectiveness Measures							
Level 1 participant reaction△	% favorable	70%	80%	85%	5% above	85%	5% above
Level 1 goal owner reaction	5-point scale	3.8	4.5	4.3	0.2 below	4.3	0.2 below
Level 2 learning#	% first-time pass rate	86%	90%	95%	5% above	95%	5% above
Level 3 intent to apply**	% content applied	53%	95%	87%	8% below	90%	5% below
Level 3 actual application††	% content applied	39%	90%	81%	9% below	85%	5% below
Program B (Design and Deliver Three New Courses to Factory B)							
Design New Courses							
Efficiency Measure: Complete by 3/31	Number	N/A	3	3	100%	3	100%
Effectiveness Measure: Goal owner reaction	5-point scale	4.0	4.5	4.5	On plan	4.5	On plan
Deliver New Courses							
Efficiency Measures							
Unique participants‡‡	Number	N/A	1,000	895	90%	1,100	110%
Total participants§§	Number	N/A	3,000	2,568	86%	3,200	107%
Completion rate (100% by July 31)	% complete, date	N/A	7/31	98%	Below plan	8/31	100%
Percentage of performance support tools used	%	N/A	100%	87%	13% below	95%	5% below
Effectiveness Measures							
Level 1 participant reaction△△	% favorable	N/A	80%	80%	On plan	80%	On plan
Level 1 goal owner reaction	5-point scale	3.8	4.5	4.1	0.4 below	4.3	0.2 below
Level 2 learning##	% first-time pass rate	N/A	90%	92%	2% above	92%	2% above
Level 3 intent to apply***	% content applied	N/A	95%	91%	4% below	91%	4% below
Level 3 actual application†††	% content applied	39%	90%	82%	8% below	87%	3% below

Appendix Figure 1. Sample Report for a Strategic Program (cont.)

Results Through June			2021				
	Metric	2020 Actual	Plan	YTD Results	YTD Results Compared to Plan	Forecast	Forecast Compared to Plan
Summary							
Total							
Courses developed	Number	1	3	3	100%	3	100%
Unique participants	Number	452	4,000	3,973	99%	4,300	108%
Total participants	Number	858	9,000	8,635	96%	9,500	106%
Direct cost	Dollars, thousands	$37	$250	$231	92%	$245	Near plan
Total cost (including opportunity cost)	Dollars, thousands	$51	$300	$273	91%	$295	Near plan
Net benefit	Dollars, thousands	N/A	$150	$90	60%	$150	On plan
ROI	Percent	N/A	50%	33%	On plan	51%	On plan

* YTD and FC impacts based on participant estimates, Level 1 and 3 results, and ongoing discussions with the goal owner

† Manufacturing leaders responsible for attendance

‡ Audience is increased to 6,300 by Swilthe

§ Completion rate at March 31 was 96%; 100% achieved April 25

△ YTD sample size = 872

YTD sample size = 6,006

** YTD sample size = 872; reinforcement plan in place

†† YTD sample size = 765; reinforcement plan in place

Manufacturing leaders responsible for attendance

§§ Audience is increased to 3,200 by Swilthe

△△ YTD sample size = 301

YTD sample size = 2,499

*** YTD sample size = 301; reinforcement plan in place

††† YTD sample size = 176; reinforcement plan in place

Appendix Figure 2. Sample Report for a Non-Strategic Program

Results Through June					2021		
Program Owner: Wang, SVP HR **Enterprise Need:** Provide onboarding for new employees	Unit of Measure	2020 Actual	Plan	YTD Results	YTD Results Compared to Plan	Forecast	Forecast Compared to Plan
Measures of Success							
Number onboarded	Number	548	700	321	46%	700	100%
Leader satisfaction with onboarding*	% favorable	67%	80%	75%	5% below	80%	On plan
Efficiency Measures							
Develop two courses by January 31[†]	% complete, date	N/A	100%	1/29	2 days early	100%	On plan
Start using by February 28[‡]	% complete, date	N/A	100%	2/18	10 days early	100%	On plan
Hire five new instructors[§]	Number	N/A	5	3	2 behind	5	On plan
Portal onboarding content accessed by new employees	Number of documents	N/A	3,500	2,154	62%	3,800	109%
Portal general content accessed by new employees	Number of documents	N/A	1,400	597	43%	1,400	100%
Unique portal usage by new employees	Number of unique users	N/A	700	700	100%	700	100%
Provide facilitator training to new instructors in their first month	% complete	N/A	100%	100%	On plan	100%	On plan
Provide refresher training to select instructors[△]	Number	7	12	12	100%	15	125%
Program duration[#]	Days	61	50	50	100%	50	On plan
Cost	Dollars, thousands	$657	$800	$393	49%	$800	On plan
Effectiveness Measures							
Level 1 participant reaction to formal learning**	% favorable	70%	80%	73%	7% below	75%	5% below
Level 1 participant reaction to informal learning[††]	% favorable	N/A	80%	81%	1% above	80%	On plan
Level 1 program owner satisfaction	5-point scale	3.7	4.5	4.2	0.3 below	4.5	On plan
Level 2 learning	% first-time pass rate	86%	90%	88%	2% below	90%	On plan

* YTD and forecast contribution based on Level 1 and 3 results and ongoing discussions with sponsor
[†] First done Jan 26, second Jan 29
[‡] Started using February 18
[§] The last two are expected to be hired in July
[△] Three additional instructors identified
[#] Shorter duration achieved with first cohort
** YTD sample size = 254
[††] YTD sample size = 560

Appendix Figure 3. Sample Operations Report

Initiatives to Improve Processes and Systems				2021			
	Unit of Measure	2020 Actual	Plan	June YTD Results	YTD Results Compared to Plan	Forecast	Forecast Compared to Plan
Informal Learning Initiatives							
Communities of Practice							
Efficiency Measures							
Number of active communities	Number	29	50	43	86%	50	100%
Number unique users	Number	312	750	512	68%	750	100%
Number of total users	Number	1,968	7,500	3,968	53%	7,000	93%
Effectiveness Measures							
User satisfaction	% favorable	67%	80%	75%	5% below	80%	On plan
Content on Portal							
Efficiency Measures							
Number of documents	Number	51	100	82	82%	100	100%
Percentage of documents accessed	%	71%	100%	87%	13% below	100%	On plan
Number unique users	Number	2,301	5,000	4,023	80%	6,000	120%
Number of total users	Number	3,590	7,500	5,423	72%	7,500	100%
Effectiveness Measures							
User satisfaction	% favorable	37%	60%	56%	4% below	60%	On plan
Performance Support							
Efficiency Measures							
Number of performance support tools	Number	N/A	20	18	90%	25	125%
Percentage of performance support tools used							
Number unique users	Number	N/A	5,000	3,000	60%	4,000	80%
Number of total users	Number	N/A	10,000	4,600	46%	6,000	60%
Effectiveness Measures							
User satisfaction	% favorable	45%	70%	59%	11% below	60%	10% below
Help Desk Initiatives							
Efficiency Measures							
Number of associates trained	Number	1	4	5	1 above	6	2 above
Completion date for training	Date	N/A	3/31	3/25	On plan	7/31	On plan
Hold time	Minutes	2.5	0.5	1.2	0.7 above	0.6	0.2 above
Dropped calls	Number	564	100	63	37 below	110	10 above
Effectiveness Measures							
User satisfaction	% favorable	47%	80%	75%	5% below	80%	On plan
Quality metric (accuracy)	5-point scale	4.1	4.5	4.3	0.2 below	4.5	On plan

Appendix Figure 3. Sample Operations Report (cont.)

Initiatives to Improve Efficiency and Effectiveness Across All Programs					2021		
	Unit of Measure	2020 Actual	Plan	June YTD Results	YTD Results Compared to Plan	Forecast	Forecast Compared to Plan
Efficiency Measures							
Total participants	Number	7,689	9,000	4,390	49%	9,000	100%
Total unique participants	Number	24,567	36,000	15,467	43%	34,000	94%
Percentage of courses meeting deadline for development	%	68%	90%	78%	12% below	85%	5% below
Percentage of courses meeting deadline for delivery	%	59%	90%	72%	18% below	82%	8% below
Reach (percent of employee reached by L&D)	%	85%	88%	72%	16% below	88%	On plan
Direct cost	Dollars, thousands	$209	$280	$137	49%	$280	100%
Effectiveness Measures							
Level 1 user satisfaction with performance support for application	% favorable	N/A	80%	76%	4% below	79%	1% below
Level 1 goal owner satisfaction with application efforts	% favorable	N/A	80%	79%	1% below	80%	On plan
Level 3 application rate (select programs)							
Intent to apply (from post-event survey at end of course)	% content applied	70%	75%	70%	5% below	72%	3% below
Actual application (from follow-up survey after three months)	% content applied	51%	65%	55%	10% below	63%	2% below

Appendix Figure 4. Sample Summary Report

| Results Through June | | | | 2021 | | | | |
Priority	Business Goals and Supporting L&D Programs	Unit of Measure	2020 Actual	Plan	YTD Results	YTD Results Compared to Plan	Forecast	Forecast Compared to Plan
1.	Increase Sales by 10%							
	Corporate goal or actual	%	6%	10%	7%	3% below	10%	On plan
	Impact of Learning on Sales: 20% contribution planned for 2021	% increase in sales	1%	2%	7%	1% below	2%	On plan
	New product features training *Consultative selling skills*							
2.	Reduce Injuries by 20%							
	Corporate goal or actual	%	10%	20%	11%	9% below	20%	On plan
	Impact of Learning on Injuries: 70% contribution planned for 2021	% decrease in injuries	3%	14%	8%	6% below	14%	On plan
	Safety programs to address top five causes of injuries							
3.	Increase Productivity by 5%							
	Corporate goal or actual	%	5%	5%	4%	1% below	7%	2% above
	Impact of Learning on Productivity: 40% contribution planned for 2021	% decrease in expenses	0%	2%	2%	On plan	3%	1% above
	Training for purchasing agents *Training for all employees on reducing costs* *Training for department heads to meet 15% goal*							
Priority	**HR Goals and Supporting L&D Programs**							
A.	Improve Leadership Score by 3 Points to 75%							
	Corporate goal or actual	Points	1 pt	3 pts	2.2 pts	0.8 below	3 pts	On plan
	Impact of Learning on Leaderships: 80% contribution to goal for 2021	Point increase in leadership	N/A	2.4 pts	1.5 pts	0.9 below	2.4 pts	On plan
	Intro to supervision *Leadership for managers* *Advanced leadership for department heads*							
B.	Increase Engagement Score by 4 Points to 69.4%							
	Corporate goal or actual	Points	1 pt	4 pts	1.9 pts	2.1 below	3 pts	1 below
	Impact of Learning on Engagement: 25% contribution to goal for 2021	Point increase in engagement	0.2 pt	1 pt	1.5 pts	0.5 below	1 pt	On plan
	IDP for each employee to include some training *Increase use of online learning and portal content for general development*							
Initiative	**Key Non-Strategic Programs**							
1.	Onboard new employees	Number of employees	548	700	321	46%	700	100%
2.	Provide basic skills training	Number of employees	896	1,400	726	52%	1,500	107%
3.	Provide compliance training	Number of employees	9,852	11,000	5,123	47%	11,500	105%
4.	Provide reskilling	Number of employees	852	1,500	756	50%	1,600	107%

Appendix Figure 4. Sample Summary Report (cont.)

Results Through June					2021		
Initiatives to Improve Efficiency and Effectiveness Across All Programs	Unit of Measure	2020 Actual	Plan	YTD Results	YTD Results Compared to Plan	Forecast	Forecast Compared to Plan
Efficiency Measures							
Total participants	Number	7,689	9,000	4,390	49%	9,000	100%
Total unique participants	Number	24,567	36,000	15,467	43%	34,000	94%
Percentage of courses meeting deadline for development	%	68%	90%	78%	12% below	85%	5% below
Percentage of courses meeting deadline for delivery	%	59%	90%	72%	18% below	82%	8% below
Reach (percent of employee reached by L&D)	%	85%	88%	72%	16% below	88%	On plan
Effectiveness Measures							
Application rate (select programs)							
Intent to apply (from post-event survey at end of course)	% content applied	70%	75%	70%	5% below	72%	3% below
Actual application (from follow-up survey after three months)	% content applied	51%	65%	55%	10% below	63%	2% below
Initiatives to Improve Processes and Systems							
Informal Learning Initiatives							
Communities of Practice							
Efficiency measure: Number of active communities	Number	29	50	43	86%	50	100%
Effectiveness measure: User satisfaction	% favorable	67%	80%	75%	5% below	80%	On plan
Content on Portal							
Efficiency Measure: Number of total users	Number	3,590	7,500	5,423	72%	7,500	100%
Effectiveness Measure: User satisfaction	% favorable	37%	60%	56%	4% below	60%	On plan
Performance Support							
Efficiency Measure: Number of total users	Number	N/A	10,000	4,600	46%	6,000	60%
Effectiveness Measure: User satisfaction	% favorable	45%	70%	59%	11% below	60%	10% below
Help Desk Initiatives							
Efficiency Measures							
Hold time	Minutes	2.5	0.5	1.2	0.7 above	0.6	0.2 above
Dropped calls	Number	564	100	63	37 below	110	10 above
Effectiveness Measures							
User satisfaction	% favorable	47%	80%	75%	5% below	80%	On plan
Quality metric (accuracy)	5-point scale	4.1	4.5	4.3	0.2 below	4.5	On plan

14

APPENDIX D
Sample TDRp Implementation Plan

As we discussed in chapter 13, an implementation plan is a critical tool for managing a large-scale change effort. The implementation plan contains:

- The major stages of the plan including:
  - Startup
  - Planning
  - Implementation (waves 1, 2, and 3)
- Detailed tasks (numbered) that show:
  - Start and end dates
  - Duration (time to complete the task)
  - Dependencies (what precedes the task and what follows it)
  - The individuals responsible for executing each task (not shown in Table D-2)
- Milestones delineated by the delta (Δ). A milestone is a task with zero duration and identifies the completion of a body of work

The plan shown in Table D-1 follows the high-level approach discussed in chapter 13. It also breaks the major areas into specific tasks required to provide the deliverable of each phase.

The cadence of your project will likely vary from the plan shown in Table D-2. However, you can use this as a framework. Your timeline will vary based on:

- the scope of your effort
- the resources available for implementation
- the urgency within your organization

Remember also to schedule periodic checkpoints with your sponsor and key stakeholders, preferably monthly and not longer than six weeks between reviews. Celebrate your wins and regularly reflect on what's working or where you can improve your process, how you engage with stakeholders, and how to sustain momentum. Use the plan to guide you and adjust as necessary.

Table D-1. High-Level Implementation Approach

Change Area	What Changes Should We Make?	Change Level	Wave
People			
Leadership and governance	• Establish an advisory board • Build leadership advocacy skills	• Medium • High	• 3 • 2
Skills and capabilities	• Adopt common measurement language • Build skills in goal setting or forecasting • Develop data literacy skills	• Medium • High • Medium	• 1 • 1 • 2
Roles and accountabilities	• Establish role level accountability	• Medium	• 2
Resources and commitments	• Reallocate resources	• Low	• 1
Process			
Alignment and planning	• Develop or execute strategic alignment process • Identify key business initiatives • Identify business outcomes; agree on L&D's contribution	• Medium • Medium • High	• 3 • 2 • 3
Measurement	• Identify measures to manage (efficiency and effectiveness) • Develop a measures library	• Medium • Medium	• 1 • 1
Goal setting	• Develop a goal-setting process • Set goals for key measures	• High • High	• 1 • 1
Data gathering and management	• Streamline data gathering for outcome data • Improve data quality of cost and activity data	• High • Medium	• 3 • 2
Leadership engagement	• Enhance interaction with business leaders during the end-to-end process	• High	• 3
Technology			
Data collection tools	• Implement new LMS • Implement data warehouse	• Medium • High	• 3 • 3
Analysis and reporting tools	• Automate analysis and reporting tools	• Medium	• 3

Table D-2. Sample Implementation Plan

		TDRp Implementation Plan					
Milestone	Task #	Task Name	Duration	Start	Finish	Predecessors	Successors
	1	Begin Project	0 days	Mon 1/4	Mon 1/4		5, 4
	2						
	3	**Startup**	**32 days**	**Mon 1/4**	**Tue 2/16**		
	4	Agree on commitment to TDRp, goals, and resources	5 days	Mon 1/4	Fri 1/8	1	6
	5	**Stakeholder analysis**	**8 days**	**Mon 1/11**	**Wed 1/20**	1	
	6	Conduct stakeholder analysis	5 days	Mon 1/11	Fri 1/15	4	7
	7	Synthesize findings	3 days	Mon 1/18	Wed 1/20	6	8
Δ	8	Initial stakeholder assessment complete	0 days	Wed 1/20	Wed 1/20	7	10
	9	**Change assessment**	**17 days**	**Thu 1/21**	**Fri 2/12**		
	10	Conduct change assessment	5 days	Thu 1/21	Wed 1/27	8	11
	11	Develop implementation approach	5 days	Thu 1/28	Wed 2/3	10	12
	12	Review recommendations with key stakeholders	5 days	Thu 2/4	Wed 2/10	11	13
	13	Modify implementation approach based on feedback	2 days	Thu 2/11	Fri 2/12	12	14
Δ	14	High-level approach complete	0 days	Fri 2/12	Fri 2/12	13	15
	15	Complete sponsor commitment plan	2 days	Mon 2/15	Tue 2/16	14	16
Δ	16	Startup complete	0 days	Tue 2/16	Tue 2/16	15	20
	17						
	18	**Planning**	**30 days**	**Wed 2/17**	**Tue 3/30**		
	19	**Implementation Planning**	**15 days**	**Wed 2/17**	**Tue 3/9**		
	20	Develop tactical plan with team	10 days	Wed 2/17	Tue 3/2	16	21
	21	Develop high-level change and communications plan	5 days	Wed 3/3	Tue 3/9	20	22
	22	Identify resource requirements	5 days	Wed 3/3	Tue 3/9	21	23
	23	Review implementation and change plan with key resources	5 days	Wed 3/10	Tue 3/16	22	24
	24	Finalize implementation plan	5 days	Wed 3/17	Tue 3/23	23	25
	25	Senior leader review and sign off	5 days	Wed 3/24	Tue 3/30	24	26
Δ	26	Planning complete	0 days	Tue 3/30	Tue 3/30	25	30
	27						
	28	**Implementation: Wave 1**	**77 days**	**Wed 3/31**	**Thu 7/15**		
	29	**Develop measures library**	**30 days**	**Wed 3/31**	**Tue 5/11**		
	30	Identify initial measures	5 days	Wed 3/31	Tue 4/6	26	31
	31	Review with key stakeholders	10 days	Wed 4/7	Tue 4/20	30	32
	32	Adjust measures based on feedback	5 days	Wed 4/21	Tue 4/27	31	33
	33	Finalize critical measures	5 days	Wed 4/28	Tue 5/4	32	34
	34	Populate measures library	5 days	Wed 5/5	Tue 5/11	33	36, 35

Table D-2. Sample Implementation Plan (cont.)

		TDRp Implementation Plan					
Milestone	Task #	Task Name	Duration	Start	Finish	Predecessors	Successors
△	35	Measures library complete	0 days	Tue 5/11	Tue 5/11	34	37
	36	**Establish goals**	**22 days**	**Wed 5/12**	**Thu 6/10**	**34**	
	37	Develop goals for prioritized measures	5 days	Wed 5/12	Tue 5/18	35	38
	38	Develop action plans to achieve goals	10 days	Wed 5/19	Tue 6/1	37	39
	39	Review with key stakeholders	5 days	Wed 6/2	Tue 6/8	38	40
	40	Finalize goals	2 days	Wed 6/9	Thu 6/10	39	41
△	41	Goals complete	0 days	Thu 6/10	Thu 6/10	40	43
	42	**Operations Report**	**25 days**	**Fri 6/11**	**Thu 7/15**		
	43	Create first draft operations reports	10 days	Fri 6/11	Thu 6/24	41	44
	44	Review and revision cycle	15 days	Fri 6/25	Thu 7/15	43	45
△	45	Operations reports complete	0 days	Thu 7/15	Thu 7/15	44	46
△	46	Wave 1 complete	0 days	Thu 7/15	Thu 7/15	45	50, 60, 66
	47						
	48	**Implementation: Wave 2**	**75 days**	**Fri 7/16**	**Thu 10/28**		
	49	**Identify key business initiatives**	**30 days**	**Fri 7/16**	**Thu 8/26**		
	50	Meet with senior sponsors to identify key business initiatives	10 days	Fri 7/16	Thu 7/29	46	51
	51	Identify appropriate areas for program reports (prioritize)	5 days	Fri 7/30	Thu 8/5	50	52
	52	Identify relevant business goals for key programs	10 days	Fri 8/6	Thu 8/19	51	53
	53	Review recommendations with business leaders	5 days	Fri 8/20	Thu 8/26	52	54
△	54	Business initiative prioritization complete	0 days	Thu 8/26	Thu 8/26	53	56
	55	**Program Reports**	**45 days**	**Fri 8/27**	**Thu 10/28**		
	56	Create first draft program reports	30 days	Fri 8/27	Thu 10/7	54	57
	57	Review and revision cycle	15 days	Fri 10/8	Thu 10/28	56	58
△	58	Program reports complete	0 days	Thu 10/28	Thu 10/28	57	
	59	**L&D skill development**	**75 days**	**Fri 7/16**	**Thu 10/28**		
	60	Develop coaching program for core skills	45 days	Fri 7/16	Thu 9/16	46	61
	61	Execute program	30 days	Fri 9/17	Thu 10/28	60	62
△	62	Wave 2 complete	0 days	Thu 10/28	Thu 10/28	61	76
	63						
	64	**Implementation: Wave 3**	**192 days**	**Fri 7/16**	**Mon 4/18**		
	65	**Business alignment and goal setting**	**90 days**	**Fri 7/16**	**Thu 11/18**		
	66	Develop or augment business alignment process	30 days	Fri 7/16	Thu 8/26	46	67
	67	Establish advisory board	30 days	Fri 8/27	Thu 10/7	66	68
	68	Identify L&D relevant strategic initiatives with senior business leaders	15 days	Fri 10/8	Thu 10/28	67	69
	69	Develop initial goals and L&D's contribution	15 days	Fri 10/29	Thu 11/18	68	70

Table D-2. Sample Implementation Plan (cont.)

		TDRp Implementation Plan					
Milestone	Task #	Task Name	Duration	Start	Finish	Predecessors	Successors
Δ	70	Initial planning complete	0 days	Thu 11/18	Thu 11/18	69	72FS+27 days
	71	**Summary Reports**	**75 days**	**Mon 1/3**	**Fri 4/15**		
	72	Create first draft summary reports	45 days	Mon 1/3	Fri 3/4	70FS+27 days	73
	73	Review and revision cycle	30 days	Mon 3/7	Fri 4/15	72	74
Δ	74	Summary reports complete	0 days	Fri 4/15	Fri 4/15	73	79
	75	**L&D Tools Development & Data Cleanup**	**90 days**	**Fri 10/29**	**Wed 3/9**		
	76	Implement new measurement tool	90 days	Fri 10/29	Wed 3/9	62	77SS
	77	Data cleanup	90 days	Fri 10/29	Wed 3/9	76SS	78
Δ	78	Tools and data cleanup complete	0 days	Wed 3/9	Wed 3/9	77	79
Δ	79	Wave 3 Complete	0 days	Mon 4/18	Mon 4/18	74, 78	82
	80						
	81	**After Action Review**	**7 days**	**Mon 4/18**	**Tue 4/26**		
	82	Project reflection	2 days	Mon 4/18	Tue 4/19	79	83
	83	Leadership review	5 days	Wed 4/20	Tue 4/26	82	84
Δ	84	Waves 1, 2, and 3 complete	0 days	Tue 4/26	Tue 4/26	83	

APPENDIX E
Glossary

The terms and definitions for this glossary come from multiple sources. We have defined many terms to ensure a common understanding of certain critical concepts in the book. In addition, we have leveraged glossaries and definitions from *The Business of Learning*, the *Center for Talent Reporting Terms and Definitions* whitepaper, the Association for Talent Development, and the Training Industry website.

aligned learning: Learning aligned to the goals of an organization. These programs contribute directly to achieving an organization's goals.

alignment: With regard to the management of learning, alignment is the practice of aligning or identifying programs with the goal or need they support. More broadly, the term refers to the extent to which the efforts of individuals and departments are aligned to the higher goals of the organization.

analysis: See **analytics**.

analytics: An in-depth exploration of the data, which may include advanced statistical techniques such as regression, to extract insights from the data or discover relationships among measures. Synonymous with **analysis**.

analyze: The process of exploring the data that may include advanced statistical techniques such as regression, to extract insights from the data or discover relationships among measures.

applicatiwon rate (Level 3): This is a measure of the extent to which the new knowledge or skills have actually been applied on the job. Application may be measured by observation or through participant self-assessment. The measure is also known as behavior (Kirkpatrick) and is commonly referred to as Level 3.

assessment: Refers to the process or act of evaluating an individual's or organization's knowledge, skills, or performance related to a particular subject, topic, or process. See also **test**.

average: The result obtained by adding together several quantities and then dividing this total by the number of quantities. Also known as a measure of central tendency.

balance sheet: One of three common financial statements that shows assets and liabilities at one point in time.

benchmarking: The practice of measuring an organization, department, or process by its strengths and weaknesses against similar organizations, for the purpose of objectively defining and improving the work of trainers and HR professionals.

blended learning: A combination of learning modalities such as instructor-led training (ILT) and e-learning.

budget: A detailed document showing planned income and expense.

burden: The dollar amount of labor and related and overhead costs that is not allocated or assigned to any specific program.

burden rate: The burden divided by the attributable or assigned hours. It is expressed as dollars per hour and must be added to the labor and related rate to calculate the fully burdened labor and related rate.

business acumen: An understanding of business concepts and their application to make better decisions.

business case: A document or presentation that describes the benefits and costs associated with a proposed investment.

business plan: A document or presentation that completely describes the goals and activities required to achieve the goals for a year. For learning this would include a discussion of strategic alignment, business case, a detailed work plan, evaluation strategy, and budget.

business unit (BU): A division or segmentation of an organization by region, line of product or service, or area of specialization.

capability development: The processes to build organizational competency and capability in the organization, typically below the senior leadership levels.

cash flow statement: One of three common financial statements showing the sources and uses of cash for operating, investing, and financing activities for a period of time.

CEO: An abbreviation for *chief executive officer*. See also **chief executive officer**.

change management: The process of guiding people affected by change from awareness through engagement to commitment to the change.

chief executive officer (CEO): The highest-ranking executive in a company, often appointed by a board of directors.

chief financial officer (CFO): The person responsible for an organization's finances and financial systems. The position oversees accounting and treasury.

chief learning officer (CLO): The person ultimately responsible for learning in an organization. This position may also be named vice president of training or director of training. If the person also has responsibility for other aspects of talent. May be called chief talent officer (CTO), chief talent development officer (CTDO), or chief human resources officer (CHRO).

class: Each physical or virtual meeting of students where content is conveyed by an instructor. A course may consist of just one class if the content can be conveyed in one sitting or it may require multiple classes to convey all the content. It is also possible that the number of students enrolled in a course exceeds the optimum class size, which necessitates multiple classes even if the content can be conveyed in a single sitting. So, a one-hour instructor-led course for 150 employees will require six classes of 25 each. The analogy at the university level is a semester-long course like Econ 101 that meets two classes per week for 10 weeks. If 300 students sign up to take Econ 101, but enrollment is limited to 100 per class, three sections will be offered with 100 students in each class.

CLO: Abbreviation for *chief learning officer*. See also **chief learning officer**.

coaching: A process in which a more experienced person (a coach), provides a worker or workers (coachee) with constructive advice and feedback with the goal of improving performance.

community of practice (CoP): A group of individuals who share a common interest and come together (usually virtually) to learn from one another. The community typically has a leader, subject matter experts (SMEs), and rules for engagement.

competency: An area of personal capability that enables one to perform. For example, competency can be knowledge, a skill, an attitude, a value, or another personal characteristic. It is necessary for the acceptable performance of a task or achievement of a goal.

competency model: A framework for defining the skill and knowledge requirements of a job. May include the level of proficiency necessary for organizational success.

compliance training: Describes mandatory requirements for workplace regulatory training as required by law or professional governing standards. OSHA, HIPPA, and Sarbanes-Oxley are three examples of regulations that require compliance training.

core talent processes: Six key processes that all talent functions must manage: talent acquisition, leadership development, learning and development, capability management, performance management, and total rewards.

corporate university: A learning organization with a governance system that aligns all learning content with the corporate or agency mission, strategy, and goals. The governance system typically includes a governing board with CEO and other senior executives, as well as a chief learning officer who has overall control of its operations.

course: A class or series of classes, an online module, or a series of online modules, prework, post-work, performance support, discussion boards, and other types of learning materials to convey related and integrated content. For example, a course on leadership may consist of four hours of prereading, two online modules, four instructor-led classes, an online discussion board, and performance support. In a corporate environment, each course will have a specific designation in the learning management system (LMS). At the university level, students will enroll in specific courses each term, such as Econ 101.

courseware: Any type of instructional or educational course delivered via a software program or over the Internet.

curriculum: A group of courses organized around a similar topic area or designed for certain roles. For example, an enterprise may create a curriculum of courses geared specifically toward the development of IT skills. In the corporate market, curriculum is synonymous with the term portfolio of courses.

custom analysis report: These reports present the results of an analysis to determine the relationship among various measures and to predict the value of a measure based on its relationship with other measures.

dashboard: These reports are more advanced than scorecards and often contain visual displays. Unlike their static scorecard counterpart, dashboards may be continuously updated, depending on the reporting cadence of the underlying data. They may also be interactive, allowing the user to access details or select measures. If the dashboard includes a threshold, it may be used for monitoring. Dashboards usually contain summary measures rather than detailed data and therefore are especially well suited to briefing leaders.

data collection: The collection of all facts, figures, statistics, and other information that is used for various types of analyses. Some examples of data collection methods or tools include examining in-house and external written sources, sending questionnaires, conducting interviews, and observing trainees or jobholders.

delivery: Any method of transferring content to learners, including instructor-led training (ILT), web-based training, books, and more.

department initiatives: Intended to improve the efficiency and effectiveness of processes and systems (such as informal learning, the learning management system, or a help desk) or improve efficiency and effectiveness measures across all programs (such as Levels 1 and 3 or the utilization rate of classrooms or e-learning programs).

design and development: In the learning context, design and development refers to the process of designing a course and then developing it or making it available on a platform. Typically, learning and development (L&D) departments have professionals who have been trained in each discipline.

development: Consists of learning activities that prepare people for additional job responsibilities and enable them to gain knowledge or skills. It may also refer to the creation of training materials or courses.

direct cost: Includes expenses incurred by the organization for the planning, design, development, delivery, management, and measurement of formal and informal learning. Direct cost also includes expenditures by the learning function for performance consulting, reinforcement of learning, and general management of the learning function. Put another way, direct cost includes every expense (entire budget) of all learning functions within an organization plus any direct expenditures on learning that occur outside the learning function (in other business units) as well as any tuition reimbursement expenditures (wherever they are budgeted).

discretionary learning: Not mandated by law, required for employees to meet the minimum competency level necessary for their position, or required to fulfill professional certification. Discretionary learning is often scaled back or eliminated during episodes of cost cutting.

effectiveness measure: A way to determine the quality of the program or initiative that is usually gathered through a survey, test, or observation. Examples include participant reaction, amount learned, application, and return on investment (ROI). One of the three Talent Development Reporting principles (TDRp) measures recommended for all programs, initiatives, and departments. See also **efficiency measure**; **outcome measure**.

efficiency measure: A way to determine the quantity or activity, answering the question "How much?" Efficiency measures include counts, percentages, rates, and whether a measure will be efficient or not in comparison to a plan, benchmark, trend, or history. Examples include number of participants, courses, hours, and costs; percentage of courses delivered on time or employees reached by learning; and utilization of courses, instructors, seats, or rooms. Synonymous with Level 0 or volume measures. One of the three Talent Development Reporting principles (TDRp) measures recommended for all programs, initiatives, and departments. See also **effectiveness measure**; **outcome measure**.

e-learning: Training provided electronically without the presence of a real-time instructor. Includes learning content hosted on a computer or mobile device.

employee count: The unique count of all employees at a point in time. Part-time employees are counted as well as full-time employees. Note: If an organization uses many contingent workers (temporary employees and contract workers), consideration should be given to using *workforce* (employees plus contingent workers) in addition to, or as replacement for, *number of employees*.

estimate: The goal owner or learning professional's reasoned guess based on partial information about a measure's past or current value. For example, the actual impact of learning for the first quarter may not be known, but an estimate is made. Used when the actual value is not yet available.

evaluate: The process of determining whether a learning program was efficient, effective, and impactful, usually employing the Katzell, Kirkpatrick, or Phillips framework.

executive vice president (EVP): Usually a direct report to the CEO.

expense: The amount of money spent (cash basis) or the value of a product or service used (accrual basis). Synonymous with cost.

facilitator: A professional who assesses learners' knowledge and helps build upon or expand it during the training experience. Often referred to as instructors or teachers. See also **trainer**.

forecast: The goal owner or learning professional's projection or reasoned guess for the future value of a measure once the year is already underway. A forecast for the year typically includes actual or estimated data in addition to the forecast for the remainder of the year. The forecast often differs from plan (the original goal). For example, the plan may have been a 10 percent increase in sales for the year, but by July it is evident that will not be achieved so the forecast is revised to a 7 percent increase in sales. Forecasts are typically made for all measures that are actively managed.

formal learning: Learning that is structured and organized or directed by someone other than the learner. This includes instructor-led training (ILT) where the instructor is physically located with the participants, virtual ILT (vILT) where the instructor is at a different location than the participants, e-learning programs, structured coaching, and structured mobile learning.

FTE: The abbreviation for *full-time equivalent*. See also **full-time equivalent**.

full-time equivalent (FTE): This is a way of measuring full-time effort (40 hours per week × 52 weeks per year) if some employees are part time and don't work 40 hours a week or 52 weeks a year. For example, if two part-time employees each work half time, the full-time equivalent of their effort is 1.0 FTE.

fully burdened labor rate: Expressed in dollars per hour, including the burden rate and fully reflecting all costs. Used in calculating quotes for projects when the goal is to fully recover costs. See also **labor rate**.

general studies training: Courses that are not directly aligned to organizational goals or part of structured programs to address organizational needs (for example, team building, communications, and cultural awareness courses). They are important and indirectly contribute to a better workforce, but don't directly contribute to the organization's top goals or to an important need like onboarding or basic skills training. Synonymous with general studies.

goal: The desired organizational outcome or objective, such as increasing sales by 10 percent next year.

goal owner: The person responsible and accountable for achieving the planned outcome for a goal, such as the senior vice president of sales. Synonymous with **sponsor**.

gross benefit: The dollar benefit of a learning program before any costs are subtracted. The dollar benefit is simply the value of the impact of learning (Level 4) on the business outcome. For example, a 3 percent increase in sales due to training may be worth $900,000 in additional net income to a company. In this case, the gross benefit is $900,000.

headcount: See **employee count**.

ILT: Abbreviation for *instructor-led training*. See also **instructor-led training**.

impact: See **isolated impact**.

income: The amount of money collected (cash basis) or earned (accrual basis). Synonymous with revenue.

income statement: The most common financial statement, which shows income (revenue) and expense (cost) in some detail. It concludes with net income or profit, which is the difference between income and expense.

indirect material and expense (IM&E): A common category of overhead expense found on departmental income statements. It often includes all external expenses (which would be shown as overhead in a corporate income statement), such as travel, consultants, printing, telephone, leases, office supplies, and so on.

inform: One of the four reasons to measure where the purpose is to share historical results or trends. To use measures to inform, learning and development (L&D) practitioners typically generate static reports to share via scorecards, dashboards, spreadsheets, or email updates.

informal learning: Learning that is not structured and is not organized or directed by someone else—participants learn on their own through self-discovery. This includes social learning, knowledge sharing, on-the-job learning, unstructured coaching, and personal learning through Internet or library exploration.

initiative: May be used in place of program but may also designate a coordinated series of actions to improve the effectiveness or efficiency of the learning and development (L&D) department. For example, there may be an initiative to reduce complaints about the learning management system, reduce department costs, or improve the application rate of learning in general across all courses. In this book, *program* is used when the effort addresses business goals, HR goals, or organizational needs (such as onboarding or basic skills training). *Initiative* is used when the effort is not directly aligned to business goals, HR goals, or organizational needs, instead focusing more on matters internal to the L&D department. See also **program**.

instructor: An individual who leads training programs, assuming responsibility for communicating and demonstrating best practices for learners. Instructors teach students the skills and knowledge necessary for particular fields and professions. Synonymous with facilitators, teachers, and lecturers. See also **trainer** or **facilitator**.

instructor-led training (ILT): Training facilitated by an instructor, either online or in a classroom setting. ILT allows learners and instructors or facilitators to interact and discuss the training material individually or in a group setting. Online instructor-led training is known as **virtual instructor-led training (vILT)**.

internal charges: A common category of overhead expense found on departmental income statements (include charges within the company like IT, HR, legal, and occupancy).

International Organization for Standardization (ISO): An international standard-setting body. Through its Technical Committee on Human Resources (TC260), ISO is working to define and standardize measures for HR and to recommend measures for both internal and external reporting.

isolated impact: The impact of learning on achieving the goal. Impact may be expressed quantitatively (a 20 percent contribution to the goal of increasing sales by 10 percent, resulting in a 2 percent increase in sales due just to learning) or qualitatively (a low, medium, or high contribution to achieving the goal). Also known as Level 4 business impact in the ROI Methodology, isolated impact serves as both an outcome measure and an effectiveness measure. See also **Level 4 (Impact)**.

job aid: Provides guidance or assistance, either audio or visual, to the performer about when to carry out tasks and steps, thereby reducing the amount of necessary recall and minimizing error. Job aids are good candidates for tasks that are performed with relatively low frequency, are highly complex, are likely to change in the future, or have a high probability of error.

key performance indicator (KPI): At one time, KPI may have been reserved for the most important measures, but it's now used commonly for any measure. We will use the term *measure* in this book. Synonymous with metric or **measure**.

Kirkpatrick, Donald: Donald Kirkpatrick was professor emeritus at the University of Wisconsin and honorary chairman of Kirkpatrick Partners until his passing in May 2014. In 1956, he wrote the article "How to Start an Objective Evaluation of Your Training Program," which presented Katzell's Hierarchy of Steps. Kirkpatrick then shared Katzell's work in conferences throughout the 1950s and published four consecutive monthly articles in ATD's magazine in 1959 and early 1960, focusing on a different step each month. The four steps became known as the four levels and L&D's first model for evaluation.

knowledge sharing: Sharing of knowledge and information typically accomplished electronically through communities of practice (CoPs).

L&D: Abbreviation for *learning and development*. See also **learning and development (L&D)**.

labor and related rate: The hourly cost of labor and related costs expressed as dollars per hour. Related costs include healthcare, vacation pay, incentive pay, profit sharing, and employer-paid employee taxes (like social security and unemployment). Used to calculate opportunity costs.

labor rate: The hourly cost of labor expressed as dollars per hour. For a group it is the total labor cost divided by the total hours.

last year's results: The results for the last complete fiscal year. Synonymous with actuals.

leadership development: The process of identifying, assessing, reviewing, and planning for leadership bench strength in the organization to enhance the overall breadth, depth, and quality of leadership.

leading indicator: A measure that changes before another measure and can provide an indication of a future result. For example, in learning and development, the amount of learning applied is considered a leading indicator of performance improvement on the job.

learner's travel-related and fee expenses: The travel-related cost for participants to attend in-house or external learning programs in addition to the program-related costs of external programs (for example, a registration fee). This information is often difficult to obtain, although some organizations provide a check box on travel expense forms to indicate the expense is related to learning.

learning and development (L&D): The name of the professional field and many training departments dedicated to increasing the knowledge, skills, and capabilities of the workforce. Other names for the L&D department include training, organization development, and talent development, although the last two may include additional responsibilities, such as succession planning.

learning (Level 2): Used as an effectiveness measure, learning is a measure of the amount of knowledge gained or how well it was learned. Learning is typically measured through a test at the end of each module or course. It is also known as Kirkpatrick Level 2 and Phillips Level 2.

learning experience portal (LXP): A system that provides a personalized, social, online learning experience for an organization's employees. The system consolidates learning resources (such as job aids, courses, videos, or people finders) into a single portal to enable ease of access to relevant content.

learning management system (LMS): Software that automates the administration of training. An LMS registers users, tracks courses in a catalog, records data from learners, and provides reports to management. An LMS typically is designed to handle courses by multiple publishers and providers.

Level 0: Refers to all efficiency measures. Also referred to as volume or activity measures. See also **efficiency measure**.

Level 1 (participant reaction or satisfaction): Refers to the first level Kirkpatrick's Four Levels of Evaluation or the Phillips ROI Methodology. See also **participant reaction or satisfaction (Level 1)**.

Level 2 (Learning): Refers to the second level Kirkpatrick's Four Levels of Evaluation or the Phillips ROI Methodology. See also **learning (Level 2)**.

Level 3 (Application): Refers to the third level Kirkpatrick's Four Levels of Evaluation or the Phillips ROI Methodology. See also **application rate (Level 3)**.

Level 4 (Impact): Refers to fourth level of the Phillips ROI Methodology and to the isolated impact of training on the business results. See also **impact**.

Level 4 (Results): Refers to fourth level of Kirkpatrick's Four Levels of Evaluation, which is the business result when training has been applied.

Level 5 (ROI): Refers to fifth level of the Phillips ROI Methodology and to the return on investment of the training program. See also **return on investment (ROI); isolated impact**.

loss: Refers to net income, which is negative (expense exceeds income).

LXP: Abbreviation for *learning experience portal*. See also **learning experience portal**.

manage: The act of creating a plan and then executing it with discipline to deliver the expected results. In contrast to monitoring, managing is used when the leaders want to achieve a value that is higher or lower than the existing value. In other words when they want to move the needle.

management report: These reports focus on enabling leaders to manage their business. Produced at a predefined cadence (monthly or quarterly), they are typically static and show progress against plan and a forecast of year-end results. There are three types of management reports: the operations report, the program report, and the summary report. See also **operations report; program report; summary report.**

mandatory learning: Learning that is required by law or the senior leadership of an organization. All employees in the target audience are expected to take mandatory learning and there are typically negative consequences for not complying.

measure: (1) As a noun, the name associated with a particular indicator. For example, the number of participants is a measure. (2) As a verb, measure is the act of finding the value of the indicator. Synonymous with **metric** and **key performance indicator (KPI)**.

measurement: The process of measuring or finding values for indicators.

measurement maturity: Indicates the level of capability, sophistication, and robustness of measurement methods and practices within an organization.

measurement methodologies: A process and suite of standards and tools that guide how practitioners execute a specific approach. The learning measurement profession uses several well-known methodologies including Kirkpatrick's Four Levels of Evaluation, the Phillips ROI Methodology, and the Brinkerhoff Success Case Method.

measures to inform: These are the most common measures that are used to answer questions and discern trends. Common questions include the number of participants, courses, or hours. Measures to inform are shared in scorecards or dashboards. No plan, target, or thresholds are required, just the value of the measure.

measures to manage: A few measures that will be actively managed throughout the year and included in three Talent Development Reporting principle (TDRp) management reports. Each measure will have a plan or target set before the year begins and monthly reporting of year-to-date results once the year is underway. Ideally, the forecast is also updated each month.

measures to monitor: More common than measures to manage but less common than measures to inform, these are those measures for which thresholds are set and dashboards or scorecards are used monthly to determine if the measures remain within, above, or below the prescribed thresholds.

metric: See **measure**.

mobile learning: Learning that takes place via a wireless device, such as a cell phone, smartphone, tablet, or laptop computer.

monitor: The act of regularly comparing the value of a measure to a threshold, benchmark, or goal. Monitoring implies that the measure has historically been within the desired threshold and is expected to remain there.

needs analysis: A structured and disciplined exploration of an organization's need and the ability of L&D to at least partially meet that need.

net benefit: Gross benefit less the program cost of learning, which includes opportunity cost.

non-strategic programs: Important, often enterprise-wide initiatives to address key organization needs like onboarding, basic skills training, and compliance. Typically, neither the CEO nor head of HR will have a high-level goal for these programs.

online or e-learning module: A single session of computer, tablet, or mobile-based instruction, which may last from five or 10 minutes to an hour or more. Each online module typically requires the user to log in and completion is recorded in the learning management system.

operations report: Includes aggregate data on the key effectiveness and efficiency measures for all programs or initiatives managed by the learning and development (L&D) department for which data are available. The operations report is one of the three standard Talent Development Reporting principles (TDRp) management reports.

opportunity cost: The value of what is given up. In learning it is at least the value of the participant's time in class and in transit (by formula: hours × labor and related rate). In some cases, like a program for salespeople, it will be the net income not generated because they were in class.

organization goal: The desired organizational outcome, such as a 10 percent increase in sales for the year. In this example, the measure is sales and the desired value is a 10 percent increase.

organizational outcome: An organization's planned or actual results. Examples of planned outcomes include a 10 percent desired increase in revenue or a 30 percent desired decrease in injuries. Examples of actual results include an 8 percent realized increase in revenue and a 35 percent realized decrease in injuries. Planned results are synonymous with **organizational goals**.

OTO: Abbreviation for *one-time-only*. Reports that are generated only once for a specific purpose may be designated as OTO.

outcome measure: The isolated impact of the learning program on the organizational goal. The outcome measure may be expressed qualitatively (using an adjective such as high, medium, low, essential, very important, or important) or quantitatively. A quantitative outcome measure using isolated impact will always be expressed in the same unit as the goal. For example, a 1 percent increase in sales due to learning in support of a goal to increase sales by 5 percent is an outcome measure for a consultative selling initiative. Outcome may also refer to the business outcome or result itself, such as the 5 percent increase in sales. One of the three Talent Development Reporting principles (TDRp) measures recommended for all programs, initiatives, and departments. See also **effectiveness measure; efficiency measure**.

overhead: A category of expense found on the income statement referring to costs not directly related to production. On many corporate income statements overhead costs will be called sales, general, and administrative (SG&A). On departmental income statements overhead costs may be called indirect material and expense (IM&E) and internal.

participant reaction or satisfaction (Level 1): The participants' reaction to or satisfaction with the training they just completed. This information is usually gathered in a post-event survey immediately following completion. Also known as Kirkpatrick Level 1 or Phillips Level 1, participant satisfaction is an effectiveness measure.

participants: Those who are actively engaged in a formal or informal learning program or initiative. There are two ways to count the number of participants: unique participants and total participants. (1) Unique participants removes any duplication caused by participants taking multiple courses. It answers the question, "How many people have been reached by learning?" (2) Total participants measures all instances of participation or opportunities for learning and allows for the same people to take multiple courses. It answers the question, "How much learning content is being provided and is directly related to the workload of the L&D function?"

percent checking top two boxes: One of two common methods for calculating Level 1 scores. Typically, the participant has a range of answers (for example, strongly agree to strongly disagree) and is asked to select the answer that best represents their opinion. This method of calculating a Level 1 score adds up the number of participants who selected the top two boxes (typically strongly agree and agree) and divides that number by the total number of responses. A five-point scale is recommended. See also **top two box score**.

percent of plan: A calculation of progress to date to achieve the plan for the measure being reported. By formula: Year-to-date results ÷ Plan (annual).

percentage favorable: See **top two box score**.

performance consulting: In the learning context, performance consulting is the disciplined process of seeking to understand the performance problem or opportunity, assessing whether L&D has a role to play in addressing the issue, and if so, determining the most appropriate learning method to address it.

performance management: The process of setting aligned performance goals and individual performance goals, creating development plans, monitoring, and evaluating progress to create accountability.

performance support: Physical or electronic aid or support to accomplish a particular task. It may provide all the help and assistance needed to complete a task and may be preferred in some cases to formal learning.

Phillips, Jack, and Patti Phillips: Jack Phillips is founder and chairman of ROI Institute, a research, benchmarking, and consulting organization. Patti Phillips is CEO of ROI Institute. Jack Phillips developed the ROI Methodology, a critical tool for measuring and evaluating programs such as training, human resources, technology, and quality programs and initiatives. In his ground-breaking and extremely comprehensive 1983 book, *Handbook of Training Evaluation*, Jack introduced return on investment (ROI) as Level 5 and a new definition for Level 4. This was the first book on training evaluation in the United States. Jack and Patti Phillips continue to refine and improve the ROI Methodology and have published more than 100 books or articles on evaluation.

plan: The quantitative or qualitative goal for the year for the measure being reported. For example, the plan may be for a 10 percent increase in sales or an application rate of 60 percent.

planned contribution from learning: The qualitative or quantitative isolated contribution of learning toward the organizational goal that was agreed to by the goal owner or sponsor and the learning manager prior to the development of the content. For example, sales training will have a high or significant contribution to a 5 percent increase in sales (qualitative) or training will have a 20 percent contribution to a 5 percent increase in sales (quantitative).

planned impact of learning: The qualitative or quantitative isolated impact of learning toward the organizational goal that was agreed to by the goal owner or sponsor and the learning manager prior to the development of the learning. For example, sales training will cause a significant increase in sales (qualitative) or sales related training will result in a 1 percent increase (quantitative).

post-test: A test given to training participants after the instruction is presented or completed. Pre-testing and post-testing can be used to show the percentage of knowledge gained.

pre-test: A test given to training participants before the instruction is presented or received. A pre-test can be used to assess which participants may not succeed in a class, to determine class content, or to set prerequisite skills. A pre-test is most valuable when participants have partial knowledge of a subject.

profit: Calculated as income (revenue) less expense. Often referred to as the bottom line. Synonymous with net income.

profit and loss (P&L): A P&L statement is the same as an income statement. See also **income statement**.

program: A course or series of courses with similar learning objectives designed to accomplish a business or HR goal or meet an organizational need. For example, a program to improve leadership may be composed of four related courses over a six-month period. At the university level, a program leading to a degree in economics may require 12 courses over a four-year period.

program evaluation report: These reports are usually done at the end of a program and present the results of the evaluation to determine the program's efficiency, effectiveness, and impact. The program report may be a PowerPoint presentation or written document.

program manager: The manager within learning and development (L&D) who is responsible for working with the goal or program owner to plan and execute the learning content in support of the goal or need. The program manager is responsible for the program report.

program owner: The owner of a process or area of interest that can be supported by learning but that is not a top goal for the CEO. For example, the program owner for onboarding might be the senior vice president of HR while the program owner for compliance might be the chief risk officer. If learning is supporting a goal of the CEO, they are considered to be goal owners.

program report: Includes the outcome measure and key effectiveness and efficiency measures for the programs or initiatives in support of one organizational goal. Typically, each important goal supported by learning will have a program report. This is one of the three standard Talent Development Reporting principles (TDRp) management reports.

qualitative impact: The isolated impact of learning on an organizational goal expressed as an adjective such as essential, low, medium, or high.

quality: This refers to content, delivery, facilities, schedule, Internet connection, and so forth. Typically there will be multiple questions on quality.

quantitative impact: The isolated impact of learning on an organizational goal expressed as a number or percentage (for example, a 1 percent increase in sales due just to learning).

reach: The percentage of employees touched by formal or informal learning, calculated as total unique participants divided by total employees. Reach is an efficiency measure.

reinforcement: In the learning context, reinforcement refers to the process where a participant's supervisor or other leaders reinforce the importance of applying the newly learned knowledge, skills, or behavior.

relevance: The relevance of the content to the participant's needs and the organization's goals.

report: A detailed account consisting of numbers or text designed to convey important information. In the Talent Development Reporting principles (TDRp) framework, reports are used to inform, monitor, evaluate, or manage.

reporting: An approach to structure measures and analysis to share results with stakeholders.

return on expectations (ROE): A process created by Don and Jim Kirkpatrick to describe their evaluation model. ROE begins with the expectations of the goal owner (stakeholders) and seeks to build a chain of evidence through leading indicators that the stakeholder's expectations were met through the training. ROE is not a measure in itself and cannot be calculated; rather, it is a process focused on identifying and meeting the expectations of the stakeholder. Contrast **return on investment (ROI)**.

return on investment (ROI): The net benefit of a program divided by the program cost, including opportunity cost. ROI is expressed as a percentage. Contrast **return on expectations (ROE)**.

sales training: Involves the personal development of skills and techniques related to creating and exploring new sales opportunities, as well as closing sales for an organization. Sales training courses often include client relationship management, better understanding customers' needs, enhancing communication with clients, providing comprehensive feedback to clients, and improving overall interactions with clients.

scorecard: These reports provide a snapshot of current performance and are typically static and without visual displays. You can generate scorecards at any cadence, but they're generally done monthly or quarterly in L&D. If the scorecard includes a threshold, it may also be used for monitoring. Scorecards usually contain detailed data and are particularly useful for answering very specific questions or identifying trends or anomalies.

seasonality: The presence of a predictable pattern in weekly, monthly, or quarterly data by the time (or season) of the year. For example, retail stores often sell more in the fourth quarter of each year due to the holidays. Thus, we would say that their sales levels have a predefined seasonality.

senior vice president (SVP): Usually a direct report to the CEO.

simple average: The average for a series of numbers in which each number is weighted equally. The simple average is found by summing the series of numbers and dividing by the number of measures in the series.

sponsor: The person responsible and accountable for achieving the planned outcome for a goal, such as the senior vice president of sales. Synonymous with **goal owner**.

stakeholder: A person, department, or organization that has a stake in the outcome of a program, initiative, or business. Stakeholders can be internal or external to the business.

strategic alignment: The process of proactively aligning or matching learning programs with organizational goals, ensuring that training addresses the highest priority goals.

strategic programs: Learning initiatives that directly align to the top goals of the CEO and head of HR. These programs address the most important priorities in the organization's business plan. High-level goals typically involve revenue, quality, efficiency, leadership, engagement, and retention.

subject matter expert (SME): A person who has special skills or knowledge on a particular job or topic. SMEs are sought out by instructional designers to extract intelligence when developing courseware and learning programs. They are also frequently called upon to serve as guest lecturers or instructors for training.

summary report: Includes the organization's key goals, the alignment and outcome measures for learning in support of those goals, and the most important effectiveness and efficiency measures aggregated at the enterprise level. This report is intended for the CEO, chief financial officer (CFO), governing board, and other senior leaders. This is one of the three standard Talent Development Reporting principles (TDRp) management reports.

supporting process: Talent processes that enable the core processes, such as talent strategy, workforce planning, metrics and analytics, talent infrastructure, organization development, communications, and change management.

synchronous training: Occurs when the trainer and the trainee interact in real time. It often refers to virtual ILT. See also **virtual instructor led training (vILT)**.

talent acquisition: The process of recruiting, evaluating candidates, selecting, and onboarding employees into the organization.

Talent Development Reporting principles (TDRp): Measurement, reporting, and management standards for learning and development and HR, including a framework for measurement (four broad reasons to measure and three types of measures) and reporting (three standard reports). The TDRp were developed in 2010–2012 by a group of industry thought leaders and leading practitioners.

test: An assessment, exam, or evaluation instrument used to gauge an individual's performance.

threshold: The upper or lower boundary of an acceptable value for a measure.

top two box score: The top two box score is the sum of percentages for the two highest values for a specific measure. The designation *top* assumes the most favorable points on the scale (for example, strong agree and agree). See also **percentage favorable**.

total cost: All costs associated with a learning program, including design, development, delivery, management, reinforcement, and opportunity costs.

total participants: One of the two measures for participants, total participants counts all instances of participation, allowing for duplication. For example, if a person takes five courses, there will be five total participants or five instances of participation. The total participant measure is correlated with the resources (staff, budget, rooms) required for learning. Contrast **total unique participants**.

total rewards: The process of allocating compensation (including bonuses) and benefits to the workforce to reward them for performance.

total unique participants: One of the two measures for participants, total unique participants is an unduplicated count of all participants. In other words, it is a by-name measure of participants. For example, if a person takes five courses, there will be five total participants but only one unique participant. The measure of total unique participants is used to calculate the reach of learning (Total unique participants ÷ Total employees). Contrast **total participants**.

trainer: A person who helps individuals improve performance by teaching, instructing, or facilitating learning. See also **facilitator** or **instructor**.

training: The process by which an individual or group of people convey or obtain skills relevant to a job or activity. Training generally deals with the physical and mental abilities associated with performing a job, sport, or activity. *Training, education,* and *learning* are often used interchangeably, but each has very different meanings and applications.

tuition reimbursement expenditure: Reimbursements to employees for educational programs at educational institutions. It is understood tuition reimbursement may not fall within the scope of all learning and development (L&D) functions.

unaligned learning: Learning content that is not directly aligned to any organizational goals.

unique participants: See **total unique participants**.

virtual classroom: An online classroom delivery tool within a virtual learning environment. A virtual classroom is part of the distance learning platform, which typically incorporates course materials, homework, tests, assessments, and other tools that are external to the classroom experience. Virtual classrooms may also include social media tools that allow learners and instructors to interact via chat or online discussion boards.

virtual instructor-led training (vILT): A real-time instructor leads the class virtually or remotely. Synonymous with synchronous learning online learning. See also **synchronous training**.

virtual training: Training done in a virtual or simulated environment, or when the learner and the instructor are in separate locations. Virtual training can be done synchronously or asynchronously. Virtual training and virtual training environments are designed to simulate the traditional classroom or learning experience. See also **web-based training (WBT)**.

web-based training (WBT): Online instruction that may be synchronous (the instructor and students meet online at the same time) or asynchronous (the lesson is recorded and students can access it any time).

webinar: Live, online learning events in which learners can obtain information or expertise on a topic, and have the ability to comment or ask questions in real time. Webinars are flexible and can be done cost efficiently for a large or small audience. A webinar is considered a form of web-based training, distance learning, and virtual training.

weighted average: The average for a series of numbers in which each number is weighted differently. This is in contrast to the simple average where each number has equal weight. Calculation of a weighted average requires a weight for each number. For example, suppose 10 participants take a class and they rate it a 4.0. Suppose 20 others take a different class and rate it a 5.0. The simple average rating for the two classes would be 4.5 ([4 + 5] ÷ 2). If we weight the responses by class size, then the weights are 10 ÷ 30 for the first class and 20 ÷ 30 for the second class. Thus, the weighted average is 4.66—(4 × [10 ÷ 30]) + (5 × [20 ÷ 30]) = 1.33 + 3.33.

year-to-date (YTD): The value of a measure from the start of the year to the present.

year-to-date results: The results from the start of the fiscal year through the most recent month for which actuals are available. Synonymous with actuals. See also **year-to-date (YTD)**.

APPENDIX F
Resources on Survey Design

Books

Dillman, D.A., J.D. Smyth, et al. 2014. *Internet, Phone, Mail, and Mixed-Mode Surveys: The Tailored Design Method.* Hoboken, NJ: Wiley.

Robinson, S.B., and K.F. Leonard. 2018. *Designing Quality Survey Questions.* Thousand Oaks, CA: SAGE Publications.

Phillips, P.P., and J.J. Phillips. 2013. *Survey Basics.* Alexandria, VA: ASTD Press.

Online Resources

· "Introduction to Survey Design and Delivery." This 24-page paper on the basics of survey design is not specific to NOAA (National Oceanic and Atmospheric Administration; coast.noaa.gov/data/digitalcoast/pdf/survey-design.pdf).

· The American Evaluation Association has a host of resources on this topic (eval.org).

Courses

· Coursera offers a course on survey design called Questionnaire Design for Social Surveys (coursera.com).

· Udemy also offers short courses on survey design (udemy.com).

References

ATD (Association for Talent Development). 2019. *2019 State of the Industry*. Alexandria, VA: ATD Press.

Bersin, J. 2008. *The Training Measurement Book*. San Francisco: Pfeiffer.

Boudreau, J., and P. Ramstad. 2007. *Beyond HR: The New Science of Human Capital*. Boston: Harvard Business School Press.

David, L. 2014. "Communities of Practice (Lave and Wenger)." *Learning Theories*, July 16. learning-theories.com/communities-of-practice-lave-and-wenger.html.

Donnelly, R., 2007. *Statistics*, 2nd ed. New York: Penguin Group.

ISO (International Organization for Standardization). 2018. *30414:2018 Human Resource Management – Guidelines for Internal and External Reporting*. December.

Katzell, R.A. 1948. "Testing a Training Program in Human Relations." *Personnel Psychology* 1:319–329.

Katzell, R.A. 1952. "Can We Evaluate Training?" Industrial Management Institute at the University of Wisconsin, Madison.

Kirkpatrick, D. 1956. "How to Start an Objective Evaluation of Your Training Program." *Journal of the America Society of Training Directors* 10–11 (May–June): 18–22.

Kirkpatrick, D. 2006. *Evaluating Training Programs: The Four Levels*. San Francisco: Berrett Koehler.

Kirkpatrick, J., and W. Kirkpatrick. 2016. *Kirkpatrick's Four Levels of Training Evaluation*. Alexandria, VA: ATD Press.

Krosnick, J.A., and S. Presser. 2010. "Question and Questionnaire Design." In *Handbook of Survey Research*, 2nd ed., 262–313. Bingley, UK: Emerald.

Lamb, T. 2005. "The Retrospective Pretest: An Imperfect but Useful Tool." *The Evaluation Exchange, Harvard Family Research Project* 11(2). archive.globalfrp.org/evaluation/the -evaluation-exchange/issue-archive/evaluation-methodology/the-retrospective -pretest-an-imperfect-but-useful-tool.

Mattox II, J., P. Parskey, and C. Hall. 2020. *Learning Analytics: Using Talent Data to Improve Business Outcomes*. London: Kogan Page.

Phillips, J.J. 2016. *The Handbook of Training Evaluation and Measurement Methods*, 4th ed. New York: Routledge.

Phillips, J.J., and P.P. Phillips. 2009. *Measuring Success: What CEOs Really Think About Their Learning Investments*. Alexandria, VA: ASTD Press.

Phillips, J.J., and P.P. Phillips. 2010. *Measuring for Success.* Alexandria, VA: ASTD Press.

Phillips, J.J., and P.P. Phillips. 2016. *Handbook of Training Evaluation and Measurement Methods,* 4th ed. New York: Routledge.

Phillips, P.P., and J.J. Phillips. 2016. *Real World Training Evaluation.* Alexandria, VA: ATD Press.

Phillips, P.P., J.J. Phillips, and R. Ray. 2020. *Proving the Value of Soft Skills.* Alexandria, VA: ATD Press.

Rivera, R. 2007. *WLP Scorecard: Why Learning Matters.* Alexandria, VA: ASTD Press.

Surowiecki, J. 2005. *The Wisdom of Crowds.* New York: Anchor.

Tukey, J.W., and M.B. Wilk. 1965. "Proceedings of the Symposium on Information Processing in Sight Sensory Systems." California Institute of Technology, Pasadena, California.

Van Adelsberg, D., and E. Trolley. 1999. *Running Training Like a Business.* San Francisco: Berrett-Koehler.

Vance, D. 2017. *The Business of Learning,* 2nd ed. Windsor, CO: Poudre River Press.

Vance, D., and P. Parskey. 2017. *Definitions of Terms and Measures.* Whitepaper, Center for Talent Reporting. dev.centerfortalentreporting.org/files/student/definitions-of-terms.pdf.

Vance, D., and P. Parskey. 2019. *Introduction to TDRp.* Whitepaper, Center for Talent Reporting. CenterforTalentReporting.org.

Wingate, L. 2016. "The Retrospective Pretest Method for Evaluating Training." EvaluATE Blog, March 16. evalu-ate.org/blog/wingate-mar2016.

Index

Pages numbers followed by *f* or *t* indicate figures or tables.

About the Authors

 **David Vance** is the executive director of the Center for Talent Reporting, a nonprofit organization dedicated to the creation and implementation of best practices and standards for human capital measurement, reporting, and management. He is the former president of Caterpillar University, which he founded in 2001. Until his retirement in January 2007, he was responsible for ensuring that the right education, training, and leadership were provided to achieve corporate goals and efficiently meet the learning needs of Caterpillar and dealer employees. Prior to this position, Dave was chief economist and head of the business intelligence group at Caterpillar with responsibility for economic outlooks, sales forecasts, market research, competitive analysis, and business information systems.

He was named 2006 Chief Learning Officer (CLO) of the Year by *Chief Learning Officer* magazine. He also was named 2004 Corporate University Leader of the Year by the International Quality and Productivity Center in their annual CUBIC (Corporate University Best in Class) Awards. Caterpillar was ranked number one in the 2005 ASTD Best Awards and was named Best Overall Corporate University in 2004 by both Corporate University Xchange and the International Quality and Productivity Center. During his tenure, Caterpillar University was honored with numerous other awards including many in the measurement and alignment arenas.

Dave is a frequent speaker at conferences and association meetings, and conducts workshops on measurement and reporting and running learning like a business. He also organizes and hosts CTR's annual conference. Dave teaches in the human capital PhD programs at Bellevue University and the University of Southern Mississippi, as well as in the executive education program at George Mason University for Chief Talent Officers. He is a member of Working Group 2 on Metrics for the International Organization for Standardization Technical Committee on Human Capital. Dave is also a trustee and lead independent director for State Farm Mutual Funds, and an intermittent chief learning officer for Defense Acquisition University. He is the author of *The Business of Learning: How to Manage Corporate Training to Improve Your Bottom Line*, 2nd edition. Dave received a bachelor of science degree in political science from MIT in 1974, a master of science degree in business administration from Indiana University, South Bend, in 1983, and a PhD in economics from the University of Notre Dame in 1988.

Dave, his wife, Barbara, and their two dogs live in Windsor, Colorado, where they moved after retiring from Caterpillar.

Peggy Parskey is the assistant director of the Center for Talent Reporting, a nonprofit organization dedicated to the creation and implementation of best practices and standards for human capital measurement, reporting, and management.

Peggy owns her own consulting firm, Parskey Consulting, enabling her clients to successfully implement strategic change initiatives that improve organizational and individual performance. She has a deep background in performance measurement and leverages her expertise in management of change and organizational design to ensure sustainable capability. Peggy is certified in management of change methodologies both at the organizational and individual performer levels. She also holds a bachelor of science degree in mathematics from Simmons College and two master's degrees from the University of Chicago in statistics and business administration.

Peggy is also a part-time principal consultant at Explorance, a firm focused on employee journey analytics. She provides business development support and delivers strategic consulting services to talent and learning organizations. In this role, Peggy consults with organizations to develop talent measurement strategies; integrate measurement into talent processes; develop action-oriented reports, scorecards, and dashboard for clients; and conduct impact studies to demonstrate the link between talent programs and business outcomes.

Prior to working with CTR and Explorance, Peggy was employed at Hewlett-Packard Company where she was responsible for global learning processes focused on creating best-in-class learning methodologies as well as enterprise-wide evaluation for the L&D function. During her tenure, training value, effectiveness, and utility measurably improved. Peggy and her team authored a paper for the *Journal of Performance Improvement* entitled "Looking in the Mirror, Performance Improvement for Performance Improvers."

Peggy has spoken at a number of conferences including those for the International Society for Performance Improvement, American Evaluation Annual Conference, Explorance Impact Symposium, and chapters of the Association of Talent Development (ATD). She has published several articles on measurement, chapters in two books, and is the co-author of the second edition of *Learning Analytics: Using Talent Data to Improve Business Outcomes.*

Peggy and her husband, Kevin McEntee, moved to Connecticut from Los Angeles in 2018 to be closer to their two daughters who live in New York and Philadelphia.